William Hickling Prescott

History of the Reign of Philip II, King of Spain

Vol. 3

William Hickling Prescott

History of the Reign of Philip II, King of Spain
Vol. 3

ISBN/EAN: 9783337241179

Printed in Europe, USA, Canada, Australia, Japan

Cover: Foto ©ninafisch / pixelio.de

More available books at **www.hansebooks.com**

HISTORY OF THE REIGN

OF

PHILIP THE SECOND,

KING OF SPAIN.

By WILLIAM H. PRESCOTT,

CORRESPONDING MEMBER OF THE INSTITUTE OF FRANCE, OF THE ROYAL
ACADEMY OF HISTORY AT MADRID, ETC.

NEW AND REVISED EDITION,

WITH THE AUTHOR'S LATEST CORRECTIONS AND
ADDITIONS.

EDITED BY JOHN FOSTER KIRK.

IN THREE VOLUMES.—VOL. III.

PHILADELPHIA:
J. B. LIPPINCOTT & CO.
1882.

Entered, according to Act of Congress, in the year 1858, by
WILLIAM H. PRESCOTT,
In the Clerk's Office of the District Court of the District of Massachusetts.

Entered, according to Act of Congress, in the year 1874, by
J. B. LIPPINCOTT & CO.,
In the Office of the Librarian of Congress, at Washington.

CONTENTS OF VOL. III.

BOOK V.

CHAPTER I.

	PAGE
THE MOORS OF SPAIN	1
Conquest of Spain by the Arabs	1
Hostility between the Two Races	2
The Country recovered by the Spaniards	4
Effect of the Struggle on the National Character	5
Religious Intolerance of the Spaniards	6
Attempts to convert the Moslems	7
Policy of Ximenes	7
Suppression of the Mahometan Worship	8
Outward Conformity to Christianity	9
Moors abandon their National Habits	10
Their Condition under Philip the Second	11
Their Industry and Commerce	12
Treatment by the Government	14
Ordinance of 1563	17
Stringent Measures called for by the Clergy	19
Prepared by the Government	20
Severity of the Enactments	23
Approval of them by Philip	26
Proclamation at Granada	27
Indignation of the Moriscoes	27
Representations to Deza	28
Appeal to the Throne	29
Rejection of their Prayers	30

CHAPTER II.

	PAGE
REBELLION OF THE MORISCOES	33
The Edict enforced	33
Plans for Resistance by the Moriscoes	34
Their Descent on Granada	37
Failure of the Attempt	39
General Insurrection	40
Election of a King	41
Character of Aben-Humeya	42
His Coronation	43
His Preparations for Defence	44
The Christian Population	45
Unsuspicious of their Danger	46
Attacked by the Moors—Panic	47
General Massacre	48
Horrible Cruelties	49
Fate of the Women and Children	52
Fierceness of Aben-Farax	53
Deposed from his Command	54

CHAPTER III.

REBELLION OF THE MORISCOES	55
Consternation in the Capital	55
Mutual Fears of the two Races	56
Garrison of the Alhambra strengthened	57
Troops mustered by Mondejar	57
Civic Militia—Feudal Levies	58
Warlike Ecclesiastics	60
March of the Army	61
Pass of Tablate	62
Bridge crossed by a Friar	64
The Army follows	64
The Moriscoes withdraw	65
Entrance into the Alpujarras	66
Night Encampment at Lanjaron	67

CONTENTS.

	PAGE
Relief of Orgiba	68
Mondejar pursues his March	69
Gloom of the Mountain Scenery	69
Defile of Alfajarali	70
Sudden Attack	71
Bravery of the Andalusian Knights	71
Precipitate Retreat of the Moriscoes	72
Capture of Bubion	73
Humanity of Mondejar	74
Sufferings of the Army	75
Capture of Jubiles	76
Prisoners protected by Mondejar	77
Massacred by the Soldiers	78
Christian Women sent to Granada	79
Welcomed by the Inhabitants	80

CHAPTER IV.

REBELLION OF THE MORISCOES	82
Mondejar's Policy	82
Aben-Humeya at Paterna	83
Offers to surrender	84
Flight to the Sierra Nevada	85
Disposition of the Moorish Prisoners	86
Attack on Las Guajaras	88
Evacuated by the Garrison	89
Massacre ordered by Mondejar	90
Cruelty of the Count of Tendilla	91
Attempt to capture Aben-Humeya	92
His Escape	93
Heroism of Aben-Aboo	93
The Marquis of Los Velez	95
His Campaign in the Alpujarras	96
Cruelties committed by the Troops	97
Celebration of a religious Fête	98
Licentiousness of the Soldiery	100
Contrast between Mondejar and Los Velez	100
Accusations against the former	102
Decision arrived at in Madrid	104

A*

Effect on the Army	105
Moorish Prisoners in Granada	106
Rumors circulated in the Capital	106
Night Attack on the Prisoners	107
Fearful Struggle and Massacre	108
Apathy of the Government	110
Renewal of the Insurrection	111

CHAPTER V.

REBELLION OF THE MORISCOES	113
Don John of Austria	113
Birth and Early History	114
Placed under the Care of Quixada	116
Secrecy in regard to his Origin	117
The young Geronimo at Yuste	118
Testamentary Dispositions of the Emperor	120
The Boy presented to the Regent	121
Curious Scene	122
Meeting appointed with the King	123
Philip acknowledges his Brother	125
Assigns him an Establishment	126
Royal Triumvirate at Alcalá	128
Chivalrous Character of Don John	128
His Adventurous Disposition	129
He is intrusted with the Command of a Fleet	131
His Cruise in the Mediterranean	132
He is selected for the Command in Granada	133
Restrictions on his Authority	134
His Reception at Granada	135
Answers to Petitioners	136
Discussions in the Council of War	138
New Levies summoned	139
Increased Power of Aben-Humeya	140
Forays into the Christian Territory	141
Movements of Los Velez	143
Extension of the Rebellion	144
Successful Expedition of Requesens	145

CONTENTS. vii

	PAGE
Moriscoes lay Siege to Seron	146
Surrender and Massacre of the Garrison	147
Decree for removing the Moriscoes from Granada	148
Their Consternation and Grief	149
Expulsion from the City	150
Farewell to their Ancient Home	152
Distribution through the Country	152
Ruinous Effects on Granada	153
Character of the Transaction	154

CHAPTER VI.

REBELLION OF THE MORISCOES	156
State of the Troops under Los Velez	156
Encounter with Aben-Humeya	158
Flight of the Morisco Prince	159
Desertions from the Spanish Camp	160
Mondejar recalled to Court	160
His Character	161
Exterminating Policy of the Government	162
Sensual Tyranny of Aben-Humeya	163
Treachery towards Diego Alguazil	165
Plan of Revenge formed by Alguazil	166
Conspiracy against Aben-Humeya	168
His Assassination	170
He is succeeded by Aben-Aboo	171
Energy of the new Chief	173
Repulse at Orgiba	173
The Place evacuated by the Garrison	174
Continual Forays	175
Conflicts in the *Vega*	176
Don John's Desire for Action	177
Philip yields to his Entreaties	178
Preparations for the Campaign	179
Surprise of Guejar	180
Mortification of Don John	181
Mendoza the Historian	182

CHAPTER VII.

	PAGE
REBELLION OF THE MORISCOES	187
Philip's Instructions to his Brother	187
Don John takes the Field	189
Discontent of Los Velez	189
His Meeting with Don John	190
He retires from the War	191
Investment of Galera	193
Description of the Place	194
Munitions and Garrison	195
Establishment of Batteries	197
The Siege opened	197
First Assault	198
Spaniards repulsed	199
Mines opened in the Rock	200
Second Assault	201
Explosion of the Mine	203
Troops rush to the Attack	204
Struggle at the Ravelin	204
Bravery of the Morisco Women	205
Ill Success of Padilla	206
Failure of the Attack	207
Insubordination of the Troops	207
Severe Loss of the Spaniards	208
Bloody Determination of Don John	209
Prudent Advice of Philip	209
Condition of the Besieged	211
Preparations for a last Attack	212
Cannonade and Explosions	213
Third Assault	214
Irresistible Fury of the Spaniards	215
Struggle in the Streets and Houses	216
Desperation of the Inhabitants	217
Inhumanity of the Conqueror	218
Wholesale Massacre	219
The Town demolished	220
Tidings communicated to Philip	221
Reputation gained by Don John	222

CHAPTER VIII.

	PAGE
Rebellion of the Moriscoes	223
Seron reconnoitred	223
Sudden Attack by the Moriscoes	224
Army thrown into Confusion	225
Indignation of Don John	226
Death of Quixada	229
His Character	229
Doña Magdalena de Ulloa	231
Rapid Successes of Don John	231
Negotiations opened with El Habaqui	232
Merciless Pursuit of the Rebels	233
Guerilla Warfare	234
Conferences at Fondon	235
Aben-Aboo consents to treat	236
Arrangement concluded	236
Submission tendered by El Habaqui	237
Dissatisfaction with the Treaty	239
Vacillation of Aben-Aboo	240
El Habaqui engages to arrest him	241
Fate of El Habaqui	242
Mission of Palacios	243
His Interview with Aben-Aboo	244
Spirited Declaration of that Chief	244
Stern Resolve of the Government	246
War of Extermination	246
Expedition of the Duke of Arcos	248
March across the Plain of Calaluz	249
Engagement with the Moriscoes	250
The Rebellion crushed	250
Edict of Expulsion	251
Removal of the Moriscoes	252
Don John's Impatience to resign	254
His final Dispositions	255
Hiding-Place of Aben-Aboo	256
Plot formed for his Capture	257
His Interview with El Senix	258

	PAGE
His Murder	259
His Body brought to Granada	259
His Head placed in a Cage	260
Remarks on his Career	261
Wasted Condition of the Country	263
The scattered Moriscoes	264
Cruelly treated by the Government	265
Their Industry and Cheerfulness	266
Increase of their Numbers	267
They preserve their National Feeling	268
Mutual Hatred of the Two Races	269
Expulsion of the Moriscoes from Spain	269
Works of Marmol and Circourt	270

CHAPTER IX.

WAR WITH THE TURKS	273
Sultan Selim the Second	273
Determines on the Conquest of Cyprus	274
Spirit of Pius the Fifth	275
His Appeals to Philip	275
King's Entrance into Seville	276
Determines to join the League	277
Capture of Nicosia	278
Vacillating Conduct of Venice	279
Meeting of Deputies at Rome	280
Treaty of Confederation	281
Ratified and proclaimed	282
Turkish Fleet in the Adriatic	283
Papal Legate at Madrid	284
Concessions to the Crown	285
Fleets of Venice and Rome	285
Preparations in Spain	286
Enthusiasm of the Nation	287
Don John's Departure	288
His Reception at Naples	289
His noble Appearance	290
Accomplishments and Popularity	291

CONTENTS.

	PAGE
Presentation of the Consecrated Standard	292
Arrival at Messina	293
Grand Naval Spectacle	294
Strength and Condition of the Fleets	294
Discretion of the Generalissimo	296
Communications from the Pope	296
Departure from Messina	297

CHAPTER X.

WAR WITH THE TURKS	298
Arrival at Corfu	298
Council of War	299
Resolution to give Battle	300
Arbitrary Conduct of Veniero	301
Passage across the Sea of Ionia	302
Fall of Famagosta	302
The Enemy in Sight	303
Preparations for Combat	304
Final Instructions of Don John	305
Approach of the Turkish Fleet	306
Its Form and Disposition	307
Change in the Order of Battle	309
Last Preparation of the Christians	310
Battle of Lepanto	311
Left Wing of the Allies turned	311
Right Wing, under Doria, broken	312
Don John and Ali Pasha engage	313
Superior Fire of the Spaniards	314
Bird's-eye View of the Scene	315
Venetians victorious on the Left	317
Continued Struggle in the Centre	318
Turkish Admiral boarded	319
Death of Ali Pasha	320
Victory of the Christians	321
Flight of Uluch Ali	322
Chase and Escape	323
Allies take Shelter in Petala	323

CHAPTER XI.

	PAGE
WAR WITH THE TURKS	324
Losses of the Combatants	324
Turkish Armada annihilated	325
Roll of Slaughter and Fame	326
Exploits of Farnese	326
Noble Spirit of Cervantes	327
Sons of Ali Pasha Prisoners	328
Generously treated by Don John	329
His Conduct towards Veniero	330
Operations suspended	331
Triumphant Return to Messina	332
Celebrations in Honor of the Victory	333
Tidings despatched to Spain	335
Philip's Reception of them	336
Acknowledgments to his Brother	337
Don John's Conduct criticised	338
Real Fruits of the Victory	340
Delay in resuming Operations	342
Death of Pius the Fifth	342
Philip's Distrust	343
Permits his Brother to sail	344
Turks decline to accept Battle	345
Anniversary of Lepanto	346
Allies disband their Forces	347
Perfidy of Venice	347
The League dissolved	348
Tunis taken by Don John	349
He provides for its Security	350
Returns to Naples	352
His Mode of Life there	352
His Schemes of Dominion	353
Tunis retaken by the Moslems	354
Don John's Mission to Genoa	355
He prepares a fresh Armament	356
His Disappointment, and Return to Madrid	357

BOOK VI.

CHAPTER I.

	PAGE
DOMESTIC AFFAIRS OF SPAIN	358
Internal Administration	358
Revolutions under Isabella and Charles V.	359
Absolute Power of the Crown	360
Contrast between Charles and Philip	361
The latter wholly a Spaniard	361
The Royal Councils	363
Principal Advisers of the Crown	363
Character of Ruy Gomez de Silva	364
Figueroa, Count of Feria	368
Cardinal Espinosa	369
Two Parties in the Council	372
Balance held by Philip	373
His Manner of transacting Business	374
His Assiduity	375
His Mode of dividing the Day	376
His Love of Solitude	377
Extent of his Information	378
Partial Confidence in his Ministers	379
His Frugality	380
His Magnificent Establishment	381
His Fatal Habit of Procrastination	383
Remonstrances of his Almoner	384
Habits of the great Nobles	385
Manners of the Court	386
Degeneracy of the Nobles	387
Splendor of their Households	388
Loss of Political Power	389
Depressed Condition of the Commons	390
Petitions of the Cortes	390
Their Remonstrance against Arbitrary Government	391
Their Regard for the National Interests	392
Erroneous Notions respecting Commerce	393

Philip.—Vol. III.—B

xiv CONTENTS.

	PAGE
Sumptuary Laws	394
Encouragement of Bull-Fights	395
Various Subjects of Legislation	396
Schools and Universities	397
Royal Pragmatics	398
Philip's Replies to the Cortes	399
Freedom of Discussion	400
Standing Army	401
Guards of Castile	401

CHAPTER II.

DOMESTIC AFFAIRS OF SPAIN	403
Philip the Champion of the Faith	403
Endowments of the Church	404
Alienations in Mortmain	405
Disputed Prerogatives	406
Appointments to Benefices	407
The Clergy dependent on the Crown	408
The Escorial	409
Motives for its Erection	410
Site selected	410
Convent founded	412
Royal Humility	413
Building commenced	414
Philip's Interest in it	415
His Architectural Taste	415
His Oversight of the Work	416
He governs the World from the Escorial	417
The Edifice endangered by Fire	418
Materials used in its Construction	419
Artists employed	421
Philip's Fondness for Art	421
Completion of the Escorial	422
The Architects	423
Character of the Structure	424
Its Whimsical Design	425
Its Magnitude	426
Interior Decorations	427

CONTENTS.

	PAGE
Ravages it has undergone	428
Its present Condition	428
Anne of Austria	429
Her Reception in Spain	430
Her Marriage with Philip	432
Her Residence at the Escorial	433
Her Character and Habits	434
Her Death	435

HISTORY

OF

PHILIP THE SECOND.

BOOK V.

CHAPTER I.

THE MOORS OF SPAIN.

Conquest of Spain by the Arabs.—Slow Recovery by the Spaniards.—Efforts to convert the Moslems.—Their Homes in the Alpujarras.—Their Treatment by the Government.—The Minister Espinosa.—Edict against the Moriscoes.—Their ineffectual Remonstrance.

1566, 1567.

IT was in the beginning of the eighth century, in the year 711, that the Arabs, filled with the spirit of conquest which had been breathed into them by their warlike apostle, after traversing the southern shores of the Mediterranean, reached the borders of those straits that separate Africa from Europe. Here they paused for a moment, before carrying their banners into a strange and unknown quarter of the globe. It was but for a moment, however, when, with accumulated strength, they descended on the sunny fields of Andalusia, met the whole Gothic array on the banks of the Guadalete, and, after that fatal battle in which King Roderick fell with the flower of his nobility, spread themselves, like an army of locusts, over every part of the Peninsula. Three years sufficed for the conquest of the country,—except that small corner in the north, where a remnant of the Goths contrived to maintain a savage independence, and where the rudeness of the soil held out to the Saracens no temptation to follow them.

It was much the same story that was repeated, more than three centuries later, by the Norman conquerors in England. The battle of Hastings was to that kingdom what the battle of the Guadalete was to Spain; though the Norman barons, as they rode over the prostrate land, dictated terms to the vanquished of a sterner character than those granted by the Saracens.

But whatever resemblance there may be in the general outlines of the two conquests, there is none in the results that followed. In England the Norman and the Saxon, sprung from a common stock, could not permanently be kept asunder by the barrier which at first was naturally interposed between the conqueror and the conquered; and in less, probably, than three centuries after the invasion, the two nations had imperceptibly melted into one, so that the Englishman of that day might trace the current that flowed through his veins to both a Norman and a Saxon origin.

It was far otherwise in Spain, where difference of race, of religion, of national tradition, of moral and physical organization, placed a gulf between the victors and the vanquished too wide to be overleaped. It is true, indeed, that very many of the natives, accepting the liberal terms offered by the Saracens, preferred remaining in the genial clime of the south to sharing the rude independence of their brethren in Asturias, and that, in the course of time, intermarriages, to some extent, took place between them and their Moslem conquerors; to what extent cannot now be known. The intercourse was certainly far greater than that between our New-England ancestors and the Indian race which they found in possession of the soil,—that ill-fated race, which seems to have shrunk from the touch of civilization, and to have passed away before it like the leaves of the forest before the breath of winter. The union was probably not so intimate as that which existed between the old Spaniards and the semi-civilized tribes that occupied the plateau of Mexico, whose descendants at this day are to be there seen filling the highest places, both social and political, and whose especial boast it is to have sprung from the countrymen of Montezuma.

The very anxiety shown by the modern Spaniard to prove that only the *sangre azul*—"blue blood"—flows through his veins, uncontaminated by any Moorish or Jewish taint, may be thought to afford some evidence of the intimacy which once existed between his forefathers and the tribes of Eastern origin. However this may be, it is certain that no length of time ever served, in the eye of the Spaniard, to give the Moslem invader a title to the soil; and after the lapse of nearly eight centuries—as long a period as that which has passed since the Norman conquest—the Arabs were still looked upon as intruders whom it was the sacred duty of the Spaniards to exterminate or to expel from the land.

This, then, was their mission. And it is interesting to see how faithfully they fulfilled it; and during the long period of the Middle Ages, when other nations were occupied with base feudal quarrels or border warfare, it is curious to observe the Spaniard intent on the one great object of reclaiming his country from the possession of the infidel. It was a work of time; and his progress, at first almost imperceptible, was to be measured by centuries. By the end of the ninth century it had reached as far as the Ebro and the Douro. By the middle of the eleventh the victorious banner of the Cid had penetrated to the Tagus. The fortunes of Christian Spain trembled in the balance on the great day of Navas de Tolosa, which gave a permanent ascendency to the Castilian arms; and by the middle of the thirteenth century the campaigns of James the First of Aragon, and of St. Ferdinand of Castile, stripping the Moslems of the other southern provinces, had reduced them to the petty kingdom of Granada. Yet on this narrow spot they still continued to maintain a national existence, and to bid defiance for more than two centuries longer to all the efforts of the Christians. The final triumph of the latter was reserved for the glorious reign of Ferdinand and Isabella. It was on the second of January, 1492, that, after a war which rivalled that of Troy in its duration and surpassed it in the romantic character of its incidents, the august pair made their solemn entry into Granada; while the large silver cross which had served as their banner through the war, sparkling in the sunbeams on the red towers of the Alhambra, announced to the Christian world that the last rood of territory in the Peninsula had passed away forever from the Moslem.

The peculiar nature of the war in which the Spaniard for eight centuries had thus been engaged exercised an important influence on the national character. Generation after generation had passed their lives in one long, uninterrupted crusade. It had something of the same effect on the character of the nation that the wars for the recovery of Palestine had on the Crusaders of the Middle Ages. Every man learned to regard himself as in an especial manner the soldier of Heaven,—forever fighting the great battle of the Faith. With a mind exalted by this sublime conviction, what wonder that he should have been ever ready to discern the immediate interposition of Heaven in his behalf?—that he should have seen again and again the patron saint of his country, charging on his milk-white steed at the head of his celestial chivalry, and restoring the wavering fortunes of the fight? In this exalted state of feeling, institutions that assumed elsewhere only a political or military aspect wore here the garb of religion. Thus the orders of chivalry, of which there were several in the Peninsula, were founded on the same principles as those of Palestine, where the members were pledged to perpetual war against the infidel.

As a consequence of these wars with the Moslems, the patriotic principle became identified with the religious. In the enemies of his country the Spaniard beheld also the enemies of God; and feelings of national hostility were still further embittered by those of religious hatred. In the palmy days of the Arabian empire, these feelings, it is true, were tempered by those of respect for an enemy who in the various forms of civilization surpassed not merely the Spaniards, but every nation in Christendom. Nor was this respect wholly abated under the princes who afterwards ruled with imperial sway over Granada, and who displayed in their little courts such a union of the courtesies of Christian chivalry with the magnificence of the East as shed a ray of glory on the declining days of the Moslem empire in the Peninsula.

But as the Arabs, shorn of their ancient opulence and power, descended in the scale, the Spaniards became more arrogant. The feelings of aversion with which they had hitherto regarded their enemies were now mingled with those of contempt. The latent fire of intolerance was fanned into a blaze by the breath of the fanatical clergy, who naturally possessed unbounded influence in a country where religious considerations entered so largely into the motives of action as they did in Spain. To crown the whole, the date of the fall of Granada coincided with that of the establishment of the Inquisition,—as if the hideous monster had waited the time when an inexhaustible supply of victims might be afforded for its insatiable maw.

By the terms of the treaty of capitulation, the people of Granada were allowed to remain in possession of their religion and to exercise its rites; and it was especially stipulated that no inducements or menaces should be held out to effect their conversion to Christianity.[1] For a few years the conquerors respected these

---

[1] "Que ningun Moro ni Mora serán apremiados á ser Christianos contra su voluntad; y que si alguna doncella, ó casada, ó viuda, por

provisions. Under the good Talavera, the first archbishop of Granada, no attempt was made to convert the Moslems except by the legitimate means of preaching to the people and of expounding to them the truths of revelation. Under such a course of instruction the work of proselytism, though steadily, went on too slowly to satisfy the impatience of some of the clergy. Among others, that extraordinary man, Cardinal Ximenes, archbishop of Toledo, was eager to try his own hand in the labor of conversion. Having received the royal assent, he set about the affair with characteristic ardor, and with as little scruple as to the means to be employed as the most zealous propagandist could have desired. When reasoning and expostulation failed, he did not hesitate to resort to bribes, and, if need were, to force. Under these combined influences the work of proselytism went on apace. Thousands were added daily to the Christian fold; and the more orthodox Mussulmans trembled at the prospect of a general defection of their countrymen. Exasperated by the unscrupulous measures of the prelate, and the gross violation they involved of the treaty, they broke out into an insurrection, which soon extended along the mountain-ranges in the neighborhood of Granada.

Ferdinand and Isabella, alarmed at the consequences, were filled with indignation at the high-handed conduct of Ximenes. But he replied that the state of things was precisely that which was most to be desired. By placing themselves in an attitude of rebellion, the Moors had re-

razon de algunos amores se quisiere tornar Christiana, tampoco será recebida, hasta ser interrogada." See the original treaty, as given *in extenso* by Marmol, Rebelion de los Moriscos (Madrid, 1797), tom. i. pp. 83-98.

nounced all the advantages secured by the treaty, and had, moreover, incurred the penalties of death and confiscation of property! It would be an act of grace in the sovereigns to overlook their offence and grant an amnesty for the past, on condition that every Moor should at once receive baptism or leave the country.[2] This precious piece of casuistry, hardly surpassed by any thing in ecclesiastical annals, found favor in the eyes of the sovereigns, who, after the insurrection had been quelled, lost no time in proposing the terms suggested by their minister as the only terms of reconciliation open to the Moors. And as but few of that unhappy people were prepared to renounce their country and their worldly prospects for the sake of their faith, the result was that in a very short space of time, with but comparatively few exceptions, every Moslem in the dominions of Castile consented to abjure his own faith and receive that of his enemies.[3]

A similar course of proceeding was attended with similar results in Valencia and other dominions of the crown of Aragon, in the earlier part of Charles the Fifth's reign; and before that young monarch had been ten years upon the throne the whole Moorish population—*Moriscoes*, as they were henceforth to be called—were brought within the pale of Christianity, or, to speak more correctly, within that of the Inquisition.[4]

[2] "Y que pues habian sido rebeldes, y por ello merecian pena de muerte y perdimento de bienes, el perdon que les concediese fuese condicional, con que se tornasen Christianos, ó dexasen la tierra." Marmol, Rebelion de los Moriscos, tom. i. p. 122.

[3] The reader curious in the matter will find a full account of it in the History of Ferdinand and Isabella, part ii. chapters 6, 7.

[4] Advertimientos de Don Geronimo Corella sobre la Conversion de los Moriscos del Reyno de Valencia, MS.

Such conversions, it may well be believed, had taken too little root in the heart to bear fruit. It was not long before the agents of the Holy Office detected, under the parade of outward conformity, as rank a growth of infidelity as had existed before the conquest. The blame might in part, indeed, be fairly imputed to the lukewarmness of the Christian laborers employed in the work of conversion. To render this more effectual, the government had caused churches to be built in the principal towns and villages occupied by the Moriscoes, and sent missionaries among them to wean them from their errors and unfold the great truths of revelation. But an act of divine grace could alone work an instantaneous change in the convictions of a nation. The difficulties of the preachers were increased by their imperfect acquaintance with the language of their hearers; and they had still further to overcome the feelings of jealousy and aversion with which the Spaniard was naturally regarded by the Mussulman. Discouraged by these obstacles, the missionary became indifferent to the results. Instead of appealing to the understanding or touching the heart of his hearer, he was willing to accept his conformity to outward ceremony as the evidence of his conversion. Even in his own performance of the sacred rites the ecclesiastic showed a careless indifference, that proved his heart was little in the work; and he scattered the purifying waters of baptism in so heedless a way over the multitude that it was not uncommon for a Morisco to assert that none of the consecrated drops had fallen upon him.[5]

[5] "Sin tratar de instruir á cada uno en particular ni de examinar

The representations of the clergy at length drew the attention of the government. It was decided that the best mode of effecting the conversion of the Moslems was by breaking up those associations which connected them with the past,—by compelling them, in short, to renounce their ancient usages, their national dress, and even their language. An extraordinary edict to that effect, designed for Granada, was accordingly published by Charles in the summer of 1526; and all who did not conform to it were to be arraigned before the Inquisition. The law was at once met, as might have been expected, by remonstrances from the men of most consideration among the Moriscoes, who, to give efficacy to their petition, promised the round sum of eighty thousand gold ducats to the emperor in case their prayers should be granted. Charles, who in his early days did not always allow considerations of religion to supersede those of a worldly policy, lent a favorable ear to the petitioners; and the monstrous edict, notwithstanding some efforts to the contrary, was never suffered to go into operation during his reign.[6]

los ni saber su voluntad los baptizaron á manadas y de modo que algunos de ellos, segun es fama, pusieron pleito que no les avia tocado el agua que en comun les hechavan." Advertimientos de Corella, MS.

[6] Marmol, Rebelion de los Moriscos, tom. i. pp. 133-155.—Bleda, Coronica de los Moros de España (Valencia, 1618), p. 656.—Advertimientos de Corella, MS.—Ferreras, Hist. générale d'Espagne, tom. ix. pp. 65, 68.—Vanderhammen, Don Juan de Austria, fol. 55.—The last writer says that, besides the largess to the emperor, the Moriscoes were canny enough to secure the good will of his ministers by a liberal supply of doubloons to them also: "Sirvieron al Emperador con ochenta mil ducados. Aprovechóles esto, y buena suma de do-

Such was the state of things on the accession of Philip the Second. Granada, Malaga, and the other principal cities of the south were filled with a mingled population of Spaniards and Moriscoes, the latter of whom,—including many persons of wealth and consideration,—under the influence of a more intimate contact with the Christians, gave evidence, from time to time, of conversion to the faith of their conquerors. But by far the larger part of the Moorish population was scattered over the mountain-range of the Alpujarras, southeast of Granada, and among the bold sierras that stretch along the southern shores of Spain. Here, amidst those frosty peaks, rising to the height of near twelve thousand feet above the level of the sea, and readily descried, from their great elevation, by the distant voyager on the Mediterranean, was many a green, sequestered valley, on which the Moorish peasant had exhausted that elaborate culture which in the palmy days of his nation was unrivalled in any part of Europe.⁷

blones que dieron à los privados para que Carlos suspendiesse la execucion deste acuerdo."

⁷ Calderon, in his "Amar despues de la Muerte," has shed the splendors of his muse over the green and sunny spots that glitter like emeralds amidst the craggy wilds of the Alpujarras;

"Porque entre puntas y puntas
Hay valles que la hermosean,
Campos que la fertilizan,
Jardines que la deleitan.
Toda ella está poblada
De villages y de aldeas;
Tal, que, cuando el sol se pone
Á las vislumbres que deja,
Parecen riscos nacidos
Cóncavos entre las peñas,
Que rodaron de la cumbre
Aunque á la falda no llegán."

His patient toil had constructed terraces from the rocky soil, and, planting them with vines, had clothed the bald sides of the sierra with a delicious verdure. With the like industry he had contrived a net-work of canals along the valleys and lower levels, which, fed by the streams from the mountains, nourished the land with perpetual moisture. The different elevations afforded so many different latitudes for agricultural production; and the fig, the pomegranate, and the orange grew almost side by side with the hemp of the north and the grain of more temperate climates. The lower slopes of the sierra afforded extensive pastures for flocks of merino sheep;[8] and the mulberry-tree was raised in great abundance for the manufacture of silk, which formed an important article of export from the kingdom of Granada.

Thus gathered in their little hamlets among the mountains, the people of the Alpujarras maintained the same sort of rugged independence which belonged to the ancient Goth when he had taken shelter from the Saracen invader in the fastnesses of Asturias. Here the Moriscoes, formed into communities which preserved their national associations, still cherished the traditions of their fathers, and perpetuated those usages and domestic institutions that kept alive the memory of ancient days. It was from the Alpujarras that, in former times, the kings of Granada had drawn the brave soldiery who enabled them for so many years to

[8] Señor de Gayangos, correcting a blunder of Casiri on the subject, tells us that the Arabic name of the Alpujarras was *Al-busherát*, signifying "mountains abounding in pastures." See that treasure of Oriental learning, the History of the Mohammedan Dynasties in Spain (London, 1843), vol. ii. p. 515.

bold defiance to their enemies. The trade of war was now at an end. But the hardy life of the mountaineer gave robustness to his frame, and saved him from the effeminacy and sloth which corrupted the inhabitants of the capital. Secluded among his native hills, he cherished those sentiments of independence which ill suited a conquered race; and, in default of a country which he could call his own, he had that strong attachment to the soil which is akin to patriotism, and which is most powerful among the inhabitants of a mountain-region.

The products of the husbandman furnished the staples of a gainful commerce with the nations on the Mediterranean, and especially with the kindred people on the Barbary shores. The treaty of Granada secured certain commercial advantages to the Moors beyond what were enjoyed by the Spaniards.[1] This, it may well be believed, was looked upon with no friendly eye by the latter, who had some ground, moreover, for distrusting the policy of an intercourse between the Moslems of Spain and those of Africa, bound together as they were by so many ties,—above all, by a common hatred of the Christians. With the feelings of political distrust were mingled those of cupidity and envy,

[1] Such was the exemption from certain duties paid by the Christians in their trade with the Barbary coast,—a singular and not very potent provision: Que si los Moros que entraren debaxo de estas capitulaciones y conciertos, quisieren ir con sus mercaderias á tratar y contratar en Berberia, se les dará licencia para poderlo hacer é bremen e, y lo mesmo en todos los lugares de Castilla y de la Andalucia, sin pagar portazgos ni los otros derechos que los Christianos acostumbran pagar. Marmol Rebelion de los Moriscos, tom. i. p. 53.

as the Spaniard saw the fairest provinces of the south still in the hands of the accursed race of Ishmael, while he was condemned to earn a scanty subsistence from the comparatively ungenial soil of the north.

In this state of things, with the two races not merely dissimilar, but essentially hostile to one another, it will readily be understood how difficult it must have been to devise any system of legislation by which they could be brought to act in harmony as members of the same political body. That the endeavors of the Spanish government were not crowned with success would hardly surprise us, even had its measures been more uniformly wise and considerate.

The government caused the Alpujarras to be divided into districts and placed under the control of magistrates, who, with their families, resided in the places assigned as the seats of their jurisdiction. There seem to have been few other Christians who dwelt among the Moorish settlements in the sierra, except, indeed, the priests who had charge of the spiritual concerns of the natives. As the conversion of these latter was the leading object of the government, they caused churches to be erected in all the towns and hamlets, and the curates were instructed to use every effort to enlighten the minds of their flocks, and to see that they were punctual in attendance on the rites and ceremonies of the Church. But it was soon too evident that attention to forms and ceremonies was the only approach made to the conversion of the heathen, and that below this icy crust of conformity the waters of infidelity lay as dark and deep as ever. The result, no doubt, was to be partly charged on the clergy themselves, many of whom grew languid in the execution of a task which seemed to them to be hopeless.[10] And what task, in truth, could be more hopeless than that of persuading a whole nation at once to renounce their long-established convictions, to abjure the faith of their fathers, associated in their minds with many a glorious recollection, and to embrace the faith of the very men whom they regarded with unmeasured hatred? It would be an act of humiliation not to be expected even in a conquered race.

In accomplishing a work so much to be desired, the Spaniards, if they cannot be acquitted of the charge of persecution, must be allowed not to have urged persecution to any thing like the extent which they had done in the case of the Protestant reformers. Whether from policy or from some natural regard to the helplessness of these benighted heathen, the bloodhounds of the Inquisition were not as yet allowed to run down their game at will; and, if they did terrify the natives by displaying their formidable fangs, the time had not yet come when they were to slip the leash and spring upon their miserable victims. It is true there were some exceptions to this more discreet policy. The Holy Office had its agents abroad, who kept watch upon the Moriscoes; and occasionally the more flagrant

[10] Such is the opinion expressed by the author of the "*Advertimientos*," whose remarks—having particular reference to Valencia—are conceived in a spirit of candor, and of charity towards the Moslems, rarely found in a Spaniard of the sixteenth century. "De donde," he says, "colije claramente que el no sanar estos enfermos hasta agora no se puede imputar à ser incurable la enfermedad, sine à averse errado la cura, y tambien se vee que hasta oy no estan bastamente descargados delante de Dios nuestro Señor aquellos á quien toca este negocio, pues no han puesto los medios que Christo nuestro Señor tiene ordenados para la cura de este mal." MS.

offenders were delivered up to its tender mercies."¹¹ But a more frequent source of annoyance arose from the teasing ordinances from time to time issued by the government, which could have answered no other purpose than to irritate the temper and sharpen the animosity of the Moriscoes. If the government had failed in the important work of conversion, it was the more incumbent on it, by every show of confidence and kindness, to conciliate the good will of the conquered people, and enable them to live in harmony with their conquerors, as members of the same community. Such was not the policy of Philip, any more than it had been that of his predecessors.

During the earlier years of his reign the king's attention was too closely occupied with foreign affairs to leave him much leisure for those of the Moriscoes. It was certain, however, that they would not long escape the notice of a prince who regarded uniformity of faith as the corner-stone of his government. The first important act of legislation bearing on these people was in 1560, when the Cortes of Castile presented a remonstrance to the throne against the use of negro slaves by the Moriscoes, who were sure to instruct them in their Mahometan tenets and thus to multiply the number of infidels in the land."¹² A royal *prag-*

---

[11] "Forzandoles con injurias y penas pecuniarias y justiciando á algunos de ellos." Advertimientos de Corella, MS.—Mendoza, speaking of a somewhat later period, just before the outbreak, briefly alludes to the fact that the Inquisition was then beginning to worry the Moriscoes more than usual : "Porque la Inquisicion les comenzó á apretar mas de lo ordinario." Guerra de Granada (Valencia, 1776), p. 20.

[12] Marmol, Rebelion de los Moriscos, tom. i. p. 135.

matic was accordingly passed, interdicting the use of African slaves by the Moslems of Granada. The prohibition caused the greatest annoyance; for the wealthier classes were in the habit of employing these slaves for domestic purposes, while in the country they were extensively used for agricultural labor.

In 1563 another ordinance was published, reviving a law which had fallen into disuse, and which prohibited the Moriscoes from having any arms in their possession but such as were duly licensed by the captain-general and were stamped with his escutcheon.[13] The office of captain-general of Granada was filled at this time by Don Iñigo Lopez de Mendoza, count of Tendilla, who soon after, on his father's death, succeeded to the title of marquis of Mondejar. The important post which he held had been hereditary in his family ever since the conquest of Granada. The present nobleman was a worthy scion of the illustrious house from which he sprang.[14] His manners were blunt, and not such as win popularity; but he was a man of integrity, with a nice sense of honor and a humane heart,—the last of not too common occurrence in the iron days of chivalry. Though bred a soldier, he was inclined to peace. His life had been passed

---

[13] Marmol, Rebelion de los Moriscos, tom. ii. p. 338.—Ordenanzas de Granada, fol. 375, ap. Circourt, Hist. des Arabes d'Espagne (Paris, 1846), tom. ii. p. 267.—The penalty for violating the above ordinance was six years' hard labor in the galleys. That for counterfeiting the stamp of the Mendoza arms was death. *Væ victis!*

[14] The name of Mendoza, which occupied for so many generations a prominent place in arms, in politics, and in letters, makes its first appearance in Spanish history as far back as the beginning of the thirteenth century.—Mariana, Historia de España, tom. i. p. 676.

much among the Moriscoes, so that he perfectly understood their humors; and, as he was a person of prudence and moderation, it is not improbable, had affairs been left to his direction, that the country would have escaped many of those troubles which afterwards befell it.

It was singular, considering the character of Mendoza, that he should have recommended so ill-advised a measure as that relating to the arms of the Moriscoes. The ordinance excited a general indignation in Granada. The people were offended by the distrust which such a law implied of their loyalty. They felt it an indignity to be obliged to sue for permission to do what they considered it was theirs of right to do. Those of higher condition disdained to wear weapons displaying the heraldic bearings of the Mendozas instead of their own. But the greater number, without regard to the edict, provided themselves secretly with arms, which, as it reached the ears of the authorities, led to frequent prosecutions. Thus a fruitful source of irritation was opened, and many, to escape punishment, fled to the mountains, and there too often joined the brigands who haunted the passes of the Alpujarras and bade defiance to the feeble police of the Spaniards.[15]

These impolitic edicts, as they were irritating to the Moriscoes, were but preludes to an ordinance of so astounding a character as to throw the whole country

---

[15] M. de Circourt, in his interesting volumes, has given a minute account—much too minute for these pages—of the first developments of the insurrectionary spirit of the Moriscoes, in which he shows a very careful study of the subject.—Hist. des Arabes d'Espagne, tom. ii. pp. 263, et seq.

into a state of revolution. The apostasy of the Moriscoes—or, to speak more correctly, the constancy with which they adhered to the faith of their fathers—gave great scandal to the old Christians—especially to the clergy, and above all to its head, Don Pedro Guerrero, archbishop of Granada. This prelate seems to have been a man of an uneasy, meddlesome spirit, and possessed of a full share of the bigotry of his time. While in Rome, shortly before this period, he had made such a representation to Pope Pius the Fourth as drew from that pontiff a remonstrance, addressed to the Spanish government, on the spiritual condition of the Moriscoes. Soon after, in the year 1567, a memorial was presented to the government by Guerrero and the clergy of his diocese, in which, after insisting on the manifold backslidings of the "new Christians," as the Moriscoes were termed, they loudly called for some efficacious measures to arrest the evil. These people, they said, whatever show of conformity they might make to the requisitions of the Church, were infidels at heart. When their children were baptized, they were careful, on returning home, to wash away the traces of baptism, and, after circumcising them, to give them Moorish names. In like manner, when their marriages had been solemnized with Christian rites, they were sure to confirm them afterwards by their own ceremonies, accompanied with the national songs and dances. They continued to observe Friday as a holy day; and, what was of graver moment, they were known to kidnap the children of the Christians and sell them to their brethren on the coast of Barbary, where they were circumcised, and nurtured in the

Mahometan religion. This last accusation, however improbable, found credit with the Spaniards, and sharpened the feelings of jealousy and hatred with which they regarded the unhappy race of Ishmael.[16]

The memorial of the clergy received prompt attention from the government, at whose suggestion, very possibly, it had been prepared. A commission was at once appointed to examine into the matter; and their report was laid before a junta consisting of both ecclesiastics and laymen, and embracing names of the highest consideration for talent and learning in the kingdom. Among its members we find the duke of Alva, who had not yet set out on his ominous mission to the Netherlands. At its head was Diego de Espinosa, at that time the favorite minister of Philip, or at least the one who had the largest share in the direction of affairs. He was a man after the king's own heart, and, from the humble station of *colegial mayor* of the college of Cuença in Salamanca, had been advanced by successive steps to the high post of president of the Council of Castile and of the Council of the Indies. He was now also bishop of Siguenza, one of the richest sees in the kingdom. He held an important office in the Inquisition, and was soon to succeed Valdés in the unenviable post of grand inquisitor. To conclude the catalogue of his honors, no long time was to elapse before, at his master's suggestion, he was to receive from Rome a cardinal's hat. The deference shown by Philip to his minister, increased as it was by this new

---

[16] Ferreras, Hist. d'Espagne, tom. ix. p. 524.—Marmol, Rebelion de los Moriscos, tom. i. p. 142.—Vanderhammen, Don Juan de Austria, fol. 55.

accession of spiritual dignity, far exceeded what he had ever shown to any other of his subjects.

Espinosa was at this time in the morning, or rather the meridian, of his power. His qualifications for business would have been extraordinary even in a layman. He was patient of toil, cheerfully doing the work of others as well as his own. This was so far fortunate that it helped to give him that control in the direction of affairs which was coveted by his aspiring nature. He had a dignified and commanding presence, with but few traces of that humility which would have been graceful in one who had risen so high by his master's favor as much as by his own deserts. His haughty bearing gave offence to the old nobility of Castile, who scornfully looked from the minister's present elevation to the humble level from which he had risen. It was regarded with less displeasure, it is said, by the king, who was not unwilling to see the pride of the ancient aristocracy rebuked by one whom he had himself raised from the dust.[17] Their mortification, however, was to be appeased ere long by the fall of the favorite,—an event as signal and unexpected by the world, and as tragical to the subject of it, as the fall of Wolsey.

The man who was qualified for the place of grand

[17] Such was the judgment of the acute Venetian who, as one of the train of the minister Tiepolo, obtained a near view of what was passing in the court of Philip the Second: "Levato di bassissimo stato dal re, e posto in tanta grandezza in pochi anni, per esser huomo da bene, libero et schietto, et perchè S. M. vuol tener bassi li grandi di Spagna, conoscendo l' alticrissima natura loro." Gachard, Relations des Ambassadeurs Vénitiens sur Charles-Quint et Philippe II. (Bruxelles, 1855), p. 175.

inquisitor was not likely to feel much sympathy for the race of unbelievers. It was unfortunate for the Moriscoes that their destinies should be placed in the hands of such a minister as Espinosa. After due deliberation, the junta came to the decision that the only remedy for the present evil was to lay the axe to the root of it,—to cut off all those associations which connected the Moriscoes with their earlier history, and which were so many obstacles in the way of their present conversion. It was recommended that they should be interdicted from employing the Arabic either in speaking or writing, for which they were to use only the Castilian. They were not even to be allowed to retain their family names, but were to exchange them for Spanish ones. All written instruments and legal documents, of whatever kind, were declared to be void and of no effect unless in the Castilian. As time must be allowed for a whole people to change its language, three years were assigned as the period at the end of which this provision should take effect.

They were to be required to exchange their national dress for that of the Spaniards; and, as the Oriental costume was highly ornamented, and often very expensive, they were to be allowed to wear their present clothes one year longer if of silk, and two years if of cotton, the latter being the usual apparel of the poorer classes. The women, moreover, both old and young, were to be required, from the passage of the law, to go abroad with their faces uncovered,—a scandalous thing among Mahometans.

Their weddings were to be conducted in public, after the Christian forms; and the doors of their houses were to be left open during the day of the ceremony, that any one might enter and see that they did not have recourse to unhallowed rites. They were further to be interdicted from the national songs and dances with which they were wont to celebrate their domestic festivities. Finally, as rumors—most absurd ones—had got abroad that the warm baths which the natives were in the habit of using in their houses were perverted to licentious indulgences, they were to be required to destroy the vessels in which they bathed, and to use nothing of the kind thereafter.

These several provisions were to be enforced by penalties of the sternest kind. For the first offence the convicted party was to be punished with imprisonment for a month, with banishment from the country for two years, and with a fine varying from six hundred to ten thousand maravedis. For a second offence the penalties were to be doubled; and for a third, the culprit, in addition to former penalties, was to be banished for life. The ordinance was closely modelled on that of Charles the Fifth, which, as we have seen, he was too politic to carry into execution.[18]

Such were the principal provisions of a law which, for cruelty and absurdity, has scarcely a parallel in history. For what could be more absurd than the attempt by an act of legislation to work such a change in the long-established habits of a nation,—to efface those

[18] This remarkable ordinance may be found in the Nueva Recopilacion (ed. 1640), lib. viii. tit. 2, leyes 13-18.—The most severe penalties were those directed against the heinous offence of indulging in warm baths. For a second repetition of this, the culprit was sentenced to six years' labor in the galleys and the confiscation of half his estate!

recollections of the past, to which men ever cling most closely under the pressure of misfortune,—to blot out by a single stroke of the pen, as it were, not only the creed but the nationality of a people,—to convert the Moslem at once both into a Christian and into a Castilian? It would be difficult to imagine any greater outrage offered to a people than the provision compelling women to lay aside their veils,—associated as these were in every Eastern mind with the obligations of modesty; or that in regard to opening the doors of the houses and exposing those within to the insolent gaze of every passer; or that in relation to the baths,—so indispensable to cleanliness and comfort, especially in the warm climate of the south.

But the masterpiece of absurdity, undoubtedly, is the stipulation in regard to the Arabic language; as if by any human art a whole population, in the space of three years, could be made to substitute a foreign tongue for its own, and that, too, under circumstances of peculiar difficulty, partly arising from the total want of affinity between the Semitic and the European languages, and partly from the insulated position of the Moriscoes, who in the cities had separate quarters assigned to them, in the same manner as the Jews, which cut them off from intimate intercourse with the Christians. We may well doubt, from the character of this provision, whether the government had so much at heart the conversion of the Moslems as the desire to entangle them in such violations of the law as should afford a plausible pretext for driving them from the country altogether. One is strengthened in this view of the subject by the significant reply of Otadin, pro-

fessor of theology at Alcalá, who, when consulted by
Philip on the expediency of the ordinance, gave his
hearty approbation of it, by quoting the appalling
Spanish proverb, " The fewer enemies, the better." [19]
It was reserved for the imbecile Philip the Third to
crown the disasters of his reign by the expulsion of the
Moriscoes. Yet no one can doubt that it was a consummation earnestly desired by the great body of the
Spaniards, who looked, as we have seen, with longing
eyes to the fair territory which they possessed, and who
regarded them with the feelings of distrust and aversion
with which men regard those on whom they have inflicted injuries too great to be forgiven.

Yet there were some in the junta with whom the proposed ordinance found no favor. Among these, one
who calls to mind his conduct in the Netherlands may
be surprised to find the duke of Alva. Here, as in
that country, his course was doubtless dictated less by
considerations of humanity than of policy. Whatever
may have been his reasons, they had little weight with
Espinosa, who probably felt a secret satisfaction in
thwarting the man whom he regarded with all the
jealousy of a rival.[20]

What was Philip's own opinion on the matter we can

[19] " De los enemijos los menos."—Circourt gives a version of the
whole of the professor's letter, with his precious commentary on this
text. (Hist. des Arabes d'Espagne, tom. ii. p. 278.) According to
Ferreras, Philip highly relished the maxim of his ghostly counsellor.
Hist. d'Espagne, tom. ix. p. 525.

[20] Cabrera, throwing the responsibility of the subsequent troubles
on Espinosa and Deza, sarcastically remarks that " two cowls had the
ordering of an affair which had been better left to men with helmets
on their heads." Cabrera, Filipe Segundo, lib. vii. cap. 21.

but conjecture from our general knowledge of his character. He professed to be guided by the decision of the "wise and learned men" to whom he had committed the subject. That this decision did no great violence to his own feelings, we may infer from the promptness with which he signed the ordinance. This he did on the seventeenth of November, 1566, when the pragmatic became a law.

It was resolved, however, not to give publicity to it at once. It was committed to the particular charge of one of the members of the junta, Diego Deza, auditor of the Holy Office, and lately raised by Espinosa to the important post of president of the chancery of Granada. This put him at once at the head of the civil administration of the province, as the marquis of Mondejar was at the head of the military. The different views of policy entertained by the two men led to a conflict of authority, which proved highly prejudicial to affairs. Deza, who afterwards rose to the dignity of cardinal, was a man whose plausible manners covered an inflexible will. He showed, notwithstanding, an entire subserviency to the wishes of his patron, Espinosa, who committed to him the execution of his plans.

The president resolved, with more policy than humanity, to defer the publication of the edict till the ensuing first of January, 1567, the day preceding that which the Spaniards commemorated as the anniversary of the surrender of the capital. This humiliating event, brought home at such a crisis to the Moriscoes, might help to break their spirits, and dispose them to receive the obnoxious edict with less resistance.

On the appointed day the magistrates of the principal tribunals, with the corregidor of Granada at their head, went in solemn procession to the Albaicin, the quarter occupied by the Moriscoes. They marched to the sound of kettle-drums, trumpets, and other instruments; and the inhabitants, attracted by the noise and fond of novelty, came running from their houses to swell the ranks of the procession on its way to the great square of *Bab el Bonat*. This was an open space, of large extent, where the people of Granada, in ancient times, used to assemble to celebrate the coronation of a new sovereign; and the towers were still standing from which the Moslem banners waved, on those days, over the heads of the shouting multitude. As the people now gathered tumultuously around these ancient buildings, the public crier, from an elevated place, read, in audible tones and in the Arabic language, the royal ordinance. One may imagine the emotions of shame, sorrow, and indignation with which the vast assembly, consisting of both sexes, listened to the words of an instrument every sentence of which seemed to convey a personal indignity to the hearers, —an outrage on all those ideas of decorum and decency in which they had been nurtured from infancy; which rudely rent asunder all the fond ties of country and kindred; which violated the privacy of domestic life, deprived them of the use of their own speech, and reduced them to a state of utter humiliation unknown to the meanest of their slaves. Some of the weaker sort gave way to piteous and passionate exclamations, wringing their hands in an agony of grief. Others, of sterner temper, broke forth into menaces and fierce invective, accompanied with the most furious gesticulations.' Others, again, listened with that dogged, determined air which showed that the mood was not the less dangerous that it was a silent one. The whole multitude was in a state of such agitation that an accident might have readily produced an explosion which would have shaken Granada to its foundations. Fortunately, there were a few discreet persons in the assembly, older and more temperate than the rest, who had sufficient authority over their countrymen to prevent a tumult. They reminded them that in their fathers' time the emperor Charles the Fifth had consented to suspend the execution of a similar ordinance. At all events, it was better to try first what could be done by argument and persuasion. When these failed, it would be time enough to think of vengeance.[21]

One of the older Moriscoes, a man of much consideration among his countrymen, was accordingly chosen to wait on the president and explain their views in regard to the edict. This he did at great length, and in a manner which must have satisfied any fair mind of the groundlessness of the charges brought against the Moslems, and the cruelty and impracticability of the

[21] Marmol, Rebelion de los Moriscos, tom. i. pp. 147-151.—Circourt, Hist. des Arabes d'Espagne, tom. ii. p. 283.—Ferreras, Hist. d'Espagne, tom. ix. p. 535.—Dr. Salazar de Mendoza considers that nothing but a real love of rebellion could have induced the Moriscoes to find a pretext for it in a measure so just and praiseworthy, and every way so conducive to their own salvation, as this ordinance: "Tomaron por achaque esta accion tan justificada y meritoria del Rey, y para sus almas tan provechosa y saludable." Monarquia de España, tom. ii. p. 137.

measures proposed by the government. The president, having granted to the envoy a patient and courteous hearing, made a short and not very successful attempt to vindicate the course of the administration. He finally disposed of the whole question by declaring that "the law was too just and holy, and had been made with too much consideration, ever to be repealed; and that, in fine, regarded as a question of interest, his majesty estimated the salvation of a single soul as of greater price than all the revenues he drew from the Moriscoes."[22] An answer like this must have effectually dispelled all thoughts of a composition, such as had formerly been made with the emperor.

Defeated in this quarter, the Moriscoes determined to lay their remonstrance before the throne. They were fortunate in obtaining for this purpose the services of Don Juan Henriquez, a nobleman of the highest rank and consideration, who had large estates at Beza, in the heart of Granada, and who felt a strong sympathy for the unfortunate natives. Having consented, though with much reluctance, to undertake the mission, he repaired to Madrid, obtained an audience of the king, and presented to him a memorial on behalf of his unfortunate subjects. Philip received him graciously, and promised to give all attention to the paper. "What I have done in this matter," said the king, "has been done by the advice of wise and con-

---

[22] "Y al fin concluyó con decirle resolutamente, que su Magestad queria mas fe que farda, y que preciaba mas salvar una alma, que todo quanto le podian dar de renta los Moriscos nuevamente convertidos." Marmol, Rebelion de los Moriscos, tom. i. p. 163.

scientious men, who have given me to understand that it was my duty."[23]

Shortly afterwards, Henriquez received an intimation that he was to look for his answer to the president of Castile. Espinosa, after listening to the memorial, expressed his surprise that a person of the high condition of Don Juan Henriquez should have consented to take charge of such a mission. "It was for that very reason I undertook it," replied the nobleman, "as affording me a better opportunity of being of service to the king." "It can be of no use," said the minister: "religious men have represented to his majesty that at his door lies the salvation of these Moors; and the ordinance which has been decreed, he has determined shall be carried into effect."[24]

Baffled in this direction, the persevering envoy laid his memorial before the councillors of state, and endeavored to interest them in behalf of his clients. In this he met with more success; and several of that body, among whom may be mentioned the duke of Alva and Luis de Avila, the grand commander of Alcántara, whom Charles the Fifth had honored with his friendship, entered heartily into his views. But it availed little with the minister, who would not even consent to delay the execution of the ordinance until time should have been given for further inquiry, or to confine the operation of it, at the outset, to one or two of the provisions, in order to ascertain what would

---

[23] "Que él habia consultado aquel negocio con hombres de ciencia y conciencia, y le decian que estaba obligado á hacer lo que hacia." Marmol, Rebelion de los Moriscos, tom. i. p. 175.

[24] "Que el negocio de la prematica estaba determinado, y su Magestad resoluta en que se cumpliese." Ibid., ubi supra.

probably be the temper of the Moriscoes.[25] Nothing would suit the peremptory humor of Espinosa but the instant execution of the law in all its details.

Nor would he abate any thing of this haughty tone in favor of the captain-general, the marquis of Mondejar. That nobleman, with good reason, had felt himself aggrieved that in discussions so materially affecting his own government he should not have been invited to take a part. From motives of expediency, as much as of humanity, he was decidedly opposed to the passage of the ordinance. It was perhaps a knowledge of this that had excluded him from a seat in the junta. His representations made no impression on Espinosa; and when he urged that, if the law were to be carried into effect, he ought to be provided with such a force as would enable him to quell any attempt at resistance, the minister made light of the danger, assuring him that three hundred additional troops were as many as the occasion demanded. Espinosa then peremptorily adjourned all further discussion, by telling the captain-general that it would be well for him to return at once to Granada, where his presence would be needed to enforce the execution of the law.[26]

It was clear that no door was left open to further discussion, and that, under the present government, no

---

[25] Marmol, Rebelion de los Moriscos, tom. i. p. 176.—Cabrera, Filipe Segundo, lib. vii. cap. 21.

[26] "A estas y otras muchas razones que el Marques de Mondejar daba, Don Diego de Espinosa le respondió, que la voluntad de su Magestad era aquella, y que se fuese al reyno de Granada, donde seria de mucha importancia su persona, atropellando como siempre todas las dificultades que le ponian por delante." Marmol, Rebelion de los Moriscos, tom. i. p. 168.

chance remained to the unfortunate Moriscoes of buying off the law by the payment of a round sum, as in the time of Charles the Fifth. All negotiations were at an end. They had only to choose between implicit obedience and open rebellion. It was not strange that they chose the latter.

CHAPTER II.

REBELLION OF THE MORISCOES.

Resistance of the Moriscoes.—Night-Assault on Granada.—Rising in the Alpujarras.—Election of a King.—Massacre of the Christians.

1568.

THE same day on which the ordinance was published in the capital, it was proclaimed in every part of the kingdom of Granada. Everywhere it was received with the same feelings of shame, sorrow, and indignation. Before giving way to these feelings by any precipitate action, the Moriscoes of the Alpujarras were discreet enough to confer with their countrymen in the Albaicin, who advised them to remain quiet until they should learn the result of the conferences going on at Madrid.

Before these were concluded, the year expired after which it would be penal for a Morisco to wear garments of silk. By the president's orders it was proclaimed by the clergy, in the pulpits throughout the city, that the law would be enforced to the letter. This was followed by more than one edict relating to other matters, but yet tending to irritate still further the minds of the Moriscoes.[1]

[1] An ordinance was passed at this time, that the Moriscoes who had come from the country to reside, with their families, in Granada, should leave the city and return whence they came, under pain of

All hope of relieving themselves of the detested ordinance having thus vanished, the leaders of the Albaicin took counsel as to the best mode of resisting the government. The first step seemed to be to get possession of the capital. There was at this time in Granada a Morisco named Farax Aben-Farax, who followed the trade of a dyer. But, though he was engaged in this humble calling, the best blood of the Abencerrages flowed in his veins. He was a man of a fierce, indeed ferocious nature, hating the Christians with his whole heart, and longing for the hour when he could avenge on their heads the calamities of his countrymen. As his occupation carried him frequently into the Alpujarras, he was extensively acquainted with the inhabitants. He undertook to raise a force there of eight thousand men and bring them down secretly by night into the *vega*, where, with the aid of his countrymen in the Albaicin, he might effect an entrance into the city, overpower the garrison in the Alhambra, put all who resisted to the sword, and make himself master of the capital. The time fixed upon for the execution of the plan was Holy Thursday, in the ensuing month of

---

death. (Marmol, Rebelion de los Moriscos, tom. i. p. 169.) By another ordinance, the Moriscoes were required to give up their children between the ages of three and fifteen, to be placed in schools and educated in the Christian doctrine and the Castilian tongue. (Ibid., p. 170.) The *Nueva Recopilacion* contains two laws passed about this time, making it a capital offence to hold any intercourse with Turks or Moors who might visit Granada, even though they came not as corsairs, but for purposes of traffic. (Lib. viii. tit. 26, leyes 16, 18.) Such a law proves the constant apprehensions in which the Spaniards lived of a treasonable correspondence between their Morisco subjects and the foreign Moslems.

April, when the attention of the Spaniards would be occupied with their religious solemnities.

A secret known to so many could not be so well kept, and for so long a time, but that some information of it reached the ears of the Christians. It seems to have given little uneasiness to Deza, who had anticipated some such attempt from the turbulent spirit of the Moriscoes. The captain-general, however, thought it prudent to take additional precautions against it; and he accordingly distributed arms among the citizens, strengthened the garrison of the Alhambra, and visited several of the great towns on the frontiers, which he placed in a better posture of defence. The Moriscoes, finding their purpose exposed to the authorities, resolved to defer the execution of it for the present. They even postponed it to as late a date as the beginning of the following year, 1569. To this they were led, we are told, by a prediction found in their religious books, that the year of their liberation would be one that began on a Saturday. It is probable that the wiser men of the Albaicin were less influenced by their own belief in the truth of the prophecy than by the influence it would exert over the superstitious minds of the mountaineers, among whom it was diligently circulated.²

Having settled on the first of January for the rising, the Moslems of Granada strove, by every outward show of loyalty, to quiet the suspicions of the government. But in this they were thwarted by the information

---

² Marmol, Rebelion de los Moriscos, tom. i. pp. 223–233.—Mendoza, Guerra de Granada (Valencia, 1776), p. 43.—Hita, Guerras de Granada, tom. ii. p. 724.

which the latter obtained through more trustworthy channels. Still surer evidence of their intentions was found in a letter which fell by accident into the hands of the marquis of Mondejar. It was addressed by one of the leaders of the Albaicin to the Moslems of the Barbary coast, invoking their aid by the ties of consanguinity and of a common faith. "We are sorely beset," says the writer, "and our enemies encompass us all around like a consuming fire. Our troubles are too grievous to be endured. Written," concludes the passionate author of the epistle, "in nights of tears and anguish, with hope yet lingering,—such hope as still survives amidst all the bitterness of the soul."[3]

But the Barbary powers were too much occupied by their petty feuds to give much more than fair words to their unfortunate brethren of Granada. Perhaps they distrusted the efficacy of any aid they could render in so unequal a contest as that against the Spanish monarchy. Yet they allowed their subjects to embark as volunteers in the war; and some good service was rendered by the Barbary corsairs, who infested the coasts of the Mediterranean, as well as by the *monfis*,—as the African adventurers were called, who took part with their brethren in the Alpujarras, where they made themselves conspicuous by their implacable ferocity against the Christians.

Meanwhile the hot blood of the mountaineers was too much inflamed by the prospect of regaining their independence to allow them to wait patiently for the

---

[1] "Escrita en noches de angustia y de lagrimas corrientes, sustentadas con esperanza, y la esperanza se deriva de la amargura." Marmol, Rebelion de los Moriscos, tom. i. p. 219.

day fixed upon for the outbreak. Before that time arrived, several acts of violence were perpetrated,—forerunners of the bloody work that was at hand. In the month of December, 1568, a body of Spanish alguazils, with some other officers of justice, were cut off in the neighborhood of Granada, on their way to that city. A party of fifty soldiers, as they were bearing to the capital a considerable quantity of muskets,—a tempting prize to the unarmed Moriscoes,—were all murdered, most of them in their beds, in a little village among the mountains where they had halted for the night.[4] After this outrage, Aben-Farax, the bold dyer of Granada, aware of the excitement it must create in the capital, became convinced it would not be safe for him to postpone his intended assault a day longer.

At the head of only a hundred and eighty followers, without waiting to collect a larger force, he made his descent, on the night of the twenty-sixth of December, a week before the appointed time, into the *vega* of Granada. It was a dreadful night. A snow-storm was raging wildly among the mountains and sweeping down in pitiless fury on the plains below.[5] Favored by the

---

[4] Marmol, Rebelion de los Moriscos, tom. i. p. 235.

[5] " La furia horrible de los torbellinos
    Cada momento mas se vee yr creciendo,
    Cubre la blanca nieve los caminos
    Tambien los hombres luego va cubriendo."

So sings, or rather says, the poet-chronicler Rufo, whose epic of four-and-twenty cantos shows him to have been much more of a chronicler than a poet. Indeed, in his preface he avows that strict conformity to truth which is the cardinal virtue of the chronicler. See the Austriada (Madrid, 1584).

commotion of the elements, Aben-Farax succeeded, without attracting observation, in forcing an entrance through the dilapidated walls of the city, penetrated at once into the Albaicin, and endeavored to rouse the inhabitants from their slumbers. Some few came to their windows, it is said, but, on learning the nature of the summons, hastily closed the casements and withdrew, telling Aben-Farax that "it was madness to undertake the enterprise with so small a force, and that he had come before his time."[6] It was in vain that the enraged chief poured forth imprecations on their perfidy and cowardice, in vain that he marched through the deserted streets, demolishing crucifixes and other symbols of Christian worship which he found in his way, or that he shouted out the watchword of the faithful, "There is but one God, and Mahomet is the prophet of God!" The uproar of the tempest, fortunately for him, drowned every other noise; and no alarm was given till he stumbled on a guard of some five or six soldiers who were huddled round a fire in one of the public squares. One of these Farax despatched; the others made their escape, raising the cry that the enemy was upon them. The great bell of St. Salvador rang violently, calling the inhabitants to

---

[6] "Pocos sois, i venís presto." Mendoza, Guerra de Granada, p. 47.—Hita gives a *cancion* in his work, the burden of which is a complaint that the mountaineers had made their attack too late instead of too early:

"Pocos sois, y venís tarde."

(Guerras de Granada, tom. ii. p. 32.) The difference is explained by the circumstance that the author of the verses—probably Hita himself—considers that Christmas Eve, not New Year's Eve, was the time fixed for the assault.

arms. Dawn was fast approaching; and the Moorish chief, who felt himself unequal to an encounter in which he was not to be supported by his brethren in the Albaicin, thought it prudent to make his retreat. This he did with colors flying and music playing, all 'n as cool and orderly a manner as if it had been only a holiday parade.

Meantime the citizens, thus suddenly startled from their beds, gathered together, with eager looks and faces white with fear, to learn the cause of the tumult; and their alarm was not diminished by finding that the enemy had been prowling round their dwellings, like a troop of mountain wolves, while they had been buried in slumber. The marquis of Mondejar called his men to horse, and would have instantly given chase to the invaders, but waited until he had learned the actual condition of the Albaicin, where a population of ten thousand Moriscoes, had they been mischievously inclined, might, notwithstanding the timely efforts of the government to disarm them, have proved too strong for the slender Spanish garrison in the Alhambra. All, however, was quiet in the Moorish quarter; and, assured of this, the captain-general sallied out, at the head of his cavalry and a small corps of foot, in quest of the enemy. But he had struck into the mountain-passes south of Granada; and Mendoza, after keeping on his track, as well as the blinding tempest would permit, through the greater part of the day, at nightfall gave up the pursuit as hopeless and brought back his way-worn cavalcade to the city.[7]

[7] Marmol, Rebelion de los Moriscos, tom. i. p. 238.—Mendoza, Guerra de Granada, pp. 45-52.—Miniana, Hist. de España, p. 367.—

Aben-Farax and his troop, meanwhile, traversing the snowy skirts of the Sierra Nevada, came out on the broad and populous valley of Lecrin, spreading the tidings everywhere, as they went, that the insurrection was begun, that the Albaicin was in movement, and calling on all true believers to take up arms in defence of their faith. The summons did not fall on deaf ears. A train had been fired which ran along the mountain-regions to the south of Granada, stretching from Almeria and the Murcian borders on the east to the neighborhood of Velez Malaga on the west. In three days the whole country was in arms. Then burst forth the fierce passions of the Arab,—all that unquenchable hate which seventy years of oppression had nourished in his bosom, and which now showed itself in one universal cry for vengeance. The bloody drama opened with the massacre of nearly every Christian man within the Moorish borders,—and that too with circumstances of a refined and deliberate cruelty of which, happily, few examples are to be found in history.

The first step, however, in the revolutionary movement had been a false one, inasmuch as the insurgents had failed to secure possession of the capital, which would have furnished so important a *point d'appui* for future operations. Yet, if contemporary chroniclers are correct, this failure should rather be imputed to miscalculation than to cowardice. According to them, the persons of most consideration in the Albaicin were many of them wealthy citizens, accustomed to the easy, luxurious way of life so well suited to the Moorish

---

Herrera, Historia general, tom. i. p. 726.—Ferreras, Hist. d'Espagne, tom. ix. pp. 573-575.

taste. They had never intended to peril their fortunes by engaging personally in so formidable a contest as that with the Castilian crown. They had only proposed to urge their simple countrymen in the Alpujarras to such a show of resistance as should intimidate the Spaniards and lead them to mitigate, if not indeed to rescind, the hated ordinance.[8] If such was their calculation, as the result showed, it miserably failed.

As the Moriscoes had now proclaimed their independence, it became necessary to choose a sovereign in place of the one whose authority they had cast aside. The leaders in the Albaicin selected for this dangerous pre-eminence a young man who was known to the Spaniards by his Castilian name of Don Fernando de Valor. He was descended in a direct line from the ancient house of the Omeyas,[9] who for nearly four centuries had sat with glory on the throne of Córdova. He was but twenty-two years of age at the time of his election, and according to a contemporary, who had seen him, possessed a comely person and engaging manners. His complexion was of a deep olive; his beard was thin; his eyes were large and dark, with eyebrows well defined and nearly approaching each other. His deportment was truly royal; and his lofty sentiments were worthy of the princely line from which

---

[8] "Creyendo que lo uno y lo otro seria parte para que por bien de paz se diese nueva orden en lo de la prematica, sin aventurar ellos sus personas y haciendas." Marmol, Rebelion de los Moriscos, tom. i. p. 239.

[9] Beni Umeyyah in the Arabic, according to an indisputable authority, my learned friend Don Pascual de Gayangos. See his Mohammedan Dynasties in Spain, *passim*.

he was descended.[10] Notwithstanding this flattering portrait from the pen of a Castilian, his best recommendation, to judge from his subsequent career, seems to have been his descent from a line of kings. He had been so prodigal in his way of life that, though so young, he had squandered his patrimony and was at this very time under arrest for debt. He had the fiery temperament of his nation, and had given evidence of it by murdering with his own hand a man who had borne testimony against his father in a criminal prosecution. Amidst his luxurious self-indulgence he must be allowed to have shown some energy of character and an unquestionable courage. He was attached to the institutions of his country; and his ferocious nature was veiled under a bland and plausible exterior, that won him golden opinions from the multitude.[11]

Soon after his election, and just before the irruption of Aben-Farax, the Morisco prince succeeded in making his escape from Granada, and, flying to the moun-

[10] " Era mancebo de veinte y dos años, de poca barba, color moreno, verdinegro, cejijunto, ojos negros y grandes, gentil hombre de cuerpo: mostraba en su talle y garbo ser de sangre real, como en verdad lo era, teniendo los pensamientos correspondientes." Hita, Guerras de Granada, tom. ii. p. 13.—Few will be disposed to acquiesce in the savage tone of criticism with which the learned Nic. Antonio denounces Hita's charming volumes as "Milesian tales, fit only to amuse the lazy and the listless." (Bibliotheca Nova, tom. i. p. 536.) Hita was undoubtedly the prince of romancers; but fiction is not falsehood; and when the novelist, who served-in the wars of the Alpujarras, tells us of things which he professes to have seen with his own eyes, we may surely cite him as an historical authority.

[11] "Usava de blandura general; queria ser tenido por Cabeza, i no por Rei: la crueldad, la codicia cubierta engañó á muchos en los principios." Mendoza, Guerra de Granada, p. 129.

tains, took refuge among his own kindred, the powerful family of the Valoris, in the village of Beznar. Here his countrymen gathered round him, and confirmed by acclamation the choice of the people of Granada. For this the young chieftain was greatly indebted to the efforts of his uncle, Aben-Jahuar, commonly called El Zaguer, a man of much authority among his tribe, who, waiving his own claims to the sceptre, employed his influence in favor of his nephew.

The ceremony of the coronation was of a martial kind, well suited to the rough fortunes of the adventurer. Four standards, emblazoned with the Moslem crescent, were spread upon the ground, with their spear-heads severally turned towards the four points of the compass. The Moorish prince, who had been previously arrayed in a purple robe, with a crimson scarf or shawl, the insignia of royalty, enveloping his shoulders, knelt down on the banners, with his face turned towards Mecca, and, after a brief prayer, solemnly swore to live and die in defence of his crown, his faith, and his subjects. One of the principal attendants, prostrating himself on the ground, kissed the footprints of the newly-elected monarch, in token of the allegiance of the people. He was then raised on the shoulders of four of the assistants, and borne aloft amidst the waving of banners and the loud shouts of the multitude, "Allah exalt Muley-Mohammed-Aben-Humeya, lord of Andalucia and Granada!"[12] Such

---

[12] Mendoza, Guerra de Granada, p. 40.—The ceremonies of the coronation make, of course, a brave show in Rufo's epic. One stanza will suffice:

" Entonces con aplauso le pusieron
  Al nuevo Rey de purpura un vestido,

were the simple forms practised in ancient times by the Spanish-Arabian princes, when their empire, instead of being contracted within the rocky girdle of the mountains, stretched over the fairest portions of the Peninsula."

The first act of Aben-Humeya was to make his appointments to the chief military offices. El Zaguer, his uncle, he made captain-general of his forces. Aben-Farax, who had himself aspired to the diadem, he removed to a distance, by sending him on an expedition to collect such treasures as could be gathered from the Christian churches in the Alpujarras. He appointed officers to take charge of the different *tahas*, or districts, into which the country was divided. Having completed these arrangements, the new monarch— the *reyezuelo*, or "little king," of the Alpujarras, as he was contemptuously styled by the Spaniards—transferred his residence to the central part of his dominions, where he repeated the ceremony of his coronation. He made a rapid visit to the most important places in the sierra, everywhere calling on the inhabitants to return to their ancient faith and to throw off the hated yoke of the Spaniards. He then established himself in the wildest parts of the Alpujarras, where he endeavored to draw

> Y a manera de beca le ciñeron
> Al cuello y ombros un cendal bruñido,
> Quatro vanderas a sus pies tendieron,
> Una házia el Levante esclarecido,
> Otra a do el sol se cubre en negro velo,
> Y otras dos a los polos dos del cielo."
>   La Austriada, fol. 24.

13 "Tal era la antigua ceremonia con que eligian los Reyes de la Andalucia, i despues los de Granada." Mendoza, Guerra de Granada, p. 40.

his forces to a head, and formed the plan of his campaign. It was such as was naturally suggested by the character of the country, which, broken and precipitous, intersected by many a deep ravine and dangerous pass, afforded excellent opportunities for harassing an invading foe, and for entangling him in those inextricable defiles, where a few mountaineers acquainted with the ground would be more than a match for an enemy far superior in discipline and numbers.

While Aben-Humeya was thus occupied in preparing for the struggle, the work of death had already begun among the Spanish population of the Alpujarras; and Spaniards were to be found, in greater or less numbers, in all the Moorish towns and hamlets that dotted the dark sides of the sierras or nestled in the green valleys at their base. Here they dwelt side by side with the Moriscoes, employed, probably, less in the labors of the loom, for which the natives of this region had long been famous, than in that careful husbandry which they might readily have learned from their Moorish neighbors, and which, under their hands, had clothed every spot with verdure, making the wilderness to blossom like the rose.[14] Thus living in the midst of those who professed the same religion with themselves, and in the occasional interchange, at least, of the kind offices of social intercourse, which sometimes led to nearer domestic ties, the Christians of the Alpujarras

---

[14] " Que en la agricultura tienen
Tal estudio, tal destreza,
Que á preñeces de su hazada
Hacen fecundas las piedras."
Calderon, Amar despues de la Muerte, Jornada II.

dwelt in blind security, little dreaming of the mine beneath their feet.

But no sooner was the first note of insurrection sounded than the scene changed as if by magic. Every Morisco threw away his mask, and, turning on the Christians, showed himself in his true aspect, as their avowed and mortal enemy.

A simultaneous movement of this kind, through so wide an extent of country, intimates a well-concerted plan of operations; and we may share in the astonishment of the Castilian writers that a secret of such a nature and known to so many individuals should have been so long and faithfully kept,—in the midst, too, of those who had the greatest interest in detecting it,[15] —some of them, it may be added, spies of the Inquisition, endowed, as they seem to have been, with almost supernatural powers for scenting out the taint of heresy.[16] It argues an intense feeling of hatred in the Morisco that he could have been so long proof against the garrulity that loosens the tongue, and against the sympathy that so often, in similar situations, unlocks the heart to save some friend from the doom of his companions. But no such instance either of levity or lenity occurred among this extraordinary people. And

[15] " Tres años tuvo en silencio
Esta traicion encubierta
Tanto número de gentes,
Cosa, que admira y eleva."
Calderon, Amar despues de la Muerte, Jornada II.

[16] " Una cosa mui de notar califica los principios desta rebelion, que gente de mediana condicion mostrada á guardar poco secreto i hablar juntos, callasen tanto tiempo, i tantos hombres, en tierra donde hai Alcaldes de corte i Inquisidores, cuya profesion es descubrir delitos."
Mendoza, Guerra de Granada, p. 36.

when the hour arrived, and the Christians discerned their danger in the menacing looks and gestures of their Moslem neighbors, they were as much astounded by it as the unsuspecting traveller on whom, as he heedlessly journeys through some pleasant country, the highwayman has darted from his covert by the roadside.

The first impulse of the Christians seems to have been very generally to take refuge in the churches; and every village, however small, had at least one church, where the two races met together to join in the forms of Christian worship. The fugitives thought to find protection in their holy places and in the presence of their venerated pastors, whose spiritual authority had extended over all the inhabitants. But the wild animal of the forest, now that he had regained his freedom, gave little heed to the call of his former keeper, —unless it were to turn and rend him.

Here, crowded together like a herd of panic-stricken deer with the hounds upon their track, the terrified people soon found the church was no place of security, and they took refuge in the adjoining tower, as a place of greater strength and affording a better means of defence against an enemy. The mob of their pursuers then broke into the church, which they speedily despoiled of its ornaments, trampling the crucifixes and other religious symbols under their feet, rolling the sacred images in the dust, and desecrating the altars by the sacrifice of swine, or by some other act denoting their scorn and hatred of the Christian worship."[17]

[17] Bleda, Cronica de España, p. 680.—" Robaron la iglesia, hicieron pedazos los retablos y imagines, destruyeron todas las cosas sagradas,

They next assailed the towers, the entrances to which the Spaniards had barricaded as strongly as they could; though, unprovided as they were with means of defence, except such arms as they had snatched in the hurry of their flight, they could have little hope of standing a siege. Unfortunately, these towers were built more or less of wood, which the assailants readily set on fire, and thus compelled the miserable inmates either to surrender or to perish in the flames. In some instances they chose the latter; and the little garrison—men, women, and children—were consumed together on one common funeral pile. More frequently they shrank from this fearful death, and surrendered at the mercy of their conquerors,—such mercy as made them soon regret that they had not stayed by the blazing rafters.

The men were speedily separated from the women, and driven, with blows and imprecations, like so many cattle, to a place of confinement. From this loathsome prison they were dragged out, three or four at a time, day after day, the longer to protract their sufferings; then, with their arms pinioned behind them, and stripped of their clothing, they were thrown into the midst of an infuriated mob, consisting of both sexes, who, armed with swords, hatchets, and bludgeons, soon felled their victims to the ground and completed the bloody work.

The mode of death was often varied to suit the capricious cruelty of the executioners. At Guecija, where the olive grew abundant, there was a convent of Augustine monks, who were all murdered by being thrown

y no dexaron maldad ni sacrilegio que no cometicron." Marmol, Rebelion de Granada, tom. i. p. 275.

into caldrons of boiling oil.[18] Sometimes the death of the victim was attended with circumstances of diabolical cruelty not surpassed by any thing recorded of our North American savages. At a place called Pitres de Ferreyra, the priest of the village was raised by means of a pulley to a beam that projected from the tower, and was then allowed to drop from a great height upon the ground. The act was repeated more than once, in the presence of his aged mother, who, in an agony of grief, embracing her dying son, besought him "to trust in God and the Blessed Virgin, who through these torments would bring him into eternal life." The mangled carcass of the poor victim, broken and dislocated in every limb, was then turned over to the Moorish women, who, with their scissors, bodkins, and other feminine implements, speedily despatched him.[19]

The women, indeed, throughout this persecution, seem to have had as rabid a thirst for vengeance as the men. Even the children were encouraged to play their part in the bloody drama; and many a miserable captive was set up as a target to be shot at with the arrows of the Moorish boys.

The rage of the barbarians was especially directed against the priests, who had so often poured forth anathemas against the religion which the Moslems loved, and who, as their spiritual directors, had so often called

[18] "Quemaron por voto un Convento de Frailes Augustinos, que se recogieron a la Torre echandoles por un horado de lo alto azeite hirviendo: sirviendose de la abundancia que Dios les dió en aquella tierra, para ahogar sus Frailes." Mendoza, Guerra de Granada, p. 60.

[19] Marmol, Rebelion de Granada, tom. i. p. 271.—Ferreras, Hist. d'Espagne, tom. ix. p. 582.

them to account for offences against the religion which they abhorred. At Coadba the priest was stretched out before a brazier of live coals until his feet, which had been smeared with pitch and oil, were burned to a cinder. His two sisters were compelled to witness the agonies of their brother, which were still further heightened by the brutal treatment which he saw them endure from their tormentors.[20]

Fire was employed as a common mode of torture, by way of retaliation, it may be, for similar sufferings inflicted on the infidel by the Inquisition. Sometimes the punishments seemed to be contrived so as to form a fiendish parody on the exercises of the Roman Catholic religion. In the town of Filix the pastor was made to take his seat before the altar, with his two sacristans, one on either side of him. The bell was rung, as if to call the people together to worship. The sacristans were each provided with a roll containing the names of the congregation, which they were required to call over, as usual, before the services, in order to see that no one was absent. As each Morisco answered to his name, he passed before the priest, and dealt him a blow with his fist, or the women plucked his beard and hair, accompanying the act with some bitter taunt, expressive of their mortal hate. When every one had thus had the opportunity of gratifying his personal grudge against his ancient pastor, the executioner stepped forward, armed with a razor, with which he scored the face of the ecclesiastic in the detested form

---

[20] "Y para darle mayor tormento traxeron alli dos hermanas doncellas que tenia, para que le viesen morir, y en su presencia las vituperaron y maltrataron." Marmol, Rebelion de Granada, tom. 1. p. 316

of the cross, and then, beginning with the fingers, deliberately proceeded to sever each of the joints of his wretched victim!"

But it is unnecessary to shock the reader with more of these loathsome details, enough of which have already been given, not merely to prove the vindictive temper of the Morisco, but to suggest the inference that it could only have been a long course of cruelty and oppression that stimulated him to such an awful exhibition of it.[22] The whole number of Christians who, in the course of a week, thus perished in these massacres,—if we are to receive the accounts of Castilian writers,—was not less than three thousand![23]

[21] "Llegó un herege á él con una navaja, y le persinó con ella, hendiendole el rostro de alto abaxo, y por través; y luego le despedazó coyuntura por coyuntura, y miembro á miembro." Marmol, Rebelion de Granada, tom. i. p. 348.—Among other kinds of torture which they invented, says Mendoza, they filled the curate of Manena with gunpowder, and then blew him up. Guerra de Granada, p. 60.

[22] Of all the Spanish historians no one discovers so insatiable an appetite for these horrors as Ferreras, who has devoted nearly fifty quarto pages to an account of the diabolical cruelties practised by the Moriscoes in this persecution,—making altogether a momentous contribution to the annals of Christian martyrology. One may doubt, however, whether the Spaniards are entirely justified in claiming the crown of martyrdom for all who perished in this persecution. Those, undoubtedly, have a right to it who might have saved their lives by renouncing their faith; but there is no evidence that this grace was extended to all; and we may well believe that the Moriscoes were stimulated by other motives besides those of a religious nature,—such motives as would naturally operate on a conquered race, burning with hatred of their conquerors and with the thirst of vengeance for the manifold wrongs which they had endured.

[23] "Murieron en pocos mas de quatro dias, con muertes exquesitas y no imaginados tormentos, mas de tres mil martires." Vanderhammen, Don Juan de Austria, fol. 70.

Considering the social relations which must to some extent have been established between those who had lived so long in the neighborhood of one another, it might be thought that, on some occasions, sympathy would have been shown for the sufferers, or that some protecting arm would have been stretched out to save a friend or a companion from the general doom. But the nearest approach to such an act of humanity was given by a Morisco who plunged his sword in the body of a Spaniard, in order to save him from the lingering death that otherwise would await him.[24]

Of the whole Christian population very few of the men who fell into the hands of the Moslems escaped with life. The women were not always spared. The Morisco women, especially, who had married Christian husbands and embraced Christianity, which they refused to abjure, became the objects of vengeance to their own sex. Sad to say, even the innocence and helplessness of childhood proved no protection against the fury of persecution. The historians record the names of several boys, from ten to twelve or thirteen years of age, who were barbarously murdered because they would not renounce the religion in which they had been nurtured for that of Mahomet. If they were too young to give a reason for their faith, they had at least learned the lesson that to renounce it was a great sin; and, when led out like lambs to the slaughter, their mothers, we are told, stifling the suggestions of natural affection in

---

[24] "Se adelantó un Moro, que solia ser grande amigo suyo, y haciendose encontradizo con él en el umbral de la puerta, le atravesó una espada por el cuerpo, diciendole: Toma, amigo, que mas vale que te mate yo que otro." Marmol, Rebelion de Granada, tom. i. p. 277.

obedience to a higher law, urged their children not to shrink from the trial, nor to purchase a few years of life at the price of their own souls.[75] It is a matter of no little gratulation to a Catholic historian that amongst all those who perished in these frightful massacres there was not one of any age or either sex who could be tempted to secure personal safety by the sacrifice of religious convictions.[76] On the contrary, they employed the brief respite that was left them in fortifying one another's courage, and in bearing testimony to the truth in so earnest a manner that they might almost seem to have courted the crown of martyrdom. Yet among these martyrs there were more than one, it is admitted, whose previous way of life showed but a dim perception of the value of that religion for which they were thus prepared to lay down their lives.[77]

The chief blame of these indiscriminate proscriptions has been laid on Aben-Farax, the famous dyer of Granada, whose appetite for blood seems to have been as insatiable as that of any wild beast in the Alpujarras. In executing the commission assigned to him by Aben-Humeya, he was obliged to visit all

---

[75] Ferreras, Hist. d'Espagne, tom. ix. p. 617.

[76] "Fue gran testimonio de nuestra fé i de compararse con la del tiempo de los Apostoles; que en tanto numero de gente como murió a manos de infieles ninguno huvo que quisiese renegar." Mendoza, Guerra de Granada, p. 61.

[77] "Todos estuvieron tan constantes en la Fé, que si bien fueron combidados con grandes riquezas y bienes á que la dejasen, con ninguno se pudo acabar; aunque entre los martyrizados huvo muchas mugeres, niños y hombres que havian vivido descompuestamente." Salazar de Mendoza, Monarquia de España, tom. ii. p. 139.

parts of the country. Wherever he came, impatient of the slower movements of his countrymen in the work of destruction, he caused the prisons to be emptied and the wretched inmates to be butchered before his eyes. At Ugijar he thus directed the execution of no less than two hundred and forty Christians, laymen and ecclesiastics.[28] His progress through the land was literally over the dead bodies of his victims.

Fierce as he was, Aben-Humeya had some touches of humanity in his nature, which made him revolt at the wholesale murders perpetrated by his lieutenant. He was the more indignant when, on hastening to Ugijar to save the lives of some of the captives, his friends, he found that he had come too late, for the man of blood had been there before him. He soon after summoned his officer into his presence, not with the impolitic design of taxing him with his cruelties, but to call him to a reckoning for the treasure he had pillaged from the churches; and, dissatisfied, or affecting to be so, with his report, he at once deposed Aben-Farax from his command. The ferocious chief submitted without a murmur. He descended into the common file, and no more appears on the scene. He was one of those miscreants who are thrown on the surface by the turmoil of a revolution, and, after floating there for a while, disappear from sight, and the wave of history closes over them forever.

[28] " Murieron este dia en Uxixar docientos y quarenta Christianos clerigos y legos, y entre ellos seis canonigos de aquella iglesia, que es colegial." Marmol, Rebelion de Granada, tom. i. p. 297.

CHAPTER III.

REBELLION OF THE MORISCOES.

Panic in Granada.—Muster of Troops.—Mondejar takes the Field.—Bold Passage at Tablate.—Retreat of the Moriscoes.—Combat at Alfajarali.—Perilous March.—Massacre at Jubiles.—The Liberated Christians.

1568, 1569.

As day after day brought tidings to the people of Granada of the barbarities perpetrated in the Alpujarras, the whole city was filled with grief and consternation. The men might be seen gathered together in knots in the public squares; the women ran about from house to house, telling the tale of horrors, which could hardly be exaggerated in the recital. They thronged to the churches, where the archbishop and the clergy were all day long offering up prayers, to avert the wrath of Heaven from Granada. The places of business were abandoned. The shops and booths were closed.[1] As men called to mind the late irruption of Aben-Farax, they were filled with apprehensions that the same thing would be attempted again; and rumors went abroad that the mountaineers were plotting another descent on

[1] "Estavan las casas yermas i tiendas cerradas, suspenso el trato, mudadas las horas de oficios divinos i humanos; atentos los Religiosos i ocupados en oraciones i plegarias, como se suele en tiempo i punto de grandes peligros." Mendoza, Guerra de Granada, p. 54.—Mendoza paints the panic of Granada with the pencil of Tacitus.

the city, and, with the aid of their countrymen in the Albaicin, would soon deluge the streets with the blood of the Christians. Under the influence of these fears, some took refuge in the fortress of the Alhambra; others fled into the country. Many kept watch during the long night, while those who withdrew to rest started from their slumbers at the least noise, supposing it to be the war-cry of the Moslem and that the enemy was at the gates.

Nor was the alarm less that was felt by the Moriscoes in the city, as it was certainly better founded,—for the Moriscoes were the weaker party of the two. They knew the apprehensions entertained of them by the Christians, and that when men have the power to relieve themselves of their fears they are not apt to be very scrupulous as to the means of doing so. They were afraid to venture into the streets by day, and at night they barricaded their houses as in a time of siege.[a] They well knew that a single act of imprudence on their part, or even the merest accident, might bring the Spaniards upon them and lead to a general massacre. They were like the traveller who sees the avalanche trembling above him, which the least jar of the elements, or his own unwary movements, may dislodge from its slippery basis and bring down in ruin on his head. Thus the two races, inhabitants of the same city, were like two hostile camps, looking on each other with watchful and malignant eyes and ready at any moment to come into deadly conflict.

In this state of things, the Moriscoes, anxious to allay the apprehensions of the Spaniards, were profuse in

[a] Circourt, Hist. des Arabes d'Espagne, tom. ii. p. 322.

their professions of loyalty and in their assurances
that there was neither concert nor sympathy between
them and their countrymen in the Alpujarras. The
government, to give still greater confidence to the
Christians, freely distributed arms among them, thus
enabling them, as far as possible, to provide for their
own security. The inhabitants enrolled themselves in
companies. The citizen was speedily converted into
the soldier; and every man, of whatever trade or profession,—the mechanic, the merchant, the lawyer,—
took his turn of military service. Even the advocates,
when attending the courts of justice, appeared with
their weapons by their side.[3]

But what contributed above all to revive the public
confidence was the care of the government to strengthen
the garrison in the Alhambra by the addition of five
hundred regular troops. When, by these various means,
the marquis of Mondejar saw that tranquillity was
restored to the capital, he bestowed all his thoughts on
an expedition into the Alpujarras, desirous to crush the
insurrection in its bud, and to rescue the unfortunate
captives, whose fate there excited the most dismal apprehensions among their friends and relatives in Granada.
He sent forth his summons accordingly to the great
lords and the cities of Andalusia to furnish him at once
with their contingents for carrying on the war. The
feudal principle still obtained in this quarter, requiring

---

[3] " En un punto se mudaron todos los oficios y tratos en soldadesca,
tanto que los relatores, secretarios, letrados, procuradores de la Audiencia entraban con espadas en los estrados, y no dexaban de parescer
muy bien en aquella coyuntura." Marmol, Rebelion de Granada,
tom. i. p. 358.

the several towns to do military service for their possessions, by maintaining, when called upon, a certain number of troops in the field, at their own expense for three months, and at the joint expense of themselves and the government for six months longer.[4] The system worked well enough in those ancient times when a season rarely passed without a foray against the Moslems. But since the fall of Granada a long period of inactivity had followed, and the citizen, rarely summoned to the field, had lost all the essential attributes of the soldier. The usual term of service was too short to supply the experience and the discipline which he needed; and, far from entering on a campaign with the patriotic or the chivalrous feeling that gives dignity to the profession of arms, he brought with him the mercenary spirit of a trader, intent only on his personal gains, and eager, as soon as he had enriched himself by a lucky foray or the sack of some ill-fated city, to return home, and give place to others, as inexperienced and possessed of as little subordination as himself.[5]

But, however deficient this civic militia might be in tactics, the men were well provided with arms and military accoutrements; and, as the motley array of troops passed over the *vega*, they made a gallant show, with their gay uniforms and bright weapons glancing in the

[4] "Servian tres meses pagados por sus pueblos enteramente, i seis meses adelante pagavan los pueblos la mitad, i otra mitad el Rei." Mendoza, Guerra de Granada, p. 53.

[5] Mendoza, with a few vigorous touches, has sketched, or rather sculptured in bold relief, the rude and rapacious character of the Andalusian soldiery: "Mal pagada i por esto no bien disciplinada; mantenida del robo, i a trueco de alcanzar o conservar este mucha libertad, poca verguenza, i menos honra." Ibid., p. 103.

sun, while they proudly displayed the ancient banners of their cities, which had waved over many a field of battle against the infidel.⁶

But no part of the warlike spectacle was so brilliant as that afforded by the chivalry of the country,—the nobles and cavaliers, who, with their retainers and household troops, had taken the field with as much alacrity on the present occasion as their fathers had ever shown when roused by the cry that the enemy was over the borders.⁷ They were much inferior in numbers to the militia of the towns. But inferiority of numbers was more than compensated by excellence of discipline, by their perfect appointments, and by that chivalrous feeling which made them discard every mercenary consideration in the pursuit of glory. Such was the feeling of Luis Paer de Castillego, the ancient regidor of Córdova. When offered an independent command, with the emoluments annexed to it, he proudly replied, "I want neither rank nor pay. I, my sons, my kindred, my whole house, will always be found ready to serve our God and our king. It is the title by which we hold our inheritance and our patent of nobility."⁸

⁶ "Toda gente lucida y bien arreada á punto de guerra, que cierto representaban la pompa y nobleza de sus ciudades." Marmol, Rebelion de Granada, tom. i. p. 396.

⁷ "Muchos capitanos fuertes,
muchos lucidos soldados,
ricas banderas tendidas,
y su estandarte dorado."
Hita, Guerras de Granada, tom. ii. p. 61.

⁸ Circourt, Hist. des Arabes d'Espagne, tom. ii. p. 326.—Seville alone furnished two thousand troops, with one of the most illustrious

With such loyal and high-mettled cavaliers to support him, Mondejar could not feel doubtful of the success of his arms. They had, however, already met with one reverse; and he received tidings that his advance-guard, sent to occupy a strong pass that led into the mountains, had been driven from its position and had sustained something like a defeat. This would have been still more decisive had it not been for the courage of certain ecclesiastics, eight in number,—four of them Franciscans and four of the Society of Jesus,—who, as the troops gave way, threw themselves into the thick of the fight and by their example shamed the soldiers into making a more determined resistance. The present war took the form of a religious war; and many a valiant churchman, armed with sword and crucifix, bore his part in it as in a crusade.

Hastening his preparations, the captain-general, without waiting for further reinforcements, marched out of Granada on the second of January, 1569, at the head of a small body, which did not exceed in all two thousand foot and four hundred horse. He was speedily joined by levies from the neighboring towns, —from Jaen, Loja, Alhama, Antequera, and other places,—which in a few days swelled his little army to double its original size. The capital he left in the hands of his son, the count of Tendilla, a man of less discretion than his father, of a sterner and more impatient temper, and one who had little sympathy for the Morisco. By his directions, the peasantry of the *vega*

cavaliers of the city at their head. They did not arrive, however, till a later period of the war. See Zuñiga, Annales de Sevilla (Madrid, 1677, fol.), p. 533.

were required to supply the army with twenty thousand pounds of bread daily.⁹ The additional troops stationed in the city, as well as those who met there, as in a place of rendezvous, on their way to the sierra, were all quartered on the inhabitants of the Albáicin, where they freely indulged in the usual habits of military license. The Moriscoes still retained much of that jealous sensibility which leads the natives of the East to seclude their wives and daughters from the eye of the stranger. It was in vain, however, that they urged their complaints in the most respectful and deprecatory terms before the governor. The haughty Spaniard only answered them with a stern rebuke, which made the Moriscoes too late repent that they had not profited by the opportunity offered them by Aben-Farax of regaining their independence.¹⁰

Leaving Granada, the captain-general took the most direct route, leading along the western slant of the Sierra Nevada, that mountain-range which, with its frosty peaks glistening in the sun like palisades of silver, fences round the city on the south, and screens it in the summer from the scorching winds of Africa. Thence he rapidly descended into the beautiful vale of Lecrin, which spreads out, like a gay carpet embroidered with many a wild flower, to the verge of the Alpujarras. It was now, however, the dead of winter,

---

⁹ "Repartió los lugares de la vega en siete partidos, y mandóles, que cada uno tuviese cuidado de llevar diez mil panes amasados de á dos libras al campo el dia que le tocase de la semana." Marmol. Rebelion de Granada, tom. i. p. 404.

¹⁰ "Pasó este negocio tan adelante, que muchos Moriscos afrentados y gastados se arrepintieron, por no haber tomado las armas quando Abenfarax los llamaba." Ibid., p. 407.

when the bright coloring of the landscape, even in this favored region, watered as it was by numerous fountains and running streams, had faded into the sombre tints more in harmony with the rude scenes on which the Spaniards were about to enter.

Halting a night at Padul to refresh his troops, Mondejar pressed forward to Durcal, which he reached barely in time to save his advance-guard from a more shameful discomfiture than it had before experienced; for the enemy, pressing it on all sides, was in possession of the principal avenues to the town. On the approach of the main body of the Spaniards, however, he made a hasty retreat and established himself in a strong position at the pass of Tablate. The place was defended by a *barranca*, or ravine, not formidable from its width, but its rocky sides swept sheer down to a depth that made the brain of the traveller giddy as he looked into the frightful abyss. The chasm extended at least eight leagues in length, thus serving, like a gigantic ditch scooped out by the hand of Nature, to afford protection to the beautiful valley against the inroads of the fierce tribes of the mountains.

Across this gulf a frail wooden bridge had been constructed, forming the only means of access from this quarter to the country of the Alpujarras. But this structure was now nearly demolished by the Moriscoes, who had taken up the floor and removed most of the supports, till the passage of the tottering fabric could not safely be attempted by a single individual, much less by an army." That they did not destroy the

[11] " Apenas podia ir por ella un hombre suelto; y aun este poco paso, le tenian descavado y solapado por los cimientos, de manera,

bridge altogether, probably arose from their desire to re-establish, as soon as possible, their communications with their countrymen in the valley.

Meanwhile the Moslems had taken up a position which commanded the farther end of the bridge, where they calmly awaited the approach of the Spaniards. Their army, which greatly fluctuated in its numbers at different periods of the campaign, was a miscellaneous body, ill disciplined and worse armed. Some of the men carried fire-arms, some cross-bows; others had only slings or javelins, or even sharp-pointed stakes,—any weapon, in short, however rude, which they had contrived to secrete from the Spanish officials charged with enforcing the laws for disarming the Moriscoes. But they were a bold and independent race, inured to a life of peril and privation; and, however inferior to the Christians in other respects, they had one obvious advantage in their familiarity with the mountain-wilds in which they had been nurtured from infancy.

As the Spaniards approached the ravine, they were saluted by the enemy, from the other side, with a shower of balls, stones, and arrows, which, falling at random, did little mischief. But as soon as the columns of the Christians reached the brow of the *barranca* and formed into line, they opened a much more effective fire on their adversaries; and when the heavy guns with which Mendoza was provided were got int . position, they did such execution on the enemy that he thought it prudent to abandon the bridge and

que si cargase mas de una persona, fuese abaxo." Marmol, Rebelion de Granada, tom. i. p. 409.

take post behind a rising ground, which screened him from the fire.

All thoughts were now turned on the mode of crossing the ravine; and many a look of blank dismay was turned on the dilapidated bridge, which, like a spider's web, trembling in every breeze, was stretched across the formidable chasm. No one was bold enough to venture on this pass of peril. At length a Franciscan monk, named Christoval de Molina, offered himself for the emprise. It was again an ecclesiastic who was to lead the way in the path of danger. Slinging his shield across his back, with his robe tucked closely around him, grasping a crucifix in his left hand, and with his right brandishing his sword, the valiant friar set his foot upon the bridge.[12] All eyes were fastened upon him, as, invoking the name of Jesus, he went courageously but cautiously forward, picking his way along the skeleton fabric, which trembled under his weight, as if about to fall in pieces and precipitate him into the gulf below. But he was not so to perish; and his safe arrival on the farther side was greeted with the shouts of the soldiery, who, ashamed of their hesitation, now pressed forward to follow in his footsteps.

The first who ventured had the same good fortune as his predecessor. The second, missing his step or becoming dizzy, lost his foothold, and, tumbling headlong, was dashed to pieces on the bottom of the ravine.

[12] "Mas un bendito frayle de la orden del serafico padre San Francisco, llamado fray Christoval de Molina, con un crucifixo en la mano izquierda, y la espada desnuda en la derecha, los habitos cogidos en la cinta, y una rodela echada á las espaldas, invocando el poderoso nombre de Jesus, llegó al peligroso paso, y se metió determinadamente por él." Marmol, Rebelion de Granada, tom. i. p. 410.

One after another, the soldiers followed, and with fewer casualties than might have been expected from the perilous nature of the passage. During all this time they experienced no molestation from the enemy, intimidated, perhaps, by the unexpected audacity of the Spaniards, and not caring to come within the range of the deadly fire of their artillery. No sooner had the arquebusiers crossed in sufficient strength than Mondejar, putting himself at their head, led them against the Moslems. He was received with a spirited volley, which had wellnigh proved fatal to him; and had it not been for his good cuirass, that turned the ball of an arquebuse, his campaign would have been brought to a close at its commencement. The skirmish lasted but a short time, as the Moriscoes, already disheartened by the success of the assailants, or in obedience to the plan of operations marked out by their leader, abandoned their position and drew off rapidly towards the mountains. It was the intention of Aben-Humeya, as already noticed, to entangle his enemies in the defiles of the sierra, where, independently of the advantage he possessed from a knowledge of the country, the rugged character of the ground, he conceived, would make it impracticable for both cavalry and artillery, with neither of which he was provided.[13]

[13] Marmol, Rebelion de Granada, tom. i. p. 410, et seq.—Mendoza, Guerra de Granada, pp. 67, 68.—Herrera, Historia general, tom. i. p. 736.—Hita has commemorated the bold passage of the bridge at Tablate in one of the *romances*, or ballads, with which he has plentifully besprinkled the second volume of his work, and which present a sorry contrast to the ballads in the preceding volume. These, which form part of the popular minstrelsy of an earlier age, have all the raciness and flavor that belong to the native wild flower of the soil.

The Spanish commander, resuming his former station, employed the night in restoring the bridge, on which his men labored to such purpose that by morning it was in a condition for both his horse and his heavy guns to cross in safety. Meanwhile he received tidings that a body of a hundred and eighty Spaniards, in the neighboring town of Orgiba, who had thrown themselves into the tower of the church on the breaking out of the insurrection, were still holding their position, and anxiously looking for succor from their countrymen. Pushing forward, therefore, without loss of time, he resumed his march across the valley, which was here defended on either side by rugged hills, that, growing bolder as he advanced, announced his entrance into the gorges of the Alpujarras. The weather was tempestuous. The roads were rendered worse than usual by the heavy rains and by the torrents that descended from the hills. The Spaniards, moreover, suffered much from straggling parties of the enemy, who had possession of the heights, whence they rolled down huge rocks and hurled missiles of every kind on the heads of the invaders. To rid himself of this annoyance, Mondejar ordered detachments of horse—one of them under the command of his son, Don Antonio de Mendoza—to scour the crests of the hills and dislodge the skirmishers. Pioneers were sent in advance, to level the ground and render it practicable for the cavalry. The service was admirably performed; and

---

The ballads in the second volume are probably the work of Hita himself,—poor imitations of the antique, and proving that, if his rich and redundant prose is akin to poetry, his poetry is still nearer allied to prose.

the mountaineers, little acquainted with the horse, which they seem to have held in as much terror as did the ancient Mexicans, were so astounded by seeing the light-footed Andalusian steed scaling the rough sides of the sierra, along paths where the sportsman would hardly venture, that, without waiting for the charge, they speedily quitted the ground and fell back on the main body of their army.

This was posted at Lanjaron, a place but a few miles off, where the Moriscoes had profited by a gentle eminence that commanded a narrow defile, to throw up a breastwork of stone and earth, behind which they were intrenched, prepared, as it would seem, to give battle to the Spaniards.

The daylight had begun to fade as the latter drew near the enemy's encampment; and, as he was unacquainted with the ground, Mondejar resolved to postpone his attack till the following morning. The night set in dark and threatening. But a hundred watchfires blazing on the hill-tops illumined the sky and sent a feeble radiance into the gloom of the valley. All night long the wild notes of the musical instruments peculiar to the Moors, mingling with their shrill war-cries, sounded in the ears of the Christians, keeping them under arms and apprehensive every moment of an attack.[14] But a night-attack was contrary to the usual tactics of the Moors. Nor, as it appeared, did

[14] "Estuvo alli aquella noche á vista de los enemigos, que teniendo ocupado el paso con grandes fuegos por aquellos cerros, no hacian sino tocar sus atabalejos, dulzaynas y xabecas, haciendo algazaras para atemorizar nuestros Christianos, que con grandisimo recato estuvieron todos con las armas en las manos." Marmol, Rebelion de Granada, tom. i. p. 413.

they intend to join battle with the Spaniards at all in this place. At least, if such had been their design, they changed it. For at break of day, to the surprise of the Spaniards, no vestige was to be seen of the Moriscoes, who, abandoning their position, had taken flight, like their own birds of prey, into the depths of the mountains.

Mondejar, not sorry to be spared the delay which an encounter must have caused him at a time when every moment was so precious, now rapidly pushed forward to Orgiba, where he happily arrived in season to relieve the garrison, reduced almost to the last extremity, and to put to flight the rabble who besieged it.

In the fulness of their hearts, and with the tears streaming from their eyes, the poor prisoners came forth from their fortress to embrace the deliverers who had rescued them from the most terrible of deaths. Their apprehensions of such a fate had alone nerved their souls to so long and heroic a resistance. Yet they must have sunk ere this from famine, had it not been for their politic precaution of taking with them into the tower several of the Morisco children, whose parents secretly supplied them with food, which served as the means of subsistence—scanty though it was—for the garrison. But, as the latter came forth into view, their wasted forms and famine-stricken visages told a tale of woe that would have softened a heart of flint.[15]

The situation of Orgiba pointed it out as suitable for

---

[15] Marmol, Rebelion de Granada, tom. i. p. 414.—Herrera, Historia general. tom. i. p. 737.—Bleda, Cronica de España, p. 684.—Mendoza, Guerra de Granada, pp. 69, 70.—Ferreras, Hist. d'Espagne, tom. x. p. 17.

a fortified post, to cover the retreat of the army, if necessary, and to protect the convoys of supplies to be regularly forwarded from Granada. Leaving a small garrison there, the captain-general, without longer delay, resumed his pursuit of the enemy.

Aben-Humeya had retreated into Poqueira, a rugged district of the Alpujarras. Here he had posted himself, with an army amounting to more than double its former numbers, at the extremity of a dangerous defile, called the Pass of Alfajarali. Behind lay the town of Bubion, the capital of the district, in which, considering it as a place of safety, many of the wealthier Moriscoes had deposited their women and their treasures.

Mondejar's line of march now took him into the heart of the wildest regions of the Alpujarras, where the scenery assumed a character of sublimity very different from what he had met with in the lower levels of the country. Here mountain rose beyond mountain, till their hoary heads, soaring above the clouds, entered far into the region of eternal snow. The scene was as gloomy as it was grand. Instead of the wide-spreading woods that usually hang round the skirts of lofty mountains, covering up their nakedness from the eye, nothing here was to be seen but masses of shattered rock, black as if scathed by volcanic fires, and heaped one upon another in a sort of wild confusion, as if some tremendous convulsion of nature had torn the hills from their foundations and thrown them into primitive chaos. Yet the industry of the Moriscoes had contrived to relieve the savage features of the landscape, by scooping out terraces wherever the rocky soil allowed it, and raising there the vine and other plants, in bright patches of variegated culture, that hung like a garland round the gaunt and swarthy sierra.

The temperature was now greatly changed from what the army had experienced in the valley. The wind, sweeping down the icy sides of the mountains, found its way through the harness of the cavaliers and the light covering of the soldiers, benumbing their limbs and piercing them to the very bone. Great difficulty was experienced in dragging the cannon up the steep heights, and along roads and passes which, however easily traversed by the light-footed mountaineer, were but ill suited to the movements of an army clad in the heavy panoply of war.

The march was conducted in perfect order, the arquebusiers occupying the van, and the cavalry riding on either flank, while detachments of infantry, the main body of which occupied the centre, were thrown out to the right and left, on the higher grounds along the route of the army, to save it from annoyance from the mountaineers.

On the thirteenth of January, Mondejar entered the narrow defile of Alfajarali, at the farther end of which the motley multitude that had gathered round the standard of Aben-Humeya were already drawn up in battle-array. His right wing rested on the bold side of the sierra. The left was defended by a deep ravine, and his position was strengthened by more than one ambuscade, for which the nature of the ground was eminently favorable.[16] Indeed, ambushes and surprises

---

[16] "A la mano derecha cubiertos con un sierro, havia emboscados quinientos arcabuceros i vallesteros, demás desto otra emboscada en

formed part of the regular strategy of the Moorish warrior, who lost heart if he failed in these,—like the lion, who, if balked in the first spring upon his prey, is said rarely to attempt another.

Putting these wily tactics into practice, the Morisco chief, as soon as the Spaniards were fairly entangled in the defile, without waiting for them to come into order of battle, gave the signal; and his men, starting up from glen, thicket, and ravine, or bursting down the hill-sides like their own winter-torrents, fell at once on the Christians,—front, flank, and rear,—assailing them on every quarter."[17] Astounded by the fiery suddenness of the assault, the rear-guard retreated on the centre, while the arquebusiers in the van were thrown into still greater disorder. For a few moments it seemed as if the panic would become general. But the voice of the leader was heard above the tumult, and by his prompt and sagacious measures he fortunately succeeded in restoring order and reviving the confidence of his men. He detached one body of cavalry, under his son-in-law, to the support of the rear, and another to the front under the command of his son, Antonio de Mendoza. Both executed their commissions with spirit; and Mendoza, outstripping his companions in the haste with which he galloped to the front, threw himself into the thickest of the fight,

---

lo hondo del barranco de mucho mayor numero de gente." Mendoza, Guerra de Granada, tom. i. p. 71.

[17] " Ellos quando pensaron que nuestra gente iva cansada acometieron por la frente, por el costado, i por la retaguardia, todo a un tiempo; de manera que quasi una hora se peleó con ellos a todas partes i a las espaldas, no sin igualdad i peligro." Ibid., ubi supra.

where he was struck from his horse by a heavy stone, and was speedily surrounded by the enemy, from whose grasp he was with difficulty, and not till after much hard fighting, rescued by his companions. His friend, Don Alonso Portocarrero, the scion of a noble house in Andalusia, whose sons had always claimed the front of battle against the infidel, was twice wounded by poisoned arrows; for the Moors of the Alpujarras tipped their weapons with a deadly poison distilled from a weed that grew wild among the mountains.[18]

A fierce struggle now ensued. For the Morisco was spurred on by hate and the recollection of a thousand wrongs. Ill provided with weapons for attack, and destitute of defensive armor, he exposed himself to the hottest of his enemy's fire, and endeavored to drag the horsemen from their saddles, while stones and arrows, with which some musket-balls were intermingled, fell like rain on the well-tempered harness of the Andalusian knights. The latter, now fully roused, plunged boldly into the thickest of the Moorish multitude, trampling them under foot, and hewing them down, right and left, with their sharp blades. The arquebusiers, at the same time, delivered a well-directed fire on the flank of the Moriscoes, who, after a brave struggle of an hour's duration, in which they were baffled on every quarter, quitted the field, covered

---

[18] This poison was extracted from the aconite, or wolf's-bane, that grew rife among the Alpujarras. It was of so malignant a nature that the historian assures us that if a drop mingled with the blood flowing from a wound the virus would ascend the stream and diffuse itself over the whole system! Quince-juice was said to furnish the best antidote. Mendoza, Guerra de Granada, tom. i. pp. 73, 74.

with their slain, as precipitately as they had entered it, and, vanishing among the mountains, were soon far beyond pursuit.[19]

From the field of battle Mondejar marched at once upon Bubion, the capital of the district, now left wholly unprotected by the Moslems. Yet many of their wives and daughters remained in it; and what rejoiced the heart of Mondejar more than all was the liberation of a hundred and eighty Christian women, who came forth, frantic with joy and gratitude, to embrace the knees of their deliverers. They had many a tale of horror to tell their countrymen, who had now rescued them from a fate worse than that of death itself; for arrangements had been made, it was said, to send away those whose persons offered the greatest attractions, to swell the harems of the fierce Barbary princes in alliance with the Moriscoes. The town afforded a rich booty to the victorious troops, in gold, silver, and jewels, together with the finest stuffs, especially of silk, for the manufacture of which the people of the country were celebrated. As the Spanish commander, unwilling to be encumbered with unnecessary baggage, had made no provision for transporting the more bulky articles, the greater part of them, in the usual exterminating spirit of war, was consigned to the flames.[20] The

---

[19] Mendoza, Guerra de Granada, tom. i. pp. 71-74.—Cabrera, Filipe Segundo, p. 554.—Marmol, Rebelion de Granada, tom. i. pp. 416-418.—Herrera, Historia general, tom. i. p. 737.—Bleda, Cronica de España, p. 684.

[20] "Mas la priesa de caminar en siguimiento de los enemigos, i la falta de bagages en que la cargar i gente con que aseguralla, fue causa de quemar la mayor parte, porque ellos no se aprovechasen." Mendoza, Guerra de Granada, tom. i. p. 75.

soldiers would willingly have appropriated to themselves the Moorish women whom they found in the place, regarding them as the spoils of victory; but the marquis, greatly to the disgust of his followers, humanely interfered for their protection.

Mondejar now learned that Aben-Humeya, gathering the wreck of his forces about him, had taken the route to Jubiles,—a place situated in the wildest part of the country, where there was a fortress of much strength, in which he proposed to make a final stand against his enemies. Desirous to follow up the blow before the enemy had time to recover from its effects, Mondejar resumed his march. He had not advanced many leagues before he reached Pitres, the principal town in the district of Ferreiras. It was a place of some importance, and was rich in the commodities usually found in the great Moorish towns, where the more wealthy of the inhabitants rivalled their brethren of Granada in their taste for sumptuous dress and in the costly decorations of their houses.

The conquerors had here the satisfaction of releasing a hundred and fifty of their poor countrywomen from the captivity in which they had been held, after witnessing the massacre of their friends and relatives. The place was given up to pillage; but the marquis, true to his principles, notwithstanding the murmurs, and even menaces, of his soldiers, would allow no injury to be done to the Moorish women who remained in it. In this he acted in obedience to the dictates of sound policy, no less than of humanity, which indeed, happily for mankind, can never be dissevered from each other. He had no desire to push the war to extremities, or to exterminate a race whose ingenuity and industry were a fruitful source of revenue to the country. He wished, therefore, to leave the door of reconciliation still open; and, while he carried fire and sword into the enemy's territory, he held out the prospect of grace to those who were willing to submit and return to their allegiance.

The route of the army lay through a wild and desolate region, which, from its great elevation, was cool even in midsummer, and which now, in the month of January, wore the dreary aspect of a polar winter. The snow, which never melted on the highest peaks of the mountains, lay heavily on their broad shoulders, and, sweeping far down their sides, covered up the path of the Spaniards. It was with no little difficulty that they could find a practicable passage, especially for the train of heavy guns, which were dragged along with incredible toil by the united efforts of men and horses. The soldiers, born and bred in the sunny plains of Andalusia, were but ill provided against an intensity of cold of which they had never formed a conception. The hands and feet of many were frozen. Others, benumbed, and exhausted by excessive toil, straggled in the rear, and sank down in the snowdrifts, or disappeared in the treacherous ravines and crevices, which, under their glittering mantle, lay concealed from the eye. It fared still worse with the Moriscoes, especially with the women and children, who, after hanging on the skirts of the retreating army, had, the better to elude pursuit, scaled the more inaccessible parts of the mountains, where, taking refuge in caverns, they perished, in great numbers, of cold and hunger.[21]

Meanwhile, Aben-Humeya, disheartened by his late reverses, felt too little confidence in the strength of his present position to abide there the assault of the Spaniards. Quitting the place, therefore, and taking with him his women and effects, he directed his course by rapid marches towards Paterna, his principal residence, which had the advantage, by its neighborhood to the Sierra Nevada, of affording him, if necessary, the means of escaping into its wild and mysterious recesses, where none but a native would care to follow him. He left in the castle of Jubiles a great number of Morisco women, who had accompanied the army in its retreat, and three hundred men, who, from age or infirmity, would be likely to embarrass his movements.

On reaching Jubiles, therefore, the Spanish general met with no resistance from the helpless garrison who occupied the fortress, which, moreover, contained a rich booty in gold, pearls, and precious stones, to gratify the cupidity of the soldiers.[22] Yet their discontent was expressed in more audacious terms than usual at the protection afforded by their commander to the Morisco women, of whom there were more than two thousand in the place. Among the women found there was also a good number of Christian captives, who roused the fierce passions of their countrymen by their

---

[21] "Los Moros tomaron lo alto de la sierra, y no pararon hasta meterse en la nieve, donde perecieron cantidad de mugeres y de criatura de frio." Marmol, Rebelion de Granada, tom. i. p. 437.

[22] "El Marques les dió á saco todo el mueble, en que habia ricas cosas de seda, oro, plata y aljofar, de que cupo la mejor y mayor parte á los que habian ido delante." Ibid., p. 444.

piteous recital of the horrors they had witnessed, of the butchery of fathers, husbands, and brothers, and of the persecutions to which they had themselves been subjected in order to convert them to Islamism. They besought the captain-general to take pity on their sufferings, and to avenge their wrongs by putting every man and woman found in the place to the sword.²³ It is evident that, however prepared they may have been to accept the crown of martyrdom rather than abjure their faith, they gave little heed to the noblest of its precepts, which enjoined the forgiveness of their enemies. In this respect Mondejar proved himself decidedly the better Christian; for while he listened with commiseration to their tale of woe, and did all he could to comfort them in their affliction,²⁴ he would not abandon the protection of his captives, male or female, nor resign them to the brutality of his soldiers.

He provided for their safety during the night by allowing them to occupy the church. But as this would not accommodate more than a thousand persons, the remainder, including all the men, were quartered in an open square in the neighborhood of the building. The Spanish troops encamped at no great distance from the spot.

In the course of the night one of the soldiers found his way into the quarters of the captives and attempted to take some freedoms with a Morisco maiden. It so happened that her lover, disguised in woman's attire,

---

²³ "No tomen, señores, á vida hombre ni muger de aquestos hereges, que tan malos han sido, y tanto mal nos han hecho." Marmol, Rebelion de Granada, tom. i. p. 440.

²⁴ "El Marques se enterneció de ver aquellas pobres mugeres tan lastimadas, y consolandolas lo mejor que pudo," etc. Ibid, ubi supra.

was at her side, having remained with her for her protection. His Moorish blood fired at the insult, and he resented it by striking his poniard into the body of the Spaniard. The cry of the latter soon roused his comrades. Rushing to the place, they fell on the young Morisco, who, now brandishing a sword which he had snatched from the disabled man, laid about him so valiantly that several others were wounded. The cry rose that there were armed men, disguised as women, among the prisoners. More soldiers poured in to the support of their comrades, and fell with fury on their helpless victims. The uproar was universal. On the one side might be heard moans and petitions for mercy; on the other, brutal imprecations, followed by deadly blows, that showed how little the prayers for mercy had availed. The hearts of the soldiers were harder than the steel with which they struck; for they called to mind the cruelties inflicted on their own countrymen by the Moriscoes. Striking to the right and left, they hewed down men and women indiscriminately,—both equally defenceless. In their blind fury they even wounded one another; for it was not easy to discern friend from foe in the obscurity, in which little light was to be had, says the chronicler, except such as came from the sparks of clashing steel or the flash of fire-arms.[25] It was in vain that the officers endeavored to call off the men from their work of butchery. The

---

[25] "Hubo muchos soldados heridos, los mas que se herian unos á otros, entendiendo los que venian de fuera, que los que martillaban con las espadas eran Moros, porque solamente les alumbraba el centellear del acero, y el relampaguear de la polvora de los arcabuces en la tenebrosa escuridad de la noche." Marmol, Rebelion de Granada, tom. i. p. 445.

hot temper of the Andalusian was fully roused, and it would have been as easy to stop the explosion of the mine when the train has been fired, as to stay his fury. It was not till the morning light showed the pavement swimming in gore, and the corpses of the helpless victims lying in heaps on one another, that his appetite for blood was satisfied. Great numbers of the women, and nearly all the men, perished in this massacre.[26] Those in the church succeeded in making fast the doors and thus excluding their enemies, who made repeated efforts to enter the building. The marquis of Mondejar, indignant at this inhuman outrage perpetrated by his followers, and at their flagrant disobedience of orders, caused an inquiry into the affair to be instantly made; and the execution of three of the most guilty proved a salutary warning to the Andalusian soldier that there were limits beyond which it was not safe to try the patience of his commander.[7]

Before leaving Jubiles, Mondejar sent off to Granada, under a strong escort, the Christian captives who, since their liberation, had remained with the army. There were eight hundred of them, women and children,—a helpless multitude, whose wants were to be provided for, and whose presence could not fail greatly to embarrass his movements. They were obliged to perform that long and wearisome journey

---

[26] "De los Moriscos quasi ninguno quedó vivo, de las Moriscas huvo muchas muertas, de los nuestros algunos heridos, que con la escuridad de la noche se bacian daño unos á otros." Mendoza, Guerra de Granada, p. 77.

[7] Ibid., ubi supra.—Bleda, Cronica de España, p. 685.—Herrera, Historia general, tom. i. p. 737.—Marmol, Rebelion de Granada, tom. i. p. 441, et seq.—Cabrera, Filipe Segundo, p. 558.

across the mountains on foot, as there were no means of transportation. And piteous was the spectacle which they presented when they reached the capital. As the way-worn wanderers entered by the gate of Bib-arranbla, the citizens came forth in crowds to welcome them. A body of cavalry was in the van,—each of the troopers holding one or two children on the saddle before him, with sometimes a third on the crupper clinging to his back. The infantry brought up the rear; while the centre of the procession was occupied by the women,—a forlorn and melancholy band, with their heads undefended by any covering from the weather; their hair, bleached by the winter's tempests, streaming wildly over their shoulders; their clothes scanty, tattered, and soiled with travel; without stockings, without shoes, to protect their feet against the cold and flinty roads; while in the lines traced upon their countenances the dullest eye might read the story of their unparalleled sufferings. Many of the company were persons who, unaccustomed to toil, and delicately nurtured, were but poorly prepared for the trials and privations of every kind to which they had been subjected.[28]

As their friends and countrymen gathered round them, to testify their sympathy and listen to the story of their misfortunes, the voices of the poor wanderers were choked with sobs and lamentations. The grief was contagious; and the sorrowing and sympathetic

---

[28] "Habia entre ellas muchas dueñas nobles, apuestas y hermosas doncellas, criadas con mucho regalo, que iban desnudas y descalzas, y tan maltratadas del trabajo del captiverio y del camino, que no solo quebraban los corazones á los que las conocian, mas aun á quien no las habia visto." Marmol, Rebelion de Granada, tom. i. p. 448.

THE LIBERATED CHRISTIANS.

multitude accompanied the procession like a train of mourners to the monastery of Our Lady of Victory, in the opposite quarter of the city, where services were performed with much solemnity and thanks were offered up for their deliverance from captivity. From the church they proceeded to the Alhambra, where they were graciously received by the marchioness of Mondejar, the wife of the captain-general, who did what she could to alleviate the miseries of their condition. Those who had friends and relations in the city found shelter in their houses; while the rest were kindly welcomed by the archbishop of Granada, and by the charitable people of the town, who provided them with raiment and whatever was necessary for their comfort.[29] The stories which the fugitives had to tell of the horrid scenes they had witnessed in the Alpujarras roused a deeper feeling of hatred in the Spaniards towards the Moriscoes, that boded ill for the security of the inhabitants of the Albaicin.

[29] " Y volviendo á las casas del Arzobispo, las que tenian parientes las llevaron á sus posadas, y las otras fueron hospedadas con caridad entre la buena gente, y de limosna se les compró de vestir y de calzar." Marmol, Rebelion de Granada, ubi supra.

CHAPTER IV.

REBELLION OF THE MORISCOES.

Situation of Aben-Humeya. — Fate of the Moorish Prisoners. — Storming of Guájaras.—Escape of Aben-Humeya.—Operations of Los Velez.—Cabal against Mondejar.—License of the Soldiers.— Massacre in Granada.—The Insurrection rekindled.

1569.

BEFORE the marquis of Mondejar quitted Jubiles, he received a visit from seventeen of the principal Moriscoes in that part of the country, who came to tender their submission, exculpating themselves, at the same time, from any share in the insurrection, and humbly suing for the captain-general's protection. This, agreeably to his policy, he promptly accorded, granting them a safe-conduct, with instructions to tell their countrymen what he had done, and persuade them, if possible, to return to their allegiance, as the only way of averting the ruin that else would speedily overtake them. This act of clemency, so repugnant to the feelings of the Spaniards, was a new cause of disgust to his soldiers, who felt that the fair terms thus secured by the rebels were little better than a victory over themselves.[1]

[1] " Los soldados no podian llevar á paciencia ver que se tratase de medios con los rebeldes; y quando otro dia se supo que los admitia, fue tan grande la tristeza en el campo, como si hubieran perdido la jornada." Marmol, Rebelion de Granada, tom. i. p. 443.

Yet the good effects of this policy were soon made visible when the marquis resumed his march. For, as his favorable dispositions became more generally known, numbers of the Moriscoes, and several places on the route, eagerly tendered their submission, imploring his mercy, and protection against his followers.

Aben-Humeya, meanwhile, who lay at Paterna, with his wives and his warriors gathered around, saw with dismay that his mountain-throne was fast sliding away from beneath him. The spirit of distrust and disaffection had crept into his camp. It was divided into two parties. One of these, despairing of further resistance, would have come instantly to terms with the enemy. The other still adhered to a bolder policy; but its leaders, if we may trust the Castilian writers, were less influenced by patriotic than by personal motives, being for the most part men who had borne so conspicuous a part in the insurrection that they could scarcely hope to be included in any amnesty granted by the Spaniards. Such, in particular, were the African adventurers, who had distinguished themselves above all others by their ferocious persecution of the Christians. They directed, at this time, the counsels of the Moorish prince, filling his mind with suspicions of the loyalty of some of his followers, especially of the father of one of his wives, a person of much authority among the Moriscoes. To suspect and to slay were words of much the same import with Aben-Humeya. He sent for his relative, and, on his entering the apartment, caused him to be despatched before his eyes.[a] He would have followed this up by the murder of some others of the family, if they had

[a] Marmol, Rebelion de Granada, tom. i. p. 455.

not eluded his grasp; thus establishing his title to a descent from those despots of the East with whom the lives of their kindred were of as little account as the vermin in their path.[3]

He was still at the head of a numerous army. Its number, indeed, amounting to six thousand men, constituted its greatest strength; for, without discipline, almost without arms, it was made up of such rude, incongruous materials, that, as he had already experienced, it could never abide the shock of battle from the militia of Castile. The Moorish prince had other causes for discouragement, in the tidings he was hourly receiving of the defection of his subjects. The clemency shown by the conqueror was doing more for him than his arms,—as the snow which the blasts of winter have only bound more closely to the hill-side loosens its hold and falls away under the soft touch of spring. Notwithstanding his late display of audacity, the unhappy young man now lost all confidence in his own fortunes and in his followers. Sorely perplexed, he knew not where to turn. He had little of the constancy or courage of the patriot who has perilled his life in a great cause; and he now had recourse to the same expedient which he had so lately punished with death in his father-in-law.

He sent a message to the marquis of Mondejar, offering to surrender, and, if time were given, to persuade his people to follow his example. Meanwhile, he

[3] Abderrahman — or, as spelt by Gayangos, Abdu-r-rhamán — the First, the founder of the dynasty from which Aben-Humeya claimed his descent, took refuge in Spain from a bloody persecution, in which every member of his numerous family is said to have perished by the scimitar or the bow-string.

requested the Spanish commander to stay his march, and thus prevent a collision with his troops. Mondejar, though he would not consent to this, advanced more leisurely, while he opened a negotiation with his enemy. He had already come in sight of the rebel forces, when he consented, at the request of Aben-Humeya, to halt for a night in the neighboring village of Iñiza, in order to give time for a personal interview. This required the troops, some of whom had now advanced within musket-range of the enemy, to fall back and take up ground in the rear of their present position. In executing this manœuvre they came almost in contact with a detachment of the Moorish army, who, in their ignorance of its real object, regarding the movement as a hostile demonstration, sent a shower of arrows and other missiles among the Spaniards, which they returned with hearty good will by a volley of musketry. The engagement soon became general. Aben-Humeya at the time was reading a letter, which he had just received from one of Mondejar's staff, arranging the place for the interview, when he was startled by the firing, and saw with consternation his own men warmly engaged with the enemy. Supposing he had been deceived by the Spaniards, he flung the letter on the ground, and, throwing himself into the saddle, without so much as attempting to rally his forces, which were now flying over the field in all directions, he took the road to the Sierra Nevada, followed by only five or six of his attendants.[4] His

---

[4] "Y como vió que los Christianos iban la sierra arriba, y que los suyos huían desvergonzadamente, entendiendo que todo lo que Don Alonso Venegas trataba era engaño, echo las cartas en el suelo, y

horse was fleet, and he soon gained the defiles of the mountains. But he was hotly pursued; and, thinking it safer to trust to himself than to his horse, he dismounted, cut the hamstrings of the animal to prevent his being of service to his pursuers, and disappeared in the obscure depths of the sierra, where it would have been fruitless to follow him.

The rout of his army was complete; and the victors might have inflicted an incalculable loss on the fugitives, had not the marquis of Mondejar called off his troops and put a stop to the work of death. He wished to keep open as widely as possible the door of reconciliation. His conduct, which was not understood and could not have been appreciated by his men, was stigmatized by them as treachery. They found some amends for their disappointment in the pillage of Paterna, the residence of Aben-Humeya, which, well provided with the costly finery so much loved by the Moriscoes, furnished a welcome booty to the conquerors.[5]

Among the Moorish captives were Aben-Humeya's mother, two of his sisters, and one of his wives, to whom, as usual, Mondejar extended his protection.

Yet the disposal of his prisoners was a subject of perplexity to the Spanish commander. His soldiers, as we have seen, would have settled it at once, had their captain consented, by appropriating them all as

subiendo á gran priesa en un caballo, dexó su familia atras, y huyo tambien la vuelta de la sierra." Marmol, Rebelion de Granada, tom. i. p. 460.

[5] Ibid., p. 458, et seq.—Ferreras, Hist. d'Espagne, tom. x. pp. 29-31.—Mendoza, Guerra de Granada, pp. 80, 81.—Cabrera, Filipe Segundo, pp. 560, 561.—Herrera, Historia general, tom. i. p. 737.

the spoils of victory. There were many persons, higher in authority than these soldiers, who were of the same way of thinking on the subject with them. The question was one of sufficient importance to come before the government. Philip referred it to the council of state; and, regarding it as a case of conscience, in which the interests of religion were concerned, he asked the opinion of the Royal Audience of Granada, over which Deza presided. The final decision was what might have been expected from tribunals with inquisitors at their head. The Moriscoes, men and women, were declared to have incurred by their rebellion the doom of slavery. What is more remarkable is the precedent cited for this judgment, it being no other than a decision of the Council of Toledo, as far back as the time of the Visigoths, when certain rebellious Jews were held to have forfeited their liberty by an act of rebellion.[6] The Morisco, it was said, should fare no better than the Jew, since he was not only, like him, a rebel and an infidel, but an apostate to boot. The decision, it was understood, was very satisfactory to Philip, who, however, "with the pious moderation that distinguished so just and considerate a prince,"[7] so far mitigated the severity of the sentence, in the pragmatic which he published, as to exempt from its operation boys under ten years of age and girls under eleven. These were to be placed in the care of responsible persons who would give them the benefits of a Chris-

[6] The decision referred to was probably one in the last Council of Toledo, A.D. 690. See Mariana, Hist. de España, tom. i. p. 452.

[7] I quote the words of Marmol: "Con una moderacion piadosa, de que quiso usar como principe considerado y justo." Rebelion de Granada, tom. i. p. 495.

tian education. Unhappily, there is reason to think that the good intentions of the government were not very conscientiously carried out in respect to this provision by those intrusted with the execution of it.[8]

While the question was pending, Jubiles fell into the hands of the victors; and Mondejar, not feeling himself at liberty to release his female captives, of whom more than a thousand, by this event, had come into his possession, delivered them in charge to three of the principal Moriscoes, to whom, it may be remembered, he had given letters of safe-conduct. They were allowed to restore the women to their families, on condition that they should all be surrendered on the demand of the government. Such an act, it must be admitted, implies great confidence in the good faith of the Moslems,—a confidence fully justified by the result. When, in obedience to the pragmatic, they were claimed by the government, they were delivered up by their families,—with the exception of some who had died in the mean time,—and the greater part of them were sold by public auction in Granada.[9]

The only place of any importance which now held out against Mondejar was Las Guájaras, situated in the plains of Salobreña, in the direction of Velez Malaga. This was a rocky, precipitous hill, on the summit of which nature, with little assistance from art, had constructed a sort of rude fortress. It was held by a fierce band of Moriscoes, who, descending from the heights,

[8] Marmol, Rebelion de Granada, tom. i. p. 495.
[9] Ibid., pp. 465, 498.—Mendoza says they were all returned.—" a thing never before seen, whether it arose from fear or obedience, or that there was such an abundance of women that they were regarded as little better than household furniture." Guerra de Granada, p. 96.

swept over the plains, carrying on devastating forays, that made them the terror of the surrounding country. Mondejar, moved by the complaints of the inhabitants, left Ugijar on the fifth of February, at the head of his whole array, now much augmented by the arrival of recent levies, and marched rapidly on Guájaras. He met with a more formidable resistance than he had expected. His first attempt to carry the place was repulsed with a heavy loss on the part of the assailants. The Moorish garrison, from its elevated position, poured a storm of missiles on their heads, and, what was worse, rolled down huge masses of rock, which, ploughing through the Castilian ranks, overthrew men and horses, and did as great execution as would have been done by artillery. Eight hundred Spaniards were left dead on the field; and many a noble house in Andalusia had to go into mourning for that day's disaster.

Mondejar, stung by this repulse,—the first reverse his arms had experienced,—determined to lead the attack in person on the following day. His approaches were made with greater caution than before; and, without much injury, he succeeded in bringing his arquebusiers on a higher level, where their fire swept the enemy's intrenchments and inflicted on him a terrible loss. Still, the sun went down, and the place had not surrendered. But El Zamar, its brave defender, without ammunition, almost without arms, felt that there was no longer hope for his little garrison. Silently evacuating the place, therefore, at dead of night, the Moriscoes, among whom were both women and children, scrambled down the precipice with the fearlessness of the mountain-goat, and made their escape without attracting the notice of the Spaniards. They left behind only such as, from age or infirmity, were unable to follow them in their perilous descent.

On the next day, when the Spanish general prepared to renew the assault, great was his astonishment to find that the enemy had vanished, except only a few wretched beings, incapable of making any resistance. All the evil passions of Mondejar's nature had been roused by the obstinate defence of the place and the lives it had cost him. In the heat of his wrath, he ordered the helpless garrison to be put to the sword. No prayer for mercy was heeded. No regard was had to age or to sex. All were cut down in the presence of the general, who is even said to have stimulated the faltering soldiers to go through with their bloody work.[10] An act so hard to be reconciled with his previous conduct has been referred by some to the annoyance which he felt at being so frequently taxed with excessive lenity to the Moriscoes, an accusation which was carried, indeed, before the crown, and which the present occasion afforded him the means of effectually disproving. However this may be, the historian must lament the tarnished honor of a brave and generous chief, whose character up to this time had been sullied by none of those acts of cruelty which distinguished this sanguinary war.[11]

[10] " Fue tanta la indignacion del Marques de Mondejar, que, sin perdonar á ninguna edad ni sexo, mandó pasar á cuchillo hombres y mugeres, quantos habia en el fuerte ; y en su presencia los hacia matar á los alabarderos de su guardia, que no bastaban los ruegos de los caballeros y capitanes, ni las piadosas lagrimas de las que pedian la miserable vida." Marmol, Rebelion de Granada, tom. i. p. 493.

[11] Ibid., p. 482, et seq.—Mendoza, Guerra de Granada, pp. 85-95

But even this cruelty was surpassed by that of his son, the count of Tendilla. El Zamar, the gallant defender of the fortress, wandered about among the crags with his little daughter, whom he carried in his arms. Famished and fainting from fatigue, he was at length overtaken by his enemies, and sent off as a prisoner to Granada, where the fierce Tendilla caused the flesh to be torn from his bones with red-hot pincers, and his mangled carcass, yet palpitating with life, to be afterwards quartered. The crime of El Zamar was that he had fought too bravely for the independence of his nation.

Having razed the walls of Guájaras to the ground, Mondejar returned with his blood-stained laurels to his headquarters at Orgiba. Tower and town had gone down before him. On every side his arms had proved victorious. But one thing was wanting,—the capture of Aben-Humeya, the "little king" of the Alpujarras. So long as he lived, the insurrection, now smothered, might be rekindled at any time. He had taken refuge, it was known, in the wilds of the Sierra Nevada, where, as the captain-general wrote, he was wandering from rock to rock with only a handful of followers."[12] Mon-

—Ferreras, Hist. d'Espagne, tom. x. pp. 32-36.—Bleda, Cronica de España, p. 688, et seq.—Herrera, Historia general, tom. i. p. 738.—Cabrera, Filipe Segundo, p. 569.—The storming of Guájaras is a favorite theme with both chroniclers and bards. Among the latter Hita has not failed to hang his garland of verse on the tombs of more than one illustrious cavalier who perished in that bloody strife, and for whose loss "all the noble dames of Seville," as he tells us, "went into mourning." Guerras de Granada, tom. ii. pp. 112-118.

[12] "Que no habia osado parar en la Alpuxarra, y con solos cincuenta ó sesenta hombres, que le seguian, andaba huyendo de peña en peña." Marmol, Rebelion de Granada, tom. i. p. 464.

dejar sent two detachments of soldiers into the sierra, to discover his haunts, if possible, and seize upon his person.

The commander of one of these parties, named Maldonado, ascertained that Aben-Humeya, secreting himself among the fastnesses of the mountains by day, would steal forth at night, and repair, with a few of his followers, to a place called Mecina, on the skirts of the sierra. Here he found shelter in the house of his kinsman, Aben-Aboo, one of those Moriscoes who, after the affair of Jubiles, had obtained a safe-conduct from Mondejar. Having gained this intelligence and learned the situation of the house, the Spanish captain marched, with his little band of two hundred soldiers, in that direction. He made his approach with the greatest secrecy. Travelling by night, he reached undiscovered the neighborhood of Aben-Aboo's residence. Advancing under cover of the darkness, he had arrived within gunshot of the dwelling, when, at this critical moment, all his precautions were defeated by the carelessness of one of his company, whose arquebuse was accidentally discharged. The report, reverberating from the hills in the silence of the night, roused the inmates of the house, who slept as the wearied mariner sleeps when his ship is in danger of foundering. One of them, El Zaguer, the uncle of Aben-Humeya, and the person who had been mainly instrumental in securing him his crown,—a crown of thorns,—was the first roused, and, springing to the window, he threw himself down, though the height was considerable, and made his way to the mountains.

His nephew, who lay in another part of the building,

was not so fortunate. When he reached the window he saw with dismay the ground in front occupied by a body of Castilian troops. Hastening to another window, he found it still the same: his enemies were everywhere around the house. Bewildered and sorely distressed, he knew not where to turn. Thus entrapped, and without the means of making any terms with his enemies, he knew he had as little to hope from their mercy as the wolf has from the hunters who have caught him in his lair. The Spaniards, meanwhile, were thundering at the door of the building for admittance. Fortunately, it was well secured. A sudden thought occurred to Aben-Humeya, which he instantly put into execution. Hastening down-stairs, he took his station behind the door, and gently drew the bolts. The noise was not heard amidst the din made by the assailants, who, finding the door give way, supposed they had forced the fastenings, and, pouring in, soon spread themselves in every direction over the house in search of the fugitive. Aben-Humeya, ensconced behind the door, escaped observation, and, when his enemies had disappeared, stole out into the darkness, and, under its friendly mantle, succeeded in finding his way to the mountains.

It was in vain that the Spaniards, enraged at the loss of the quarry, questioned Aben-Aboo as to the haunts of his kinsman, and of El Zaguer, his uncle, in the sierra. Nor could the most excruciating tortures shake his constancy. "I may die," said the brave Morisco, "but my friends will live." Leaving him for dead, the soldiers returned to the camp, taking with them a number of prisoners, his companions. There was no one of them, however, that was not provided with a safe-conduct from the marquis, who accordingly set them at liberty, showing a respect for his engagements in which, unhappily, as we shall see hereafter, he was not too well imitated by his soldiers. The heroic Aben-Aboo, though left for dead, did not die, but lived to head another insurrection and to take ample vengeance on his enemies.[13]

While the arms of the marquis of Mondejar were thus crowned with success, the war raged yet more fiercely on the eastern slopes of the Alpujarras, where a martial race of mountaineers threatened a descent on Almeria and the neighboring places, keeping the inhabitants in perpetual alarm. They accordingly implored the government at Granada to take some effectual measures for their relief. The president, Deza, in consequence, desired the marquis of Los Velez, who held the office of adelantado of the adjoining province of Murcia, to muster a force and provide for the defence of the frontier. This proceeding was regarded by Mondejar's friends as an insult to that nobleman, whose military authority extended over the country menaced by the Moriscoes. The act was the more annoying that the person invited to assume the command was a rival, between whose house and that of the Mendozas there existed an ancient feud. Yet

[13] The Castilian chronicler cannot refuse his admiration—somewhat roughly expressed—to this brave Morisco,—" este barbaro," as he calls him, " hijo de aspereza y frialdad indomable, y menospreciador de la muerte." (Marmol, Rebelion de Granada, tom. i. p. 503.) The story of the escape of Aben-Humeya is also told, and with little discrepancy, by Cabrera (Filipe Segundo, p. 573) and Ferreras (Hist. d'Espagne, tom. x. pp. 39, 40).

the king sanctioned the proceeding, thinking perhaps that Mondejar was not in sufficient force to protect the whole region of the Alpujarras. However this may be, Philip, by this act, brought two commanders of equal authority on the theatre of action, men who in their characters and habitual policy were so opposed to each other that little concert could be expected between them.

Don Luis Fajardo, marquis of Los Velez, was a nobleman somewhat advanced in years, most of which had been passed in the active duties of military life. He had studied the art of war under the great emperor, and had acquired the reputation of a prompt and resolute soldier, bold in action, haughty, indeed overbearing, in his deportment, and with an inflexible will, not to be shaken by friend or foe. The severity of his nature had not been softened under the stern training of the camp; and, as his conduct in the present expedition showed, he was troubled with none of those scruples on the score of humanity which so often turned the edge of Mondejar's sword from the defenceless and the weak. The Moriscoes, who understood his character well, held him in terror, as they proved by the familiar *sobriquet* which they gave him of the " iron-headed devil." [14]

[14] " Quando entendieron que peleaban contra el campo del Marques de los Velez, á quien los Moros de aquella tierra solian llamar Ibiliz Arraez el Hadid, que quiere decir, *diabolo cabeza de hierro*, perdieron esperanza de vitoria." Marmol, Rebelion de Granada, tom. i. p. 451. —Hita, who was a native of Murcia, and followed Los Velez to the war, gives an elaborate portrait of this powerful chief, whom he extols as one of the most valiant captains in the world, rivalling in his achievements the Cid, Bernardo del Carpio, or any other hero of greatest renown in Spain. Guerras de Granada, tom. ii. p. 68, et seq.

The marquis, on receiving the invitation of Deza, lost no time in gathering his kindred and numerous vassals around him; and they came with an alacrity which showed how willingly they obeyed the summons to a foray over the border. His own family was a warlike race, reared from the cradle amidst the din of arms. In the present expedition he was attended by three of his sons, the youngest of whom, a boy of thirteen, had the proud distinction of carrying his father's banner.[15] With the levies promptly furnished from the neighboring places, Los Velez soon found himself supported by a force of greater strength than that which followed the standard of Mondejar. At the head of this valiant but ill-disciplined array, he struck into the gloomy gorges of the mountains, resolved on bringing the enemy at once to battle.

Our limits will not allow room for the details of a campaign which in its general features bears so close a resemblance to that already described. Indeed, the contest was too unequal to afford a subject of much interest to the general reader, while the details are of still less importance in a military view, from the total ignorance shown by the Moriscoes of the art of war.

The fate of the campaign was decided by three battles, fought successively at Huécija, Filix, and Ohanez,—places all lying in the eastern ranges of the Alpujarras. That of Filix was the most sanguinary. A great number of stragglers hung on the skirts of the Morisco army; and besides six thousand—many of them women[16]—left dead upon the field, there were

---

[15] Circourt, Hist. des Arabes en Espagne, tom. ii. p. 346.

[16] " Mas mugeres que hombres," says Mendoza, Guerra de Granada, p. 83.

two thousand children, we are told, butchered by the Spaniards.[17] Some fled for refuge to the caves and thickets; but they were speedily dragged from their hiding-places and massacred by the soldiers in cold blood. Others, to escape death from the hands of their enemies, threw themselves headlong down the precipices,—some of them with their infants in their arms,—and thus miserably perished. "The cruelties committed by the troops," says one of the army, who chronicles its achievements, "were such as the pen refuses to record.[18] I myself," he adds, "saw the corpse of a Morisco woman, covered with wounds, stretched upon the ground, with six of her children lying dead around her. She had succeeded in protecting a seventh, still an infant, with her body; and, though the lances which pierced her had passed through its clothes, it had marvellously escaped any injury. It was clinging," he continues, "to its dead mother's bosom, from which it drew milk that was mingled with blood. I carried it away and saved it."[19] For the credit of human nature he records some other instances of the like kind, showing that a spark of humanity might occa-

[17] "En menos de dos horas fueron muertas mas de seis mil personas entre hombres y mugeres; y de niños, desde uno hasta diez años, habia mas de dos mil degollados." Hita, Guerras de Granada, tom. ii. p. 126.—We may hope this is an exaggeration of the romancer. Mendoza says nothing of the children, and reduces the slain to seven hundred. But Hita was in the action.

[18] "La soldadesca que andaba suelta por el lugar cometió crueldades inauditas, y que la pluma se resiste á transcribir." Ibid., p. 125.

[19] "El niño arrastrando como pudó se llegó á ella, y movido del deseo de mamar, se asió de los pechos de la madre, sacando leche mezclada con la sangre de las heridas." Ibid., p. 126.

sionally be struck out from the flinty breasts of these marauders.

The field of battle afforded a rich harvest for the victors, who stripped the dead, and rifled the bodies of the women, of collars, bracelets, ornaments of gold and silver, and costly jewels, with which the Moorish female loved to decorate her person. Sated with plunder, the soldiers took the first occasion to leave their colors and return to their homes. Their places were soon supplied, as the display of their riches sharpened the appetites of their countrymen, who eagerly flocked to the banner of a chief that was sure to lead them on to victory and plunder. But that chief, with all his stern authority, was no match for the spirit of insubordination that reigned among his troops; and when he attempted to punish one of their number for a gross act of disobedience, he was made to understand that there were three thousand in the camp ready to stand by their comrade and protect him from injury.[20]

The wild excesses of the soldiery were strangely mingled with a respect for the forms of religion that intimated the nature of the war in which they were engaged. Before entering into action the whole army knelt down in prayer, solemnly invoking the protection of Heaven on its champions. After the battle of Ohanez, where the mountain-streams were so polluted with gore that the Spaniards found it difficult to slake their thirst, they proceeded to celebrate the *fête* of the

---

[20] "Advirtiendo al mismo tiempo que hay tres mil hombres paisanos suyos puestos sobre las armas, y decididos á perder la vida por salvarle." Hita, Guerras de Granada, tom. ii. p. 132.

Purification of the Virgin.[21] A procession was formed to the church, which was headed by the marquis of Los Velez and his chivalry, clad in complete mail and bearing white tapers in their hands. Then came the Christian women who had been rescued from captivity, dressed, by the general's command, in robes of blue and white, as the appropriate colors of the Virgin.[22] The rear was brought up by a body of friars and other ecclesiastics who had taken part in the crusade. The procession passed slowly between the files of the soldiery, who saluted it with volleys of musketry as it entered the church, where *Te Deum* was chanted, and the whole company prostrated themselves in adoration of the Lord of Hosts, who had given his enemies into their hands.

From this solemn act of devotion the troops proceeded to the work of pillage, in which the commander, unlike his rival, the marquis of Mondejar, joined as heartily as the meanest of his followers. The Moorish captives, to the number of sixteen hundred, among whom, we are told, were many young and beautiful maidens, instead of meeting with the protection they

[21] Hita has devoted one of the most spirited of his *romances* to the rout of Ohanez. The opening stanza may show the tone of it:
> " Las tremolantes banderas
> del grande Fajardo parten
> para las Nevadas Sierras,
> y van camino de Ohanez.
> Ay de Ohanez!"

[22] " Todos los caballeros y capitanes en la procesion armados de todas sus armas, con velas de cera blanca en las manos, que se las habian enviado para aquel dia desde su casa, y todas las Christianas en medio vestidas de azul y blanco, que por ser colores aplicados á nuestra Señora, mandó el Marques que las vistiesen de aquella manera á su costa." Marmol, Rebelion de Granada, tom. i. p. 469.

had received from the more generous Mondejar, were delivered up to the licentious soldiery; and for a fortnight there reigned throughout the camp a carnival of the wildest riot and debauchery.[73] In this strange confusion of the religious sentiment and of crimes most revolting to humanity we see the characteristic features of the crusade. Nowhere do we find such a free range given to the worst passions of our nature as in the wars of religion,—where each party considers itself as arrayed against the enemies of God, and where the sanctity of the cause throws a veil over the foulest transgressions, that hides their enormity from the eye of the transgressor.

While the Moriscoes were stunned by the fierce blows thus dealt in rapid succession by the iron-hearted marquis, the mild and liberal policy of his rival was still more effectually reducing his enemies to obedience. Disheartened by their reverses, exhausted by fatigue and hunger, as they roved among the mountains, without raiment to clothe or a home to shelter them, the wretched wanderers came in one after another to sue for pardon. Nearly all the towns and villages in the district assigned to Mondejar, oppressed with like feelings of despondency, sent deputations to the Spanish quarters, to tender their submission and to sue for his protection. While these were graciously received, the general provided for the future security of his conquests, by establishing garrisons in the principal places, and by

---

[73] "Trayéndose muchas moras hermosas, pues pasaron de trescientas las que se tomaron allí; y habiéndolas tenido los soldados á su voluntad mas de quince dias, al cabo de ellos mandó el marqués que las llevasen á la iglesia." Hita, Guerras de Granada, tom. ii. p. 155.

sending small detachments to different parts, to act as a sort of armed police for the maintenance of order In this way, says a contemporary, the tranquillity of the country was so well established that small parties of ten or a dozen soldiers wandered unmolested from one end of it to the other.[24]

Mondejar, at the same time, wrote to the king, to acquaint him with the actual state of things. He besought his master to deal mercifully with the conquered people, and thus afford him the means of redeeming the pledges he had given for the favorable dispositions of the government.[25] He made another communication to the marquis of Los Velez, urging that nobleman to co-operate with him in the same humane policy, as the one best suited to the interests of the country. But his rival took a very different view of the matter; and he plainly told the marquis of Mondejar that it would require more than one pitched battle yet to break the spirit of the Moriscoes, and that, since they thought so differently on the subject, the only way left was for each commander to take the course he judged best.[26]

[24] " Por manera que ya estaba la Alpuxarra tan llana, que diez y doce soldados iban de unos lugares en otros, sin hallar quien los enojase." Marmol, Rebelion de Granada, tom. i. p. 498.—Mendoza fully confirms Marmol's account of the quiet state of the country. Guerra de Granada, pp. 96, 97.

[25] " Le suplicase de su parte los admitiese, habiendose misericordiosamente con los que no fuesen muy culpados, para que él pudiese cumplir la palabra que tenia ya dada á los reducidos, entendiendo ser aquel camino el mas breve para acabar con ellos por la via de equidad." Marmol, Rebelion de Granada, tom. i. p. 483.

[26] " Que hiciese por su parte lo que pudiese, porque ansi haria él de la suya." Ibid., p. 470.

Unfortunately, there were others—men, too, of influence at the court—who were of the same stern way of thinking as the marquis of Los Velez; men acting under the impulse of religious bigotry, of implacable hatred of the Moslems, and of a keen remembrance of the outrages they had committed. There were others who, more basely, thought only of themselves and of the profit they should derive from the continuance of the war.

Among those of the former class was the president, Deza, with the members of the Audience and the civil authorities in Granada. Always viewing the proceedings of the captain-general with an unfriendly eye, they loudly denounced his policy to the king, condemning his ill-timed lenity to a crafty race, who would profit by it to rally from their late disasters and to form new plans of rebellion. It was not right, they said, that outrages like those perpetrated against both *divine and human majesty* should go unpunished.[27] Mondejar's enemies did not stop here, but accused him of defrauding the exchequer of its dues,—the fifth of the spoils of war gained in battle from the infidel. Finally, they charged him with having shown want of respect for the civil authorities of Granada, in omitting to communicate to them his plan of operations.

The marquis, advised by his friends at court of these malicious attempts to ruin his credit with the government, despatched a confidential envoy to Madrid, to present his case before his sovereign and to refute the

---

[27] "Dexar sin castigo exemplar á quien tantos crimenes habian cometido contra la Magestad *divina y humana*." Marmol, Rebelion de Granada, tom. i. p. 499.

accusations of his enemies. The charge of peculation seems to have made no impression on the mind of a prince who would not have been slow to suspect had there been any ground for suspicion. There may have been stronger grounds for the complaint of want of deference to the civil authorities of Granada. The best vindication of his conduct in this particular must be found in the character and conduct of his adversaries. From the first, Deza and the municipality had regarded him with jealousy and done all in their power to thwart his plans and circumscribe his authority. It is only confidence that begets confidence. Mondejar, early accustomed to command, was probably too impatient of opposition.[28] He chafed under the obstacles and annoyances thrown in his way by his narrow-minded rivals. We have not the means before us of coming to a conclusive judgment on the merits of the controversy; but from what we know of the marquis's accusers, with the wily inquisitor at their head, we shall hardly err by casting our sympathies into the scale of the frank and generous-hearted soldier, who, while those that thus censured him were living at ease in the capital, had been fighting and following up the enemy amidst the winter's tempests and across mountains covered with snow, and who in little more than a month, without other aid than the disorderly levies of the cities, had quelled a dangerous revolt and restored tranquillity to the land.

[28] "El Marques," says Mendoza, "hombre de estrecha i rigurosa disciplina, criado al favor de su abuelo i padre en gran oficio, sin igual ni contradictor, impaciente de tomar compañia, comunicava sus consejos consigo mismo." Guerra de Granada, p. 103.

Philip was greatly perplexed by the different accounts sent to him of the posture of affairs in Granada. Mondejar's agent suggested to the council of state that it would be well if his majesty would do as his father, Charles the Fifth, would have done in the like case,—repair himself to the scene of action, and observe the actual state of things with his own eyes. But the suggestion found no favor with the minister, Espinosa, who affected to hold the Moriscoes in such contempt that a measure of this kind, he declared, would be derogatory to the royal dignity. A better course would be for his majesty to send some one as his representative, clothed with full powers to take charge of the war, and of a rank so manifestly pre-eminent that neither of the two commanders now in the field could take umbrage at his appointment over their heads.

This suggestion, as the politic minister doubtless had foreseen, was much more to Philip's taste than that of his going in person to the scene of strife; for, however little he might shrink from any amount of labor in the closet, he had, as we have seen, a sluggish temperament, that indisposed him to much bodily exertion. The plan of sending some one to represent the monarch at the seat of war was accordingly approved; and the person selected for this responsible office was Philip's bastard brother, Don John of Austria.[29]

Rumors of what was going on in the cabinet at Madrid, reaching Granada from time to time, were followed by the most mischievous consequences. The

---

[29] Mendoza, Guerra de Granada, p. 115, et seq.—Marmol, Rebelion de Granada, tom. i. pp. 511-513.—Miniana, Historia de España, p. 376.—Cabrera, Filipe Segundo, pp. 573, 574.

troops, in particular, had no sooner learned that the marquis of Mondejar was about to be superseded in the command than they threw off the little restraint he had been hitherto able to impose on them, and abandoned themselves to the violence and rapine to which they were so well disposed, and which seemed now to be countenanced by the president and the authorities in Granada. The very patrols whom Mondejar had commissioned to keep the peace were the first to set the example of violating it. They invaded the hamlets and houses they were sent to protect, plundered them of their contents, and committed the foulest outrages on their inmates. The garrisons in the principal towns imitated their example, carrying on their depredations, indeed, on a still larger scale. Even the capital, under the very eyes of the count of Tendilla, sent out detachments of soldiers, who with ruthless violence trampled down the green plantations in the valleys, sacked the villages, and dragged away the inhabitants from the midst of their blazing dwellings into captivity.[30]

It was with the deepest indignation that the marquis of Mondejar saw the fine web of policy he had been so busily contriving thus wantonly rent asunder by the very hands that should have protected it. He now longed as ardently as any in the province for the coming of some one intrusted with authority to enforce obedience from the turbulent soldiery,—a task of still greater difficulty than the conquest of the enemy. While such was the state of things, an event occurred in Granada

---

[30] Marmol, Rebelion de Granada, tom. ii. p. 8, et seq.—Mendoza, Guerra de Granada, pp. 97, 128.—Miniana, Historia de España, p. 376.—Cabrera, Filipe Segundo, pp. 575, 576.

E*

which, in its general character, may remind one of some of the most atrocious scenes of the French Revolution.

In the beginning of the troubles, the president had caused a number of Moriscoes, amounting to not less than a hundred and fifty, it is said, to be arrested and thrown into the prison of the Chancery. Certain treasonable designs, of which they had been suspected for a long time, furnished the feeble pretext for this violent proceeding. Some few, indeed, were imprisoned for debt. But the greater number were wealthy men, who enjoyed the highest consideration among their countrymen. They had been suffered to remain in confinement during the whole of the campaign, thus serving, in some sort, as hostages for the good behavior of the people of the Albaicin.

Early in March, a rumor was circulated that the mountaineers, headed by Aben-Humeya, whose father and brother were among the prisoners, were prepared to make a descent on the city by night, and, with the assistance of the inhabitants of the Albaicin, to begin the work of destruction by assaulting the prison of the Chancery and liberating their countrymen. This report, readily believed, caused the greatest alarm among the citizens, boding no good to the unhappy prisoners. On the evening of the seventeenth, Deza received intelligence that lights had been seen on some of the neighboring mountains, which seemed to be of the nature of signals, as they were answered by corresponding lights in some of the houses in the Albaicin. The assault, it was said, would doubtless be made that very night. The president appears to have taken no measures for the protection of the city. But on receiving the information he at once communicated it to the alcayde of the prison and directed him to provide for the security of his prisoners. The alcayde lost no time in gathering his friends about him, and caused arms to be distributed among a body of Spaniards, of whom there appears to have been a considerable number confined in the place at this time. Thus prepared, they all remained, as in silent expectation of some great event.

At length, some time before midnight, the guard posted in the Campana, one of the towers of the Alhambra, struck the bell with a succession of rapid strokes, such as were used to give an alarm. In a moment every Spaniard in the prison was on his feet; and, the alcayde throwing open the doors and leading the way, they fell at once on their defenceless victims, confined in another quarter of the building. As many of these were old and infirm, and most of them inoffensive citizens, whose quiet way of life had little fitted them for brawl or battle, and who were now destitute of arms of any kind, they seemed to be as easy victims as the sheep into whose fold the famishing wolves have broken in the absence of the shepherd. Yet they did not give up their lives without an effort to save them. Despair lent them strength, and, snatching up chairs, benches, or any other article of furniture in their cells, they endeavored to make good their defence against the assailants. Some, exerting a vigor which despair only could have given, succeeded in wrenching stones from the walls or iron bars from the windows, and thus supplied themselves with the means not merely of defence, but of doing some mischief to the assailants in their turn. They fought, in short, like men who are fighting for their lives. Some, however, losing all hope of escape, piled together a heap of mats, bedding, and other combustibles, and, kindling them with their torches, threw themselves into the flames, intending in this way to set fire to the building and to perish in one general conflagration with their murderers.[31] But the flames they had kindled were soon extinguished in their own blood, and their mangled remains were left to blacken among the cinders of their funeral pile.

For two hours the deadly conflict between parties so unequally matched had continued; the one shouting its old war-cry of "Santiago," as if fighting on an open field; the other, if we may take the Castilian account, calling on their prophet to come to their assistance. But no power, divine or human, interposed in their behalf; and, notwithstanding the wild uproar caused by men engaged in a mortal struggle, by the sound of heavy blows and falling missiles, by the yells of the victors and the dying moans and agonies of the vanquished, no noise to give token of what was going on—if we are to credit the chroniclers—found its way beyond the walls of the prison. Even the guard stationed in the court-yard, we are assured, were not roused from their slumbers.[32]

At length some rumor of what was passing reached the city, where the story ran that the Moriscoes were

[31] "Otros, como desesperados, juntando esterás, tascos y otras cosas secas, que pudiesen arder, se metian entre sus mesmas llamas, y las avivaban, para que ardiendo la carcel y la Audiencia, pereciesen todos los que estaban dentro." Marmol, Rebelion de Granada, tom. i. p. 517.

[32] Ibid., ubi supra.

in arms against their keepers and would soon probably get possession of the gaol. This report was enough for the people, who, roused by the alarm-bell, were now in a state of excitement that disposed them to any deed of violence. Snatching up their weapons, they rushed, or rather flew, like vultures snuffing the carrion from afar, to the scene of slaughter. Strengthened by this reinforcement, the assailants in the prison soon completed the work of death; and when the morning light broke through the grated windows it disclosed the full extent of the tragedy. Of all the Moriscoes only two had escaped,—the father and brother of Aben-Humeya, over whom a guard had been especially set. Five Spaniards were slain, and seventeen wounded,—showing the fierce resistance made by the Moslems, though destitute of arms.[33]

Such was the massacre in the prison of the Chancery of Granada, which, as already intimated, nowhere finds a more fitting parallel than in the murders perpetrated on a still larger scale during the French Revolution, in the famous massacres of September. But the miscreants who perpetrated these enormities were the tools of a sanguinary faction, that was regarded with horror by every friend of humanity in the country. In Granada, on the other hand, it was the government itself, or at least those of highest authority in it, who were responsible for the deed. For who can doubt that a proceeding, the success of which depended on the concurrence

---

[33] "Los mataron á todos, sin dexar hombre á vida, sino fueron los dos que defendió la guardia que tenian." Marmol, Rebelion de Granada, tom. i. p. 517.—See also Mendoza, Guerra de Granada, p. 122; Herrera, Historia general, tom. i. p. 744.

of so many circumstances as to preclude the idea of accident, must have been countenanced, if not contrived, by those who had the direction of affairs?

Another feature, not the least striking in the case, is the apathy shown by contemporary writers,—men who on more than one occasion have been willing to testify their sympathy for the sufferings of the Moriscoes. One of these chroniclers, after telling the piteous tale, coolly remarks that it was a good thing for the alcayde of the prison, who pocketed a large sum of money which had been found on the persons of the wealthy Moors. Another, after noticing the imputation of an intended rising on the part of the prisoners as in the highest degree absurd, dismisses the subject by telling us that "the Moriscoes were a weak, scatter-brained race, with just wit enough to bring on themselves such a *mishap*,"—as he pleasantly terms the massacre.[34] The government of Madrid received the largest share of the price of blood. For when the wives and families of the deceased claimed the inheritance of their estates, in some cases very large, their claims were rejected— on what grounds we are not told—by the alcaldes of the Court of Audience in Granada, and the estates were confiscated to the use of the crown. Such a decision, remarks a chronicler, may lead one to infer that the prisoners had been guilty of even more heinous offences than those commonly imputed to them.[35] The

---

[34] "Havia en ellos culpados en platicas i demonstraciones, i todos en deseo; gente flaca, liviana, inhabil para todo, sino para dar ocasion a su desventura." Mendoza, Guerra de Granada, p. 122.

[35] "Las culpas de los quales debieron ser mayores de lo que aqui se escribe, porque despues pidiendo las mugeres y hijos de los muertos

impartial reader will probably come to a very different conclusion; and, since it was the opulent burghers who were thus marked out for destruction, he may naturally infer that the baser passion of avarice mingled with the feelings of fear and hatred in bringing about the massacre.

However this may be, so foul a deed placed an impassable gulf between the Spaniards and the Moriscoes. It taught the latter that they could no longer rely on their perfidious enemy, who, while he was holding out to them one hand in token of reconciliation, was raising the other to smite them to the ground. A cry of vengeance ran through all the borders of the Alpujarras. Again the mountaineers rose in arms. They cut off stragglers, waylaid the patrols whom Mondejar had distributed throughout the country, and even menaced the military posts of the Spaniards. On some occasions they encountered the latter with success in the open field, and in one instance defeated and slew a large body of Christians as they were returning from a foray laden with plunder. Finally, they invited Aben-Humeya to return and resume the command, promising to stand by him to the last. The chief obeyed the call, and, leaving his retreat in the Sierra Nevada, again took possession of his domains, and, planting his blood-red flag on his native hills,[36] soon gathered around him

sus doles y haciendas ante los alcaldes del crimen de aquella Audiencia, y saliendo el fiscal á la causa, se formó proceso en forma; y por sentencias y revista fueron condenados, y aplicados todos sus bienes al Real fisco." Marmol, Rebelion de Granada, tom. i. p. 517.

[36] "Levantó un Estandarte bermejo, que mostrava el lugar de la persona del Rei a manera de Guion." Mendoza, Guerra de Granada, p. 118.

a more formidable host than before. He even affected a greater pomp than he had before displayed. He surrounded himself with a body-guard of four hundred arquebusiers.[37] He divided his army into battalions and companies, and endeavored to introduce into it something of the organization and tactics of the Spaniards.[38] He sent his brother Abdallah to Constantinople, to represent his condition to the sultan and to implore him to make common cause with his Moslem brethren in the Peninsula. In short, rebellion assumed a more audacious front than at any time during the previous campaign; and the Christians of Andalusia and Granada looked with the greatest anxiety for the coming of a commander possessed of sufficient authority to infuse harmony into the counsels of the rival chiefs, to enforce obedience from the turbulent soldiery, and to bring the war to a speedy conclusion.

[37] " Para seguridad de su persona pagó arcabuceria de guardia, que fue creciendo hasta quatrocientos hombres." Mendoza, Guerra de Granada, p. 118.

[38] " Siguió nuestra orden de Guerra, repartió la gente por esquadras, juntóla en compañias, nombró Capitanes." Ibid., ubi supra.

CHAPTER V.

REBELLION OF THE MORISCOES.

Early Life of Don John of Austria.—Acknowledged by Philip.—His Thirst for Distinction.—His Cruise in the Mediterranean.—Made Commander-in-Chief.—The War renewed.—Removal of the Moriscoes.

1569.

As Don John of Austria is to occupy an important place, not only in the war with the Moriscoes, but in some of the most memorable scenes in the remainder of this history, it will be proper to acquaint the reader with what is known of the earlier part of his career. Yet it is precisely over this part of it that a veil of mystery hangs, which no industry of the historian has been able wholly to remove.

It seems probable that he was born in the year 1547.[1] The twenty-fourth of February is assigned by common consent—I hardly know on what ground—as the day of his birth. It was also, it may be remembered, the birthday of his father, Charles the Fifth. His mother,

[1] This, which is two years later than the date commonly assigned by historians, seems to be settled by the researches of Lafuente. (See Historia general de España (Madrid, 1854), tom. xiii. p. 437, note.) Among other evidence adduced by the historian is that of a medal struck in honor of Don John's victory at Lepanto, in the year 1571, the inscription on which expressly states that he was twenty-four years of age.

Barbara Blomberg, was an inhabitant of Ratisbon, in Germany. She is described as a beautiful young girl, who attracted the emperor's notice several years after the death of the Empress Isabella.[2] The Spanish chroniclers claim a noble descent for Barbara.[3] Indeed, it would go hard but a Spaniard could make out a pedigree for his hero. Yet there are several circumstances which suggest the idea that the mother of Don John must have occupied a very humble position.

Subsequently to her connection with Charles she married a German named Kegell, on whom the emperor bestowed the office of commissary.[4] The only other notice, so far as I am aware, which Charles took of his former mistress, was the settlement on her of a yearly pension of two hundred florins, which he made the day before his death.[5] It was certainly not a princely legacy, and infers that the object of it must have been in a humble condition in life to have rendered it important to her comfort. We are led to the same conclusion by the mystery thrown around the birth of the child,

[2] Vanderhammen, Don Juan de Austria, fol. 3.—Villafañe, Vida y Virtudes de Doña Magdalena de Ulloa (Salamanca, 1722), p. 36.— See also Lafuente, Historia de España, tom. xiii. p. 432. This last historian has made the parentage of John of Austria the subject of a particular discussion in the Revista de Ambos Mundos, No. 3.

[3] Vanderhamnien, alluding to the doubts thrown on the rank of his hero's mother, consoles himself with the reflection that, if there was any deficiency in this particular, no one can deny that it was more than compensated by the proud origin of her imperial lover. Don Juan de Austria, fol. 3.

[4] Lafuente, Hist. de España, tom. xiii. p. 432, note.

[5] Gachard, Retraite et Mort de Charles-Quint, tom. ii. p. 506.—In a private interview with Luis Quixada, the evening before his death, the emperor gave him six hundred gold crowns to purchase the above-mentioned pension.

forming so strong a contrast to the publicity given to the birth of the emperor's natural daughter, Margaret of Parma, whose mother could boast that in her veins flowed some of the best blood of the Netherlands.

For three years the boy, who received the name of Geronimo, remained under his mother's roof, when, by Charles's order, he was placed in the hands of a Fleming named Maffi, a musician in the imperial band. This man transferred his residence to Leganes, a village in Castile, not far from Madrid. The instrument still exists that contains the agreement by which Maffi, after acknowledging the receipt of a hundred florins, engages for fifty florins annually to bring up the child with as much care as if he were his own.[6] It was a moderate allowance, certainly, for the nurture of one who was some day to come before the world as the son of an emperor. It showed that Charles was fond of a bargain,—though at the expense of his own offspring.

No instruction was provided for the child except such as he could pick up from the parish priest, who, as he knew as little as Maffi did of the secret of Geronimo's birth, probably bestowed no more attention on him than on the other lads of the village. And we cannot doubt that a boy of his lively temper must have preferred passing his days in the open fields, to confinement in the house and listening to the homilies of his teacher. As he grew in years, he distinguished himself above his young companions by his courage. He took

---

[6] This interesting document was found among the testamentary papers of Charles the Fifth. A copy of it has been preserved among the manuscripts of Cardinal Granvelle. Papiers d'État, tom. iv. pp. 499. 500.

the lead in all their rustic sports, and gave token of his belligerent propensities by making war on the birds in the orchards, on whom he did great execution with his little cross-bow.[7]

Four years were passed in this hardy way of life, which, if it did nothing else for the boy, had the advantage of strengthening his constitution for the serious trials of manhood, when the emperor thought it was time to place him in a situation where he would receive a better training than could be found in the cottage of a peasant. He was accordingly transferred to the protection of Luis Quixada, Charles's trusty major-domo, who received the child into his family at Villagarcia, in the neighborhood of Valladolid. The emperor showed his usual discernment in the selection of a guardian for his son. Quixada, with his zeal for the faith, his loyalty, his nice sentiment of honor, was the very type of the Castilian hidalgo in his best form; while he possessed all those knightly qualities which made him the perfect mirror of the antique chivalry. His wife, Doña Magdalena de Ulloa, sister of the marquis of Mota, was a lady yet more illustrious for her virtues than for her rank. She had naturally the most to do with the training of the boy's earlier years; and under her discipline it was scarcely possible that one of so generous a nature should fail to acquire the courtly breeding and refinement of taste which shed a lustre over the stern character of the soldier.

However much Quixada may have reposed on his wife's discretion, he did not think proper to try it, in

[7] "Gastava buena parte del dia en tirar con una ballestilla a los paxaros." Vanderhammen, Don Juan de Austria, fol. 10.

the present instance, by communicating to her the secret of Geronimo's birth. He spoke of him as the son of a great man, his dear friend, expressing his desire that his wife would receive him as her own child. This was the less difficult, as Magdalena had no children of her own. The solicitude shown by her lord may possibly have suggested to her the idea that the boy was more nearly related to him than he chose to acknowledge,— in short, that he was the offspring of some intrigue of Quixada previous to his marriage.[8] But an event which took place not long after the child's introduction into the family is said to have awakened in her suspicions of an origin more in accordance with the truth. The house at Villagarcia took fire; and, as it was in the night, the flames gained such head that they were not discovered till they burst through the windows. The noise in the street roused the sleeping inmates; and Quixada, thinking first of his charge, sprang from his bed, and, rushing into Geronimo's apartment, snatched up the affrighted child and bore him in his arms to a place of safety. He then re-entered the house, and, forcing his way through the smoke and flames, succeeded in extricating his wife from her perilous situation. This sacrifice of love to loyalty is panegyrized by a Castilian chronicler as "a rare achievement, far transcending any act of heroism of which antiquity could boast."[9] Whether Magdalena looked with the same

[8] "Y puede ser llegase á sospechar, si acaso tendria por Padre á su Esposo." Villafañe, Vida de Magdalena de Ulloa, p. 38.

[9] "Accion singular y rara, y que dexa atras quantas la Antiguedad celebra por peregrinas." Vanderhammen, Don Juan de Austria, fol. 31.—According to another biographer, two fires occurred to Quixada, one in Villagarcia and one in Valladolid. On each of these occasions

complacency on the proceeding we are not informed. Certain it is, however, that the interest shown by her husband in the child had no power to excite any feeling of jealousy in her bosom. On the contrary, it seemed rather to strengthen her own interest in the boy, whose uncommon beauty and affectionate disposition soon called forth all the tenderness of her nature. She took him to her heart, and treated him with all the fondness of a mother,—a feeling warmly reciprocated by the object of it, who, to the day of his death, regarded her with the truest feelings of filial love and reverence.

In 1558, the year after his retirement to Yuste, Charles the Fifth, whether from a wish to see his son, or, as is quite as probable, in the hope of making Quixada more contented with his situation, desired his major-domo to bring his family to the adjoining village of Cuacos. While there, the young Geronimo must doubtless sometimes have accompanied his mother, as he called Doña Magdalena, in her visits to the monastery. Indeed, his biographer assures us that the sight of him operated like a panacea on the emperor's health.[10] We find no allusion to him, however, in any of the letters from Yuste; and, if he did go there, we may be sure that Charles had sufficient control over himself not to betray, by any indiscreet show of fond-

the house was destroyed, but his ward was sayed, borne off by the good knight in his arms. (Villafañe, Vida de Magdalena de Ulloa, pp. 44, 53.) The coincidences are too much opposed to the doctrine of chances to commend themselves readily to our faith. Vanderhammen's reflection was drawn forth by the second fire, the only one he notices. It applies, however, equally well to both.

[10] Vanderhammen, Don Juan de Austria, fol. 16.

ness, his relationship to the child." One tradition respecting him lingered to a late period among the people of Cuacos, where the peasants, it is said, pelted him with stones as he was robbing their orchards. It was the first lesson in war of the future hero of Lepanto.

There is no reason to doubt that the boy witnessed the obsequies of the emperor. One who was present tells us that he saw him there, dressed in full mourning, and standing by the side of Quixada, for whose page he passed among the brethren of the convent.[11] We may well believe that a spectacle so solemn and affecting as these funeral ceremonies must have sunk deep into his young mind, and heightened the feelings of veneration with which he always regarded the memory of his father. It was perhaps the appearance of Geronimo as one of the mourners that first suggested the idea of his relationship to the emperor. We find a letter from Quixada to Philip, dated soon after, in which he speaks of rumors on the subject as current in the neighborhood.[13]

Among the testamentary papers of Charles was found one in an envelope sealed with his private seal, and

[11] Indeed, Siguenza, who may have had it from the monks of Yuste, tells us that the "boy sometimes was casually seen by the emperor, who was careful to maintain his usual reserve and dignified demeanor, so that no one could suspect his secret. Once or twice," adds the Jeronymite father, "the lad entered the apartment of his father, who doubtless spoke to him as he would have spoken to any other boy." Historia de la Orden de San Geronimo, tom. iii. p. 205.

[12] Relation d'un Religieux de Yuste, ap. Gachard, Retraite et Mort de Charles-Quint, tom. ii. p. 55.

[13] "Hallo tan público aquí lo que toca aquella persona que V. M^{tad} sabe que está á mi cargo que me ha espantado, y espántame mucho mas las particularidades que sobrello oyo." Ibid., tom. i. p. 449.

addressed to his son, Philip, or, in case of his death, to his grandson, Carlos, or whoever might be in possession of the crown. It was dated in 1554, before his retirement to Yuste. It acknowledged his connection with a German maiden, and the birth of a son named Geronimo. The mother's name was not given. He pointed out the quarter where information could be got respecting the child, who was then living with the violin-player at Leganes. He expressed the wish that he should be trained up for the ecclesiastical profession, and that, when old enough, he should enter a convent of one of the reformed orders. Charles would not, however, have any constraint put on the inclinations of the boy, and in case of his preferring a secular life he would have a suitable estate settled on him in the kingdom of Naples, with an annual income of between thirty and forty thousand ducats. Whatever course Geronimo might take, the emperor requested that he should receive all the honor and consideration due to him as his son. His letter concluded by saying that, although for obvious reasons he had not inserted these directions in his will, he wished them to be held of the same validity as if he had.[14] Philip seems from the first to have so regarded them, though, as he was then in Flanders, he resolved to postpone the public acknowledgment of his brother till his return to Spain.

Meanwhile, the rumors in regard to Geronimo's birth had reached the ears of the regent, Joanna. With

[14] A copy of this interesting document was found in the collection of Granvelle at Besançon, and has been lately published in the beautiful edition of the cardinal's papers. Papiers d'État, tom. iv. p. 495, et seq.

natural curiosity, she ordered her secretary to write to Quixada and ascertain the truth of the report. The trusty hidalgo endeavored to evade the question by saying that some years since a friend of his had intrusted a boy to his care, but, as no allusion whatever was made to the child in the emperor's will, the story of their relationship to each other should be treated as idle gossip.[15] The reply did not satisfy Joanna, who seems to have settled it in her own mind that the story was well founded. She took an occasion soon after to write to Doña Magdalena, during her husband's absence from home, expressing her wish that the lady would bring the boy where she could see him. The place selected was at an *auto de fe* about to be celebrated in Valladolid. Doña Magdalena, reluctant as she was, felt herself compelled to receive the request from such a source as a command which she had no right to disobey. One might have thought that a ceremony so heart-rending and appalling in its character as an *auto de fe* would be the last to be selected for the indulgence of any feeling of a light and joyous nature. But the Spaniard of that and of a much later age regarded this as the sweetest sacrifice that could be offered to the Almighty; and he went to it with the same indifference to the sufferings of the victim—probably with the same love of excitement—which he would have felt in going to a bull-fight.

On the day which had been named, Magdalena and

---

[15] "Que pues Su M^{tad}, en su testamento ni codecilo, no hazia memoria dél, que era razon tenello por burla, y que no sabia que poder responder otra cosa, en público ni en secreto." Gachard, Retraite et Mort de Charles-Quint, tom. i. p. 446.

her charge took their seats on the carpeted platform reserved for persons of rank, in full view of the scaffold appropriated to the martyrs who were to suffer for conscience' sake. It was in the midst of the august company here assembled that the son of Charles the Fifth was to receive his first lesson in the school of persecution; that he was to learn to steel his heart against sympathy with human suffering; to learn, above all, that compassion for the heretic was a crime of the deepest dye. It was a terrible lesson for one so young,—of an age when the mind is most open to impressions; and the bitter fruits of it were to be discerned ere long in the war with the Moriscoes.

As the royal train approached the place occupied by Doña Magdalena, the regent paused and looked around for the boy. Magdalena had thrown her mantle about him, to conceal him as much as possible from the public eye. She now drew it aside; and Joanna looked so long and earnestly on the child that he shrank abashed from her gaze. It was not, however, before she had recognized in his bright blue eyes, his ample forehead, and the rich yellow locks that clustered round his head, some of the peculiarities of the Austrian line, though happily without the deformity of the protruding lip, which was no less its characteristic. Her heart yearned with the tenderness of a sister, as she felt convinced that the same blood flowed in his veins as in her own; and, stooping down, she threw her arms around his neck, and, kissing him, called him by the endearing name of brother.[16] She would have persuaded him to go with

---

[16] "La Princesa al punto arrebatada del amor, le abraçò, y besò, sin reparar en el lugar que estava, y el acto que exercia. Llamòle

her and sit by her side. But the boy, clinging closely to his foster-mother, refused to leave her for the stranger lady.

This curious scene attracted the attention of the surrounding spectators, which was hardly diverted from the child by the appearance of the prisoners on the scaffold to receive their sentences. When these had been pronounced, and the wretched victims led away to execution, the multitude pressed so eagerly round Magdalena and the boy that it was with difficulty the guards could keep them back, till the regent, seeing the awkwardness of their situation, sent one of her train, the count of Osorno, to their relief; and that nobleman, forcing his way through the crowd, carried off Geronimo in his arms to the royal carriage."[17]

It was not long before all mystery was dispelled by the public acknowledgment of the child as the son of the emperor. One of the first acts of Philip after his return to Spain, in 1559, was to arrange an interview with his brother. The place assigned for the meeting was an extensive park, not far from Valladolid, in the neighborhood of the convent of *La Espina*, a spot much resorted to by the Castilian princes of the older time for the pleasures of the chase.

hermano, y tratóle de Alteza." Vanderhammen, Don Juan de Austria, fol. 23.

[17] " Llego el caso a estado, que le huvo de tomar en braços el Conde Osorno hasta la carroça de la Princesa, porque le gozassen todos." Vanderhammen, Don Juan de Austria, fol. 25.—The story must be admitted to be a strange one, considering the punctilious character of the Castilian court and the reserved and decorous habits of Joanna. But the author, born and bred in the palace, had access, as he tells us, to the very highest sources of information, oral and written.

On the appointed day, Quixada, richly dressed, and mounted on the best horse in his stables, rode forth, at the head of his vassals, to meet the king, with the little Geronimo, simply attired and on a common palfrey, by his side. They had gone but a few miles when they heard through the woods the sound of horses' hoofs, announcing the approach of the royal cavalcade. Quixada halted, and, alighting, drew near to Geronimo, with much deference in his manner, and, dropping on one knee, begged permission to kiss his hand. At the same time he desired his ward to dismount, and take the charger which he had himself been riding. Geronimo was sorely bewildered by what he would have thought a merry jest on the part of his guardian, had not his sedate and dignified character forbidden the supposition. Recovering from his astonishment, he complied with his guardian's directions; and the vision of future greatness must have flashed on his mind, if, as we are told, when preparing to mount, he turned round to Quixada, and with an affected air of dignity told him that, "since things were so, he might hold the stirrup for him."[18]

They had not proceeded far when they came in sight of the royal party. Quixada pointed out the king to his ward, adding that his majesty had something of importance to communicate to him. They then dismounted; and the boy, by his guardian's instructions, drawing near to Philip, knelt down and begged leave

[18] "Vuelto ya en si de la suspension primera, alargó la mano, y montó en el caballo; y aun se dice que con airosa Grandeza, añadió, Pues si eso es asi tened el estribo." Villafañe, Vida de Doña Magdalena de Ulloa, p. 51.

to kiss his majesty's hand. The king, graciously extending it, looked intently on the youth, and at length broke silence by asking "if he knew who was his father." Geronimo, disconcerted by the abruptness of the question, and indeed, if the reports of his origin had ever reached his ears, ignorant of their truth, cast his eyes on the ground and made no answer. Philip, not displeased with his embarrassment, was well satisfied, doubtless, to read in his intelligent countenance and noble mien an assurance that he would do no discredit to his birth. Alighting from his horse, he embraced Geronimo, exclaiming, "Take courage, my child; you are descended from a great man. The Emperor Charles the Fifth, now in glory, is your father as well as mine."[19] Then, turning to the lords who stood around, he presented the boy to them as the son of their late sovereign, and his own brother. The courtiers, with the ready instinct of their tribe, ever prompt to worship the rising sun, pressed eagerly forward to pay their obeisance to Geronimo. The scene was concluded by the king's buckling a sword on his brother's side and throwing around his neck the sparkling collar of the Golden Fleece.

The tidings of this strange event soon spread over the neighborhood, for there were many more witnesses of the ceremony than those who took part in it; and the king and his retinue found, on their return, a multitude of people gathering along the route, eager to get a glimpse of this newly-discovered gem of

---

[19] "Macte, inquit, animo puer, prænobilis viri filius es tu: Carolus Quintus Imperator, qui cœlo degit, utriusque nostrûm pater est." Strada, De Bello Belgico, tom. i. p. 608.

royalty. The sight of the handsome youth called forth a burst of noisy enthusiasm from the populace, and the air rang with their tumultuous *vivas* as the royal party rode through the streets of the ancient city of Valladolid. Philip expressed his satisfaction at the events of the day, by declaring that "he had never met better sport in his life, or brought back game so much to his mind."[20]

Having thus publicly acknowledged his brother, the king determined to provide for him an establishment suited to his condition. He assigned him for his residence one of the best mansions in Madrid. He was furnished with a numerous band of retainers, and as great state was maintained in his household as in that of a prince of the blood. The count of Priego acted as his chief major-domo; Don Luis Carrillo, the eldest son of that noble, was made captain of the guard; and Don Luis de Córdova master of the horse. In short, nobles and cavaliers of the best blood in Castile did not disdain to hold offices in the service of the peasant-boy. With one or two exceptions, of little importance, he enjoyed all the privileges that belonged to the royal *infantes*. He did not, like them, have apartments in the palace; and he was to be addressed by the title of "Excellency," instead of "Highness," which was their peculiar prerogative. The distinction was not always scrupulously observed.[21]

[20] "Jamás habia tenido dia de caza mas gustoso, ni logrado presa que le hubiese dado tanto contento." Villafañe, Vida de Doña Magdalena de Ulloa, p. 52.—This curious account of Philip's recognition of his brother is told, with less discrepancy than usual, by various writers of that day.

[21] Vanderhammen, Don Juan de Austria, fol. 27.—"Mandóle llamar

A more important change took place in his name, which from *Geronimo* was now converted into *John of Austria*,—a lofty name, which intimated his descent from the imperial house of Hapsburg, and on which his deeds in after-life shed a lustre greater than the proudest title that sovereignty could confer.

Luis Quixada kept the same place after his pupil's elevation as before. He continued to be his *ayo*, or governor, and removed with Doña Magdalena to Madrid, where he took up his residence in the house of Don John. Thus living in the most intimate personal relations with him, Quixada maintained his influence unimpaired till the hour of his own death.

Philip fully appreciated the worth of the faithful hidalgo, who was fortunate in thus enjoying the favor of the son in as great a degree as he had done that of the father,—and, as it would seem, with a larger recompense for his services. He was master of the horse to Don Carlos, the heir to the crown; he held the important post of president of the Council of the Indies; and he possessed several lucrative benefices in the military order of Calatrava. In one of his letters to the king, we find Quixada remarking that he had endeavored to supply the deficiencies of his pupil's early education by training him in a manner better suited to his destinies in after-life.[22] We cannot doubt that in the

Ecelencia; pero sus Reales costunbres le dieron adelante titulo de Alteza i de señor entre los Grandes i menores." Cabrera, Filipe Segundo, lib. v. cap. 3.

[22] "Tengo mucho cuidado que aprenda y se le enseñen las cosas necesarias, conforme á su edad y á la calidad de su persona, que, segun la estrecheza en que se crió y ha estado hasta que vino á mi poder, es bien menester con todo cuidado tener cuenta con él." Gachard, Retraite et Mort de Charles-Quint, tom. i. p. 450.

good knight's estimate of what was essential to such a training the exercises of chivalry must have found more favor than the monastic discipline recommended by the emperor. However this may have been, Philip resolved to give his brother the best advantages for a liberal education by sending him to the University of Alcalá, which, founded by the great Ximenes a little more than a century before, now shared with the older school of Salamanca the glory of being the most famous seat of science in the Peninsula. Don John had for his companions his two nephews, Don Carlos, and Alexander Farnese, the son of Margaret of Parma. They formed a triumvirate each member of which was to fill a large space in the pages of history,—Don Carlos from his errors and misfortunes, and the two others from their military achievements. They were all of nearly the same age. Don John, according to a writer of the time, stood foremost among the three for the comeliness, or rather beauty, of his person, no less than for the charm of his manners;[23] while his soul was filled with those nobler qualities which gave promise of the highest excellence.[24]

His biographers tell us that Don John gave due attention to his studies; but the studies which found most favor in his eyes were those connected with the art of war. He was perfect in all chivalrous accomplishments; and he sighed for some field on which he could display them. The knowledge of his real

[23] "Longè tamen anteibat Austriacus et corporis habitudine, et morum suavitate. Facies illi non modò pulchra, sed etiam venusta." Strada, De Bello Belgico, tom. i. p. 609.

[24] "Eminebat in adolescente comitas, industria, probitas, et, ut in novæ potentiæ hospite, verecundia." Ibid., loc. cit.

parentage fired his soul with a generous ambition, and he longed by some heroic achievement to vindicate his claim to his illustrious descent.

At the end of three years, in 1564, he left the university. The following year was that of the famous siege of Malta; and all Christendom hung in suspense on the issue of the desperate conflict which a handful of warriors, on their lonely isle, were waging against the whole strength of the Ottoman empire. The sympathies of Don John were roused in behalf of the Christian knights; and he resolved to cast his own fortunes into the scale with theirs, and win his maiden laurels under the banner of the Cross. He did not ask the permission of his brother. That, he knew, would be refused to him. He withdrew secretly from the court, and with only a few attendants took his way to Barcelona, whence an armament was speedily to sail to carry succor to the besieged. Everywhere on the route he was received with the respect due to his rank. At Saragossa he was lodged with the archbishop, under whose roof he was detained by illness. While there he received a letter from the king, who had learned the cause of his departure, commanding him to return, as he was altogether too young to take part in this desperate strife. Don John gave little heed to the royal orders. He pushed on to Barcelona, where he had the mortification to find that the fleet had sailed. He resolved to cross the mountains and take ship at Marseilles. The viceroy of Catalonia could not dissuade the hot-headed youth from his purpose, when another despatch came from court, in which Philip, in a more peremptory tone than before, repeated his orders for his brother to return, under pain of his severe displeasure. A letter from Quixada had warned him of the certain disgrace which awaited him if he continued to trifle with the royal commands. Nothing remained but to obey; and Don John, disappointed in his scheme of ambition, returned to the capital.[25]

This adventure caused a great sensation throughout the country. The young nobles and cavaliers about the court, fired by Don John's example, which seemed like a rebuke on their own sluggishness, had hastened to buckle on their armor and follow him to the war.[26] The common people, peculiarly sensible in Spain to deeds of romantic daring, were delighted with the adventurous spirit of the young prince, which gave promise that he was one day to take his place among the heroes of the nation. This was the beginning of the popularity of John of Austria with his countrymen, who in time came to regard him with feelings little short of idolatry. Even Philip, however necessary he may have thought it to rebuke the insubordination of his brother, must in his heart have been pleased with the generous spirit he had exhibited. At least, the favor with which he continued to regard the offender showed that the royal displeasure was of no long continuance.

The sudden change in the condition of Don John might remind one of some fairy-tale, where the poor

[25] Strada, De Bello Belgico, tom. ii. pp. 609, 610.—Vanderhammen, Don Juan de Austria, fol. 34-36.—Cabrera, Filipe Segundo, lib. vi. cap. 24.

[26] "La fama de la partida de Don Juan sacó del ocio a muchos cavalleros de la Corte i Reynos, que avergonçados de quedarse en el, le siguieron." Cabrera, Filipe Segundo, loc. cit.

peasant-boy finds himself all at once converted by enchantment into a great prince. A wiser man than he might well have had his head turned by such a rapid revolution of the wheel of fortune; and Philip may naturally have feared that the idle dalliance of a court, to which his brother was now exposed, might corrupt his simple nature and seduce him from the honorable path of duty. Great, therefore, must have been his satisfaction when he saw that, far from this, the elevation of the youth had only served to give a wider expansion to his views and to fill his bosom with still higher and nobler aspirations.

The discreet conduct of Don John in regard to his nephew, Don Carlos, when the latter would have engaged him in his wild and impracticable schemes, established him still more firmly in the royal favor.[7]

In the spring of the year 1568 an opportunity occurred for Philip to gratify his brother's ambition, by intrusting him with the command of a fleet then fitting out, in the port of Carthagena, against the Barbary corsairs, who had been making alarming depredations of late on the Spanish commerce. But, while giving him this appointment, the king was careful to supply the lack of experience in his brother by naming as second in command an officer in whose abilities he perfectly confided. This was Antonio de Zuñiga y Requesens, grand commander of St. James, an eminent personage, who will come frequently before the reader in the progress of the narrative. Requesens, who at this time filled the post of ambassador at Rome, was possessed of the versatility of talent so important in an

---

[7] *Ante*, vol. ii. book iv. ch. 6.

age when the same individual was often required to exchange the duties of the cabinet for those of the camp. While Don John appeared before the public as the captain of the fleet, the actual responsibility for the conduct of the expedition rested on his lieutenant.

On the third of June, Don John sailed out of port, at the head of as brave an armament as ever floated on the waters of the Mediterranean. The prince's own vessel was a stately galley, gorgeously fitted up, and decorated with a profusion of paintings, the subjects of which, drawn chiefly from ancient history and mythology, were of didactic import, intended to convey some useful lesson to the young commander. The moral of each picture was expressed by some pithy maxim inscribed beneath it in Latin. Thus, to whatever quarter Don John turned his eyes, they were sure to fall on some homily for his instruction; so that his galley might be compared to a volume richly filled with illustrations, that serve to impress the contents on the reader's memory.[28]

The cruise was perfectly successful; and Don John, on his return to port, some eight months later, might boast that, in more than one engagement, he had humbled the pride of the corsairs, and so far crippled them that it would be long before they could resume their depredations; that, in fine, he had vindicated the honor of his country's flag throughout the Mediterranean.

[28] Vanderhammen has given a minute description of this royal galley, with its pictorial illustrations. Among the legends emblazoned below them, that of "*Dolum reprimere dolo*" savors strongly of the politic monarch. Don Juan de Austria, fol. 44-48.

His return to Madrid was welcomed with the honors of a triumph. Courtier and commoner, men of all classes, in short, vied with each other in offering up the sweet incense of adulation, filling his young mind with lofty visions of the future, that beckoned him forward in the path of glory.

When the insurrection of the Moriscoes broke out, in 1568, the eyes of men naturally turned on Don John of Austria, as the person who would most likely be sent to suppress it. But Philip thought it would be safer to trust the command to those who, from their long residence in the neighborhood, were better acquainted with the character of the country and of its inhabitants. When, however, the dissensions of the rival chiefs made it necessary to send some one invested with such powers as might enable him to overawe this factious spirit and enforce greater concert of action, the council of state recommended Don John to the command. Their recommendation was approved by the king, if indeed it was not originally made at his suggestion.

Still, the "prudent" monarch was careful not to invest his brother with that independent command which the public supposed him to possess. On the contrary, his authority was restricted within limits almost as narrow as those which had curbed it in the Mediterranean. A council of war was appointed, by whose opinions Don John was to be guided in every question of moment. In case of a division of opinion, the question was to be referred to the decision of Philip.*

* "Su comision fue sin limitacion ninguna; mas su libertad tan atada, que de cosa grande ni pequeña podia disponer sin comuni-

The chief members of this body, in whom the supreme power was virtually lodged, were the marquis of Mondejar, who from this time does not appear to have taken the field in person; the duke of Sesa, grandson of the Great Captain, Gonsalvo de Córdova, and endowed with no small portion of the military talent of his ancestor; the archbishop of Granada, a prelate possessed of as large a measure of bigotry as ever fell to the lot of a Spanish ecclesiastic; Deza, president of the Audience, who hated the Moriscoes with the fierce hatred of an inquisitor; and, finally, Don John's faithful *ayo*, Quixada, who had more influence over him than was enjoyed by any other, and who had come to witness the first of his pupil's campaigns, destined, alas! to be the closing one of his own.[30]

There could hardly have been a more unfortunate device than the contrivance of so cumbrous a machinery as this council, opposed as it was, from its very nature, to the despatch so indispensable to the success of military operations. The mischief was increased by the necessity of referring every disputed point to the decision of the king. As this was a contingency that often occurred, the young prince soon found almost as many embarrassments thrown in his way by his friends as by his foes,—embarrassments which nothing but an uncommon spirit of determination on his own part could have overcome.

cacion i parecer de los Consegeros, i mandado del Rei." Mendoza, Guerra de Granada, p. 139.

[30] Ibid., p. 130, et seq.—Vanderhammen, Don Juan de Austria, fol. 81.—Marmol, tom. i. pp. 511-513.—Villafañe, Vida de Doña Magdalena de Ulloa, p. 73.--Cabrera, Filipe Segundo, lib. ix. cap. 1.

On the sixth of April, 1569, Don John took leave of the king, then at Aranjuez, and hastened towards the south. His coming was eagerly expected by the inhabitants of Granada: by the Christians, from their hopes that it would remedy the disorders in the army and bring the war to a speedy conclusion; by the Moriscoes, from the protection they anticipated he would afford them against the violence of the Spaniards. Preparations were made in the capital for giving him a splendid reception. The programme of the ceremonies was furnished by Philip himself.[31] At some miles from the city, Don John was met by the count of Tendilla, at the head of a small detachment of infantry, wearing uniforms partly of the Castilian fashion, partly of the Morisco,—presenting altogether a strange and picturesque spectacle, in which silks, velvets, and rich embroidery floated gayly amidst the iron mail and burnished weapons of the warrior.[32] As the prince proceeded along his route, he was met by a long train of ecclesiastical and civic functionaries, followed by the principal cavaliers and citizens of Granada. At their head were the archbishop and the president, the latter of whom was careful to assert his rank by walking on the right of the prelate. Don John showed them both the greatest deference; and, as they drew near, he dismounted from his horse, and, embracing the two churchmen, stood with hat in hand, for some

---

[31] "Ya el Presidente tenia orden de su Magestad de la que se habia de tener en el recibimiento de su hermano." Marmol, Rebelion de Granada, tom. ii. p. 17.

[32] "De manera que entre gala y guerra hacian hermosa y agradable vista." Ibid., ubi supra.

moments, while conversing with them.[33] As their train came up, the president presented the most eminent persons to the prince, who received them with that frank and graceful courtesy which won the hearts of all who approached him. He then resumed his route, escorted on either side by the president and the archbishop. The neighboring fields were covered with spectators, and on the plains of Béyro he found a large body of troops, not less than ten thousand, drawn up to receive him. As he approached, they greeted him with salvoes of musketry, delivered with admirable precision. As Don John glanced over their beautiful array and beheld their perfect discipline and appointments, his eyes brightened and his cheek flushed with a soldier's pride.

Hardly had he entered the gates of Granada when he was surrounded by a throng of women, who gathered about him in an attitude of supplication. They were the widows, the mothers, and the daughters of those who had so miserably perished in the massacres of the Alpujarras. They were clad in mourning, some of them so scantily as too plainly to reveal their poverty. Falling on their knees, with tears streaming from their eyes, and their words rendered almost inarticulate by their sobs, they demanded justice,—justice on the murderers of their kindred. They had seen their friends fall, they said, beneath the blows of their executioners; but the pain with which their hearts were

---

[33] " El qual lo recibió muy bien, y con el sombrero en el mano, y le tuvo un rato abrazado. Y apartandose á un lado, llegó el Arzobispo, y hizo lo mismo con él." Marmol, Rebelion de Granada, tom. ii. p. 18.

then rent was not so great as what they now felt on learning that the cruel acts of these miscreants were to go unpunished.[34] Don John endeavored to calm their agitation by expressions of the deepest sympathy for their misfortunes,—expressions of which none who saw his countenance could doubt the truth; and he promised that he would do all in his power to secure them justice.

A livelier scene awaited him as the procession held its way along the streets of the ancient capital. Everywhere the houses were gayly decorated with tapestries of cloth of gold. The multitude who thronged the avenues filled the air with their loyal acclamations. Bright eyes glanced from balconies and windows, where the noblest matrons and maidens of Granada, in rich attire, were gathered to look upon the splendid pageant and the young hero who was the object of it.[35] In this state he moved along until he reached the palace of the Royal Audience, where, by the king's command, apartments had been sumptuously fitted up for his accommodation.[36]

[34] "Que no sintieron tanto dolor con oir los crueles golpes de las armas con que los hereges los mataban á ellos y á sus hijos, hermanos y parientes, como el que sienten en ver que han de ser perdonados." Marmol, Rebelion de Granada, tom. ii. p. 19.—From this it would seem that the love of revenge was a stronger feeling with these Christian women than the love of friends.

[35] "Y mas galas y regocijos, porque estaban las ventanas de las calles, por donde habia de pasar, entoldadas de paños de oro y seda, y mucho numero de damas y doncellas nobles en ellas, ricamente ataviadas, que habian acudido de toda la ciudad por verle." Ibid., ubi supra.

[36] Ibid., pp. 17-19.—Vanderhammen, Don Juan de Austria, fol. 83 —Mendoza, Guerra de Granada, p. 133.

The following day, a deputation waited on Don John from the principal Moriscoes of the city, claiming his protection against the injuries and insults to which they were exposed whenever they went abroad. They complained especially of the Spanish troops quartered on them, and of the manner in which they violated the sanctity of their dwellings by the foulest outrages. Don John replied in a tone that expressed little of the commiseration which he had shown to the female petitioners on the preceding day. He told the Moriscoes that he had been sent to restore order to Granada, and that those who had proved loyal would find themselves protected in all their rights. Those, on the contrary, who had taken part in the late rebellion would be chastised with unsparing rigor.[37] He directed them to state their grievances in a memorial, with a caution to set down nothing which they could not prove, or it would go hard with them. The unfortunate Moriscoes found that they were to expect such justice only as comes from the hand of an enemy.

The first session of the council showed how defective was the system for conducting the war. In the discussions that ensued, Mondejar remarked that the contest, in his opinion, was virtually at an end; that the Moriscoes, for the most part, were in so favorable a mood that he would undertake, if the affair were placed in his hands, to bring them all to submission in a very short time. This proposal was treated with contempt by the haughty president, who denounced them as a

---

[37] "Juntamente con usar de equidad y clemencia con los que lo merecieren, los que no hubieren sido tales serán castigados con grandisimo rigor." Marmol, Rebelion de Granada, tom. ii. p. 21.

false-hearted race, on whose promises no one could rely. The war, he said, would never be ended so long as the Moriscoes of the capital were allowed to communicate with their countrymen in the mountains and to furnish them with secret intelligence respecting what was passing in the Christian camp. The first step was to remove them all from Granada into the interior; the second, to make such an example of the miscreants who had perpetrated the massacres in the Alpujarras as should strike terror into the hearts of the infidels and deter them from any further resistance to authority. In this division of opinion the members took different sides according to the difference of their tempers. The commander-in-chief and Quixada both leaned to Mondejar's opinion. After a protracted discussion, it became necessary to refer the question to the king, who was by no means distinguished for the promptness with which he came to his conclusions. All this required much time, during which active operations could not be resumed.[*]

Yet Don John did not pass it idly. He examined the state of the works in Granada and its neighborhood; he endeavored to improve the condition of the army, and to quell the spirit of insubordination which had risen in some portions of it; finally, he sent his commands for enforcing levies, not merely in Andalusia and the adjoining provinces, but in Castile. The appeal was successful; and the great lords in the south, more particularly, gathering their retainers, hastened

[*] Marmol, Rebelion de Granada, tom. ii. pp. 23, 24.—Vanderhammen, Don Juan de Austria, fol. 85.—Cabrera, Filipe Segundo, lib. ix. cap. 1.—Herrera, Historia general, tom. i. pp. 744, 745.

to Granada, to draw their swords under this popular chieftain.[39]

Meanwhile, the delay was attended with most mischievous consequences, as it gave the enemy time to recover from the disasters of the previous campaign. Aben-Humeya had returned, as we have seen in the former chapter, to his mountain-throne, where he soon found himself in greater strength than before. Even the "Moriscoes of the peace," as they were called, who had resumed their allegiance to the crown, exasperated by the outrages of the Spanish soldiery and the contempt which they showed for the safe-conduct of the marquis of Mondejar, now came in great numbers to Aben-Humeya's camp, offering their services and promising to stand by him to the last. Other levies he drew from Africa. The Moslem princes to whom he had applied for succor, though refusing to embark openly in his cause, as he had desired, allowed such of their subjects as chose to join his standard. In consequence, a considerable body of Barbary Moors crossed the sea and entered into the service of the Morisco chief. They were a fierce, intrepid race, accustomed to a life of wild adventure, and possessing a better acquaintance with military tactics than belonged to the Spanish mountaineers.[40]

While strengthened by these recruits, Aben-Humeya

---

[39] Mendoza, Guerra de Granada, p. 141.—Vanderhammen, Don Juan de Austria, fol. 85.—Marmol, Rebelion de Granada, tom. ii. p. 27.—Cabrera, Filipe Segundo, lib. ix. cap. 1.

[40] The historian of the Morisco rebellion tells us that these Africans wore garlands round their heads, intimating their purpose to conquer or to die like martyrs in defence of their faith. Marmol, Rebelion de Granada, tom. ii. p. 73.

drew a much larger revenue than formerly from his more extended domains." Though showy and expensive in his tastes, he did not waste it all on the maintenance of the greater state which he now assumed in his way of living. He employed it freely in the pay of foreign levies, and in procuring arms and munitions for his own troops; and he profited by his experience in the last campaign, and by the example of his African mercenaries, to introduce a better system of tactics among his Morisco warriors. The policy he adopted, as before, was to avoid pitched battles, and to confine himself chiefly to the guerilla warfare better suited to the genius of the mountaineer. He fell on small detachments of Spaniards who were patrolling the country, cut off the convoys, and thus greatly straitened the garrisons in their supplies. He made forays into the Christian territories, penetrating even into the *vega*, and boldly carried the war up to the walls of Granada.

His ravages in this quarter, it is true, did not continue long after the arrival of Don John, who took effectual measures for protecting the capital from insult. But the prince was greatly chagrined by seeing the rapid extension of the Morisco domain. Yet he could take no decisive measures to check it until the council had determined on some plan of operations. He was moreover fettered by the king's orders not to take the

---

[41] Besides a tenth of the produce of the soil, one source of his revenue, we are told, was the confiscated property of such Moriscoes as refused to yield him obedience. Another was a fifth of the spoil taken from the enemy. Marmol, Rebelion de Granada, tom. ii. p. 35. —Also Mendoza, Guerra de Granada, p. 120.

field in person, but to remain and represent him in Granada, where he would find enough to do in regulating the affairs and providing for the safety of the city.[42] Philip seems to have feared that Don John's adventurous spirit would lead him to some rash act, that might unnecessarily expose him to danger. He appears, indeed, as we may gather from numerous passages in his letters, to have been more concerned for the safety of his brother than for the success of the campaign.[43] He may have thought, too, that it was better to trust the war to the hands of the veteran chief, the marquis of Los Velez, who could boast so much larger experience than Don John, and who had possessed the king with a high idea of his military talents.

This nobleman still held the command of the country east of the Alpujarras, in which lay his own large property. He had, as we have seen, a hard and arrogant nature, which could ill brook the paramount authority of the young commander-in-chief, to whom he rarely condescended to write, preferring to make his communications directly to the king.[44] Philip, prompted by

[42] "Y la vuestra, ya yo os dixe que la queria para cosas mayores, y que asi agora yo no os embiaba á las de la guerra sino á esa ciudad á dar desde ella la orden en todo que conbiniese: Pues yo por otras ocupaciones y cartas no lo podia hazer." Carta del Rey á Don Juan de Austria, 10 de Mayo, 1569, MS.

[43] Don John seems to have chafed under the restrictions imposed on him by the king. At least we may infer so from a rebuke of Philip, who tells his brother that, "though for the great love he bears him he will overlook such language this time, it will not be well for him to repeat it." Carta del Rey á Don Juan de Austria, 20 de Mayo, 1569, MS.

[44] Vanderhammen, Don Juan de Austria, fol. 94.—Marmol, with

his appetite for power, winked at this irregular proceeding, which enabled him to take a more direct part in the management of affairs than he could otherwise have done. It was a most injudicious step, and was followed, as we shall see, by disastrous consequences.

The marquis, without waiting for orders, resolved to open the campaign by penetrating into the Alpujarras with the small force he had under his command. But a body of some four hundred troops, which he had caused to occupy the pass of Ravaha, was cut off by the enemy; and the haughty chieftain reluctantly obeyed the orders of Don John to abandon his design. Aben-Humeya's success encouraged him to attack the marquis in his new quarters at Verja. It was a well-concerted enterprise, but unfortunately, before the time arrived for its execution, it was betrayed by a prisoner to the Spanish commander. It consequently failed. Aben-Humeya penetrated into the heart of the town, where he found himself in the midst of an ambuscade, and with difficulty, after a heavy loss, effected his retreat. But if the victory remained with the Spaniards, the fruits of it fell to the Moriscoes. The spirit shown by the Moslem prince gave new life to his countrymen, and more than counterbalanced the effects of his defeat. The rich and populous country of the Rio de Almanzora rose in arms. The marquis of Los Velez found it expedient to abandon his present position, and

one or two vigorous *coups de pinceau*, gives the portrait of the marquis: " No se podia determinar qual era en él mayor extremo, su esfuerzo, valentía y discrecion, ó la arrogancia y ambicion de honra, acompañada de aspereza de condicion." Rebelion de Granada, tom ii. p. 99.

to transfer his quarters to Adra, a sea-port on the Mediterranean, which would afford him greater facilities for receiving reinforcements and supplies.[45]

The spirit of insurrection now spread rapidly over other parts of the Alpujarras, and especially along the sierra of Bentomiz, which stretches from the neighborhood of Alhama towards the south. Here the mountaineers, who had hitherto taken no part in the troubles of the country, ranging themselves under the crimson banner of Aben-Humeya, broke forth into open rebellion. The inhabitants of Velez and of the more important city of Malaga were filled with consternation, trembling lest the enemy should descend on them from the mountains and deluge their streets with blood. They hastily mustered the militia of the country, and made preparations for their defence.

Fortunately, at this conjuncture, they were gladdened by the sight of the Grand Commander Requesens, who sailed into the harbor of Velez Malaga with a squadron from Italy, having on board several battalions of Spanish veterans who had been ordered home by the government to reinforce the army of the Alpujarras. There were no better troops in the service, seasoned as they were by many a hard campaign, and all under the most perfect discipline. The first step of Requesens—the same officer, it will be remembered, who had acted as the lieutenant of Don John of Austria in his cruise in the Mediterranean—was to request of his young general the command of the expedition against the rebels of

[45] Marmol, Rebelion de Granada, tom. ii. p. 73. et seq.—Vanderhammen, Don Juan de Austria, fol. 94.—Mendoza, Guerra de Granada, p. 175. et seq.—Miniana, Historia de España, p. 377.

Bentomiz. These were now gathered in great force on the lofty table-land of Fraxiliana, where they had strengthened the natural defences of the ground by such works as rendered the approach to it nearly impracticable. The request was readily granted; and the grand commander of St. James, without loss of time, led his battalions into the heart of the sierra.

We have not space for the details. It is enough to say that the expedition was one of the best-conducted in the war. The enemy made a desperate resistance; and, had it not been for the timely arrival of the bold burghers of Malaga, the grand commander would have been driven from the field. The Morisco women fought by the side of their husbands; and, when all was lost, many threw themselves headlong from the precipices rather than fall into the hands of the Spaniards.[46] Two thousand of the enemy were slain; and three thousand captives, with an immense booty of gold, silver, jewels, and precious stuffs, became the spoil of the victors. The spirit of rebellion was effectually crushed in the sierra of Bentomiz.

Yet it was not a bloodless victory. Full six hundred of the Christians fell on the field of battle. The loss bore most heavily on the troops from Italy. Nearly every captain in this valiant corps was wounded.[47] The bloody roll displayed, moreover, the name of more than one cavalier as distinguished for his birth as for his bravery. Two thousand Moriscoes succeeded in making

---

[46] " Quando vieron el fuerte perdido, se despeñaron por las peñas mas agrias, quiriendo mas morir hechas pedazos, que venir en poder de Christianos." Marmol, Rebelion de Granada, tom. ii. p. 89.

[47] " Casi todos los capitanes." Ibid., loc. cit.

their escape to the camp of Aben-Humeya. They proved a seasonable reinforcement; for that chief was meditating an assault on Seron.[48]

This was a strongly-fortified place, perched like an eagle's eyry on the summit of a bold cliff that looked down on the Rio de Almanzora and commanded its formidable passes. It was consequently a most important post, and at this time was held by a Spanish garrison under an officer named Mirones. Aben-Humeya sent a strong detachment against it, intending to carry it by storm. But the Moriscoes had no battering-train, and, as it soon appeared, were little skilled in the art of conducting a siege. It was resolved, therefore, to abandon the present plan of operations, and to reduce the place by the slower but surer way of blockade. Five thousand men, accordingly, sat down before the town on the eighteenth of June, and effectually cut off all communication from abroad.

The garrison succeeded in conveying intelligence of their condition to Don John, who lost no time in ordering Alonso de Carbajal to march with a body of troops and a good supply of provisions to their relief. But

---

[48] The fierce encounter at Fraxiliana is given in great detail by Mendoza (Guerra de Granada, pp. 165-169) and Marmol (Rebelion de Granada, tom. ii. pp. 86-90). No field of fight was better contested during the war; and both historians bear testimony to the extraordinary valor of the Moriscoes, worthy of the best days of the Arabian empire. Philip, while he commends the generous ardor shown by the grand commander in the expedition, condemns him for having quitted his fleet to engage in it: "El comendador mayor tubo buen suceso como deseais, y como entiendo yo que lo merece su zelo y su intencion, mas salir su persona en tierra, teniendo en vuestra ausencia el cargo de la mas, fué cosa digna de mucha reprehension." Carta del Rey á Don Juan, 25 de Junio, 1569, MS.

just after his departure Don John received information that the king had intrusted the marquis of Los Velez with the defence of Seron. He therefore, by Quixada's advice, countermanded his orders to Carbajal, and directed him to return. That officer, who had approached within a short distance of the place, reluctantly obeyed, and left Seron to its fate. The marquis of Los Velez, notwithstanding the jealousy he displayed of the interference of Don John in the affair, showed so little alacrity in providing for the safety of the beleaguered fortress that the garrison, reduced to extremity, on the eleventh of July surrendered on honorable terms. But no sooner had they given up the place than the victors, regardless of the terms of capitulation, murdered in cold blood every male over twelve years of age, and made slaves of the women and children. This foul act was said to have been perpetrated by the secret command of Aben-Humeya. The Morisco chief might allege, in vindication of his perfidy, that he had but followed the lesson set him by the Spaniards.[49]

The loss of Seron caused deep regret to the army. Nor could this regret be mitigated by the reflection that its loss was to be attributed not so much to the valor of the Moslems as to the misconduct of their own commanders, or rather to the miserable system adopted for carrying on the war. The triumph of the Moriscoes, however, was greatly damped by the intelligence which they had received, shortly before the surrender of

---

[49] Marmol, Rebelion de Granada, tom. ii. pp. 108-111.—Ferreras, Hist. d'Espagne, tom. x. pp. 83, 84.—Cabrera, Filipe Segundo, lib. ix. cap. 6.

Seron, of disasters that had befallen their countrymen in Granada.

Philip, after much hesitation, had given his sanction to Deza's project for the removal of the Moriscoes from the capital into the interior of the country. The day appointed for carrying the measure into effect was the twenty-third of June. A large body of troops, with the principal commanders, was secretly assembled in the capital, to enforce the execution of the plan. Meanwhile, rumors were current that the Moriscoes in the city were carrying on a secret communication with their countrymen in the Alpujarras; that they supplied the mountaineers with arms and money; that the young men were leaving Granada to join their ranks; finally, that a conspiracy had been planned for an assault on the city, and even that the names of the leaders were given. It is impossible, at this time, to say what foundation there was for these charges; but the reader may recollect that similar ones had been circulated previous to the barbarous massacre in the prison of the Chancery.

On the twenty-third of the month, on the eve of St. John's, an edict was published, commanding all the Morisco males in Granada between ten and sixty years of age to repair to the parish churches to which they respectively belonged, where they were to learn their fate. The women were to remain some time longer in the city, to dispose of the most valuable effects, such as could not easily be transported. This was not difficult, at the low prices for which, in their extremity, they were obliged to part with their property. We are left in ignorance of the fate of the children, who, no doubt, remained in the hands of the government, to be nurtured in the Roman Catholic faith.[50]

Nothing could exceed the consternation of the Moriscoes on the publication of this decree, for which, though so long suspended by a thread, as it were, over their heads, they were wholly unprepared. It is not strange, as they recalled the atrocious murders perpetrated in the prison of the Chancery, that they should have been led to believe that nothing less than a massacre of the whole Moorish population was now designed. It was in vain that the marquis of Mondejar endeavored to allay their fears. They were somewhat comforted by the assurance of the President Deza, given under his own hand, that their lives were in no danger. But their apprehensions on this point were not wholly quieted till Don John had pledged his royal word that no harm should come to their persons,—that, in short, the great object of the government was to secure their safety. They then submitted without any attempt at resistance. Resistance, indeed, would have been hardly possible, destitute as they were of weapons or other means of defence, and surrounded on all quarters by the well-armed soldiery of Castile. They accordingly entered the churches assigned to them, at the doors of which strong guards were stationed during the night.

On the following morning the Moriscoes were marched out and formed into a procession, which was to take its

---

[50] Mendoza, Guerra de Granada, p. 146.—Marmol, Rebelion de Granada, tom. ii. p. 100.—Bleda (Cronica de España, p. 705), in this part of his work, has done nothing more than transcribe the pages of Mendoza, and that in so blundering a style as to mistake the date of this event by a month.

way to the great hospital in the suburbs. This was a noble building, erected by the good Queen Isabella the Catholic, not long after the Conquest. Here they were to stay till the arrangements were completed for forming them into divisions according to their several places of destination. It was a sad and solemn spectacle, that of this company of exiles, as they moved with slow and uncertain step, bound together by cords,[51] and escorted, or rather driven along like a gang of convicts, by the fierce soldiery. There they were, the old and the young, the rich and the poor, now, alas! brought to the same level, the forms of most of them bowed down, less by the weight of years than of sorrow, their hands meekly folded on their breasts, their cheeks wet with tears, as they gazed for the last time on their beautiful city, the sweet home of their infancy, the proud seat of ancient empire, endeared to them by so many tender and glorious recollections.[52]

The march was conducted in an orderly manner, with but a single interruption, which, however, was near being attended by the most disastrous consequences. A Spanish alguazil, offended at some words that fell from one of the prisoners, — for so they might be called, — requited them with a blow from his staff. But the youth whom he struck had the fiery blood of

---

[51] "Puestos en la cuerda, con guarda de infanteria i cavalleria por una i otra parte." Mendoza, Guerra de Granada, p. 147.

[52] "Fue un miserable espectaculo," says an eye-witness, "ver tantos hombres de todas edades, las cabezas baxas, las manos cruzadas y los rostros bañados de lagrimas, con semblante doloroso y triste, viendo que dexaban sus regaladas casas, sus familias, su patria, y tanto bien como tenian, y aun no sabian cierto lo que se haria de sus cabezas." Marmol, Rebelion de Granada, tom. ii. p. 102.

the Arab in his veins. Snatching up a broken tile, he dealt such a blow on the offender's head as nearly severed his ear from it. The act cost him his life. He was speedily cut down by the Spaniards, who rushed to the assistance of their wounded comrade. A rumor now went round that the Moriscoes had attempted the life of Don John, whose dress resembled in its color that of the alguazil. The passions of the soldiery were roused. They flocked to the scene of violence, uttering the most dreadful imprecations. Their swords and lances glittered in the air, and in a few moments would have been sheathed in the bodies of their terrified victims.

Fortunately, the quick eye of Don John discerned the confusion. Surrounded by a body-guard of arquebusiers, he was there in person to superintend the removal of the Moriscoes. Spurring his horse forward into the midst of the tumult, and showing himself to the troops, he exclaimed that no one had offered him any harm. He called on them to return to their duty, and not to dishonor him, as well as themselves, by offering violence to innocent men, for whose protection he had so solemnly pledged his word. The soldiers, abashed by the rebuke of their young chief, and satisfied with the vengeance they had taken on the offender, fell back into their ranks. The trembling Moriscoes gradually recovered from their panic, the procession resumed its march, and without further interruption reached the hospital of Isabella.[53]

There the royal *contadores* were not long in ascer-

[53] Marmol, Rebelion de Granada, tom. ii. p. 103.—Mendoza, Guerra de Granada, p. 147.—Both historians were present on this occasion.

taining the number of the exiles. It amounted to thirty-five hundred. That of the women, who were soon to follow, was much greater.[54] The names, the ages, and the occupations of the men were all carefully registered. The following day they were marched into the great square before the hospital, where they were distributed into companies, each under a strong escort, to be conducted to their various places of destination. These, far from being confined to Andalusia, reached into New Castile. In this arrangement we may trust that so much respect was paid to the dictates of humanity as not to separate those of the same kindred from one another. But the chroniclers give no information on the subject,—probably regarding details of this sort in regard to the fallen race as below the dignity of history.

It was on the twenty-fifth of June, 1569, that, bidding a sad farewell to the friends and companions of their youth, from whom they were now to be forever parted, they set forth on their doleful pilgrimage. The morning light had broken on the red towers of the Alhambra, as the bands of exiles, issuing from the gates of their beloved capital, the spot dearest to them upon earth, turned their faces towards their new homes,—homes which many of them were destined never to behold. The government, with shameful indifference, had neglected to provide for the poor wanderers the most common necessaries of life. Some actually perished of hunger by the way. Others, especially those accustomed from infancy to a delicate nurture, sank down

---

[54] "Los que salieron por todos tres mil i quinientos, el numero de mugeres mucho mayor." Mendoza, Guerra de Granada, p. 147.

and died of fatigue. Some were seized by the soldiers, whose cupidity was roused by the sight of their helplessness, and were sold as slaves. Others were murdered by their guards in cold blood.[55] Thus reduced far below their original number, they reached their appointed places, there to linger out the remainder of their days in the midst of a population who held them in that abhorrence with which a good Catholic of the sixteenth century regarded "the enemies of God."[56]

But the evils which grew out of this stern policy of the government were not wholly confined to the Moriscoes. This ingenious people were so far superior to the Spaniards in the knowledge of husbandry and in the various mechanic arts that they formed the most important part of the population of Granada. The only art in which their rivals excelled them was that which thrives at the expense of every other,—the art of war. Aware of this, the government had excepted some of the best artisans in the capital from the doom of exile which had fallen on their countrymen, and they had accordingly remained in the city. But their number was too small to produce the result desired; and it was not long before the quarter of the town which had been occupied by the Moriscoes exhibited a scene of woeful desolation. The light and airy edifices, which displayed in their forms the fantastic graces of Arabian

[55] "Muchos murieron por los caminos de trabajo, de cansancio, de pesar, de hambre; a hierro, por mano de los mismos que los havian de guardar, robados, vendidos por cautivos." Mendoza, Guerra de Granada, p. 148.

[56] "Los enemigos de Dios,"—the charitable phrase by which Moriscoes, as well as Moors, came now to be denominated by the Christians.

G*

architecture, fell speedily into decay. The parterres and pleasure-grounds, filled with exotics and glowing in all the exuberance of southern vegetation, became a wilderness of weeds; and the court-yards and public squares, where tanks and sparkling fountains, fed by the streams of the Sierra Nevada, shed a refreshing coolness over the atmosphere in the sultriest months of summer, were soon converted into a melancholy heap of rubbish.

The mischiefs growing out of the removal of the Moriscoes fell sorely on the army. The men had been quartered, as we have seen, in the houses of the Moriscoes. From the present occupants, for the most part needy and thriftless speculators, they met with very different fare from what they had enjoyed under the former wealthy and luxurious proprietors. The troops supplied the deficiency, as far as they could, by plundering the citizens. Hence incessant feuds arose between the people and the army, and a spirit of insubordination rapidly grew up in the latter, which made it more formidable to its friends than to its foes.[57]

An eye-witness of these troubles closes his narrative of the removal of the Moriscoes by remarking that it was a sad spectacle to one who reflected on the former policy and prosperity of this ill-starred race; who had seen their sumptuous mansions in the day of their glory, their gardens and pleasure-grounds, the scene of many a gay revel and jocund holiday, and who now contrasted all this with the ruin into which every thing had fallen.[58] "It seems," he concludes, "as if Provi-

---

[57] Mendoza, Guerra de Granada, pp. 148-150.

[58] "Quedó grandisima lastima á los que habiendo visto la prosperi-

dence had intended to show, by the fate of this beautiful city, that the fairest things in this world are the most subject to decay."[59] To the philosopher of the present age it may seem rather the natural result of that system of religious intolerance which had converted into enemies those who, under a beneficent rule, would have been true and loyal subjects, and who by their industry and skill would have added incalculably to the resources of the country.

dad, la policía, y el regalo de las casas, carmenes y guertas, donde los Moriscos tenian todas sus recreaciones y pasatiempos, y desde á pocos dias lo vieron todo asolado y destruido." Marmol, Rebelion de Granada, tom. ii. p. 104.

[59] "Parecia bien estar sujeta aquella felicisima ciudad á tal destruicion, para que se entienda que las cosas mas esplendidas y floridas entre la gente están mas aparejadas á los golpes de fortuna." Marmol, ubi supra.

CHAPTER VI.

REBELLION OF THE MORISCOES.

Operations of Los Velez.—Conspiracy against Aben-Humeya.—His Assassination.—Election of Aben-Aboo.—Vigorous Prosecution of the War.—Fierce Combats in the Vega.—Impetuous Spirit of Don John.—Surprise of Guejar.

1569.

WHILE the events related in the preceding chapter were occurring, the marquis of Los Velez lay, with a considerable force, at Adra, a port on the Mediterranean, at the foot of the Alpujarras, which he had selected chiefly from the facilities it would afford him for getting supplies for his army. In this he was disappointed. Before the month of June had expired, his troops had begun to be straitened for provisions. The evil went on increasing from day to day. His levies, composed chiefly of raw recruits from Andalusia, were full of that independent and indeed turbulent spirit which belongs to an ill-disciplined militia. There was no lack of courage in the soldiery. But the same men who had fearlessly braved the dangers of the campaign, now, growing impatient under the pinch of hunger, abandoned their colors in great numbers.

There were various causes for the deficiency of supplies. The principal one of these may probably be found in the remissness of the council of war, several of whose members regarded the marquis with an evil eye and were not sorry to see his embarrassments.

Some vigorous measures were instantly to be taken, or the army, it was evident, would soon altogether melt away. By the king's command, orders were despatched to Requesens, who lay with his squadron off the port of Velez Malaga, to supply the camp with provisions, while it received reinforcements, as before, principally from the Andalusian militia. The army received a still more important accession in the well-disciplined veterans who had followed the grand commander from Italy. Thus strengthened, and provisioned for a week or more, Los Velez, at the head of twelve thousand men, set forth on the twenty-sixth of July and struck at once into the Alpujarras. He had been directed by the council to establish himself at Ugijar, which by its central position would enable him to watch the movements of Aben-Humeya and act on any point as occasion required.

The marquis, without difficulty, defeated a force of some five or six thousand men who had been stationed to oppose his entrance into the mountain-country. He then pressed forward, and on the high lands beyond Ugijar—which place he had already occupied—he came in sight of Aben-Humeya, with the flower of his troops, drawn up to receive him.

The two chiefs, in their characters, their persons, and their equipments, might be considered as no bad types of the European and the Arab chivalry. The marquis, sheathed in complete mail of a sable color, and mounted on his heavy war-horse also covered with armor, was to be seen brandishing a lance which, short and thick, seemed rather like a truncheon, as he led his men boldly on, prepared to plunge at once into the thick of the fight.[1] He was the very emblem of brute force. Aben-Humeya, on the other hand, gracefully managing his swift-footed snow-white Andalusian, with his Morisco mantle of crimson floating lightly from his shoulders, and his Turkish turban wreathed around his head,[2] instead of force, suggested the opposite ideas of agility and adroitness, so characteristic of the children of the East.

Riding along his lines, the Morisco prince exhorted his followers not to fear the name of Los Velez; for in the hour of danger God would aid his own; and better was it, at any rate, to die like brave men in the field, than to live dishonored.[3] Notwithstanding these magnanimous words, it was far from Aben-Humeya's wish to meet his enemy in a fair field of fight. It was contrary to the genius and the habit of his warfare, which was of the guerilla kind, abounding in sallies and surprises, in which, seeking some vulnerable point, he could deal his blow and retreat precipitately among the mountains.

Yet his followers, though greatly inferior in numbers to the enemy, behaved with spirit; and the field was

[1] "Armado de unas armas negras de la color del acero, y una celada en la cabeza llena de plumages, y una gruesa lanza en la mano mas recia que larga." Marmol, Rebelion de Granada, tom. ii. p. 133.

[2] "Andaba Aben Umeya vistoso delante de todos en un caballo blanco con una aljuba de grana vestida y un turbante turquesco en la cabeza." Ibid., p. 134.

[3] "No temiesen el vano nombre del Marques de los Velez, porque en los mayores trabajos acudia Dios á los suyos; y quando les faltase, no les podria faltar una honrosa muerte con las armas en las manos, que les estaba mejor que vivir deshonrados." Ibid., p. 134.

well contested, till a body of Andalusian horse, making a *détour* under cover of some rising ground, fell unexpectedly on the rear of the Moriscoes and threw them into confusion. The marquis pressing them at the same time vigorously in front, they broke, and soon gave way on all sides. Aben-Humeya, perceiving the day lost, gave the rein to his high-mettled genet, who swiftly bore him from the field; and, though hotly pursued, he soon left his enemies behind. On reaching the foot of the Sierra Nevada the chief dismounted, and, hamstringing his noble animal, plunged into the depths of the mountains, which again opened their friendly arms to receive him.[4] Yet he did not remain there long before he was joined by his followers; and no sooner was he in sufficient strength than he showed himself on the eastern skirts of the sierra, whence, like an eagle stooping on his prey, he rushed down upon the plains below, sweeping through the rich valley of the Rio de Almanzora, and carrying fire and sword to the very borders of Murcia. Here he revenged himself on Los Velez by falling on his town of Las Cuevas, firing his dwellings, ravaging his estates, and rousing his Morisco vassals to rebellion.[5]

Meanwhile, the marquis, instead of following up his victory, remained torpid within the walls of Calahorra. Here he had desired the council to provide stores for the subsistence of his army. To his dismay, none had

[4] " Y apeandose del caballo, le hizo desjarretar, y se embreñó en las sierras." Marmol, Rebelion de Granada, loc. cit.—Hita commemorates the flight of the "little king" of the Alpujarras in one of his ballads. Guerras de Granada, tom. ii. p. 310.

[5] Mendoza, Guerra de Granada, p. 209.—Marmol, Rebelion de Granada, tom. ii. p. 150.—Hita, Guerras de Granada, tom. ii. p. 233.

been provided; and, as his own attempts to procure them were unsuccessful, he soon found himself in the same condition as at Adra. The famine-stricken troops, with little pay and less plunder, first became discontented, then mutinous, and at length deserted in great numbers. It was in vain that the irascible old chief poured out his wrath in menaces and imprecations. His arrogant temper had made him hated even more than he was feared by his soldiers. They now went off, not stealthily and by night, but in the open day, whole companies at a time, their arquebuses on their shoulders and their matches lighted.[6] When Don Diego Fajardo, the marquis's son, endeavored to stay them, one, more audacious than the rest, lodged a musket-ball in his body. It was not long before the gallant array with which the marquis had so proudly entered the Alpujarras was reduced to less than three thousand men. Among them were the Italian veterans, who refused to tarnish their well-earned laurels by thus basely abandoning their commander.

The council of war complained loudly to the king of the fatal inactivity of the marquis, and of his neglect to follow up the advantages he had gained. Los Velez angrily retorted by throwing the blame on that body, for neglecting to furnish him with the supplies which would have enabled him to do so. Philip, alarmed, with reason, at the critical aspect of affairs, ordered the marquis of Mondejar to repair to court, that he might confer with him on the state of the country.

[6] "I tan adelante pasó la desorden, que se juntaron quatrocientos arcabuceros, i con las mechas en las serpentinas salieron a vista del campo." Mendoza, Guerra de Granada, p. 195.

This was the avowed motive for his recall. But in truth it seems probable that the king, aware of that nobleman's leaning to a pacific policy and of his personal hostility to Los Velez, deemed it best to remove him altogether from any share in the conduct of the war. This he did most effectually, by sending him into honorable exile, first appointing him viceroy of Valencia, and afterwards raising him to the important post of viceroy of Naples. From this period the name of Mondejar no more appears on the theatre of the Morisco war.[7]

The marquis did not win the favor to which he was entitled by his deserts. He seems to have possessed some of the best qualities of a good captain. Bold in action, he was circumspect in council. Slow and sagacious in the formation of his plans, he carried them out with singular perseverance. He knew the country well which was the seat of the insurrection, and perfectly understood the character of its inhabitants. What was more rare, he made allowance for the excesses into which they had been drawn by a long course of insult and oppression. The humanity of his disposition combined with his views of policy to make him rely more on conciliatory measures than on fear, for the reduction of the enemy. How well this worked we have seen. Had he been properly supported by those engaged with him in the direction of affairs, we can hardly doubt of his ultimate success. But, unhappily, the two most prominent of these, the President Deza and the marquis of Los Velez, were narrow-minded,

[7] Mendoza, Guerra de Granada, p. 198, et seq.—Marmol, Rebelion de Granada, tom. ii. p. 146.

implacable bigots, who, far from feeling compassion for the Moriscoes, looked on the whole race as "God's enemies." Unfortunately, these views found favor with the government; and Philip, who rightly thought that the marquis of Mondejar would only prove a hinderance to carrying on hostilities with vigor, acted consistently in sending him from the country. Yet, while he was thus removed from the conduct of the war, it may be thought an unequivocal acknowledgment of Mondejar's deserts that he was transferred to the most considerable post in the gift of the crown.

Before the marquis's departure, Philip had transferred his court to Córdova, in order to facilitate his communication with the seat of war. He hoped, too, that the knowledge of his being so near would place some check on the disorderly temper of the soldiery and animate them with more loyal and patriotic feelings. In this way of proceeding he considered himself as imitating the example of his great ancestors, Ferdinand and Isabella, who, during the war of Granada, usually transferred their court to one of the capitals of the south. He did not, however, think it necessary, like them, to lead his armies in person and share in the toils of the campaign.

On the nineteenth of October, Philip published an edict which intimated his design of following up the war with vigor. It commanded that such of the Moriscoes as had hitherto been allowed to remain in Granada should now be removed from it, in order that no means of communication might be left to them with their brethren in the mountains. It was further proclaimed that the war henceforth was to be carried on with "fire and blood,"[8]—in other words, that no mercy was to be shown the insurgents. This was the first occasion on which this fierce denunciation had been made by the government. To reconcile the militia of the towns to the service, their pay was to be raised to a level with that of the Italian volunteers; and to relieve the towns, the greater part of the expense was to be borne by the crown. Before the publication of this ordinance the king had received intelligence of an event unexpected alike by Christian and by Moslem,—the death of Aben-Humeya, and that by the hands of some of his own followers.

The Morisco prince, after carrying the war up to the borders of Murcia, laid siege to two or three places of strength in that quarter. As might have been expected, he failed in these attempts, from his want of battering-artillery. Thus foiled, he led back his forces into the Alpujarras, and established his quarters in the ancient Moorish palace of Lanjaron, on the slopes of the mountains commanding the beautiful valley of Lecrin. Here the torpid condition of the Spaniards under Los Velez allowed the young monarch to remain, and give himself up to those sensual indulgences with which the Moslem princes of the East were apt to solace their leisure in the intervals of war. His harem rivalled that of any Oriental satrap in the number of its inmates. This was strange to the Moriscoes, who, since their nominal conversion to Christianity, had of course repudiated polygamy. In the eyes of the Moslems it might pass for good evidence of their prince's orthodoxy.

[8] "Que se publicase la guerra á fuego y á sangre." Marmol, Rebelion de Granada, tom. ii. p. 160.

Ever since Aben-Humeya's ascent to the throne he had been declining in popularity. His handsome person, the courtesy of his manners, his chivalrous spirit, and his devotion to the cause had easily won him the affections of his subjects. But a too sudden elevation had unfortunately that effect on him which it is wont to have on weak minds without any settled principles or lofty aim to guide them. Possessed of power, he became tyrannical in the use of it.[9] His arbitrary acts created enemies, not the less dangerous that they were concealed. The consciousness of the wrongs he had committed made him suspicious. He surrounded himself with a body-guard of four hundred men. Sixteen hundred more were quartered in the place where he was residing; and the principal avenues to it, we are told, were defended by barricades.[10] Those whom he suspected he treated with particular kindness. He drew them around his person, overwhelmed them with favors, and, when he had won them by a show of confidence, he struck the fatal blow.[11] During the short period of his reign no less than three hundred and fifty persons, we are assured, fell victims to his jealousy or his revenge.[12]

[9] "Vivia ya con estado de Rei, pero con arbitrio de tirano." Mendoza, Guerra de Granada, p. 209.

[10] "Teniendo barreadas las calles del lugar de manera, que nadie pudiese entrar en él sin ser visto ó sentido." Marmol, Rebelion de Granada, tom. ii. p. 163.

[11] Mendoza, Guerra de Granada, p. 210.—Such is the Tiberius-like portrait given of him by an enemy,—by one, however, it may be added, who for liberal views and for discrimination of character was not surpassed by any chronicler of his time.

[12] "Los cuales pasaron de trescientos cincuenta, segun yo he sido informado de varios moriscos que seguian sus banderas: y de tal

Among Aben-Humeya's officers was one named Diego Alguazil, who had a beautiful kinswoman, with whom he lived, it is said, on terms of greater intimacy than was justified by the relationship of the parties. As he was one day imprudently speaking of her to Aben-Humeya in the glowing language of a lover, the curiosity of the king was so much inflamed by it that he desired to see her. In addition to her personal charms, the fair Zahara was mistress of many accomplishments which rendered her still more attractive. She had a sweet voice, which she accompanied bewitchingly on the lute, and in her dancing displayed all the soft and voluptuous movements of the dark-eyed beauties of Andalusia.[13] When brought before the king, she did her best to please him; for, though attached, as it seems, to her kinsman, the ambitious coquette had no objection to having a royal suitor in her chains. In this she perfectly succeeded; and the enamored prince intimated his desire to Alguazil that he would resign to him the possession of his mistress. But the Morisco

manera procedia el reyecillo, que vino á ser odioslsimo á los suyos por sus crueldades." Hita, Guerras de Granada, tom. ii. p. 303.

[13] " Que no la hay mas hermosa
en toda la Andalucía:
blanca es y colorada,
como la rosa mas fina;

" Tañe, danza, canta á estremo,
que es un encanto el oirla;
es moza, bella y graciosa
nadie vió tal en su vida."
Ibid., tom. ii. p. 324.

The severer pencil of Mendoza does not disdain the same warm coloring for the portrait of the Morisco beauty. Guerra de Granada, p. 213.

loved her too well; and neither threats nor promises of the most extravagant kind were able to extort his consent. Thus baffled, the reckless Aben-Humeya, consulting only his passion, caused the perhaps not reluctant Zahara to be taken by force and lodged in his harem. By this act he made a mortal enemy of Alguazil.

Nor did he long enjoy the favor of his new mistress, who, come of an ancient lineage in Granada,[14] had hoped to share the throne of the Morisco monarch. But Aben-Humeya's passion did not carry him to this extent of complaisance; and Zahara, indignant at finding herself degraded to the rank and file of the seraglio, soon breathed only a desire for vengeance. In this state of things she found the means of communicating with her kinsman, and arranged with him a plan for carrying their murderous intent into execution.

The most important corps in the Morisco army was that of the Turkish mercenaries. But they were so fierce and turbulent a race that Aben-Humeya paid dear for their services. A strong body of these troops lay on the frontiers of Orgiba, under the command of Aben-Aboo,—a near relative of the Morisco prince, whose life, it may be remembered, he had once saved, by submitting to every extremity of torture rather than betray his lurking-place. To this commander Aben-Humeya despatched a messenger, directing him to engage the Turks in a certain expedition, which would serve both to give them employment and to satisfy their appetite for plunder.

[14] "Muger igualmente hermosa i de linage." Mendoza, Guerra de Granada, p. 213.

The time named for the messenger's departure was communicated by Zahara to her kinsman, who caused him to be waylaid and murdered and his despatches to be secured. He then had a letter written to Aben-Aboo, which bore apparently the royal signature. This was counterfeited by his nephew, a young man then holding the post of secretary to Aben-Humeya, with whom he had lately conceived some cause of disgust. The letter stated that the insubordination of the Turks made them dangerous to the state, and that in some way or other they must be removed, and that speedily. With this view, Aben-Aboo was directed to march them to Mecina, on the frontiers of the Sierra Nevada, where he would be joined by Diego Alguazil, with a party of soldiers, to assist him in carrying the plan into execution. The best mode, it was suggested, of getting rid of the Turks would be by poison.

This letter was despatched by a courier, who was speedily followed by Alguazil and a hundred soldiers, as the cunning conspirator desired to present himself before Aben-Aboo without leaving him time for consideration.

He found that commander in a state of the utmost perplexity and consternation. Alguazil declared that he had come in consequence of certain instructions he had received from the king, of too atrocious a nature for him to execute. Aben-Aboo had as little mind to perform the bloody work assigned to him. He had no distrust of the genuineness of the letter. Hosceyn, the commander of the Turks, happening to pass the house at that time, was called in, and the despatches were shown to him. The fiery chief insisted on communicating them to some of his comrades. The greatest indignation prevailed among the Turkish leaders, outraged by this base treachery of the very man whom they had come to serve at the peril of their lives. They one and all demanded, not his deposition, but his death. Diego Alguazil saw that his scheme was working well. He artfully fanned the flame, and professed to share deeply in the indignation of the Moslems. It was at length agreed to put the tyrant to death and to offer the crown to Aben-Aboo.

This chieftain enjoyed a high reputation for sagacity and prudence. His passions, unlike those of Aben-Humeya, seemed ever under the control of his reason; and, far from indulging an ill-regulated ambition, he had been always faithful to his trust. But the present temptation was too strong for his virtue. He may have thought that, since the throne was to be vacant, the descendant of the Omeyas had a better claim to it than any other. Whatever may have been the sophistry to which he yielded, he knew that those who now promised him the crown had the power to make their promise good. He gave his assent, on condition that in the course of three months his election should be confirmed by the dey of Algiers, as the representative of the Turkish sultan.

Having arranged their plans, the conspirators lost no time in putting them in execution. They set out that very hour, on the evening of the third of October, for Lanjaron, with a body of four hundred troops,—one half being Turks, the other Moriscoes. By midnight they reached their place of destination. Diego Alguazil and the Turkish captains were too well known as enjoying the confidence of Aben-Humeya to meet with any opposition to their entrance into the town. Nor, though the Morisco king had retired to rest, did the guard oppose any difficulty to their passing into his dwelling. Proceeding to his chamber, they found the doors secured, but speedily forced an entrance. Neither arm nor voice was raised in his defence.[15]

Aben-Humeya, roused from sleep by the tumult, would have sprung from his couch; but the faithless Zahara held him fast in her embrace until Diego Alguazil and some others of the conspirators, rushing in, bound his arms together with a Moorish veil.[16] Indeed, he was so much bewildered as scarcely to attempt resistance.

The Turkish commander then showed him the letter. Aben-Humeya recognized the writing of his secretary, but declared that he had never dictated such a letter, nor was the signature his. How far his assertion gained credit we are not informed. But the conspirators had already gone too far to be forgiven. To recede was death. Either Aben-Humeya or they must be sacrificed. It was in vain that he protested his innocence, and that he offered to leave the question to the sultan, or to the dey of Algiers, or to any person competent to decide it. But little heed was given to his protestations, as the conspirators dragged him into an adjoining apartment. The unhappy young man perceived that his hour was come,—that there was no one of all his friends or menials to interpose between him and his

---

[15] " Ninguno huvo que tomase las armas, ni bolviese de palabra por él." Mendoza, Guerra de Granada, p. 217.

[16] " Ataronle las manos con un almaizar." Ibid., p. 218.

fate. From that moment he changed his tone, and assumed a bearing more worthy of his station. "They are mistaken," he said, "who suppose me to be a follower of the Prophet. I die, as I have lived, in the Christian faith. I accepted the post of head of the rebellion that I might the better avenge the wrongs heaped on me and my family by the Spaniards. They have been avenged in full measure, and I am now ready to die. Neither," said he, turning to Aben-Aboo, his destined successor, "do I envy you. It will not be long before you will follow me." He then, with his own hands, coolly arranged around his neck the cord with which he was to be strangled, adjusted his robes, and, covering his face with his mantle, submitted himself, without a struggle, to his executioners."[17]

His body was thrown into a neighboring sewer, with as little concern as if it had been that of a dog. There it continued, till Don John of Austria, hearing that Aben-Humeya had died a Christian, caused his remains to be removed to Guadix and laid in the ground with the solemnities of Christian burial.[18]

That Aben-Humeya should have come to so miserable

[17] "El mismo se dió la buelta como le hiciesen menos mal; concertó la ropa, cubrióse el rostro." Mendoza, Guerra de Granada, p. 219.

[18] There is less discrepancy than usual in the accounts both of Aben-Humeya's assassination and of the circumstances which led to it. These circumstances have a certain Oriental coloring, which makes them not the less probable, considering the age and country in which they occurred. Among the different authorities in prose and verse, see Marmol, Rebelion de Granada, tom. ii. pp. 162-169,—Mendoza, Guerra de Granada, pp. 212-220,—Rufo, La Austriada, cantos 13. 14.—Hita, Guerras de Granada, tom. ii. p. 337, et seq.,—Vanderhammen, Don Juan de Austria, fol. 103 105.

an end is not strange. The recklessness with which he sacrificed all who came between him and the gratification of his passions surrounded him with enemies, the more dangerous in a climate where the blood is hot and the feeling of revenge is easily kindled in the bosom. At the beginning of his reign his showy qualities won him a popularity which, however, took no root in the affections of the people, and which faded away altogether when the defects of his character were more fully brought to light by the exigencies of his situation; for he was then found to possess neither the military skill necessary to insure success in the field, nor those higher moral attributes which command respect and obedience at home.

Very different was the character of his successor, Aben-Aboo. Instead of displaying the frivolous and licentious tastes of Aben-Humeya, his private life was without reproach. He was much older than his predecessor; and, if he had not the same fiery enthusiasm and dashing spirit of adventure which belonged to Aben-Humeya, he discovered both forecast in the formation of his plans and singular courage in carrying them into execution. All confided in his integrity; while the decorum and gravity of his demeanor combined with the more substantial qualities of his character to inspire a general feeling of reverence in the people.[19]

[19] "Con la reputacion de valiente i hombre del campo, con la afabilidad, gravedad, autoridad de la presencia, fue bien quisto, respetado, obedecido, tenido como Rei generalmente de todos." Mendoza, Guerra de Granada, p. 224.—This was painting him *en beau*. For a portrait of an opposite complexion, see Miniana, who represents him as "audaz, perfido, suspicaz, y de pésimas costumbres." (Historia de España, p. 378.) Fortunately for Aben-Aboo, the first mentioned

It was not till the time of his proposed elevation to the supreme power that the lustre of these qualities was darkened by the perpetration of one foul deed,— his connivance at the conspiracy against his sovereign. But if he were really the dupe, as we are told, of Alguazil's plot, he might plead, to some extent, the necessity of self-preservation; for he may well have believed that, if he refused to aid Aben-Humeya in the execution of his bloody purpose in reference to the Turks, the tyrant would not long suffer him to live in possession of a secret so perilous to himself. At all events, the part he had taken in the conspiracy seems to have given no disgust to the people, who, weary of the despotism under which they had been living, welcomed with enthusiasm the accession of the new sovereign. Many places which had hitherto taken no part in the struggle for independence now sent in their adhesion to Aben-Aboo, who soon found himself the ruler over a wider extent of territory than at any time had acknowledged the sway of his predecessor.

It was not long before the confirmation of his election arrived from Algiers; and Aben-Aboo, assuming the regal name of Muley Abdallah Mohammed as a prefix to his own, went through the usual simple forms of a coronation of a king of Granada. In his right hand, on this occasion, he bore a banner inscribed with the legend, "More I could not desire, less would not have contented me."[20] Such an inscription may be thought

writer, a contemporary, must be admitted to be the better authority of the two.

[20] "No pude desear mas, ni contentarme con menos." Marmol, Rebelion de Granada, tom. ii. p. 168.—See also, for the account of this martial ceremony, Mendoza, Guerra de Granada, p. 222.

to intimate that a more aspiring temper lurked within his bosom than the world had given him credit for.

The new sovereign did not, like his predecessor, waste his time in effeminate sloth. He busied himself with various important reforms, giving, especially, a new organization to the army, and importing a large quantity of arms and munitions from Barbary. He determined not to allow his men time for discontent, but to engage them at once in active service. The first object he proposed was the capture of Orgiba, a fortified place which commanded the route to Granada, and which served as a point of communication between that capital and remoter parts of the country.

Aben-Aboo got every thing in readiness with such despatch that on the twenty-sixth of October, a few weeks only after the death of Aben-Humeya, he set out on his expedition at the head of a well-appointed army, consisting of more than ten thousand men, partly foreign mercenaries and partly natives. Hastening his march, he soon presented himself before Orgiba and laid siege to the place. He pushed matters forward so vigorously that in a few days he was prepared to storm the works. Four times he brought his men to the assault; but though on the fourth he succeeded in throwing himself, with a small body of troops, on the ramparts, he was met with such determined resistance by the garrison and their brave commander, Francisco de Molina, that he was obliged to fall back with loss into his trenches. Thus repulsed, and wholly destitute of battering-ordnance, the Morisco chief found it expedient to convert the siege into a blockade.

The time thus consumed gave opportunity to Don

John of Austria to send a strong force, under the duke of Sesa, to the relief of the garrison. Aben-Aboo, desirous to intercept his enemy's march and occupy one of those defiles that would give him the advantage of position, silently broke up his encampment, under cover of the night, and took the direction of Lanjaron. Here he came so suddenly on the advanced guard of the Christians that, taken by surprise, it gave way, and, falling back, after considerable loss, on the main body of the army, threw the whole into confusion. Happily, the duke of Sesa, though laboring at the time under a sharp attack of gout, by extraordinary exertions was enabled to rally his men and inspire them with courage to repulse the enemy,—thus retrieving his own honor and the fortunes of the day.

Meanwhile, the brave Molina and his soldiers no sooner learned that the besiegers had abandoned their works, than, eager to profit by their temporary absence, the cause of which they suspected, they dismantled the fortress, and, burying their guns in the ground, hastily evacuated the place. The duke of Sesa, finding that the great object of his expedition, the safety of the garrison, was now accomplished, and not feeling himself in sufficient strength to cope with the Morisco chief, instantly began his retreat on Granada. In this he was not molested by Aben-Aboo, who was only too glad to be allowed without interruption to follow up the siege of Orgiba. But finding this place, to his surprise, abandoned by the enemy, he entered it without bloodshed, and with colors flying, as a conqueror.[21]

[21] Ferreras, Hist. d'Espagne, tom. x. pp. 111-118.—Marmol, Rebe-

These successes in the commencement of his reign furnished a brilliant augury for the future. The fame of Aben-Aboo spread far and wide through the country; and the warlike peasantry thronged from all quarters to his standard. Tidings now arrived that several of the principal places on the eastern skirts of the Alpujarras had proclaimed their adherence to the Morisco cause; and it was expected that the flame of insurrection would soon spread to the adjoining provinces of Murcia and Valencia. So widely, indeed, had it already spread, that, of all the Morisco territory south of Granada, the country around Malaga and the sierra of Ronda, on the extreme west, were the only portions that still acknowledged the authority of Castile.[22]

The war now took the same romantic aspect that it wore in the days of the conquest of Granada. Beacon-fires were to be seen along the highest peaks of the sierra, throwing their ominous glare around for many a league, and calling the bold mountaineers to the foray. Then came the gathering of the wild militia of the country, which, pouring down on the lower levels, now in the faded green of autumn, swept away herds and flocks and bore them off in triumph to their fastnesses.

Sometimes marauders penetrated into the *vega*, the beautiful *vega*, every inch of whose soil was fertilized with human blood, and which now, as in ancient times,

lion de Granada, tom. ii. pp. 169-189.—Mendoza, Guerra de Granada, p. 225, et seq.—Miniana, Hist. de España, p. 378.

[22] "Desta manera quedaron levantados todos los Moriscos del Reino, sino los de la Hoya de Malaga i Serrania de Ronda." Mendoza, Guerra de Granada, p. 241.

became the battle-ground of Christian and Moslem cavaliers. Almost always it was the former who had the advantage, as was intimated by the gory trophies, the heads and hands of the vanquished, which they bore on the points of their lances, when, amidst the shouts of the populace, they came thundering on through the gates of the capital.[73]

Yet sometimes fortune lay in the opposite scale. The bold infidels, after scouring the *vega*, would burst into the suburbs, or even into the city, of Granada, filling the place with consternation. Then might be seen the terror-stricken citizens hurrying to and fro, while the great alarm-bell of the Alhambra sent forth its summons, and the chivalry, mounting in haste, shouted the old war-cry of *Saint Iago* and threw themselves on the invaders, who, after a short but bloody fray, were sure to be driven in confusion across the *vega* and far over the borders.

Don John on these occasions was always to be descried in the front of battle, as if rejoicing in his element and courting danger like some paladin of romance. Indeed, Philip was obliged again and again to rebuke his brother for thus wantonly exposing his life in a manner, the king intimated, wholly unbecoming his

---

[73] "Llevando los escuderos las cabezas y las manos de los Moros en los hierros de las lanzas." Marmol, Rebelion de Granada, tom. ii. p. 159.—The head of an enemy was an old perquisite of the victor—whether Christian or Moslem—in the wars with the Spanish Arabs. It is frequently commemorated in the Moorish *romances* as among the most honorable trophies of the field, down to as late a period as the war of Granada. See, among others, the ballad beginning

"A vista de los dos Reyes."

rank.[24] But it would have been as easy to rein in the war-horse when the trumpet was sounding in his ears as to curb the spirits of the high-mettled young chieftain when his followers were mustering to the charge. In truth, it was precisely these occasions that filled him with the greatest glee; for they opened to him the only glimpses he was allowed of that career of glory for which his soul had so long panted. Every detachment that sallied forth from Granada on a warlike adventure was an object of his envy; and as he gazed on the blue mountains that rose as an impassable barrier around him, he was like the bird vainly beating its plumage against the gilded wires of its prison-house and longing to be free.

He wrote to the king in the most earnest terms, representing the forlorn condition of affairs, — the Spaniards losing ground day after day, and the army under the marquis of Los Velez wasting away its energies in sloth or exerting them in unprofitable enterprises. He implored his brother not to compel him to remain thus cooped up within the walls of Granada, but to allow him to have a real as well as nominal command, and to conduct the war in person.[25]

The views presented by Don John were warmly supported by Requesens, who wrote to Philip, denouncing in unqualified terms the incapacity of Los Velez.

[24] " Y que salir á tales rebatos es desautoridad vuestra, siendo quien sois y teniendo el cargo que tenis." Carta de Felipe Segundo á Don Juan de Austria, 30 de Setiembre, 1569, MS.

[25] " Le suplico mire que ni á quien soy, ni á la edad que tengo, ni á otra cosa alguna conviene encerrarme, cuando mas razon es que me muestre." Carta de Don Juan de Austria al Rey, 23 de Setiembre, 1569, MS.

Philip had no objection to receive complaints, even against those whom he most favored. He could not shut his eyes to the truth of the charges now brought against the hot-headed old chief who had so long enjoyed his confidence, but whose campaigns of late had been a series of blunders. He saw the critical aspect of affairs and the danger that the rebellion, which had struck so deep root in Granada, unless speedily crushed, would spread over the adjoining provinces. Mondejar's removal from the scene of action had not brought the remedy that Philip had expected.

Yet it was with reluctance that he yielded to his brother's wishes; whether distrusting the capacity of one so young for an independent command, or, as might be inferred from his letters, apprehending the dangers in which Don John's impetuous spirit would probably involve him. Having formed his plans, he lost no time in communicating them to his brother. The young warrior was to succeed Los Velez in the command of the eastern army, which was to be strengthened by reinforcements, while the duke of Sesa, under the direction of Don John, was to establish himself, with an efficient corps, in the Alpujarras, in such a position as to cover the approaches to Granada.

A summons was then sent to the principal towns of Andalusia, requiring them to raise fresh levies for the war, who were to be encouraged by promises of better pay than had before been given. But these promises did not weigh so much with the soldiers as the knowledge that Don John of Austria was to take charge of the expedition; and nobles and cavaliers came thronging to the war, with their well-armed retainers, in such numbers that the king felt it necessary to publish another ordinance, prohibiting any, without express permission, from joining the service.[26]

All now was bustle and excitement in Granada, as the new levies came in and the old ones were receiving a better organization. Indeed, Don John had been closely occupied, for some time, with introducing reforms among the troops quartered in the city, who, from causes already mentioned, had fallen into a state of the most alarming insubordination. A similar spirit had infected the officers, and to such an extent that it was deemed necessary to suspend no less than thirty-seven out of forty-five captains from their commands.[27] Such were the difficulties under which the youthful hero was to enter on his first campaign.

Fortunately, in the retainers of the great lords and cavaliers he had a body of well-appointed and well-disciplined troops, who were actuated by higher motives than the mere love of plunder.[28] His labors, moreover, did much to restore the ancient discipline of the regiments quartered in Granada. But the zeal with which he had devoted himself to the work of reform had impaired his health. This drew forth a kind re-

[26] "Entendióse por España la fama de su ida sobre Galera, i movióse la nobleza della con tanto calor, que fue necesario dar al Rei a entender que no era con su voluntad ir Cavalleros sin licencia a servir en aquella empresa." Mendoza, Guerra de Granada, p. 256.

[27] "Havian las desordenes pasado tan adelante, que fue necesario para remediallas hacer demostracion no vista ni leída en los tiempos pasados, en la guerra: suspender treinta i dos Capitanes de quarenta i uno que havia, con nombre de reformacion." Ibid., p. 237.

[28] "Tambien la gente embiada por los Señores, escogida, igual, disciplinada, movidos por obligacion de virtud i deseo de acreditar sus personas." Ibid., p. 234.

monstrance from Philip, who wrote to his brother not thus to overtask his strength, but to remember that he had need of his services; telling him to remind Quixada that he must watch over him more carefully. "And God grant," he concluded, "that your health may be soon re-established." The affectionate solicitude constantly shown for his brother's welfare in the king's letters was hardly to have been expected in one of so phlegmatic a temperament and who was usually so little demonstrative in the expression of his feelings.

Before entering on his great expedition, Don John resolved to secure the safety of Granada in his absence by the reduction of "the robbers' nest," as the Spaniards called it, of Guejar. This was a fortified place near the confines of the Alpujarras, held by a warlike garrison, that frequently sallied out over the neighboring country, sometimes carrying their forays into the *vega* of Granada and causing a panic in the capital. Don John formed his force into two divisions, one of which he gave to the duke of Sesa, while the other he proposed to lead in person. They were to proceed by different routes, and, meeting before the place, to attack it simultaneously from opposite quarters.

The duke, marching by the most direct road across the mountains, reached Guejar first, and was not a little surprised to find that the inhabitants, who had received notice of the preparations of the Spaniards, were already evacuating the town, while the garrison was formed in order of battle to cover their retreat. After a short skirmish with the rear-guard, in which some lives were lost on both sides, the victorious Spaniards, without following up their advantage, marched into the town and took possession of the works abandoned by the enemy.

Great was the surprise of Don John, on arriving some hours later before Guejar, to see the Castilian flag floating from its ramparts; and his indignation was roused as he found that the laurels he had designed for his own brow had been thus unceremoniously snatched from him by another. "With eyes," says the chronicler, "glowing like coals of fire,"[29] he turned on the duke of Sesa and demanded an explanation of the affair. But he soon found that the blame, if blame there were, was to be laid on one whom he felt that he had not the power to rebuke. This was Luis Quixada, who, in his solicitude for the safety of his ward, had caused the army to be conducted by a circuitous route, that brought it thus late upon the field. But, though Don John uttered no word of rebuke, he maintained a moody silence, that plainly showed his vexation; and, as the soldiers remarked, not a morsel of food passed his lips until he had reached Granada.[30]

The constant supervision maintained over him by Quixada, which, as we have seen, was encouraged by the king, was a subject of frequent remark among the troops. It must have afforded no little embarrassment and mortification to Don John,—alike ill suited as it was to his age, his aspiring temper, and his station. For his station as commander-in-chief of the army made him responsible, in the eyes of the world, for the

---

[29] "Pusieronsele los ojos encendidos como brasa de puro corage." Marmol, Rebelion de Granada, tom. ii. p. 224.

[30] "Sin comer bocado en todo aquel dia se volvió á la ciudad de Granada." Ibid., p. 225.

measures of the campaign. Yet, in his dependent situation, he had the power neither to decide on the plan of operations nor to carry it into execution. Not many days were to elapse before the death of his kind-hearted monitor was to relieve him from the jealous oversight that so much chafed his spirit, and to open to him an independent career of glory such as might satisfy the utmost cravings of his ambition.

One of the authorities of the greatest importance, and most frequently cited in this Book, as the reader may have noticed, is Diego Hurtado de Mendoza. He belonge 1 to one of the most illustrious houses in Castile,—a house not more prominent for its rank than for the great abilities displayed by its members in the various walks of civil and military life, as well as for their rare intellectual culture. No one of the great families of Spain has furnished so fruitful a theme for the pen of both the chronicler and the bard.

He was the fifth son of the marquis of Mondejar, and was born in the year 1503 at Granada, where his father filled the office held by his ancestors of captain-general of the province. At an early age he was sent to Salamanca, and passed with credit through the course of studies taught in its venerable university. While there, he wrote- for, though printed anonymously, there seems no good reason to distrust the authorship—his famous " Lazarillo de Tormes," the origin of that class of *picaresco* novels, as they are styled, which constitutes an important branch of Castilian literature, and the best specimen of which, strange to say, was furnished by the hand of a foreigner,—the " Gil Blas" of Le Sage.

Mendoza had been destined to the church, for which the extensive patronage of his family offered obvious advantages. But the taste of the young man, as might be inferred from his novel, took another direction, and he persuaded his father to allow him to enter the army and take service under the banner of Charles the Fifth. Mendoza's love of letters did not desert him in the camp ; and he availed himself of such intervals as occurred between the campaigns to continue his studies, especially in the ancient languages, in the principal universities of Italy.

It was impossible that a person of such remarkable endowments as Mendoza, the more conspicuous from his social position, should escape the penetrating eye of Charles the Fifth, who, independently of his scholarship, recognized in the young noble a decided talent for political affairs. In 1538 the emperor appointed him ambassador to Venice, a capital for which the literary enterprises of the Aldi were every day winning a higher reputation in the republic of letters. Here Mendoza had the best opportunity of accomplishing a work which he had much at heart,—the formation of a library. It was a work of no small difficulty in that day, when books and manuscripts were to be gathered from obscure, often remote, sources, and at the large cost paid for objects of *virtù*. A good office which he had the means of rendering the sultan, by the redemption from captivity of a Turkish prisoner of rank, was requited by a magnificent present of Greek manuscripts, worth more than gold in the eyes of Mendoza. It was from his collection that the first edition of Josephus was given to the world. While freely indulging his taste for literary occupations in his intervals of leisure, he performed the duties of his mission with an ability that fully vindicated his appointment as minister to the wily republic. On the opening of the Council of Trent, he was one of the delegates sent to represent the emperor in that body. He joined freely in the discussions of the conclave, and enforced the views of his sovereign with a strength of reasoning and a fervid eloquence that produced a powerful impression on his audience. The independence he displayed recommended him for the delicate task of presenting the remonstrances of Charles the Fifth to the papal court against the removal of the council to Bologna. This he did with a degree of frankness to which the pontifical ear was but little accustomed, and which, if it failed to bend the proud spirit of Paul the Third, had its effect on his successor.

Mendoza, from whatever cause, does not seem to have stood so high in the favor of Philip the Second as in that of his father. Perhaps he had too lofty a nature to stoop to that implicit deference which Philip exacted from the highest as well as the humblest who approached him. At length, in 1568, Mendoza's own misconduct brought him, with good reason, into disgrace with his master. He engaged in a brawl with another courtier in the palace; and the scandalous scene, of which the reader will find an account in the preceding volume, took place when the prince of Asturias, Don Carlos, was breathing his last. The offending parties were punished first by imprisonment, and then by banishment from Madrid. Mendoza, who was sixty-five years of age at this time, withdrew to Granada, his native place. But he had passed too much of his life in the atmosphere of a court to be content with a provincial residence. He accordingly made repeated efforts to soften his sovereign's displeasure and to obtain some mitigation of his sentence. These efforts, as may be believed, were unavailing; and the illustrious exile took at length the wiser course of submitting to his fate and seeking consolation in the companionship of his books,—steady friends, whose worth he now fully proved in the hour of adversity. He devoted himself to the study of Arabic, to which he was naturally led by his residence in a capital filled with the monuments of Arabian art. He also amused his leisure by writing verses; and his labors combined with those of Boscan and Garcilasso de la Vega to naturalize in Castile those more refined forms of Italian versification that made an important epoch in the national literature.

But the great work to which he devoted himself was the history of the insurrection of the Moriscoes, which, occurring during his residence in Granada, may be said to have passed before his eyes. For this he had, moreover, obvious facilities, for he was the near kinsman of the captain-general, and was personally acquainted with those who had the direction of affairs. The result of his labors was a work of inestimable value, though of no great bulk,—being less a history of events than a commentary on such a history. The author explores the causes of these events. He introduces the reader into the cabinet of Madrid, makes him acquainted with the intrigues of the different factions, both in the court and in the camp, unfolds the policy of the government and the plans of the campaigns,—in short, enables him to penetrate into the interior, and see the secret working of the machinery, so carefully shrouded from the vulgar eye.

The value which the work derived from the author's access to these recondite sources of information is much enhanced by its independent spirit. In a country where few dared even think for themselves, Mendoza both thought with freedom and freely expressed his thoughts. Proof of this is afforded by the caustic tone of his criticism on the conduct of the government, and by the candor which he sometimes ventures to display when noticing the wrongs of the Moriscoes. This independence of the historian, we may well believe, could have found little favor with the administration. It may have been the cause that the book was not published till after the reign of Philip the Second, and many years after its author's death.

The literary execution of the work is not its least remarkable feature. Instead of the desultory and gossiping style of the Castilian chronicler, every page is instinct with the spirit of the ancient classics. Indeed, Mendoza is commonly thought to have deliberately formed his style on that of Sallust; but I agree with my friend Mr. Ticknor, who, in a luminous criticism on Mendoza, in his great work on Spanish Literature, expresses the opinion that the Castilian historian formed his style quite as much on that of Tacitus as of Sallust. Indeed, some of Mendoza's most celebrated passages are obvious imitations of the former historian, of whom he constantly reminds us by the singular compactness and energy of his diction, by his power of delineating a portrait by a single stroke of the pencil, and by his free criticism on the chief actors of the drama, conveyed in language full of that practical wisdom which, in Mendoza's case, was the result of a large acquaintance with public affairs. We recognize also the defects incident to the style he has chosen,—rigidity and constraint, with a frequent use of ellipsis in a way that does violence to the national idiom, and, worst of all, that obscurity which arises from the effort to be brief. Mendoza hurts his book, moreover, by an unseasonable display of learning, which, however it may be pardoned by the antiquary, comes like an impertinent episode to break the thread of the narrative. But, with all its defects, the work is a remarkable production for the time, and, appearing in the midst of the *romantic* literature of Spain, we regard it with the same feeling of surprise which the traveller might experience who should meet with a classic Doric temple in the midst of the fantastic structures of China or Hindostan.

Not long after Mendoza had completed his history, he obtained permission to visit Madrid, not to reside there, but to attend to some personal affairs. He had hardly reached the capital when he was attacked by a mortal illness, which carried him off in April, 1575, in the seventy-third year of his age. Shortly before his death he gave his rich collection of books and manuscripts to his obdurate master, who placed them, agreeably to the donor's desire, in the Escorial, where they still form an interesting portion of a library of which so much has been said, and so little is really known by the world.

The most copious notice, with which I am acquainted, of the life of Mendoza, is that attributed to the pen of Iñigo Lopez de Avila, and prefixed to the Valencian edition of the "Guerra de Granada," published in 1776. But his countrymen have been ever ready to do honor to the memory of one who, by the brilliant success which he achieved as a statesman, a diplomatist, a novelist, a poet, and an historian, has established a reputation for versatility of genius second to none in the literature of Spain.

CHAPTER VII.

REBELLION OF THE MORISCOES.

Don John takes the Field.—Investment of Galera.—Fierce Assaults.—Preparations for a last Attack.—Explosion of the Mines.—Desperation of the Moriscoes.—Cruel Massacre.—Galera demolished.

1570.

Don John lost no time in completing the arrangements for his expedition. The troops, as they reached Granada, were for the most part sent forward to join the army under Los Velez, on the east of the Alpujarras, where that commander was occupied with the siege of Galera, though with but little prospect of reducing the place. He was soon, however, to be superseded by Don John.

Philip, unable to close his ears against the representations of his brother, as well as those of more experienced captains in the service, had at length reluctantly come to a conviction of the unfitness of Los Velez for the command. Yet he had a partiality for the veteran; and he was willing to spare him, as far as possible, the mortification of seeing himself supplanted by his young rival. In his letters the king repeatedly enjoined it on his brother to treat the marquis with the utmost deference, and to countenance no reports circulated to his prejudice. In an epistle filled with instructions for the campaign, dated the twenty-sixth of November, the king told Don John to be directed on all occasions by the counsels of Quixada and Requesens. He was to show the greatest respect for the marquis, and to give him to understand that he should be governed by his opinions. "But in point of fact," said Philip, "should his opinion clash at any time with that of the two other counsellors, you are to be governed by theirs."[1]

On Quixada and Requesens he was indeed always to rely, never setting up his own judgment in opposition to theirs. He was to move with caution, and, instead of the impatient spirit of a boy, to show the circumspection of one possessed of military experience. "In this way," concluded his royal monitor, "you will not only secure the favor of your sovereign, but establish your reputation with the world."[2] It is evident that Philip had discerned traits in the character of Don John which led him to distrust somewhat his capacity for the high station in which he was placed. Perhaps it may be thought that the hesitating and timid policy of Philip was less favorable to success in military operations than the bold spirit of enterprise which belonged to his brother. However this may be, Don John, notwithstanding his repeated protestations to the contrary,

[1] "Y porque podria ser que ordenase al marqués de los Velez que quedase con vos y os aconsejase, convendrá en este caso que vos le mostreis muy buena cara y le trateis muy bien y le deis á entender que tomais su parecer, mas que en efecto tomeis el de los que he dicho cuando fuesen diferentes del suyo." Carta del Rey á D. Juan de Austria, 26 de Noviembre, 1569, MS.

[2] "Y que os goberneis como si hubiésedes visto mucha guerra y halládoos en ella, que os digo que comigo y con todos ganeis harta mas reputacion en gobernaros desta manera, que no haciendo alguna mocedad que á todos nos costare caro." Ibid., MS.

was of too ardent a temperament to be readily affected by these admonitions of his prudent adviser.

The military command in Granada was lodged by the prince in the hands of the duke of Sesa, who, as soon as he had gathered a sufficient force, was to march into the western district of the Alpujarras and there create a diversion in favor of Don John. A body of four thousand troops was to remain in Granada; and the commander-in-chief, having thus completed his dispositions for the protection of the capital, set forth on his expedition on the twenty-ninth of December, at the head of a force amounting only to three thousand foot and four hundred horse. With these troops went a numerous body of volunteers, the flower of the Andalusian chivalry, who had come to win renown under the banner of the young leader.

He took the route through Guadix, and on the third day reached the ancient city of Baza, memorable for the siege it had sustained under his victorious ancestors, Ferdinand and Isabella. Here he was met by Requesens, who, besides a reinforcement of troops, brought with him a train of heavy ordnance and a large supply of ammunition. The guns were sent forward, under a strong escort, to Galera; but, on leaving Baza, Don John received the astounding tidings that the marquis of Los Velez had already abandoned the siege, and drawn off his whole force to the neighboring town of Guescar.

In fact, the rumor had no sooner reached the ears of the testy old chief that Don John was speedily coming to take charge of the war than he swore in his wrath that if the report were true he would abandon the siege and throw up his command. Yet those who knew him best did not think him capable of so mad an act. He kept his word, however; and when he learned that Don John was on the way he broke up his encampment, and withdrew, as above stated, to Guescar. By this course he left the adjacent country open to the incursions of the Moriscoes of Galera; while no care was taken to provide even for the safety of the convoys which from time to time came laden with supplies for the besieging army.

This extraordinary conduct gave no dissatisfaction to his troops, who, long since disgusted with the fiery yet imbecile character of their general, looked with pleasure to the prospect of joining the standard of so popular a chieftain as John of Austria. Even the indignation felt by the latter at the senseless proceeding of the marquis was forgotten in the satisfaction he experienced at being thus relieved from the embarrassments which his rival's overweening pretensions could not have failed to cause him in the campaign. Don John might now, with a good grace and without any cost to himself, make all the concessions to the veteran so strenuously demanded by Philip. It was in this amiable mood that the prince pushed forward his march, eager to prevent the disastrous consequences which might arise from the marquis's abandonment of his post.

As he drew near to Guescar, he beheld the old nobleman riding towards him at the head of his retainers, with a stiff and stately port, like one who had no concessions or explanations to make for himself. Without alighting from his horse, as he drew near the prince, he tendered him obeisance by kissing the hand which the latter graciously extended towards him. "Noble marquis," said Don John, "your great deeds have shed a lustre over your name. I consider myself fortunate in having the opportunity of becoming personally acquainted with you. Fear not that your authority will be in the least abridged by mine. The soldiers under my command will obey you as implicitly as myself. I pray you to look on me as a son, filled with feelings of reverence for your valor and your experience, and designing on all occasions to lean on your counsels for support."[3]

The courteous and respectful tone of the prince seems to have had its effect on the iron nature of the marquis, as he replied, "There is no Spaniard living who has a stronger desire than I have to be personally acquainted with the distinguished brother of my sovereign, or who would probably be a greater gainer by serving under his banner. But, to speak with my usual plainness, I wish to withdraw to my own house; for it would never do for me, old as I am, to hold the post of a subaltern."[4] He then accompanied Don John back to the town, giving him, as they rode along, some account of the siege and of the strength of the place. On reaching the quarters reserved for the commander-in-chief, Los Velez took leave of the prince; and, without further ceremony, gathering his knights and followers about him, and escorted by a company of horse, he

---

[3] " I que seais obedecido de toda mi gente, haciendolo yo asimismo como hijo vuestro, acatando vuestro valor i canas, i amparandome en todas ocasiones de vuestros consejos." Mendoza, Guerra de Granada, p. 260.

[4] " Pues no conviene a mi edad anciana haver de ser cabo de esquadra." Ibid., loc. cit.

rode off in the direction of his town of Velez Blanco, which was situated at no great distance, amidst the wild scenery stretching towards the frontiers of Murcia. Here among the mountains he lived in a retirement that would have been more honorable had it not been purchased by so flagrant a breach of duty.[5]

The whole story is singularly characteristic, not merely of the man, but of the times in which he lived. Had so high-handed and audacious a proceeding occurred in our day, no rank, however exalted, could have screened the offender from punishment. As it was, it does not appear that any attempt was made at an inquiry into the marquis's conduct. This is the more remarkable considering that it involved such disrespect to a sovereign little disposed to treat with lenity any want of deference to himself. The explanation of the lenity shown by him on the present occasion may perhaps be found, not in any tenderness for the reputation of his favorite, but in Philip's perceiving that the further prosecution of the affair would only serve to give greater publicity to his own egregious error in retaining Los Velez in the command, when his conduct and the warnings of others should long ago have been regarded as proof of his incapacity.

On the marquis's departure Don John lost no time in resuming his march, at the head of a force which now amounted to twelve thousand foot and eight hun-

[5] The marquis of Los Velez was afterwards summoned to Madrid, where he long continued to occupy an important place in the council of state, apparently without any diminution of the royal favor.—For the preceding pages consult Marmol, Rebelion de Granada, tom. ii. pp. 229-232,—Mendoza, Guerra de Granada, pp. 257-260,—Herrera, Hist. general, tom. i. pp. 777, 778,—Bleda, Cronica, pp. 733, 734.

dred horse, besides a brilliant array of chivalry, who, as we have seen, had come to seek their fortunes in the war. A few hours brought the troops before Galera; and Don John proceeded at once to reconnoitre the ground. In this survey he was attended by Quixada, Requesens, and the greater part of the cavalry. Having completed his observations, he made his arrangements for investing the place.

The town of Galera occupied a site singularly picturesque. This, however, had been selected certainly not from any regard to its romantic beauty, still less for purposes of convenience, but for those of defence against an enemy,—a circumstance of the first importance in a mountain-country so wild and warlike as that in which Galera stood. The singular shape of the rocky eminence which it covered was supposed, with its convex summit, to bear some resemblance to that of a galley with its keel uppermost. From this resemblance the town had derived its name.[6]

The summit was crowned by a castle, which in the style of its architecture bore evident marks of antiquity. It was defended by a wall, much of it in so ruinous a

[6] The punning attractions of the name were too strong to be resisted by the ballad-makers of the day. See in particular the *romance* (one of the best, it may be added,—and no great praise,—in Hita's second volume) beginning

"Mastredages marineros
de Huescar y otro lugar
han armado una Galera
que no la hay tal en la mar
No tiene velas, ni remos,
y navegar, y hace mal,"—

and so on, for more stanzas than the reader will care to see. Guerras de Granada, tom. ii. p. 469.

condition as to be little better than a mass of stones loosely put together. At a few paces from the fortress stood a ravelin. But neither this outwork nor the castle itself could boast of any other piece of artillery than two falconets, captured from Los Velez during his recent siege of the place, and now mounted on the principal edifice. Even these had been so injudiciously placed as to give little annoyance to an enemy.

The houses of the inhabitants stretched along the remainder of the summit, and descended by a bold declivity the northwestern side of the hill to a broad plain known as the *Eras*, or "Gardens." Through this plain flowed a stream of considerable depth, which, as it washed the base of the town on its northern side, formed a sort of moat for its protection on that quarter. On the side towards the Gardens the town was defended by a ditch and a wall now somewhat dilapidated. The most remarkable feature of this quarter was a church with its belfry or tower, now converted into a fortress, which, in default of cannon, had been pierced with loopholes and filled with musketeers,—forming altogether an outwork of considerable strength, and commanding the approaches to the town.

On two of its sides, the rock on which Galera rested descended almost perpendicularly, forming the walls of a ravine fenced in on the opposite quarter by precipitous hills, and thus presenting a sort of natural ditch on a gigantic scale for the protection of the place. The houses rose one above another, on a succession of terraces, so steep that in many instances the roof of one building scarcely reached the foundation of the one above it. The houses which occupied the same terrace, and stood therefore on the same level, might be regarded as so many fortresses. Their walls, which, after the Moorish fashion, were ill provided with lattices, were pierced with loopholes, that gave the marksmen within the command of the streets on which they fronted; and these streets were still further protected by barricades thrown across them at only fifty paces' distance from each other.[7] Thus the whole place bristled over with fortifications, or rather seemed like one great fortification itself, which nature had combined with art to make impregnable.

It was well victualled for a siege, at least with grain, of which there was enough in the magazines for two years' consumption. Water was supplied by the neighboring river, to which access had been obtained by a subterranean gallery lately excavated in the rock. These necessaries of life the Moriscoes could command. But they were miserably deficient in what, in their condition, was scarcely less important,—fire-arms and ammunition. They had no artillery except the two falconets before noticed; and they were so poorly provided with muskets as to be mainly dependent on arrows, stones, and other missiles, such as had filled the armories of their ancestors. To these might be added swords and some other weapons for hand-to-hand combat. Of defensive armor they were almost wholly destitute. But they were animated by an heroic spirit, of more worth

[7] " Las tenian los Moros barreadas de cincuenta en cincuenta pasos, y hechos muchos traveses de una parte y de otro en las puertas y paredes de las casas, para herir á su salvo á los que fuesen pasando." Marmol, Rebelion de Granada, tom. ii. p. 234.—The best and by far the most minute account of the topography of Galera is given by this author.

than breastplate or helmet, and to a man they were prepared to die rather than surrender.

The fighting-men of the place amounted to three thousand, not including four hundred mercenaries, chiefly Turks and adventurers from the Barbary shore. The town was, moreover, encumbered with some four thousand women and children; though, as far as the women were concerned, they should not be termed an encumbrance in a place where there was no scarcity of food; for they showed all the constancy and contempt of danger possessed by the men, whom they aided not only by tending the sick and wounded, but by the efficient services they rendered them in action. The story of this siege records several examples of these Morisco heroines, whose ferocious valor emulated the doughtiest achievements of the other sex. It is not strange that a place so strong in itself, where the women were animated by as brave a spirit as the men, should have bid defiance to all the efforts of an enemy like Los Velez, though backed by an army in the outset at least as formidable in point of numbers as that which now sat down before it under the command of John of Austria.[8]

---

[8] Marmol, Rebelion de Granada, tom. i. p. 233, et seq.—Vanderhammen, Don Juan de Austria, fol. 112, 113.—Hita, Guerras de Granada, tom. ii. p. 377, et seq.—Hita tells us he was not present at the siege of Galera; but he had in his possession the diary of a Murcian officer named Tomás Perez de Hevia, who served through the siege, and of whom Hita speaks as a person well known for his military science. He says he has conformed implicitly to Hevia's journal, which he commends for its scrupulous veracity. According to the judgment of some critics, the Murcian officer, if he merits this encomium, may be thought to have the advantage of Hita himself.

Having concluded his survey of the ground, the Spanish general gave orders for the construction of three batteries, to operate at the same time on different quarters of the town. The first and largest of these batteries, mounting ten pieces of ordnance, was raised on an eminence on the eastern side of the ravine. Though at a greater distance than was desirable, the position was sufficiently elevated to enable the guns to command the castle and the highest parts of the town.

The second battery, consisting of six heavy cannon, was established lower down the ravine, towards the south, at the distance of hardly more than seventy paces from the perpendicular face of the rock. The remaining battery, composed of only three guns of smaller calibre, was erected in the Gardens, and so placed as to operate against the tower, which, as already noticed, was attached to the church.

The whole number of pieces of artillery belonging to the besiegers did not exceed twenty. But they were hourly expecting a reinforcement of thirteen more from Cartagena. The great body of the forces was disposed behind some high ground on the east, which effectually sheltered the men from the fire of the besieged. The corps of Italian veterans, the flower of the army, was stationed in the Gardens, under command of a gallant officer named Pedro de Padilla. Thus the investment of Galera was complete.

The first object of attack was the tower in the Gardens, from which the Moorish garrison kept up a teasing fire on the Spaniards, as they were employed in the construction of the battery, as well as in digging a trench, in that quarter. No sooner were the guns in position than they delivered their fire, with such effect that an opening was speedily made in the flimsy masonry of the fortress. Padilla, to whom the assault was committed, led forward his men gallantly to the breach, where he was met by the defenders with a spirit equal to his own. A fierce combat ensued. It was not a long one; for the foremost assailants were soon reinforced by others, until they overpowered the little garrison by numbers, and such as escaped the sword took refuge in the defences of the town that adjoined the church.

Flushed with his success in thus easily carrying the tower, which he garrisoned with a strong body of arquebusiers, Don John now determined to make a regular assault on the town, and from this same quarter of the Gardens, as affording the best point of attack. The execution of the affair he intrusted, as before, to Juan de Padilla and his Italian regiment. The guns were then turned against the rampart and the adjoining buildings. Don John pushed forward the siege with vigor, stimulating the men by his own example, carrying fagots on his shoulders for constructing the trenches, and, in short, performing the labors of a common soldier.[9]

By the twenty-fourth of January, practicable breaches had been effected in the ancient wall; and at the appointed signal Padilla and his veterans moved swiftly forward to the attack. They met with little difficulty from the ditch or from the wall, which, never formidable from its height, now presented more than one

---

[9] "Para que los soldados se animasen al trabajo, iba delante de todos á pie, y traía su haz acuestas como cada uno, hasta ponerlo en la trinchea." Marmol, Rebelion de Granada, tom. ii. p. 237.

opening to the assailants. They experienced as little resistance from the garrison. But they had not penetrated far into the town before the aspect of things changed. Their progress was checked by one of those barricades already mentioned as stretched across the streets, behind which a body of musketeers poured well-directed volleys into the ranks of the Christians. At the same time, from the loopholes in the walls of the buildings came incessant showers of musket-balls, arrows, stones, and other missiles, which swept the exposed files of the Spaniards, soon covering the streets with the bodies of the slain and the wounded. It was in vain that the assailants stormed the houses and carried one intrenchment after another. Each house was a separate fortress; and each succeeding barricade, as the ascent became steeper, gave additional advantage to its defenders, by placing them on a greater elevation above their enemy.

Thus beset in front, flank, and rear, the soldiers were completely blinded and bewildered by the pitiless storm which poured on them from their invisible foe. Huddled together, in their confusion they presented an easy mark to the enemy, who shot at random, knowing that every missile would carry its errand of death. It seemed that the besieged had purposely drawn their foes into the snare, by allowing them to enter the town without resistance, until, hemmed in on all sides, they were slaughtered like cattle in the shambles.

The fight had lasted an hour, when Padilla, seeing his best and bravest falling around him, and being himself nearly disabled by a wound, gave the order to retreat,—an order obeyed with such alacrity that the

Spaniards left numbers of their wounded comrades lying in the streets, vainly imploring not to be abandoned to the mercy of their enemies. A greater number than usual of officers and men of rank perished in the assault, their rich arms making them a conspicuous mark amidst the throng of assailants. Among others was a soldier of distinction named Juan de Pacheco. He was a knight of the order of St. James. He had joined the army only a few minutes before the attack, having just crossed the seas from Africa. He at once requested Padilla, who was his kinsman, to allow him to share in the glory of the day. In the heat of the struggle Padilla lost sight of his gallant relative, whose insignia, proclaiming him a soldier of the Cross, made him a peculiar object of detestation to the Moslems; and he soon fell, under a multitude of wounds.[10]

The disasters of the day, however mortifying, were not a bad lesson to the young commander-in-chief, who saw the necessity of more careful preparation before renewing his attempt on the place. He acknowledged the value of his brother's counsel to make free use of artillery and mines before coming to close quarters with the enemy.[11] He determined to open a mine in the perpendicular side of the rock, towards the east, and to run it below the castle and the neighboring

[10] Marmol, Rebelion de Granada, tom. ii. pp. 236-238.—Hevia, ap. Hita, Guerras de Granada, tom. ii. pp. 386, 387.—Vanderhammen, Don Juan de Austria, fol. 113.—Ferreras, Hist. d'Espagne, tom. x. p. 140.

[11] "Convendrá por no aventurar mas gente buena que se haga todo lo que sea posible con las minas y artilleria, ántes de venir á las manos." Carta del Rey á D. Juan de Austria, 6 de Febrero, 1570, MS.

houses on the summit. For this he employed the services of Francesco de Molina, who had so stoutly defended Orgiba, and who was aided in the present work by a skilful Venetian engineer. The rock, consisting of a light and brittle sandstone, was worked with even less difficulty than had been expected. In a short time the gallery was completed, and forty-five barrels of powder were lodged in it. Meanwhile the batteries continued to play with great vivacity on the different quarters of the town and castle. A small breach was opened in the latter, and many buildings on the summit of the rock were overthrown. By the twenty-seventh of January all was ready for the assault.

It was Don John's purpose to assail the place on opposite quarters. Padilla, who still smarted from his wound, was to attack the town, as before, on the side towards the Gardens. The chief object of this manœuvre was to create a diversion in favor of the principal assault, which was to be made on the other side of the rock, where the springing of the mine, it was expected, would open a ready access to the castle. The command on this quarter was given to a brave officer named Antonio Moreno. Don John, at the head of four thousand men, occupied a position which enabled him to overlook the scene of action.

On the twenty-seventh, at eight in the morning, the signal was given by the firing of a cannon; and Padilla, at the head of his veterans, moved forward to the attack. They effected their entrance into the town, with even less opposition than before; for the cannonade from the Gardens had blown away most of the houses, garrisoned by the Moslems, near the wall. But as the assailants pushed on they soon became entangled, as before, in the long and narrow defiles. The enemy, intrenched behind their redoubts thrown across the streets, poured down their murderous volleys into the close ranks of the Spaniards, who were overwhelmed, as on the former occasion, with deadly missiles of all kinds from the occupants of the houses. But experience had prepared them for this; and they had come provided with mantelets, to shelter them from the tempest. Yet, when the annoyance became intolerable, they would storm the dwellings; and a bloody struggle usually ended in putting their inmates to the sword. Each barricade too, as the Spaniards advanced, became the scene of a desperate combat, where the musket was cast aside, and men fought hand to hand, with sword and dagger. Now rose the fierce battle-cries of the combatants, one party calling on Saint Jago, the other on Mohammed, thus intimating that it was still the same war of the Cross and the Crescent which had been carried on for more than eight centuries in the Peninsula."[12] The shouts of the combatants, the clash of weapons, the report of musketry from the adjoining houses, the sounds of falling missiles, filled the air with an unearthly din, that was reverberated and prolonged in countless echoes through the narrow streets, converting the once peaceful city into a pandemonium. Still the Spaniards, though slowly winning their way through every obstacle, were far from the table-land on the

---

[12] " Unos llaman á Mahoma,
otros dicen *Santiago*,
Otros gritan *cierra España*,
muera el bando renegado."
Romance, ap. Hita, Guerras de Granada, tom. ii. p. 456.

summit, where they hoped to join their countrymen from the other quarter of the town. At this crisis a sound arose which overpowered every other sound in this wild uproar, and for a few moments suspended the conflict.

This was the bursting of the mine, which Don John, seeing Padilla well advanced in his assault, had now given the order to fire. In an instant came the terrible explosion, shaking Galera to its centre, rending the portion of the rock above the gallery into fragments, toppling down the houses on its summit, and burying more than six hundred Moriscoes in the ruins. As the smoke and dust of the falling buildings cleared away, and the Spaniards from below beheld the miserable survivors crawling forth, as well as their mangled limbs would allow, they set up a fierce yell of triumph. The mine, however, had done but half the mischief intended; for, by a miscalculation in the direction, it had passed somewhat to the right of the castle, which, as well as the ravelin, remained uninjured. Yet a small breach had been opened by the artillery in the former; and, what was more important, through the shattered sides of the rock itself a passage had been made, which, though strewn with the fallen rubbish, might afford a practicable entrance to the storming-party.

The soldiers, seeing the chasm, now loudly called to be led to the assault. Besides the thirst for vengeance on the rebels who had so long set them at defiance, they were stimulated by the desire of plunder; for Galera, from its great strength, had been selected as a place of deposit for the jewels, rich stuffs, and other articles of value belonging to the people in the neighborhood. The officers, before making the attack, were anxious to examine the breach and have the rubbish cleared away, so as to make the ascent easier for the troops. But the fierce and ill-disciplined levies were too impatient for this. Without heeding the commands or remonstrances of their leaders, one after another they broke their ranks, and, crying the old national war-cries, "*San Jago!*" "*Cierra España!*" "St. James!" and "Close up Spain!" they rushed madly forward, and, springing lightly over the ruins in their pathway, soon planted themselves on the summit. The officers, thus deserted, were not long in following, resolved to avail themselves of the enthusiasm of the men.

Fortunately, the Moriscoes, astounded by the explosion, had taken refuge in the town, and thus left undefended a position which might have given great annoyance to the Spaniards. Yet the cry no sooner rose that the enemy had scaled the heights than, recovering from their panic, they hurried back to man the defences. When the assailants, therefore, had been brought into order and formed into column for the attack, they were received with a well-directed fire from the falconets, and with volleys of musketry from the ravelin, that for a moment checked their advance. But then, rallying, they gallantly pushed forward through the fiery sleet, and soon found themselves in face of the breach which had been made in the castle by their artillery. The opening, scarcely wide enough to allow two to pass abreast, was defended by men as strong and stout-hearted as their assailants. A desperate struggle ensued, in which the besieged bravely held their ground, though a Castilian ensign, named Zapata, succeeded in forcing his way into the place, and even in planting his standard on the battlements. But it was speedily torn down by the enemy, while the brave cavalier, pierced with wounds, was thrown headlong on the rocky ground below, still clutching the standard with his dying grasp.

Meanwhile, the defenders of the ravelin kept up a plunging fire of musketry on the assailants; while stones, arrows, javelins, fell thick as rain-drops on their heads, rattling on the harness of the cavaliers, and inflicting many a wound on the ill-protected bodies of the soldiery. The Morisco women bore a brave part in the fight, showing the same indifference to danger as their husbands and brothers, and rolling down heavy weights on the ranks of the besiegers. These women had a sort of military organization, being formed into companies. Sometimes they even joined in hand-to-hand combats with their enemies, wielding their swords and displaying a prowess worthy of the stronger sex. One of these Amazons, whose name became famous in the siege, was seen on this occasion to kill her antagonist and bear away his armor as the spoils of victory. It was said that, before she received her mortal wound, several Spaniards fell by her hand.[13]

Thus, while the besieged, secure within their de-

[13] No less than eighteen, according to Hevia. But this number, notwithstanding Hita's warrant for the writer's scrupulous accuracy, is somewhat too heavy a tax on the credulity of the reader: " Esta brava mora se llamaba la Zarzamodonia, era corpulenta, recia de miembros, y alcanzaba grandísima fuerza: se averiguó que en este dia mató ella sola por su mano á diez y ocho soldados, no de los peores del campo." Hita, Guerras de Granada, tom. ii. p. 393.

fences, suffered comparatively little, the attacking column was thrown into disorder. Most of its leaders were killed or wounded. Its ranks were thinned by the incessant fire from the ravelin and castle; and, though it still maintained a brave spirit, its strength was fast ebbing away. Don John, who, from his commanding position, had watched the field, saw the necessity of sending to the support of his troops six companies of the reserve, which were soon followed by two others. Thus reinforced, they were enabled to keep their ground.

Meanwhile, the Italian regiment under Padilla had penetrated far into the town. But they had won their way inch by inch, and it had cost them dear. There was not an officer, it was said, that had not been wounded. Four captains had fallen. Padilla, who had not recovered from his former wound, had now received another still more severe. His men, though showing a bold front, had been so roughly handled that it was clear they could never fight through the obstacles in their way and join their comrades on the heights. While little mindful of his own wounds, Padilla saw with anguish the blood of his brave followers thus poured out in vain; and, however reluctantly, he gave the order to retreat. This command was the signal for a fresh storm of missiles from the enemy. But the veterans of Naples, closing up their ranks as a comrade fell, effected their retreat in the same cool and orderly manner in which they had advanced, and, though woefully crippled, regained their position in the trenches.

Thus disengaged from the conflict on this quarter,

the victorious Moslems hastened to the support of their countrymen in the castle, where they served to counterbalance the reinforcement received by the assailants. They fell at once on the rear of the Christians, whose front ranks were galled by the guns from the enemy's battery,—though clumsily served,—while their flanks were sorely scathed by the storm of musketry that swept down from the ravelin. Thus hemmed in on all sides, they were indeed in a perilous situation. Several of the captains were killed. All the officers were either killed or wounded; and the narrow ground on which they struggled for mastery was heaped with the bodies of the slain. Yet their spirits were not broken; and the tide of battle, after three hours' duration, still continued to rage with impotent fury around the fortress. They still strove, with desperate energy, to scale the walls of the ravelin and to force a way through the narrow breach in the castle. But the besieged succeeded in closing up the opening with heavy masses of stone and timber, which defied the failing strength of the assailants.

Another hour had now elapsed, and Don John, as from his station he watched the current of the fight, saw that to prolong the contest would only be to bring wider ruin on his followers. He accordingly gave the order to retreat. But the men who had so impetuously rushed to the attack in defiance of the commands of their officers now showed the same spirit of insubordination when commanded to leave it; like the mastiff, who, maddened by the wounds he has received in the conflict, refuses to loosen his hold on his antagonist, in spite of the chiding of his master. Seeing his orders thus unheeded, Don John, accompanied by his staff, resolved to go in person to the scene of action and enforce obedience by his presence. But on reaching the spot he was hit on his cuirass by a musket-ball, which, although it glanced from the well-tempered metal, came with sufficient force to bring him to the ground. The watchful Quixada, not far distant, sprang to his aid; but it appeared he had received no injury. His conduct, however, brought down an affectionate remonstrance from his guardian, who, reminding him of the king's injunctions, besought him to retire, and not thus expose a life, so precious as that of the commander-in-chief, to the hazards of a common soldier.

The account of the accident soon spread, with the usual exaggerations, among the troops, who, after the prince's departure, yielded a slow and sullen obedience to his commands. Thus for a second time the field of battle remained in possession of the Moslems; and the banner of the Crescent still waved triumphantly from the battlements of Galera.[14]

The loss was a heavy one to the Spaniards, amounting, according to their own accounts,—which will not be suspected of exaggeration,—to not less than four hundred killed and five hundred wounded. That of the enemy, screened by his defences, must have been comparatively light. The loss fell most severely on the Spanish chivalry, whose showy dress naturally drew the

---

[14] For an account of the second assault, see Mendoza, Guerra de Granada, pp. 264, 265,—Marmol, Rebelion de Granada, tom. ii. pp. 240-243.—Vanderhammen, Don Juan de Austria, fol. 113, 114,— Hevia, ap. Hita, Guerras de Granada, tom. ii. p. 389, et seq.,—. Cabrera, Filipe Segundo, pp. 629, 630.

attention of the well-trained Morisco marksmen. The bloody roll is inscribed with the names of many a noble house in both Andalusia and Castile.

This second reverse of his arms stung Don John to the quick. The eyes of his countrymen were upon him; and he well knew the sanguine anticipations they had formed of his campaign, and that they would hold him responsible for its success. His heart was filled with mourning for the loss of his brave companions in arms. Yet he did not give vent to unmanly lamentation; but he showed his feelings in another form, which did little honor to his heart. Turning to his officers, he exclaimed, " The infidels shall pay dear for the Christian blood they have spilt this day. The next assault will place Galera in our power; and every soul within its walls—man, woman, and child—shall be put to the sword. Not one shall be spared. The houses shall be razed to the ground; and the ground they covered shall be sown with salt."[15] This inhuman speech was received with general acclamations. As the event proved, it was not an empty menace.

The result of his operations showed Don John the prudence of his brother's recommendation to make good use of his batteries and his mines before coming to close quarters with the enemy. Philip, in a letter written some time after this defeat, alluding to the low state of discipline in the camp, urged his brother to give greater attention to the morals of the soldiers,—to

[15] "Yo hundiré á Galera, y la asolaré, y sembraré toda de sal; y por el riguroso filo de la espada pasarán chicos y grandes, quantos están dentro, por castigo de su pertinacia, y en venganza de la sangre que han derramado." Marmol, Rebelion de Granada, tom. ii. p. 244.

guard especially against profanity and other offences to religion, that by so doing he might secure the favor of the Almighty.[16] Don John had intimated to Philip that, under some circumstances, it might be necessary to encourage his men by leading them in person to the attack. But the king rebuked the spirit of the knight-errant, as not suited to the commander, and admonished his brother that the place for him was in the rear; that there he might be of service in stimulating the ardor of the remiss; adding that those who went forward promptly in the fight had no need of his presence to encourage them.[17]

Don John lost no time in making his preparations for a third and last assault. He caused two new mines to be opened in the rock, on either side of the former one, and at some thirty paces' distance from it. While this was going on, he directed that all the artillery should play without intermission on the town and castle. His battering-train, meantime, was reinforced by the arrival of fourteen additional pieces of heavy ordnance from Cartagena.

The besieged were no less busy in preparing for their defence. The women and children toiled equally with the men in repairing the damages in the works. The

---

[16] "No puedo yo dejar de encargaros que le tengais muy grande de que él no sea deservido en ese campo, ni haya las maldades y desórdenes que decis, que siendo tales no pueden hacer cosa buena, y así lo procurad, y que no haya juramentos ni otras ofensas de Dios, que con esto él nos ayudará y todo se hará bien." Carta del Rey á D. Juan de Austria, 6 de Febrero, 1570, MS.

[17] "Y con esa gente, segun lo que decis, mas importará estar detras dellos deteniéndolos y castigándolos que no delante, pues para los que lo están y hacen lo que deben no es menester." Ibid.

breaches were closed with heavy stones and timber. The old barricades were strengthened, and new ones thrown across the streets. The magazines were filled with fresh supplies of stones and arrows. Long practice had made the former missile a more formidable weapon than usual in the hands of the Moriscoes. They were amply provided with water, and, as we have seen, were well victualled for a siege longer than this was likely to prove. But in one respect, and that of the last importance, they were miserably deficient. Their powder was nearly all expended. They endeavored to obtain supplies of ammunition, as well as reinforcements of men, from Aben-Aboo. But the Morisco prince was fully occupied at this time with maintaining his ground against the duke of Sesa in the west. His general, El Habaqui, who had charge of the eastern army, encouraged the people of Galera to remain firm, assuring them that before long he should be able to come to their assistance. But time was precious to the besieged.[18]

The Turkish auxiliaries in the garrison greatly doubted the possibility of maintaining themselves, with no better ammunition than stones and arrows, against the well-served artillery of the Spaniards. Their leaders accordingly, in a council of war, proposed that the troops

[18] It is singular that no one of the chroniclers gives us the name of the Moorish chief who commanded in Galera. A romance of the time calls him Abenhozmin:

"Marinero que la rige
Sarracino es natural,
criado acá en nuestra España
por su mal y nuestro mal:
Abenhozmin ha por nombre,
y es hombre de gran caudal."
          Hita, Guerras de Granada, tom. ii. p. 490.

should sally forth and cut their way through the lines of the besiegers, while the women and children might pass out by the subterranean avenue which conducted to the river, the existence of which, we are told, was unknown to the Christians. The Turks, mere soldiers of fortune, had no local attachment or patriotic feeling to bind them to the soil. But when their proposal was laid before the inhabitants, they all, women as well as men, treated the proposition with disdain, showing their determination to defend the city to the last, and to perish amidst its ruins rather than surrender.

Still sustained by the hope of succor, the besieged did what they could to keep off the day of the assault. They did not, indeed, attempt to countermine; for, if they had possessed the skill for this, they had neither tools nor powder. But they made sorties on the miners, and, though always repulsed with loss, they contrived to hold the camp of the besiegers in a constant state of alarm.

On the sixth of February the engineers who had charge of the mines gave notice that their work was completed. The following morning was named for the assault. The orders of the day prescribed that a general cannonade should open on the town at six in the morning. It was to continue an hour, when the mines were to be sprung. The artillery would then play for another hour; after which the signal for the attack would be given. The signal was to be the firing of one gun from each of the batteries, to be followed by a simultaneous discharge from all. The orders directed the troops to show no quarter to man, woman, or child.

On the seventh of February, the last day of the Car-

nival, the besiegers were under arms with the earliest
dawn. Their young commander attracted every eye by
the splendor of his person and appointments. He was
armed *cap-à-pie*, and wore a suit of burnished steel
richly inlaid with gold. His casque, overshadowed
by brilliant plumes, was ornamented with a medallion
displaying the image of the Virgin.[19] In his hand he
carried the baton of command; and as he rode along
the lines, addressing a few words of encouragement to
the soldiers, his perfect horsemanship, his princely
bearing, and the courtesy of his manners, reminded
the veterans of the happier days of his father, the
emperor. The cavaliers by whom he was surrounded
emulated their chief in the richness of their appointments;
and the Murcian chronicler, present on that
day, dwells with complacency on the beautiful array
of Southern chivalry gathered together for the final
assault upon Galera.[20]

From six o'clock till seven, a furious cannonade was
kept up from the whole circle of batteries on the devoted
town. Then came the order to fire the mines. The
deafening roar of ordnance was at once hushed into a
silence profound as that of death, while every soldier
in the trenches waited, with nervous suspense, for the
explosion. At length it came, overturning houses,
shaking down a fragment of the castle, rending wider

[19] " Relumbrante y fortisimo morrion adornado de un penacho bello
y elegante, sentado sobre una rica medalla de la imagen de nuestra
Señora de la Concepcion." Hevia, ap. Hita, Guerras de Granada,
tom. ii. p. 429.

[20] " Igualmente se arreó lo mejor que pudo toda la caballería, y era
cosa digna de ver la elegancia y hermosura de un ejército tan lucido
y gallardo." Ibid., loc. cit.

the breach in the perpendicular side of the rock, and throwing off the fragments with the force of a volcano. Only one mine, however, exploded. It was soon followed by the other, which, though it did less damage, spread such consternation among the garrison that, fearing there might still be a third in reserve, the men abandoned their works and took refuge in the town.

When the smoke and dust had cleared away, an officer with a few soldiers was sent to reconnoitre the breach. They soon returned with the tidings that the garrison had fled and left the works wholly unprotected. On hearing this, the troops, with furious shouts, called out to be led at once to the assault. It was in vain that the officers remonstrated, enforcing their remonstrances, in some instances, by blows with the flat of their sabres. The blood of the soldiery was up; and, like an ill-disciplined rabble, they sprang from their trenches in wild disorder, as before, and, hurrying their officers along with them, soon scaled the perilous ascent, and crowned the heights without opposition from the enemy. Hurrying over the *débris* that strewed the ground, they speedily made themselves masters of the deserted fortress and its outworks,—filling the air with shouts of victory.

The fugitives saw their mistake, as they beheld the enemy occupying the position they had abandoned. There was no more apprehension of mines. Eager to retrieve their error, they rushed back, as by a common impulse, to dispute the possession of the ground with the Spaniards. It was too late. The guns were turned on them from their own battery. The arquebusiers who lined the ravelin showered down on their heads missiles more formidable than stones and arrows. But, though their powder was nearly gone, the Moriscoes could still make fight with sword and dagger, and they boldly closed in a hand-to-hand contest with their enemy. It was a deadly struggle, calling out—as close personal contest is sure to do—the fiercest passions of the combatants. No quarter was given; none was asked. The Spaniard was nerved by the confidence of victory, the Morisco by the energy of despair. Both fought like men who knew that on the issue of this conflict depended the fate of Galera. Again the war-cries of the two religions rose above the din of battle, as the one party invoked their military apostle and the other called on Mahomet. It was the same war-cry which for more than eight centuries had sounded over hill and valley in unhappy Spain. These were its dying notes, soon to expire with the exile or extermination of the conquered race.

The conflict was at length terminated by the arrival of a fresh body of troops on the field with Padilla. That chief had attacked the town by the same avenue as before; everywhere he had met with the same spirit of resistance. But the means of successful resistance were gone. Many of the houses on the streets had been laid in ruins by the fire of the artillery. Such as still held out were defended by men armed with no better weapons than stones and arrows. One after another, most of them were stormed and fired by the Spaniards, and those within were put to the sword or perished in the flames.

It fared no better with the defenders of the barricades. Galled by the volleys of the Christians, against whom their own rude missiles did comparatively little execution, they were driven from one position to another; as each redoubt was successively carried, a shout of triumph went up from the victors, which fell cheerily on the ears of their countrymen on the heights; and when Padilla and his veterans burst on the scene of action, it decided the fortunes of the day.

There was still a detachment of Turks whose ammunition had not been exhausted, and who were maintaining a desperate struggle with a body of Spanish infantry, in which the latter had been driven back to the very verge of the precipice. But the appearance of their friends under Padilla gave the Spaniards new heart; and Turk and Morisco, overwhelmed alike by the superiority of the numbers and of the weapons of their antagonists, gave way in all directions. Some fled down the long avenues which led from the summit of the rock. They were hotly pursued by the Spaniards. Others threw themselves into the houses and prepared to make a last defence. The Spaniards scrambled along the terraces, letting themselves down from one level to another by means of the Moorish ladders used for that purpose. They hewed openings in the wooden roofs of the buildings, through which they fired on those within. The helpless Moriscoes, driven out by the pitiless volleys, sought refuge in the street. But the fierce hunters were there, waiting for their miserable game, which they shot down without mercy, — men, women, and children; none were spared. Yet they did not fall unavenged; and the corpse of many a Spaniard might be seen stretched on the bloody pavement, lying side by side with that of his Moslem enemy.

More than one instance is recorded of the desperate

courage to which the women as well as the men were roused in their extremity. A Morisco girl, whose father had perished in the first assault in the Gardens, after firing her dwelling, is said to have dragged her two little brothers along with one hand, and, wielding a scimitar with the other, to have rushed against the foe, by whom they were all speedily cut to pieces. Another instance is told, of a man who, after killing his wife and his two daughters, sallied forth, and, calling out, "There is nothing more to lose; let us die together!" threw himself madly into the thick of the enemy.[21] Some fell by their own weapons, others by those of their friends, preferring to receive death from any hands but those of the Spaniards.

Some two thousand Moriscoes were huddled together in a square not far from the gate, where a strong body of Castilian infantry cut off the means of escape. Spent with toil and loss of blood, without ammunition, without arms, or with such only as were too much battered or broken for service, the wretched fugitives would gladly have made some terms with their pursuers, who now closed darkly around them. But the stag at bay might as easily have made terms with his hunters and the fierce hounds that were already on his haunches. Their prayers were answered by volley after volley, until not a man was left alive.

More than four hundred women and children were gathered together without the walls, and the soldiers, mindful of the value of such a booty, were willing to spare their lives. This was remarked by Don John,

---

[21] These anecdotes are given by Hevia, ap. Hita, Guerras de Granada, tom. ii. pp. 449-451.

and no sooner did he observe the symptoms of lenity in the troops than the flinty-hearted chief rebuked their remissness and sternly reminded them of the orders of the day. He even sent the halberdiers of his guard and the cavaliers about his person to assist the soldiers in their bloody work; while he sat, a calm spectator, on his horse, as immovable as a marble statue, and as insensible to the agonizing screams of his victims and their heart-breaking prayers for mercy."

While this was going on without the town, the work of death was no less active within. Every square and enclosure that had afforded a temporary refuge to the fugitives was heaped with the bodies of the slain. Blood ran down the kennels like water after a heavy shower. The dwellings were fired, some by the conquerors, others by the inmates, who threw themselves madly into the flames rather than fall into the hands of their enemies. The gathering shadows of evening —for the fight had lasted nearly nine hours[73]—were dispelled by the light of the conflagration, which threw an ominous glare for many a league over the country, proclaiming far and wide the downfall of Galera.

At length Don John was so far moved from his original purpose as to consent that the women, and the children under twelve years of age, should be spared. This he did, not from any feeling of compunction, but from deference to the murmurs of his followers, whose

[20] "Los quales mataron mas de une quientas mugeres y niños ... y ansi hizo matar muchos en su posada á los alabarderos de su guardia." Marmol, Rebelion de Granada, tom. ii. p. 248.

[73] "Duró el combate, despues de entrado el lugar, desde las ocho de la mañana hasta las cinco de la tarde." Hevia, ap. Hita, Guerras de Granada, tom. ii. p. 448.

discontent at seeing their customary booty snatched from them began to show itself in a way not to be disregarded.[24] Some fifteen hundred women and children, in consequence of this, are said to have escaped the general doom of their countrymen.[25] All the rest, soldiers and citizens, Turks, Africans, and Moriscoes, were mercilessly butchered. Not one man, if we may trust the Spaniards themselves, escaped alive! It would not be easy, even in that age of blood, to find a parallel to so wholesale and indiscriminate a massacre.

Yet, to borrow the words of the Castilian proverb, "If Africa had cause to weep, Spain had little reason to rejoice."[26] No success during the war was purchased at so high a price as the capture of Galera. The loss fell as heavily on the officers and men of rank as on the common file. We have seen the eagerness with which they had flocked to the standard of John of Austria. They showed the same eagerness to distinguish themselves under the eye of their leader. The Spanish chivalry were sure to be found in the post of danger. Dearly did they pay for that pre-eminence; and many

---

[24] "Y no paráran hasta acabarlas á todas, si las quejas de los soldados, á quien se quitaba el premio de la vitoria, no le movieran; mas esto fue quando se entendió que la villa estaba ya por nosotros, y no quiso que se perdonase á varon que pasase de doce años." Marmol, Rebelion de Granada, tom. ii. p. 248.

[25] "Se cautivaron hasta otras mil y quinientas personas de mugeres y niños, porque á hombre ninguno se tomó con vida, habiendo muerto todos sin quedar uno en este dia, y en los asaltos pasados." Hevia, ap. Hita, Guerras de Granada, tom. ii. p. 448.—Marmol, while he admits that not a man was spared, estimates the number of women and children saved at three times that given in the text.

[26] "Si Africa llora, España no rie."

a noble house in Spain wept bitter tears when the tidings came of the conquest of Galera.[27]

Don John himself was so much exasperated, says the chronicler, by the thought of the grievous loss which he had sustained through the obstinate resistance of the heretics,[28] that he resolved to carry at once into effect his menace of demolishing the town, so that not one stone should be left on another. Every house was accordingly burnt or levelled to the ground, which was then strewed with salt, as an accursed spot, on which no man was to build thereafter. A royal decree to that effect was soon afterwards published; and the village of straggling houses, which, undefended by a wall, still clusters round the base of the hill, in the Gardens occupied by Padilla, is all that now serves to remind the traveller of the once flourishing and strongly fortified city of Galera.

In the work of demolition Don John was somewhat retarded by a furious tempest of sleet and rain, which set in the day after the place was taken. It was no uncommon thing at that season of the year. Had it come on a few days earlier, the mountain-torrents would infallibly have broken up the camp of the besiegers and compelled them to suspend operations. That the storm

---

[27] For the account of the final assault, as told by the various writers, with sufficient inconsistency in the details, compare Marmol, Rebelion de Granada, tom. ii. pp. 244-249,—Mendoza, Guerra de Granada, pp. 266-268,—Vanderhammen, Don Juan de Austria, fol. 114, 115,—Hevia, ap. Hita, Guerras de Granada, tom. ii. p. 429, et seq.,—Cabrera, Filipe Segundo, pp. 630, 631.—Bleda, Cronica, p. 734,—Ferreras, Hist. d'Espagne, tom. x. pp. 143, 144.

[28] " Tanto le crecia la ira, pensando en el daño que aquellos hereges habian hecho." Marmol, Rebelion de Granada, tom. ii. p. 248.

was so long delayed was regarded by the Spaniards as a special interposition of Heaven.

The booty was great which fell into the hands of the victors; for Galera, from its great strength, had been selected by the inhabitants of the neighboring country as a safe place of deposit for their effects,—especially their more valuable treasures of gold, pearls, jewels, and precious stuffs. Besides these there was a great quantity of wheat, barley, and other grain stored in the magazines, which afforded a seasonable supply to the army.

No sooner was Don John master of Galera than he sent tidings of his success to his brother. The king was at that time paying his devotions at the shrine of Our Lady of Guadalupe. The tidings were received with exultation by the court,—by Philip with the stolid composure with which he usually received accounts either of the success or the discomfiture of his arms. He would allow no public rejoicings of any kind. The only way in which he testified his satisfaction was by offering up thanks to God and the Blessed Virgin, " to whom," says the chronicler, " he thought the cause should be especially commended, as one in which more glory was to be derived from peace than from a bloody victory." [29] With such humane and rational sentiments, it is marvellous that he did not communicate them to his brother, and thus spare the atrocious massacre of his Morisco vassals at Galera.

But, however revolting this massacre may appear in

---

[29] " Solo dar gracias á Dios y á la gloriosa virgen Maria, encomendandoles el Catholico Rey aquel negocio, por ser de calidad, que deseaba mas gloria de la concordia y paz, que de la vitoria sangrienta." Marmol, Rebelion de Granada, tom. ii. p. 249.

our eyes, it seems to have left no stain on the reputation of John of Austria in the eyes of his contemporaries. In reviewing this campaign, we cannot too often call to mind that it was regarded not so much as a war with rebellious vassals as a war with the enemies of the Faith. It was the last link in that long chain of hostilities which the Spaniard for so many centuries had been waging for the recovery of his soil from the infidel. The sympathies of Christendom were not the less on his side that now, when the trumpet of the crusader had ceased to send forth its notes in other lands, they should still be heard among the hills of Granada. The Moriscoes were everywhere regarded as infidels and apostates; and there were few Christian nations whose codes would not at that day have punished infidelity and apostasy with death. It was no harder for them that they should be exterminated by the sword than by the fagot. So far from the massacre of the Moriscoes tarnishing the reputation of their conqueror, it threw a gloomy *éclat* over his achievement, which may have rather served to add to its celebrity. His own countrymen, thinking only of the extraordinary difficulties which he had overcome, with pride beheld him entering on a splendid career, that would place his name among those of the great paladins of the nation. In Rome he was hailed as the champion of Christendom; and it was determined to offer him the baton of generalissimo of the formidable league which the pope was at this time organizing against the Ottoman Empire.[30]

[30] "Cela faict, par sa renommée qui voloit par le monde, tant des chrestiens que des infidelles, il fut faict general de la saincte ligue." Brantôme, Œuvres, tom. i. p. 326.

CHAPTER VIII.

REBELLION OF THE MORISCOES.

Disaster at Seron.—Death of Quixada.—Rapid Successes of Don John.—Submission of the Moriscoes.—Fate of El Habaqui.—Stern Temper of Aben-Aboo.—Renewal of the War.—Expulsion of the Moors.—Don John returns to Madrid.—Murder of Aben-Aboo.—Fortunes of the Moriscoes.

1570–1571.

DON JOHN was detained some days before Galera by the condition of the roads, which the storm had rendered impassable for heavy wagons and artillery. When the weather improved, he began his march, moving south in the direction of Baza. Passing through that ancient town, the scene of one of the most glorious triumphs of the good Queen Isabella the Catholic, he halted at Caniles. Here he left the main body of his army, and, putting himself at the head of a detachment of three thousand foot and two hundred horse, hastened forward to reconnoitre Seron, which he purposed next to attack.

Seron was a town of some strength, situated on the slope of the sierra, and defended by a castle held by a Morisco garrison. On his approach, most of the inhabitants, and many of the soldiers, evacuated the place and sought refuge among the mountains. Don John formed his force into two divisions, one of which he placed under Quixada, the other under Requesens. He took up a position himself, with a few cavaliers and a small body of arquebusiers, on a neighboring eminence, which commanded a view of the whole ground.

The two captains were directed to reconnoitre the environs by making a circuit from opposite sides of the town. Quixada, as he pressed forward with his column, drove the Morisco fugitives before him until they vanished in the recesses of the mountains. In the mean time the beacon-fires, which for some hours had been blazing from the topmost peaks of the sierra, had spread intelligence far and wide of the coming of the enemy. The whole country was in arms; and it was not long before the native warriors, mustering to the number of six thousand, under the Morisco chief El Habaqui, who held command in that quarter, came pouring through the defiles of the mountains and fell with fury on the front and flank of the astonished Spaniards. The assailants were soon joined by the fugitives from Seron; and the Christians, unable to withstand this accumulated force, gave way, though slowly and in good order, before the enemy.

Meanwhile, a detachment of Spanish infantry, under command of Lope de Figueroa, *maestro del campo*, had broken into the town, where they were busily occupied in plundering the deserted houses. This was a part of the military profession which the rude levies of Andalusia well understood. While they were thus occupied, the advancing Moriscoes, burning for revenge, burst into the streets of the town, and, shouting their horrid war-cries, set furiously on the marauders. The Spaniards, taken by surprise and encumbered with their booty, offered little resistance. They were seized with a panic, and fled in all directions. They were soon mingled with their retreating comrades under Quixada, everywhere communicating their own terror, till the confusion became general. It was in vain that Quixada and Figueroa, with the other captains, endeavored to restore order. The panic-stricken soldiers heard nothing, saw nothing, but the enemy.

At this crisis Don John, who from his elevated post had watched the impending ruin, called his handful of brave followers around him, and at once threw himself into the midst of the tumult. "What means this, Spaniards?" he exclaimed. "From whom are you flying? Where is the honor of Spain? Have you not John of Austria, your commander, with you? At least, if you retreat, do it like brave men, with your front to the enemy."[1] It was in vain. His entreaties, his menaces, even his blows, which he dealt with the flat of his sabre, were ineffectual to rouse any thing like a feeling of shame in the cowardly troops. The efforts of his captains were equally fruitless, though in making them they exposed their lives with a recklessness which cost some of them dear. Figueroa was disabled by a wound in the leg. Quixada was hit by a musket-ball on the left shoulder, and struck from his saddle. Don John, who was near, sprang to his assistance and placed him in the hands of some troopers, with directions to bear him at once to Caniles. In doing this the young

---

[1] "Qué es esto, Españoles? de qué huis? dónde está la honra de España? No teneis delante á Don Juan de Austria, vuestro capitan? de qué temeis? Retiraos con orden como hombres de guerra con el rostro al enemigo." Marmol, Rebelion de Granada, tom. ii. p. 257.

commander himself had a narrow escape; for he was struck on his helmet by a ball, which, however, fortunately glanced off without doing him injury.[2] He was now hurried along by the tide of fugitives, who made no attempt to rally for the distance of half a league, when the enemy ceased his pursuit. Six hundred Spaniards were left dead on the field. A great number threw themselves into the houses, prepared to make good their defence. But they were speedily enveloped by the Moriscoes, the houses were stormed or set on fire, and the inmates perished to a man.[3]

Don John, in a letter dated the nineteenth of February, two days after this disgraceful affair, gave an account of it to the king, declaring that the dastardly conduct of the troops exceeded any thing he had ever witnessed, or indeed could have believed, had he not seen it with his own eyes. "They have so little heart in the service," he adds, "that no effort that I can make, not even the fear of the galleys or the gibbet, can prevent them from deserting. Would to Heaven I could think that they are moved to this by the desire to return to their families, and not by fear of the enemy!"[4] He gave the particulars of Quixada's acci-

[2] "Acudiendo á todas las necesidades con peligro de su persona, porque le dieron un escopetazo en la cabeza sobre una celada fuerte que llevaba, que á no ser tan buena, le mataran." Marmol, Rebelion de Granada, tom. ii. p. 258.

[3] Carta de D. Juan de Austria al Rey, 19 de Febrero, 1570, MS.—Marmol, Rebelion de Granada, tom. ii. p. 253. et seq.—Mendoza, Guerra de Granada, p. 273.—Villafañe, Vida de Magdalena de Ulloa.—Vanderhammen, Don Juan de Austria, fol. 116, 117.

[4] "Conforme á esto entenderá V. M. la poca costancia y aficion que tienen á la guerra, estos que la dejan al mejor tiempo sin poderles reprimir galeras, ni horca ni cuantas diligencias se hacen. Y plega á

dent, stating that the surgeons had made six incisions before they could ascertain where the ball, which had penetrated the shoulder, was lodged, and that, with all their efforts, they had as yet been unable to extract it. "I now deeply feel," he says, "how much I have been indebted to his military experience, his diligence and care, and how important his preservation is to the service of your majesty. I trust in God he may be permitted to regain his health, which is now in a critical condition."[5]

In his reply to this letter, the king expressed his sense of the great loss which both he and his brother would sustain by the death of Quixada. "You will keep me constantly advised of the state of his health," he says. "I know well it is unnecessary for me to impress upon you the necessity of watching carefully over him." Philip did not let the occasion pass for administering a gentle rebuke to Don John for so lightly holding the promise he had made to him from Galera, not again to expose himself heedlessly to danger. "When I think of your narrow escape at Seron, I cannot express the pain I have felt at your rashly incurring such a risk. In war, every one should confine himself to the duties of his own station; nor should the general affect to play the part of the soldier, any more than the soldier that of the general."[6]

Dios que el amor de los hijos y parientes sea la causa y no miedo de los enemigos." Carta de D. Juan de Austria al Rey, 19 de Febrero, 1570, MS.

[5] Ibid.

[6] "Que cada uno ha de hacer su oficio y no el general de soldado, ni el soldado el de general." Carta del Rey á D. Juan de Austria, 24 de Febrero, 1570, MS.

It seems to have been a common opinion that Don John was more fond of displaying his personal prowess than became one of his high rank; in short, that he showed more the qualities of a knight-errant than those of a great commander.[7]

Meanwhile, Quixada's wound, which from the first had been attended with alarming symptoms, grew so much worse as to baffle all the skill of the surgeons. His sufferings were great, and every hour he grew weaker. Before a week had elapsed, it became evident that his days were numbered.

The good knight received the intelligence with composure,—for he did not fear death. He had not the happiness in this solemn hour to have her near him on whose conjugal love and tenderness he had reposed for so many years.[8] But the person whom he cherished

---

[7] One evidence of this is afforded by the frankness of his friend Ruy Gomez de Silva. "La primera," he writes to Don John, "que por cuanto V. Ex.ª está reputado de atrevido y de hombre que quiere mas ganar crédito de soldado que de general, que mude este estilo y se deje gobernar." (Carta de 4 de Marzo, 1570, MS.) It is to Don John's credit that, in his reply, he thanks Ruy Gomez warmly for his admonition, and begs his monitor to reprove him without hesitation whenever he deems it necessary, since, now that his guardian is gone, there is no other who can take this liberty. Carta de D. Juan de Austria á Ruy Gomez de Silva, MS.

[8] According to Villafañe, Doña Magdalena left Madrid on learning her husband's illness, and travelled with such despatch that she arrived in time to receive his last sighs. Hita also speaks of her presence at his bedside. But, as seven days only elapsed between the date of the knight's wound and that of his death, one finds it difficult to believe that this could have allowed time for the courier who brought the tidings, and for the lady afterwards, whether in the saddle or litter, to have travelled a distance of over four hundred and fifty miles, along execrable roads, with much of the way lying through the wild passes of the Alpujarras.

next to his wife, Don John of Austria, was by his bedside, watching over him with the affectionate solicitude of a son, and ministering those kind offices which soften the bitterness of death. The dying man retained his faculties to the last, and dictated, though he had not the strength to sign, a letter to the king, requesting some favor for his widow in consideration of his long services. He then gave himself up wholly to his spiritual concerns; and on the twenty-fourth of February, 1570, he gently expired, in the arms of his foster-son.

Quixada received a soldier's funeral. His obsequies were celebrated with the military pomp suited to his station. His remains, accompanied by the whole army, with arms reversed and banners trailing in the dust, were borne in solemn procession to the church of the Jeronymites in Caniles; and "we may piously trust," says the chronicler, "that the soul of Don Luis rose up to heaven with the sweet incense which burned on the altars of St. Jerome; for he spent his life, and finally lost it, in fighting like a valiant soldier the battles of the faith."[9]

Quixada was austere in his manners, and a martinet in enforcing discipline. He was loyal in his nature, of spotless integrity, and possessed so many generous and knightly qualities that he commanded the respect of his comrades; and the regret for his loss was uni-

[9] " Creemos piadosamente que el alma de D. Luis subiria al cielo con el oloroso inciænso que se quemó en los altares de S. Gerónimo, porque siempre habia empleado la vida en pelear contra enemigos de nuestra santa fé, y por último murió batallando con ellos como soldado valeroso." Hita, Guerras de Granada, tom. ii. p. 487.

versal. Philip, writing to Don John, a few days after the event, remarks, "I did not think that any letter from you could have given me so much pain as that acquainting me with the death of Quixada. I fully comprehend the importance of his loss both to myself and to you, and cannot wonder you should feel it so keenly. It is impossible to allude to it without sorrow. Yet we may be consoled by the reflection that, living and dying as he did, he cannot fail to have exchanged this world for a better." [10]

Quixada's remains were removed, the year following, to his estate at Villagarcia, where his disconsolate widow continued to reside. Immediately after her lord's decease, Don John wrote to Doña Magdalena, from the camp, a letter of affectionate condolence, which came from the fulness of his heart: "Luis died as became him, fighting for the glory and safety of his son, and covered with immortal honor. Whatever I am, whatever I shall be, I owe to him by whom I was formed, or rather begotten in a nobler birth. Dear sorrowing widowed mother! I only am left to you; and to you indeed do I of right belong, for whose sake Luis died and you have been stricken with this woe. Moderate your grief with your wonted wisdom. Would that I were near you now, to dry your tears, or mingle mine with them! Farewell, dearest and most honored mother! and pray to God to send back your son from these wars to your bosom." [11]

[10] Carta del Rey á D. Juan de Austria, 3 de Marzo, 1570, MS.

[11] The letter is translated by Stirling from a manuscript, entitled "Joannis Austriaci Vita, auctore Antonio Ossorio," in the National Library at Madrid. See Cloister Life of Charles the Fifth (Am. ed.), p. 286.

Doña Magdalena survived her husband many years, employing her time in acts of charity and devotion. From Don John she ever experienced the same filial tenderness which he evinces in the letter above quoted. Never did he leave the country or return to it without first paying his respects to his mother, as he always called her. She watched with maternal pride his brilliant career; and when that was closed by an early death, the last link which had bound her to this world was snapped forever. Yet she continued to live on till near the close of the century, dying in 1598, and leaving behind her a reputation for goodness and piety little less than that of a saint.

Don John, having paid the last tribute of respect to the memory of his guardian, collected his whole strength and marched at once against Seron. But the enemy, shrinking from an encounter with so formidable a force, had abandoned the place before the approach of the Spaniards. The Spanish commander soon after encountered El Habaqui in the neighborhood, and defeated him. He then marched on Tijola, a town perched on a bold cliff, which a resolute garrison might have easily held against an enemy. But the Moriscoes, availing themselves of the darkness of the night, stole out of the place, and succeeded, without much loss, in escaping through the lines of the besiegers.[12] The fall of Tijola was followed by that of Purchena. In a short

[12] Tijola is the scene of the story, familiar to every lover of Castilian romance, and better suited to romance than history, of the Moor Tuzani and his unfortunate mistress, the beautiful Maleha. It forms a most pleasing episode in Hita's second volume (pp. 523-540), and is translated with pathos and delicacy by Circourt, Hist. des Arabes d'Espagne, tom. iii. p. 345, et seq.

time the whole Rio de Almanzora was overrun, and the victorious general, crossing the southeastern borders of the Alpujarras, established his quarters, on the second of May, at Padules, about two leagues from Andarax.

These rapid successes are not to be explained simply by Don John's superiority over the enemy in strength or military science. Philip had turned a favorable ear to the pope's invitation to join the league against the Turk, in which he was complimented by having the post of commander-in-chief offered to his brother, John of Austria. But before engaging in a new war it was most desirable for him to be released from that in which he was involved with the Moriscoes. He had already seen enough of the sturdy spirit of that race to be satisfied that to accomplish his object by force would be a work of greater time than he could well afford. The only alternative, therefore, was to have recourse to the conciliatory policy which had been so much condemned in the marquis of Mondejar. Instructions to that effect were accordingly sent to Don John, who, heartily weary of this domestic contest, and longing for a wider theatre of action, entered warmly into his brother's views. Secret negotiations were soon opened with El Habaqui, the Morisco chief, who received the offer of such terms for himself and his countrymen as left him in no doubt, at least, as to the side on which his own interest lay. As a preliminary step, he was to withdraw his support from the places in the Rio de Almanzora; and thus the war, brought within the narrower range of the Alpujarras, might be more easily disposed of. This part of his agreement had been faithfully executed; and the rebellious district on the eastern borders of the Alpujarras had, as we have seen, been brought into subjection with little cost of life to the Spaniards.

Don John followed this up by a royal proclamation, promising an entire amnesty for the past to all who within twenty days should tender their submission. They were to be allowed to state the grievances which had moved them to take up arms, with an assurance that these should be redressed. All who refused to profit by this act of grace, with the exception of the women, and of children under fourteen years of age, would be put to the sword without mercy.

What was the effect of the proclamation we are not informed. It was probably not such as had been anticipated. The Moriscoes, distressed as they were, did not trust the promises of the Spaniards. At least we find Don John, who had now received a reinforcement of two thousand men, distributing his army into detachments, with orders to scour the country and deal with the inhabitants in a way that should compel them to submit. Such of the wretched peasantry as had taken refuge in their fastnesses were assailed with shot and shell and slaughtered by hundreds. Some, who had hidden with their families in the caves in which the country abounded, were hunted out by their pursuers, or suffocated by the smoke of burning fagots at the entrance of their retreats. Everywhere the land was laid waste, so as to afford sustenance for no living thing. Such were the conciliatory measures employed by the government for the reduction of the rebels.[13]

[13] Marmol, Rebelion de Granada, tom. ii. pp. 290-320, 340-346.—

Meanwhile, the duke of Sesa had taken the field on the northern border of the Alpujarras, with an army of ten thousand foot and two thousand horse. He was opposed by Aben-Aboo with a force which in point of numbers was not inferior to his own. The two commanders adopted the same policy; avoiding pitched battles, and confining themselves to the desultory tactics of guerilla warfare,—to skirmishes and surprises; while each endeavored to distress his adversary by cutting off his convoys and by wasting the territory with fire and sword. The Morisco chief had an advantage in the familiarity of his men with this wild mountain-fighting, and in their better knowledge of the intricacies of the country. But this was far more than counterbalanced by the superiority of the Spaniards in military organization, and by their possession of cavalry, artillery, and muskets, in all of which the Moslems were lamentably deficient. Thus, although no great battle was won by the Christians, although they were sorely annoyed, and their convoys of provisions frequently cut off, by the skirmishing-parties of the enemy, they continued steadily to advance, driving the Moriscoes before them, and securing the permanency of their conquests by planting a line of forts, well garrisoned, along the wasted territory in their rear. By the beginning of May the duke of Sesa had reached the borders of the Mediterranean, and soon after united his forces, greatly diminished by desertion, to those of Don John of Austria at Padules.[14]

Vanderhammen, Don Juan de Austria, fol. 119, et seq.—Ferreras, Hist. d'Espagne, tom. x. p. 170, et seq.

[14] Mendoza, Guerra de Granada, p. 271, et seq.—Marmol, Rebelion

Negotiations during this time had been resumed with El Habaqui, who, with the knowledge, if not the avowed sanction, of Aben-Aboo, had come to a place called Fondon de Andarax, not far distant from the headquarters of the Spanish commander-in-chief. He was accompanied by several of the principal Moriscoes, who were to take part in the discussions. On the thirteenth of May they were met by the deputies from the Castilian camp, and the conference was opened. It soon appeared that the demands of the Moriscoes were wholly inadmissible. They insisted not only on a general amnesty, but that things should be restored to the situation in which they were before the edicts of Philip the Second had given rise to the rebellion. The Moorish commissioners were made to understand that they were to negotiate only on the footing of a conquered race. They were advised to prepare a memorial preferring such requests as might be reasonably granted; and they were offered the services of Juan de Soto, Don John's secretary, to aid them in drafting the document. They were counselled, moreover, to see their master, Aben-Aboo, and obtain full powers from him to conclude a definitive treaty.

Aben-Aboo, ever since his elevation to the stormy sovereignty of the Alpujarras, had maintained his part

---

de Granada, tom. ii. pp. 283-289, 303-315, 321, et seq.—In a letter without date, of the duke of Sesa, forming part of a mass of correspondence which I was so fortunate as to obtain from the collection at Holland House, he insists on starvation as a much more effectual means of reducing the enemy than the sword: " Esta guerra parece que no puede acabarse por medio mas cierto que el de la hambre que necesitará á los enemigos á rendirse ó perecer, y esta los acabará primero que el espada." MS.

with a spirit worthy of his cause. But as he beheld town after town fall away from his little empire, his people butchered or swept into slavery, his lands burned and wasted, until the fairest portions were converted into a wilderness,—above all, when he saw that his cause excited no sympathy in the bosoms of the Moslem princes, on whose support he had mainly relied,—he felt more and more satisfied of the hopelessness of a contest with the Spanish monarchy. His officers, and indeed the people at large, had come to the same conviction ; and nothing but an intense hatred of the Spaniards, and a distrust of their good faith, had prevented the Moriscoes from throwing down their arms and accepting the promises of grace which had been held out to them. The disastrous result of the recent campaign against the duke of Sesa tended still further to the discouragement of the Morisco chief; and El Habaqui and his associates returned with authority from their master to arrange terms of accommodation with the Spaniards.

On the nineteenth of May the commissioners from each side again met at Fondon de Andarax. A memorial drafted by Juan de Soto was laid before Don John, whose quarters, as we have seen, were in the immediate neighborhood. No copy of the instrument has been preserved, or at least none has been published. From the gracious answer returned by the prince, we may infer that it contained nothing deemed objectionable by the conquerors.

The deputies were not long in agreeing on terms of accommodation,—or rather of submission. It was settled that the Morisco captain should proceed to the

Christian camp, and there, presenting himself before the commander-in-chief, should humbly crave forgiveness and tender submission on behalf of his nation; that in return for this act of humiliation a general amnesty should be granted to his countrymen, who, though they were no longer to be allowed to occupy the Alpujarras, would be protected by the government wherever they might be removed. More important concessions were made to Aben-Aboo and El Habaqui. The last-mentioned chief, as the chronicler tells us, obtained all that he asked for his master, as well as for himself and his friends.[15] Such politic concessions by the Spaniards had doubtless their influence in opening the eyes of the Morisco leaders to the folly of protracting the war in their present desperate circumstances.

The same evening on which the arrangement was concluded, El Habaqui proceeded to his interview with the Spanish commander. He was accompanied by one only of the Morisco deputies. The others declined to witness the spectacle of their nation's humiliation. He was attended, however, by a body of three hundred arquebusiers. On entering the Christian lines, his little company was surrounded by four regiments of Castilian infantry and escorted to the presence of John of Austria, who stood before his tent, attended by his officers, from whom his princely bearing made him easily distinguished.

El Habaqui, alighting from his horse and prostrating himself before the prince, exclaimed, "Mercy! We

---

[15] "Con estas cosas y otras particulares que El Habaqui pidió para Aben Aboo, y para los amigos, y para sí mismo, que todas se le concedieron." Marmol, Rebelion de Granada, tom. ii. p. 360.

implore your highness, in the name of his majesty, to show us mercy, and to pardon our transgressions, which we acknowledge have been great!"[16] Then unsheathing his scimitar, he presented it to Don John, saying that he surrendered his arms to his majesty in the name of Aben-Aboo and the rebel chiefs for whom he was empowered to act. At the same time the secretary, Juan de Soto, who had borne the Moorish banner, given him by El Habaqui, on the point of his lance, cast it on the ground before the feet of the prince. The whole scene made a striking picture, in which the proud conqueror, standing with the trophies of victory around him, looked down on the representative of the conquered race, as he crouched in abject submission at his feet. Don John, the predominant figure in the tableau, by his stately demeanor tempered with a truly royal courtesy, reminded the old soldiers of his father the emperor, and they exclaimed, "This is the true son of Charles the Fifth!"

Stooping forward, he graciously raised the Morisco chief from the ground, and, returning him his sword, bade him employ it henceforth in the service of the king. The ceremony was closed by flourishes of trumpets and salvoes of musketry, as if in honor of some great victory.

El Habaqui remained some time after his followers had left the camp, where he met with every attention, was feasted and caressed by the principal officers, and was even entertained at a banquet by the bishop of

---

[16] "Misericordia, Señor, misericordia nos conceda vuestra Alteza en nombre de su Magestad, y perdon de nuestras culpas, que conocemos haber sido graves." Marmol, Rebelion de Granada, tom. ii. p. 361.

Guadix. He received, however, as we have seen, something more substantial than compliments. Under these circumstances it was natural that he should become an object of jealousy and suspicion to the Moriscoes. It was soon whispered that El Habaqui, in his negotiations with the Christians, had been more mindful of his own interests than of those of his countrymen."

Indeed, the Moriscoes had little reason to congratulate themselves on the result of a treaty which left them in the same forlorn and degraded condition as before the breaking out of the rebellion,—which in one important respect, indeed, left them in a worse condition, since they were henceforth to become exiles from the homes of their fathers. Yet, cruel and pitiable in the extreme as was the situation of the Moriscoes, the Spanish monks, as Don John complains to his brother, inveighed openly in their pulpits against the benignity and mercy of the king;[18] and this too, he adds, when it should rather have been their duty to intercede for poor wretches who for the most part had sinned through ignorance.[19] The ecclesiastic on whom his censure most heavily falls is the President Deza,—a man held in such abhorrence by the Moriscoes as to have been one principal cause of their insurrection; and he beseeches the king to consult the interests of Granada

[17] The fullest account of these proceedings is to be found in Marmol, Rebelion de Granada, tom. ii. pp. 355-362.

[18] " Predicando en los púlpitos publicamente contra la benignidad y clemencia que V. M. ha mandado usar con esta gente." Carta de D. Juan de Austria al Rey, 7 de Junio, 1570, MS.

[19] " Que los religiosos que habrian de interceder con V. M. por estos miserables, que cierto la mayor parte ha pecado con ignorancia, hagan su esfuerzo en reprender la clemencia." Ibid.

by bestowing on him a bishopric, or some other dignity, which may remove him from the present scene of his labors.[20]

Among those disappointed at the terms of the treaty, as it soon appeared, was Aben-Aboo himself. At first he affected to sanction it, and promised to do all he could to enforce its execution. But he soon cooled, and, throwing the blame on El Habaqui, declared that this officer had exceeded his powers, made a false report to him of his negotiations, and sacrificed the interests of the nation to his own ambition.[21] The attentions lavished on that chief by the Spaniards, his early correspondence with them, and the liberal concessions secured to him by the treaty, furnished plausible grounds for such an accusation.

According to the Spanish accounts, however, Aben-Aboo at this time received a reinforcement of two hundred soldiers from Barbary, with the assurance that he would soon have more effectual aid from Africa. This, we are told, changed his views. Nor is it impossible that the Morisco chief, as the hour approached, found it a more difficult matter than he had anticipated to resign his royal state and descend into the common

[20] "The wise king," as Bleda tells us, "did not forget Deza's eminent services. He became one of the richest cardinals, passing the remainder of his days in Rome, where he built a sumptuous palace for his residence." (Cronica de España, p. 753.) Unfortunately, this happy preferment did not take place till some time later,—too late for the poor Moriscoes to profit by it.

[21] "Que el Habaqui habia mirado mal por el bien comun, contentandose con lo que solamente Don Juan de Austria le habia querido conceder, y procurando el bien y provecho para si y para sus deudos." Marmol, Rebelion de Granada, tom. ii. p. 390.

rank and file of the vassals of Castile,—the degraded caste of Moorish vassals, whose condition was little above that of serfs.

However this may be, the Spanish camp was much disquieted by the rumors which came in of Aben-Aboo's vacillation. It was even reported that, far from endeavoring to enforce the execution of the treaty, he was secretly encouraging his people to further resistance. No one felt more indignant at his conduct than El Habaqui, who had now become as loyal a subject as any other in Philip's dominions. Not a little personal resentment was mingled with his feeling towards Aben-Aboo; and he offered, if Don John would place him at the head of a detachment, to go himself, brave the Morisco prince in his own quarters, and bring him as a prisoner to the camp. Don John, though putting entire confidence in El Habaqui's fidelity,[22] preferred, instead of men, to give him money; and he placed eight hundred gold ducats in his hands, to enable him to raise the necessary levies among his countrymen.

Thus fortified, El Habaqui set out for the headquarters of Aben-Aboo, at his ancient residence in Mecina de Bombaron. On the second day the Morisco captain fell in with a party of his countrymen lingering idly by the way, and he inquired, with an air of authority, why they did not go and tender their submission to the Spanish authorities, as others had done. They replied, they were waiting for their master's

[22] "En lo que á esto toca, no tengo mas prendas que la palabra del Habaqui, el cual me podria engañar; pero certifico á V. M. que en su manera de proceder me paresce hombre que tracta verdad, y tal fama tiene." Carta de D. Juan de Austria al Rey, 21 de Mayo, 1570, MS.

orders. To this El Habaqui rejoined, "All are bound to submit; and if Aben-Aboo, on his part, shows unwillingness to do so, I will arrest him at once and drag him at my horse's tail to the Christian camp."[73] This foolish vaunt cost the braggart his life.

One of the party instantly repaired to Mecina and reported the words to Aben-Aboo. The Morisco prince, overjoyed at the prospect of having his enemy in his power, immediately sent a detachment of a hundred and fifty Turks to seize the offender and bring him to Mecina. They found El Habaqui at Burchal, where his family were living. The night had set in when the chieftain received tidings of the approach of the Turks; and under cover of the darkness he succeeded in making his escape into the neighboring mountains. The ensuing morning the soldiers followed closely on his track; and it was not long before they descried a person skulking among the rocks, whose white mantle and crimson turban proved him to be the object of their pursuit. He was immediately arrested and carried to Mecina. His sentence was already passed. Aben-Aboo, upbraiding him with his treachery, ordered him to be removed to an adjoining room, where he was soon after strangled. His corpse, denied the rites of burial, having been first rolled in a mat of reeds, was ignominiously thrown into a sewer; and the fate of the unhappy man was kept a secret for more than a month.[24]

---

[73] "Que quando Aben Aboo de su voluntad no lo hiciese, le llevaria él atado á la cola de su caballo." Marmol, Rebelion de Granada, tom. ii. p. 392.

[24] "Lo hizo ahogar secretamente, y mandó echar el cuerpo en un

His absence, after some time, naturally excited suspicions in the Spanish camp. A cavalier, known to Aben-Aboo, wrote to him to obtain information respecting El Habaqui, and was told in answer, by the wily prince, that he had been arrested and placed in custody for his treacherous conduct, but that his family and friends need be under no alarm, as he was perfectly safe. Aben-Aboo hinted, moreover, that it would be well to send to him some confidential person with whom he might arrange the particulars of the treaty,—as if these had not been already settled. After some further delay, Don John resolved to despatch an agent to ascertain the real dispositions of the Moriscoes towards the Christians, and to penetrate, if possible, the mystery that hung round the fate of El Habaqui.

The envoy selected was Hernan Valle de Palacios, a cavalier possessed of a courageous heart, yet tempered by a caution that well fitted him for the delicate and perilous office. On the thirteenth of July he set out on his mission. On the way he encountered a Morisco, a kinsman of the late monarch, Aben-Humeya, and naturally no friend to Aben-Aboo. He was acquainted with the particulars of El Habaqui's murder, of which he gave full details to Palacios. He added that the Morisco prince, far from acquiescing in the recent treaty, was doing all in his power to prevent its execution. He could readily muster, at short notice, said the informer, a force of five thousand men, well armed, and provisioned for three months; and he was using

muladar envuelto en un zarzo de cañas, donde estuvo mas de treinta dias sin saberse de su muerte." Marmol, Rebelion de Granada, tom. ii. p. 393.

all his efforts to obtain further reinforcements from Algiers.

Instructed in these particulars, the envoy resumed his journey. He was careful, however, first to obtain a safe-conduct from Aben-Aboo, which was promptly sent to him. On reaching Mecina, he found the place occupied by a body of five hundred arquebusiers; but by the royal order he was allowed to pass unmolested. Before entering the presence of "the little king of the Alpujarras," as Aben-Aboo, like his predecessor, was familiarly styled by the Spaniards, Palacios was carefully searched, and such weapons as he carried about him were taken away.

He found Aben-Aboo stretched on a divan, and three or four Moorish girls entertaining him with their national songs and dances. He did not rise, or indeed change his position, at the approach of the envoy, but gave him audience with the lofty bearing of an independent sovereign.

Palacios did not think it prudent to touch on the fate of El Habaqui. After expatiating on the liberal promises which he was empowered by Don John of Austria to make, he expressed the hope that Aben-Aboo would execute the treaty, and not rekindle a war which must lead to the total destruction of his country. The chief listened in silence; and it was not till he had called some of his principal captains around him that he condescended to reply. He then said that God and the whole world knew it was not by his own desire, but by the will of the people, that he had been placed on the throne. "I shall not attempt," he said, "to prevent any of my subjects from submitting that prefer to do so. But tell your master," he added, "that, while I have a single shirt to my back, I shall not follow their example. Though no other man should hold out in the Alpujarras, I would rather live and die a Mussulman than possess all the favors which King Philip can heap on me. At no time, and in no manner, will I ever consent to place myself in his power."[25] He concluded this spirited declaration by adding that, if driven to it by necessity, he could bury himself in a cavern, which he had stowed with supplies for six years to come, during which it would go hard but he would find some means of making his way to Barbary. The desperate tone of these remarks effectually closed the audience. Palacios was permitted to return unmolested, and to report to his commander the failure of his mission.

The war, which Don John had flattered himself he had so happily brought to a close, now, like a fire smothered but not quenched, burst forth again with redoubled fury. The note of defiance was heard loudest among the hills of Ronda, a wild sierra on the western skirts of the Alpujarras, inhabited by a bold and untamed race, more formidable than the mountaineers of any other district of Granada. Aben-Aboo did all he could to fan the flame of insurrection in this quarter, and sent his own brother, El Galipe, to take the command.

[25] " Que quando no quedase otro sino él en la Alpuxarra con sola la camisa que tenia vestida, estimaba mas vivir y morir Moro, que todas quantas mercedes el Rey Filipe le podia hacer; y que fuese cierto, que en ningun tiempo, ni por ninguna manera, se pondria en su poder." Marmol, Rebelion de Granada, tom. ii. p. 410

The Spanish government, now fully aroused, made more vigorous efforts to crush the spirit of rebellion than at any time during the war. Don John was ordered to occupy Guadix, and thence to scour the country in a northerly direction. Another army, under the Grand Commander Requesens, marching from Granada, was to enter the Alpujarras from the north, and, taking a route different from that of the duke of Sesa in the previous campaign, was to carry a war of extermination into the heart of the mountains. Finally, the duke of Arcos, the worthy descendant of the great marquis of Cadiz, whose name was so famous in the first war of Granada, and whose large estates in this quarter he had inherited, was intrusted with the operations against the rebels of the Serrania de Ronda.

The grand commander executed his commission in the same remorseless spirit in which it had been dictated. Early in September, quitting Granada, he took the field at the head of five thousand men. He struck at once into the heart of the country. All the evils of war in its most horrid form followed in his train. All along his track it seemed as if the land had been swept by a conflagration. The dwellings were sacked and burned to the ground. The mulberry and olive groves were cut down; the vines were torn up by the roots; and the ripening harvests were trampled in the dust. The country was converted into a wilderness. Occasionally small bodies of the Moriscoes made a desperate stand. But for the most part, without homes to shelter or food to nourish them, they were driven, like unresisting cattle, to seek a refuge in the depths of the mountains, and in the caves in which this part of the country abounded.

Their pursuers followed up the chase with the fierce glee with which the hunter tracks the wild animal of the forest to his lair. There they were huddled together, one or two hundred frequently in the same cavern. It was not easy to detect the hiding-place amidst the rocks and thickets which covered up and concealed the entrance. But when it was detected it was no difficult matter to destroy the inmates. The green bushes furnished the materials for a smouldering fire, and those within were soon suffocated by the smoke, or, rushing out, threw themselves on the mercy of their pursuers. Some were butchered on the spot; others were sent to the gibbet or the galleys; while the greater part, with a fate scarcely less terrible, were given up as the booty of the soldiers and sold into slavery.[26]

Aben-Aboo had a narrow escape in one of these caverns, not far from Bérchul, where he had secreted himself with a wife and two of his daughters. The women were suffocated, with about seventy other persons. The Morisco chief succeeded in making his escape through an aperture at the farther end, which was unknown to his enemies.[27]

Small forts were erected at short intervals along the ruined country. No less than eighty-four of these towers were raised in different parts of the land, twenty-nine of which were to be seen in the Alpujarras and the

---

[26] It is the language of Marmol, who will not be suspected of exaggerating the cruelties of his countrymen. He does not seem, indeed, to regard them as cruelties: "Unos enviaba el Comendador mayor á las galeras, otros hacia justicia de ellos, y los mas consentia que los vendiesen los soldados para que fuesen aprovechados." Rebelion de Granada, tom. ii. p. 436.

[27] Ibid., p. 433.

vale of Lecrin alone.[28] There they stood, crowning every peak and eminence in the sierra, frowning over the horrid waste, the sad memorials of the conquest. This was the stern policy of the victors. Within this rocky girdle, long held as it was by the iron soldiery of Castile, it was impossible that rebellion should again gather to a head.

The months of September and October were consumed in these operations. Meanwhile, the duke of Arcos had mustered his Andalusian levies, to the number of four thousand men, including a thousand of his own vassals. He took with him his son, a boy of not more than thirteen years of age,—following in this, says the chronicler, the ancient usage of the valiant house of Ponce de Leon.[29] About the middle of September he began his expedition into the Sierra Vermeja, or Red Sierra. It was a spot memorable in Spanish history for the defeat and death of Alonso de Aguilar, in the time of Ferdinand and Isabella, and has furnished the theme of many a plaintive *romance* in the beautiful minstrelsy of the South. The wife of the duke of Arcos was descended from Alonso de Aguilar, as he himself was the grandson of the good count of Ureña, who, with better fortune than his friend, survived the disasters of that day. The route of the army

[28] Circourt gives a precise enumeration of the fortresses in different districts of the country. Hist. des Arabes d'Espagne, tom. iii. pp. 135, 136.

[29] "Llevando cerca de sí a su hijo, mozo quasi de trece años Don Luis Ponce de Leon, cosa usada en otra edad en aquella Casa de los Ponces de Leon, criarse los muchachos peleando con los Moros, i tener a sus padres por maestros." Mendoza, Guerra de Granada, p. 318.

led directly across the fatal field. As they traversed the elevated plain of Calaluz, the soldiers saw everywhere around the traces of the fight. The ground was still covered with fragments of rusty armor, bits of broken sword-blades, and heads of spears. More touching evidence was afforded by the bones of men and horses, which, in this solitary region, had been whitening in the blasts of seventy winters. The Spaniards knew well the localities, with which they had become familiar from boyhood in the legends and traditions of the country. Here was the spot where the vanguard, under its brave commander, had made its halt in the obscurity of the night. There were the faint remains of the enemy's intrenchments, which time had nearly levelled with the dust; and there, too, the rocks still threw their dark shadows over the plain, as on the day when the valiant Alonso de Aguilar fell at their base in combat with the renowned Fèri de Ben Estepar. The whole scene was brought home to the hearts of the Spaniards. As they gazed on the unburied relics lying around them, the tears, says the eloquent historian who records the incident, fell fast down their iron cheeks, and they breathed a soldier's prayer for the repose of the noble dead. But these holier feelings were soon succeeded by others of a fierce nature, and they loudly clamored to be led against the enemy.[30]

[30] For the celebrated description of this event by Mendoza, see Guerra de Granada, pp. 301, 302. The Castilian historian, who probably borrowed the hint of it from Tacitus (Annales, lib. i. sec. 31), has painted the scene with a consummate art that raises him from the rank of an imitator to that of a rival. The reader may find a circumstantial account of Alonso de Aguilar's disastrous ex-

The duke of Arcos, profiting by the errors of Alonso de Aguilar, had made his arrangements with great circumspection. He soon came in sight of the Moriscoes, full three thousand strong. But, though well posted, they made a defence little worthy of their ancient reputation, or of the notes of defiance which they had so boldly sounded at the opening of the campaign. They indeed showed mettle at first, and inflicted some loss on the Christians. But the frequent reverses of their countrymen seemed to have broken their spirits, and they were soon thrown into disorder, and fled in various directions into the more inaccessible tracts of the sierra. The Spaniards followed up the fugitives, who did not attempt to rally. Nor did they ever again assemble in any strength, so effectual were the dispositions made by the victorious general. The insurrection of the Sierra Vermeja was at an end.[31]

The rebellion, indeed, might be said to be everywhere crushed within the borders of Granada. The more stout-hearted of the insurgents still held out among the caves and fastnesses of the Alpujarras, supporting a precarious existence until they were hunted down by detachments of the Spaniards, who were urged to the pursuit by the promise from government of twenty ducats a head for every Morisco. But nearly all felt the impracticability of further resistance. Some succeeded in making their escape to Barbary. The rest, broken in spirit, and driven to extremity by want of

---

pedition, in 1501, in the History of Ferdinand and Isabella, part ii. ch. 7.

[31] Mendoza, Guerra de Granada, pp. 298-314.—Marmol, Rebelion de Granada, tom. ii. pp. 425-431.

food in a country now turned into a desert, consented at length to accept the amnesty offered them, and tendered their submission.

On the twenty-eighth of October Don John received advices of a final edict of Philip, commanding that all the Moriscoes in the kingdom of Granada should be at once removed into the interior of the country. None were to be excepted from this decree, not even the *Moriscos de la Paz*, as those were called who had loyally refused to take part in the rebellion.[20] The arrangements for this important and difficult step were made with singular prudence, and, under the general direction of Don John of Austria, the Grand Commander Requesens, and the dukes of Sesa and Arcos, were carried into effect with promptness and energy.

By the terms of the edict, the lands and houses of the exiles were to be forfeited to the crown. But their personal effects—their flocks, their herds, and their grain—would be taken, if they desired it, at a fixed valuation by the government. Every regard was to be paid to their personal convenience and security; and it was forbidden, in the removal, to separate parents from children, husbands from wives, in short, to divide

[20] Circourt quotes a remarkable passage from the *Ordenanzas de Granada*, which well illustrates the conscientious manner in which the government dealt with the Moriscoes. It forms the preamble of the law of February 24th, 1571. "The Moriscoes who took no part in the insurrection ought not to be punished. We should not desire to injure them; but they cannot hereafter cultivate their lands; and then it would be an endless task to attempt to separate the innocent from the guilty. We shall indemnify them, certainly. Meanwhile, their estates must be confiscated, like those of the rebel Moriscoes." Hist. des Arabes d'Espagne, tom. iii. p. 143.

the members of a family from one another,—"an act of clemency," says a humane chronicler, "which they little deserved; but his majesty was willing in this to content them."[33]

The country was divided into districts, the inhabitants of which were to be conducted, under the protection of a strong military escort, to their several places of destination. These seem to have been the territory of La Mancha, the northern borders of Andalusia, the Castiles, Estremadura, and even the remote province of Galicia. Care was taken that no settlement should be made near the borders of Murcia or Valencia, where large numbers of the Moriscoes were living in comparative quiet on the estates of the great nobles, who were exceedingly jealous of any interference with their vassals.

The first of November, All-Saints' Day, was appointed for the removal of the Moriscoes throughout Granada. On that day they were gathered in the principal churches of their districts, and, after being formed into their respective divisions, began their march. The grand commander had occupied the passes of the Alpujarras with strong detachments of the military. The different columns of emigrants were placed under the direction of persons of authority and character. The whole movement was conducted with singular order,—resistance being attempted in one or two places only, where the blame, it may be added, as intimated by a Castilian chronicler, was to be charged on the brutality of the

---

[33] "Que las casas fuesen y estuviesen juntas; porque aunque lo merecian poco, quiso su Magestad que se les diese este contento." Marmol, Rebelion de Granada, tom. ii. p. 439.

soldiers.[34] Still, the removal of the Moriscoes, on the present occasion, was attended with fewer acts of violence and rapacity than the former removal, from Granada. At least this would seem to be inferred by the silence of the chroniclers; though it is true such silence is far from being conclusive, as the chroniclers, for the most part, felt too little interest in the sufferings of the Moriscoes to make a notice of them indispensable. However this may be, it cannot be doubted that, whatever precautions may have been taken to spare the exiles any unnecessary suffering, the simple fact of their being expelled from their native soil is one that suggests an amount of misery not to be estimated. For what could be more dreadful than to be thus torn from their pleasant homes, the scenes of their childhood, where every mountain, valley, and stream were as familiar friends,—a part of their own existence,—to be rudely thrust into a land of strangers, of a race different from themselves in faith, language, and institutions, with no sentiment in common but that of a deadly hatred? That the removal of a whole nation should have been so quietly accomplished, proves how entirely the strength and spirit of the Moriscoes must have been broken by their reverses.[35]

[34] "Saquearon los soldados las casas del lugar, y tomaron todas las mugeres por esclavas; cosa que dió harta sospecha de que la desorden habia nacido de su cudicia." Marmol, Rebelion de Granada, tom. ii. p. 444.—The better feelings of the old soldier occasionally—and it is no small praise, considering the times—triumph over his national antipathies.

[35] For the removal and dispersion of the Moriscoes, see Marmol, Rebelion de Granada, tom. ii. pp. 437-444.—Ferreras, Hist. d'Espagne, tom. x. pp. 227, 228,—Vanderhammen, Don Juan de Austria, fol. 126, —It may well seem strange that an event of such moment as the

The war thus terminated, there seemed no reason for John of Austria to prolong his stay in the province. For some time he had been desirous to obtain the king's consent to his return. His ambitious spirit, impatient of playing a part on what now seemed to him an obscure field of action, pent up within the mountain-barrier of the Alpujarras, longed to display itself on a bolder theatre before the world. He aspired, too, to a more independent command. He addressed repeated letters to the king's ministers,—to the Cardinal Espinosa and Ruy Gomez de Silva in particular,—to solicit their influence in his behalf. "I should be glad," he wrote to the latter, "to serve his majesty, if I might be allowed, on some business of importance. I wish he may understand that I am no longer a boy. Thank God, I can begin to fly without the aid of others' wings, and it is full time, as I believe, that I was out of swaddling-clothes."[36] In another letter he expresses his desire to have some place more fitting the brother of such a monarch as Philip and the son of such a father as Charles the Fifth.[37] On more than one occasion he

removal of the Moriscoes should have been barely noticed, when indeed noticed at all, by the general historian. It is still more strange that it should have been passed over in silence by a writer like Mendoza, to whose narrative it essentially belonged, and who could bestow thirty pages or more on the expedition into the Serrania de Ronda. But this was a tale of Spanish glory. The haughty Castilian chronicler held the race of unbelievers in too great contempt to waste a thought on their calamities, except so far as they enabled him to exhibit the prowess of his countrymen.

[36] " Querria tambien que allá se entendiese que ya no soy mochacho, y que puedo, á Dios gracias, comenzar en alguna manera á volar sin alas ajenas, y sospecho ques ya tiempo de salir de pañales." Carta de D. Juan de Austria á Ruy Gomez de Silva, 16 de Mayo, 1570, MS.

[37] " No teniendo el lugar y auctoridad que ha de tener hijo de tal

alludes to the command against the Turk as the great object of his ambition.

His importunity to be allowed to resign his present office had continued from the beginning of summer, some months before the proper close of the campaign. It may be thought to argue an instability of character, of which a more memorable example was afforded by him at a later period of life. At length he was rejoiced by obtaining the royal consent to resign his command and return to court.

On the eleventh of November, Don John repaired to Granada. Till the close of the month he was occupied with making the necessary arrangements preparatory to his departure. The greater part of the army was paid off and disbanded. A sufficient number was reserved to garrison the fortresses, and to furnish detachments which were to scour the country and hunt down such Moriscoes as still held out in the mountains. As Requesens was to take part in the expedition against the Ottomans, the office of captain-general was placed in the hands of the valiant duke of Arcos. On the twenty-ninth of November, Don John, having completed his preparations, quitted Granada and set forth on his journey to Madrid, where the popular chieftain was welcomed with enthusiasm by the citizens, as a conqueror returned from a victorious campaign. By Philip and his newly-married bride, Anne of Austria, he was no less kindly greeted; and it was not long before the king gave a substantial proof of his contentment with his brother, by placing in his hands the

padre, y hermano de tal hermano." Carta de D. Juan de Austria á Ruy Gomez de Silva, 4 de Junio, 1570, MS.

baton offered by the allies of generalissimo in the war against the Turks.

There was still one Morisco insurgent who refused to submit, and who had hitherto eluded every attempt to capture him, but whose capture was of more importance than that of any other of his nation. This was Aben-Aboo, the "little king" of the Alpujarras. His force of five thousand men had dwindled to scarcely more than four hundred. But they were men devoted to his person, and seemed prepared to endure every extremity rather than surrender. Like the rest of his nation, the Morisco chief took refuge in the mountain-caves, in such remote and inaccessible districts as had hitherto baffled every attempt to detect his retreat. In March, 1571, an opportunity presented itself for making the discovery.

Granada was at this time the scene of almost daily executions. As the miserable insurgents were taken, they were brought before Deza's tribunal, where they were at once sentenced by the inexorable president to the galleys or the gibbet, or the more horrible doom of being torn in pieces with red-hot pincers. Among the prisoners sentenced to death was one Zatahari, who was so fortunate as to obtain a respite of his punishment at the intercession of a goldsmith named Barredo, a person of much consideration in Granada. From gratitude for this service, or perhaps as the price of it, Zatahari made some important revelations to his benefactor respecting Aben-Aboo. He disclosed the place of his retirement and the number of his followers, adding that the two persons on whom he most relied were his secretary, Abou-Amer, and a Moorish captain named

El Senix. The former of these persons was known to Barredo, who in the course of his business had frequent occasion to make journeys into the Alpujarras. He resolved to open a correspondence with the secretary, and, if possible, win him over to the Spanish interests. Zatahari consented to bear the letter, on condition of a pardon. This was readily granted by the president, who approved the plan, and who authorized the most liberal promises to Abou-Amer in case of his co-operation with Barredo.

Unfortunately,—or, rather, fortunately for Zatahari, as it proved,—he was intercepted by El Senix, who, getting possession of the letter, carried it to Abou-Amer. The loyal secretary was outraged by this attempt to corrupt him. He would have put the messenger to death, had not El Senix represented that the poor wretch had undertaken the mission only to save his life.

Privately the Moorish captain assured the messenger that Barredo should have sought a conference with him, as he was ready to enter into negotiations with the Christians. In fact, El Senix had a grudge against his master, and had already made an attempt to leave his service and escape to Barbary.

A place of meeting was accordingly appointed in the Alpujarras, to which Barredo secretly repaired. El Senix was furnished with an assurance, under the president's own hand, of a pardon for himself and his friends, and of an annual pension of a hundred thousand maravedis, in case he should bring Aben-Aboo, dead or alive, to Granada.

The interview could not be conducted so secretly but

that an intimation of it reached the ears of Aben-Aboo, who resolved to repair at once to the quarters of El Senix and ascertain the truth for himself. That chief had secreted himself in a cavern in the neighborhood. Aben-Aboo took with him his faithful secretary and a small body of soldiers. On reaching the cave, he left his followers without, and, placing two men at the entrance, he, with less prudence than was usual with him, passed alone into the interior.

There he found El Senix, surrounded by several of his friends and kinsmen. Aben-Aboo, in a peremptory tone, charged him with having held a secret correspondence with the enemy, and demanded the object of his late interview with Barredo. Senix did not attempt to deny the charge, but explained his motives by saying that he had been prompted only by a desire to serve his master. He had succeeded so well, he said, as to obtain from the president an assurance that if the Morisco would lay down his arms he should receive an amnesty for the past and a liberal provision for the future.

Aben-Aboo listened scornfully to this explanation; then, muttering the word "Treachery!" he turned on his heel and moved towards the mouth of the cave, where he had left his soldiers, intending probably to command the arrest of his perfidious officer. But he had not given them, it appears, any intimation of the hostile object of his visit to El Senix; and the men, supposing it to be on some matter of ordinary business, had left the spot to see some of their friends in the neighborhood. El Senix saw that no time was to be lost. On a signal which he gave, his followers attacked the two guards at the door, one of whom was killed on the spot, while the other made his escape. They then all fell upon the unfortunate Aben-Aboo. He made a desperate defence. But though the struggle was fierce, the odds were too great for it to be long. It was soon terminated by the dastard Senix coming behind his master and with the butt-end of his musket dealing him a blow on the back of his head, that brought him to the ground, where he was quickly despatched by a multitude of wounds.[38]

The corpse was thrown out of the cavern. His followers, soon learning their master's fate, dispersed in different directions. The faithful secretary fell shortly after into the hands of the Spaniards, who, with their usual humanity in this war, caused him to be drawn and quartered.

The body of Aben-Aboo was transported to the neighborhood of Granada, where preparations were made for giving the dead chief a public entrance into the city, as if he had been still alive. The corpse was set astride on a mule, and supported erect in the saddle by a wooden frame, which was concealed beneath ample robes. On one side of the body rode Barredo; on the other, El Senix, bearing the scimitar and arquebuse of his murdered master. Then followed the kinsmen and friends of the Morisco prince, with their arms by their side. A regiment of Castilian infantry and a troop of horse brought up the rear. As the procession defiled along the street of Zacatin, it was saluted by

[38] Marmol, Rebelion de Granada, tom. ii. pp. 449-454.—Mendoza, Guerra de Granada, pp. 324-327.—Bleda, Cronica de España, p. 752.—Herrera, Historia general, tom. i. p. 781.—Vanderhammen, Don Juan de Austria, fol. 123.

salvoes of musketry, accompanied by peals of artillery from the ancient towers of the Alhambra, while the population of Granada, with eager though silent curiosity, hurried out to gaze on the strange and ghastly spectacle.

In this way the company reached the great square of Vivarambla, where were assembled the president, the duke of Arcos, and the principal cavaliers and magistrates of the city. On coming into their presence, El Senix dismounted, and, kneeling before Deza, delivered to him the arms of Aben-Aboo. He was graciously received by the president, who confirmed the assurances which had been given him of the royal favor. The miserable ceremony of a public execution was then gone through with. The head of the dead man was struck off. His body was given to the boys of the city, who, after dragging it through the streets with scoffs and imprecations, committed it to the flames. Such was one of the lessons by which the Spaniards early stamped on the minds of their children an indelible hatred of the Morisco.

The head of Aben-Aboo, enclosed in a cage, was set up over the gate which opened on the Alpujarras. There, with the face turned towards his native hills, which he had loved so well and which had witnessed his brief and disastrous reign, it remained for many a year. None ventured, by removing it, to incur the doom which an inscription on the cage denounced on the offender: "This is the head of the traitor, Aben-Aboo. Let no one take it down, under penalty of death." [39]

[39] "Esta es la cabeza del traidor de Abenabó. Nadie la quite so

Such was the sad fate of Aben-Aboo, the last of the royal line of the Omeyades who ever ruled in the Peninsula. Had he lived in the peaceful and prosperous times of the Arabian empire in Spain, he might have swayed the sceptre with as much renown as the best of his dynasty. Though the blood of the Moor flowed in his veins, he seems to have been remarkably free from some of the greatest defects in the Moorish character. He was temperate in his appetites, presenting in this respect a contrast to the gross sensuality of his predecessor. He had a lofty spirit, was cool and circumspect in his judgments, and, if he could not boast that fiery energy of character which belonged to some of his house, he had a firmness of purpose not to be intimidated by suffering or danger. Of this he gave signal proof when, as the reader may remember, the most inhuman tortures could not extort from him the disclosure of the lurking-place of his friends.[40] His qualities, as I have intimated, were such as peculiarly adapted him to a time of prosperity and peace. Unhappily, he had fallen upon evil times, when his country lay a wreck at his feet; when the people, depressed by long servitude, were broken down by the recent calamities of war; when, in short, it would not have been possible for the wisest and most warlike of his predecessors to animate them to a successful resistance against odds so overwhelming as those presented by the Spanish monarchy in the zenith of its power.

pena de muerte." Mendoza, Guerra de Granada, p. 329.—Marmol, Rebelion de Granada, tom. ii. pp. 455, 456.—Bleda, Cronica de España, p. 752.—Miniana, Hist. de España, p. 383.

[40] *Ante*, p. 93.

The Castilian chroniclers have endeavored to fix a deep stain on his memory, by charging him with the murder of El Habaqui, and with the refusal to execute the treaty to which he had given his sanction. But in criticising the conduct of Aben-Aboo we must not forget the race from which he sprang, or the nature of its institutions. He was a despot, and a despot of the Oriental type. He was placed in a situation—much against his will, it may be added—which gave him absolute control over the lives and fortunes of his people. His word was their law. He passed the sentence, and enforced its execution. El Habaqui he adjudged to be a traitor; and in sentencing him to the bowstring he inflicted on him only a traitor's doom.

With regard to the treaty, he spoke of himself as betrayed, saying that its provisions were not such as he had intended. And when we consider that the instrument was written in the Spanish tongue, that it was drafted by a Spaniard, finally, that the principal Morisco agent who subscribed the treaty was altogether in the Spanish interest, as the favors heaped on him without measure too plainly proved, it can hardly be doubted that there were good grounds for the assertion of Aben-Aboo. From the hour of his accession he seems to have devoted himself to the great work of securing the independence of his people. He could scarcely have agreed to a treaty which was to leave that people in even a worse state than before the rebellion. From what we know of his character, we may more reasonably conclude that he was sincere when he told the Spanish envoy Palacios, who had come to press the execution of the treaty and to remind him of the royal promises of grace, that "his people might do as they listed, but, for himself, he would rather live and die a Mussulman than possess all the favors which the king of Spain could heap on him." His deeds corresponded with his words; and, desperate as was his condition, he still continued to bid defiance to the Spanish government, until he was cut off by the hand of a traitor.

The death of Aben-Aboo severed the last bond which held the remnant of the Moriscoes together. In a few years the sword, famine, and the gallows had exterminated the outcasts who still lurked in the fastnesses of the mountains. Their places were gradually occupied by Christians, drawn thither by the favorable terms which the government offered to settlers. But it was long before the wasted and famine-stricken territory could make a suitable return to the labors of the colonists. They were ignorant of the country, and were altogether deficient in the agricultural skill necessary for turning its unpromising places to the best account. The Spaniard, adventurous as he was, and reckless of danger and difficulty in the pursuit of gain, was impatient of the humble drudgery required for the tillage of the soil; and many a valley and hill-side, which under the Moriscoes had bloomed with all the rich embroidery of cultivation, now relapsed into its primitive barrenness.

The exiles carried their superior skill and industry into the various provinces where they were sent. Scattered as they were, and wide apart, the presence of the Moriscoes was sure to be revealed by the more minute and elaborate culture of the soil,—as the secret course of the mountain-stream is betrayed by the brighter green of the meadow. With their skill in husbandry they combined a familiarity with various kinds of handicraft, especially those requiring dexterity and fineness of execution, that was unknown to the Spaniards. As the natural result of this superiority, the products of their labor were more abundant and could be afforded at a cheaper rate than those of their neighbors. Yet this industry was exerted under every disadvantage which a most cruel legislation could impose on it. It would be hard to find in the pages of history a more flagrant example of the oppression of a conquered race than that afforded by the laws of this period in reference to the Moriscoes. The odious law of 1566, which led to the insurrection, was put in full force. By this the national songs and dances, the peculiar baths of the Moriscoes, the *fêtes* and ceremonies which had come down to them from their ancestors, were interdicted under heavy penalties. By another ordinance, dated October 6th, 1572, still more cruel and absurd, they were forbidden to speak or to write the Arabic, under penalty of thirty days' imprisonment in irons for the first offence, double that term for the second, and for the third a hundred lashes and four years' confinement in the galleys. By another monstrous provision in the same edict, whoever read, or even had in his possession, a work written or printed in the Arabic, was to be punished with a hundred stripes and four years in the galleys. Any contract or public instrument made in that tongue was to be void, and the parties to it were condemned to receive two hundred lashes and to tug at the oar for six years."

But the most oppressive part of this terrible ordinance related to the residence of the Moriscoes. No one was allowed to change his abode, or to leave the parish or district assigned to him, without permission from the regular authorities. Whoever did so, and was apprehended beyond these limits, was to be punished with a hundred lashes and four years' imprisonment in the galleys. Should he be found within ten leagues of Granada, he was condemned, if between ten and seventeen years of age, to toil as a galley-slave the rest of his days; if above seventeen, he was sentenced to death![42] On the escape of a Morisco from his limits, the hue and cry was to be raised as for the pursuit of a criminal. Even his own family were required to report his absence to the magistrate; and in case of their failure to do this, although it should be his wife or his children, says the law, they incurred the penalty of a whipping and a month's imprisonment in the common jail.[43]

Yet in the face of these atrocious enactments we find the Moriscoes occasionally making their escape into the province of Valencia, where numbers of their countrymen were living as serfs on the estates of the great nobles, under whose powerful protection they enjoyed a degree of comfort, if not of independence, unknown

[41] Nueva Recopilacion, lib. viii. tit. ii. ley 19.
[42] "Si estos tales que se huvieren huydo, y ausentados fueren hallados en el dicho Reyno de Granada, ò dentro de diez leguas cercanas à el, caygan è incurran en pena de muerte, que sea en sus personas executada." Ibid., ubi supra.
[43] Ibid., loc. cit.

to their race in other parts of the country. Some few also, finding their way to the coast, succeeded in crossing the sea to Barbary. The very severity of the law served in some measure to defeat its execution. Indeed, Philip, in more than one instance in which he deemed that the edicts pressed too heavily on his Moorish vassals, judged it expedient to mitigate the penalty, or even to dispense with it altogether,—an act of leniency which seems to have found little favor with his Castilian subjects.[44]

Yet, strange to say, under this iron system the spirits of the Moriscoes, which had been crushed by their long sufferings in the war of the rebellion, gradually rose again as they found a shelter in their new homes and resumed their former habits of quiet industry. Though deprived of their customary amusements, their *fêtes*, their songs, and their dances,—though debarred from the use of the language in which they had lisped from the cradle, which embodied their national traditions and was associated with their fondest recollections,— they were said to be cheerful, and even gay. They lived to a good age, and examples of longevity were found among them to which it was not easy to find a parallel among the Spaniards. The Moorish stock, like the Jewish, seems to have thriven under persecution.[45]

One would be glad to find any authentic data for an account of the actual population at the time of their

[44] Examples of this are cited by Circourt, Hist. des Arabes en Espagne, tom. iii. pp. 150, 151.

[45] Ibid., p. 163.—M. de Circourt has collected, from some authentic and not very accessible sources, much curious information relative to this part of his subject.

expulsion from Granada. But I have met with none. They must have been sorely thinned by the war of the insurrection and the countless woes it brought upon the country. One fact is mentioned by the chroniclers which shows that the number of the exiles must have been very considerable. The small remnant still left in Granada, with its lovely *vega* and the valley of Lecrin, alone furnished, we are told, over six thousand.[46] In the places to which they were transported they continued to multiply to such an extent that the cortes of Castile, in the latter part of the century, petitioned the king not to allow the census to be taken, lest it might disclose to the Moriscoes the alarming secret of their increase of numbers.[47] Such a petition shows, as strongly as language can show, the terror in which the Spaniards still stood of this persecuted race.

Yet the Moriscoes were scattered over the country in small and isolated masses, hemmed in all around by the Spaniards. They were transplanted to the interior, where, at a distance from the coast, they had no means of communicating with their brethren of Africa. They were without weapons of any kind; and, confined to their several districts, they had not the power of acting in concert together. There would seem to have been little to fear from a people so situated. But the weakest individual, who feels that his wrongs are too great to be forgiven, may well become an object of dread to the person who has wronged him.

[46] Ferreras, Hist. d'Espagne, tom. x. p. 227.
[47] "Ils representèrent que ce recensement allait leur révéler le secret de leur nombre effrayant; qu'ils fourmillaient." Circourt, Hist. des Arabes en Espagne, tom. iii. p. 164.

The course of the government in reference to the Moriscoes was clearly a failure. It was as impolitic as it was barbarous. Nothing but the blindest fanaticism could have prevented the Spaniards from perceiving this. The object of the government had been to destroy every vestige of nationality in the conquered race. They were compelled to repudiate their ancient usages, their festivals, their religion, their language,—all that gave them a separate existence as a nation. But this served only to strengthen in secret the sentiment of nationality. They were to be divorced forever from the past. But it was the mistake of the government that it opened to them no future. Having destroyed their independence as a nation, it should have offered them the rights of citizenship and raised them to an equality with the rest of the community. Such was the policy of ancient Rome towards the nations which she conquered; and such has been that of our own country towards the countless emigrants who have thronged to our shores from so many distant lands. The Moriscoes, on the contrary, under the policy of Spain, were condemned to exist as foreigners in the country,—as enemies in the midst of the community into which they were thrown. Experience had taught them prudence and dissimulation; and in all outward observances they conformed to the exactions of the law. But in secret they were as much attached to their national institutions as were their ancestors when the caliphs of Córdova ruled over half the Peninsula. The Inquisition rarely gleaned an apostate from among them to swell the horrors of an *auto de fe;* but whoever recalls the facility with which, in the late rebellion, the whole population had relapsed into their ancient faith, will hardly doubt that they must have still continued to be Mahometans at heart.

Thus the gulf which separated the two races grew wider and wider every day. The Moriscoes hated the Spaniards for the wrongs which they had received from them. The Spaniards hated the Moriscoes the more that they had themselves inflicted these wrongs. Their hatred was further embittered by the feeling of jealousy caused by the successful competition of their rivals in the various pursuits of gain,—a circumstance which forms a fruitful theme of complaint in the petition of the cortes above noticed.[48] The feeling of hate became in time mingled with that of fear, as the Moriscoes increased in opulence and numbers; and men are not apt to be over-scrupulous in their policy towards those whom they both hate and fear.

With these evil passions rankling in their bosoms, the Spaniards were gradually prepared for the consummation of their long train of persecutions by that last act, reserved for the reign of the imbecile Philip the Third,—the expulsion of the Moriscoes from the Peninsula,—an act which deprived Spain of the most industrious and ingenious portion of her population, and which must be regarded as one of the principal causes of the subsequent decline of the monarchy.

[48] "Qu'ils accaparaient tous les métiers, tout le commerce." Circourt, Hist. des Arabes en Espagne, loc. cit.

An historian less renowned than Mendoza, but of more importance to one who would acquaint himself with the story of the Morisco rebellion, is Luis del Marmol Carbajal. Little is known of him but what is to be gathered from brief notices of himself in his works. He was a native of Granada, but we are not informed of the date of his birth. He was of a good family, and followed the profession of arms. When a mere youth, as he tells us, he was present at the famous siege of Tunis, in 1535. He continued in the imperial service two-and-twenty years. Seven years he was a captive, and followed the victorious banner of Mohammed, Scherif of Morocco, in his campaigns in the west of Africa. His various fortunes and his long residence in different parts of the African continent, especially in Barbary and Egypt, supplied him with abundant information in respect to the subjects of his historical inquiries; and, as he knew the Arabic, he made himself acquainted with such facts as were to be gleaned from books in that language. The fruits of his study and observation he gave to the world in his "*Descripcion general de Africa,*" a work in three volumes, folio, the first part of which appeared at Granada in 1573. The remainder was not published till the close of the century.

The book obtained a high reputation for its author, who was much commended for the fidelity and diligence with which he had pushed his researches in a field of letters into which the European scholar had as yet rarely ventured to penetrate.

In the year 1600 appeared, at Malaga, his second work, the "*Historia del Rebelion y Castigo de los Moriscos del Reyno de Granada,*" in one volume, folio. For the composition of this history the author was admirably qualified, not only by his familiarity with all that related to the character and condition of the Moriscoes, but by the part which he had personally taken in the war of the insurrection. He held the office of commissary in the royal army, and served in that capacity from the commencement of the war to its close. In the warm coloring of the narrative, and in the minuteness of its details, we feel that we are reading the report of one who has himself beheld the scenes which he describes. Indeed, the interest which, as an actor, he naturally takes in the operations of the war, leads to an amount of detail which may well be condemned as a blemish by those who do not feel a similar interest in the particulars of the struggle. But if his style have somewhat of the rambling, discursive manner of the old Castilian chronicler, it has a certain elegance in the execution, which brings it much nearer to the standard of a classic author. Far from being chargeable with the obscurity of Mendoza, Marmol is uncommonly perspicuous. With a general facility of expression, his language takes the varied character suited to the theme, sometimes kindled into eloquence and occasionally softened into pathos, for which the melancholy character of his story afforded too many occasions. Though loyal to his country and his faith, yet he shows but few gleams of the fiery intolerance that belonged to his nation, and especially to that portion of it which came into collision with the Moslems. Indeed, in more than one passage of his work we may discern gleams of that Christian charity which in Castile was the rarest, as it was, unhappily, the least precious of virtues, in the age in which he lived.

In the extensive plan adopted by Marmol, his history of the rebellion embraces a preliminary notice of the conquest of Granada, and of that cruel policy of the conquerors which led to the insurrection. The narrative, thus complete, supplied a most important hiatus in the annals of the country. Yet notwithstanding its importance in this view, and its acknowledged merit as a literary composition, such was the indifference of the Spaniards to their national history that it was not till the close of the last century, in 1797, that a second edition of Marmol's work was permitted to appear. This was in two volumes, octavo, from the press of Sancha, at Madrid,—the edition used in the preparation of these pages.

The most comprehensive and by far the most able history of the Moors of Spain with which I am acquainted is that of the Count Albert de Circourt,—"*Histoire des Arabes en Espagne.*" Beginning with the beginning, the author opens his narrative with the conquest of the Peninsula by the Moslems. He paints in glowing colors the magnificent empire of the Spanish caliphs. He dwells with sufficient minuteness on those interminable feuds which, growing out of a diversity of races and tribes, baffled every attempt at a permanent consolidation under one government. Then comes the famous war of Granada, with the conquest of the country by the "Catholic Kings;" and the work closes with the sad tale of the subsequent fortunes of the conquered races until their final expulsion from the Peninsula. Thus the rapidly shifting scenes of this most picturesque drama, sketched by a master's hand, are brought in regular succession before the eye of the reader.

In conducting his long story, the author, far from confining himself to a dry record of events, diligently explores the causes of these events. He scrutinizes with care every inch of debatable ground which lies in his path. He enriches his narrative with copious disquisitions on the condition of the arts, and the progress made by the Spanish Arabs in science and letters, thus presenting a complete view of that peculiar civilization which so curiously blended together the characteristic elements of European and Oriental culture.

If, in pursuing his speculations, M. de Circourt may be sometimes thought to refine too much, it cannot be denied that they are distinguished by candor and by a philosophical spirit. Even when we may differ from his conclusions, we must allow that they are the result of careful study and display an independent way of thinking. I may regret that in one important instance—the policy of the government of Ferdinand and Isabella—he should have been led to dissent from the opinions which I had expressed in my history of those sovereigns. It is possible that the predilection which the writer, whether historian or novelist, naturally feels for his hero when his conduct affords any ground for it, may have sometimes seduced me from the strict line of impartiality in my estimate of character and motives of action. I see, however, no reason to change the conclusions at which I had arrived after a careful study of the subject. Yet I cannot deny that the labors of the French historian have shed a light upon more than one obscure passage in the administration of Ferdinand and Isabella, for which the student of Spanish history owes him a debt of gratitude.

CHAPTER IX

WAR WITH THE TURKS.

League against the Turks.—Preparations for the War.—Don John Commander-in-Chief.—His Reception at Naples.—His Departure from Messina.

1570–1571.

WHILE Philip was occupied with the Morisco insurrection, his attention was called to another quarter, where a storm was gathering that menaced Spain in common with the rest of Christendom. In 1566, Solyman the Magnificent closed his long and prosperous reign. His son and successor, Selim the Second, possessed few of the qualities of his great father. Bred in the seraglio, he showed the fruits of his education in his indolent way of life and in the free indulgence of the most licentious appetites. With these effeminate tastes, he inherited the passion for conquest which belonged not only to his father, but to the whole of his warlike dynasty. Not that, like them, he headed his armies in the field. These were led by valiant commanders, who had learned the art of war under Solyman. Selim was, above all, fortunate in possessing for his grand vizier a minister whose untiring industry and remarkable talents for business enabled him to bear on his own shoulders the whole burden of government. It was fortunate for the state, as well as for the sultan, that Mahomet had the art to win the confidence of his master and to maintain it unshaken through the whole of his reign.

The scheme which most occupied the thoughts of Selim was the conquest of Cyprus. This island, to which Nature had been so prodigal of her gifts, belonged to Venice. Yet, placed at the extremity of the Mediterranean, it seemed in a manner to command the approaches to the Dardanelles, while its line of coast furnished convenient ports, from which swarms of cruisers might sally forth in time of war and plunder the Turkish commerce.

Selim, resolved on the acquisition of Cyprus, was not slow in devising a pretext for claiming it from Venice as a part of the Ottoman empire. The republic, though willing to make almost any concession rather than come to a rupture with the colossal power under whose shadow she lay, was not prepared to surrender without a struggle the richest gem in her colonial diadem. War was accordingly declared against her by the Porte, and vast preparations were made for fitting out an armament against Cyprus. Venice, in her turn, showed her usual alacrity in providing for the encounter. She strained her resources to the utmost. In a very short time she equipped a powerful fleet, and took measures to place the fortifications of Cyprus in a proper state of defence. But Venice no longer boasted a navy such as in earlier days had enabled her to humble the pride of Genoa and to ride the unquestioned mistress of the Mediterranean. The defences of her colonies, moreover, during her long repose, had gradually fallen into decay. In her extremity, she turned to the Christian powers of Europe, and besought them to make common cause with her against the enemy of Christendom.

Fortunately, the chair of St. Peter was occupied, at this crisis, by Pius the Fifth, one of those pontiffs who seem to have been called forth by the exigencies of the time, to uphold the pillars of Catholicism as they were yet trembling under the assaults of Luther. Though he was near seventy years of age, the fire of youth still glowed in his veins. He possessed all that impetuous eloquence which, had he lived in the days of Peter the Hermit, would have enabled him, like that enthusiast, to rouse the nations of Europe to a crusade against the infidel. But the days of the crusades were past; and a summons from the Vatican had no longer the power to stir the souls of men like a voice from heaven. The great potentates of Europe were too intent on their own selfish schemes to be turned from these by the apprehension of a danger so remote as that which menaced them from the East. The forlorn condition of Venice had still less power to move them; and that haughty republic was now made to feel, in the hour of her distress, how completely her perfidious and unscrupulous policy had estranged from her the sympathies of her neighbors.

There was one monarch, however, who did not close his ears against the appeal of Venice,—and that monarch one of more importance to her cause than any other, perhaps all others united. In the spring of 1570, Luigi Torres, clerk of the apostolic chamber, was sent to Spain by Pius the Fifth to plead the cause of the republic. He found the king at Ecija, on the route from Córdova, where he had been for some time presiding over a meeting of the cortes. The legate was graciously received by Philip, to whom he presented a letter from his holiness, urging the monarch, in the most earnest and eloquent language, to give succor to Venice and to unite with her in a league against the infidel. Philip did not hesitate to promise his assistance in the present emergency; but he had natural doubts as to the expediency of binding himself by a league with a power on whose good faith he had little reliance. He postponed his decision until his arrival at Seville. Accompanied by the legate, on the first of May he made his solemn entry into the great commercial capital of the South. It was his first visit there, and he was received with tumultuous joy by the loyal inhabitants. Loyalty to their monarchs has ever been a predominant trait of the Spaniards; and to none of their princes did they ever show it in larger measure than to Philip the Second. No one of them, certainly, was more thoroughly Spanish in his own nature, or more deeply attached to Spain.

After swearing to respect the privileges of the city, the king received the homage of the authorities. He then rode through the streets under a gorgeous canopy upheld by the principal magistrates, and visited the churches and monasteries, hearing *Te Deum*, and offering up his prayers in the cathedral. He was attended by a gay procession of nobles and cavaliers, while the streets of the populous city were thronged with multitudes, filled with enthusiasm at the presence of their sovereign. By this loyal escort Philip was accompanied to the place of his residence, the royal alcazar of Seville. Here he prolonged his stay for a fortnight, witnessing the shows and festivals which had been prepared for his entertainment. At his departure he received a more substantial proof of the attachment of the citizens, in a donation of six hundred thousand ducats. The object of this magnificent present was to defray in part the expenses of the king's approaching marriage with his fourth wife, Anne of Austria, the daughter of his cousin, the Emperor Maximilian. The fair young bride had left her father's court, and was already on her way to Madrid, where her nuptials were to be celebrated, and where she was to take the place of the lovely Isabella, whose death, not two years since, had plunged the nation into mourning.[1]

While at Seville, Philip laid the subject of the league before his ministers. Some of these, and among the number Espinosa, president of the council of Castile, entertained great doubts as to the policy of binding Spain by a formal treaty with the Venetian republic. But, with all his distrust of that power, Philip took a broader view of the matter than his ministers. Independently of his willingness to present himself before the world as the great champion of the Faith, he felt that such an alliance offered the best opportunity for crippling the maritime power of Turkey and thus providing for the safety of his own colonial possessions

---

[1] Ferreras, Hist. d'Espagne, tom. x. pp. 239, 240.—Cabrera, Filipe Segundo, p. 641.—Zuñiga, Anales de Sevilla, pp. 536-538.—The chroniclers paint in glowing colors the splendors of the royal reception at Seville, which, enriched by the Indian trade, took its place among the great commercial capitals of Christendom in the sixteenth century. It was a common saying,—

"Quien no ha visto à Sevilla
No ha visto à maravilla."

in the Mediterranean. After much deliberation, he dismissed the legate with the assurance that, notwithstanding the troubles which pressed on him both in the Low Countries and in Granada, he would furnish immediate succors to Venice, and would send commissioners to Rome, with full powers to unite with those of the pope and the republic in forming a treaty of alliance against the Ottoman Porte. The papal envoy was charged with a letter to the same effect, addressed by Philip to his holiness.

The ensuing summer, the royal admiral, the famous John Andrew Doria, who was lying with a strong squadron off Sicily, put to sea, by the king's orders. He was soon after reinforced by a few galleys which were furnished by his holiness and placed under the command of Mark Antonio Colonna, the representative of one of the most ancient and illustrious houses in Rome. On the last of August, 1570, the combined fleet effected its junction with the Venetians at Candia, and a plan of operations was immediately arranged. It was not long before the startling intelligence arrived that Nicosia, the capital of Cyprus, had been taken and sacked by the Turks, with all the circumstances of cruelty which distinguish wars in which the feeling of national hostility is embittered by religious hatred. The plan was now to be changed. A dispute arose among the commanders as to the course to be pursued. No one had authority enough to enforce compliance with his own opinion. The dispute ended in a rupture. The expedition was abandoned; and the several commanders returned home with their squadrons, without having struck a blow for the cause. It was a bad omen for the success of the league.*

Still, the stout-hearted pontiff was not discouraged. On the contrary, he endeavored to infuse his own heroic spirit into the hearts of his allies, giving them the most cheering assurances for the future if they would but be true to themselves. Philip did not need this encouragement. Once resolved, his was not a mind lightly to be turned from its purpose. Venice, on the other hand, soon showed that the Catholic king had good reason for distrusting her fidelity. Appalled by the loss of Nicosia, with her usual inconstancy, she despatched a secret agent to Constantinople to see if some terms might not yet be made with the sultan. The negotiation could not be managed so secretly, however, but that notice of it reached the ears of Pius the Fifth. He forthwith despatched an envoy to the republic to counteract this measure and to persuade the Venetians to trust to their Christian allies rather than to the Turks, the enemies of their country and their religion. The person selected for this mission was Colonna, who was quite as much distinguished for his address as for his valor. He performed his task well. He represented so forcibly to the government that the course he recommended was the one dictated not less by interest than by honor, that they finally acquiesced, and recalled their agent from Constantinople. It must be acknowledged that Colonna's arguments were greatly strengthened by the cold reception given to the Venetian envoy at Constantinople, where it was soon seen that

---

* Herrera, Historia general, tom. i. p. 798, et seq.—Cabrera, Filipe Segundo, lib. vi. cap. 17.—Sagredo, Monarcas Othomanos, p. 277.

the conquest of the capital had by no means tended to make the sultan relax his hold on Cyprus.[3]

Towards the close of 1570, the deputies from the three powers met in Rome to arrange the terms of the league. Spain was represented by the Cardinals Granvelle and Pacheco, together with the ambassador, Juan de Zuñiga, all three at that time being resident in Rome. It will readily be believed that the interests of Spain would not suffer in the hands of a commission with so skilful a tactician as Granvelle to direct it.

Yet, though the parties seemed to be embarked in a common cause, there was found much difficulty in reconciling their different pretensions. The deputies from Venice, in the usual spirit of her diplomacy, regarded the league as exclusively designed for her benefit,—in other words, for the protection of Cyprus against the Turks. The Spanish commissioners took a wider view, and talked of the war as one waged by the Christian against the Infidel,—against the Moors no less than the Turks. In this politic view of the matter, the Catholic king was entitled to the same protection for his colonies on the coast of Africa as Venice claimed for Cyprus.

Another cause of disagreement was the claim of each of the parties to select a commander-in-chief for the expedition from its own nation. This pre-eminence was finally conceded to Spain, as the power that was to bear the largest share of the expenses.

It was agreed that the treaty should be permanent in

---

[3] Cabrera, Filipe Segundo, p. 667.—Sagredo, Monarcas Othomanos, p. 277.

its duration, and should be directed against the Moors of Tunis, Tripoli, and Algiers, as well as against the Turks; that the contracting parties should furnish two hundred galleys, one hundred transports and smaller vessels, fifty thousand foot, and four thousand five hundred horse, with the requisite artillery and munitions; that by April, at farthest, of every succeeding year, a similar force should be held in readiness by the allies for expeditions to the Levant; and that any year in which there was no expedition in common, and either Spain or the republic should desire to engage in one on her own account against the infidel, the other confederates should furnish fifty galleys towards it; that if the enemy should invade the dominions of any of the three powers, the others should be bound to come to the aid of their ally; that three-sixths of the expenses of the war should be borne by the Catholic King, two-sixths by the republic, the remaining sixth by the Holy See; that the Venetians should lend his holiness twelve galleys, which he was to man and equip at his own charge, as his contribution towards the armament; that each power should appoint a captain-general; that the united voices of the three commanders should regulate the plan of operations; that the execution of this plan should be intrusted to the captain-general of the league, and that this high office should be given to Don John of Austria; that, finally, no one of the parties should make peace, or enter into a truce with the enemy, without the knowledge and consent of the others.[4]

[4] A copy of the treaty, in Latin, dated May 25th, 1571, exists in the library of the Academy of History, at Madrid. Señor Rosell has

Such were the principal provisions of the famous treaty of the Holy League. The very first article declares this treaty perpetual in its nature. Yet we should be slow to believe that the shrewd and politic statesmen who directed the affairs of Spain and the republic could for a moment believe in the perpetuity of a contract which imposed such burdensome obligations on the parties. In fact, the league did not hold together two years. But it held together long enough to accomplish a great result, and as such occupies an important place in the history of the times.

Although a draft of the treaty had been prepared in the latter part of the preceding year, it was not ratified till 1571.[5] On the twenty-fourth of May the pope caused it to be read aloud in full consistory. He then, laying his hand on his breast, solemnly swore to the observance of it. The ambassadors of Spain and Venice made oath to the same effect, on behalf of their governments, placing their hands on a missal with a copy of the Gospels beneath it. On the day following, after mass had been performed, the treaty was publicly proclaimed in the church of St. Peter.[6]

The tidings of the alliance of the three powers caused a great sensation throughout Christendom. Far from dismaying the sultan, however, it only stimulated him to greater exertions. Availing himself of the resources of his vast empire, he soon got together a

transferred it to the appendix of his work, Historia del Combate naval de Lepanto (Madrid, 1853), pp. 180-189.

[5] A copy from the first draft of the treaty, as prepared in 1570, is incorporated in the Documentos inéditos (tom. iii. p. 337, et seq.). The original is in the library of the duke of Ossuna.

[6] Rosell, Combate naval de Lepanto, p. 56.

powerful fleet, partly drawn from his own dominions, and in part from those of the Moslem powers on the Mediterranean, who acknowledged allegiance to the Porte. The armada was placed under the command of Selim's brother-in-law, the Pacha Piali, a man of an intrepid spirit, who had given many proofs of a humane and generous nature,—qualities more rare among the Turks, perhaps among all nations, than mere physical courage.

Early in the spring of 1571 the Ottoman admiral sailed out of the Golden Horn and directed his course towards Candia. Here he remained until joined by a strong Algerine force under the redoubtable corsair, Uluch Ali,—a Calabrian renegade, who had risen from the humblest condition to the post of dey of Algiers. Early in the season the combined fleets sailed for the Adriatic; and Piali, after landing and laying waste the territory belonging to the republic, detached Uluch with his squadron to penetrate higher up the gulf. The Algerine, in executing these orders, advanced so near to Venice as to throw the inhabitants of that capital into a consternation such as they had not felt since the cannon of the Genoese, two centuries before, had resounded over their waters. But it was not the dey's purpose to engage in so formidable an enterprise as an assault upon Venice; and, soon drawing off, he joined the commander-in-chief at Corfu, where they waited for tidings of the Christian fleet.[7]

The indefatigable Pius, even before the treaty was signed, had despatched his nephew, Cardinal Alessan-

[7] Paruta, Guerra di Cipro, p. 120, et seq.—Herrera, Hist. general, tom. ii. pp. 14, 15.

drino, to the different courts, to rouse the drooping spirits of the allies and to persuade other princes of Christendom to join the league. In the middle of May, the legate, attended by a stately train of ecclesiastics, appeared at Madrid. Philip gave him a reception that fully testified his devotion to the Holy See. The king's brother, Don John, and his favorite minister, Ruy Gomez de Silva, with some of the principal nobles, waited at once on the cardinal, who had taken up his quarters in the suburbs, at the Dominican monastery of Atocha, tenanted by brethren of his own order. On the following morning the papal envoy made his entrance in great state into the capital. He was mounted on a mule, gorgeously caparisoned, the gift of the city. John of Austria rode on his right; and he was escorted by a pompous array of prelates and grandees, who seemed to vie with one another in the splendor of their costumes. On the way he was met by the royal cavalcade. As the legate paid his obeisance to the monarch, he remained with his head uncovered; and Philip, with a similar act of courtesy, while he addressed a few remarks to the churchman, held his hat in his hand.[8] He then joined the procession, riding between the legate on the right and his brother on the left, who was observed from time to time to take part in the conversation, a circumstance occasioning some surprise, says an historian, as altogether contrary to the established etiquette of the punctilious Castilian court.[9]

[8] Cabrera, Filipe Segundo, lib. ix. cap. 22.—Ferreras, Hist. d'Espagne, tom. x. pp. 247, 248.—Vanderhammen, Don Juan de Austria, fol. 152.

[9] " No poco se maravillaron los curiosos, viéndole, ó por casualidad

The ceremonies were concluded by religious services in the church of Santa Maria, where the legate, after preaching a discourse, granted all present a full remission of the pains of Purgatory for two hundred years.[10] A gift of more worth, in a temporal view, was the grant to the king of the *cruzada*, the *excusada*, and other concessions of ecclesiastical revenue, which the Roman see knows so well how to bestow on the champions of the Faith. These concessions came in good time to supply the royal coffers, sorely drained by the costly preparations for the war.

Meanwhile, the Venetians were pushing forward their own preparations with their wonted alacrity,—indeed, with more alacrity than thoroughness. They were prompt in furnishing their quota of vessels, but discreditably remiss in their manner of equipping them. The fleet was placed under the charge of Sebastian Veniero, a noble who had grown gray in the service of his country. Zanne, who had had the command of the fleet in the preceding summer, was superseded on the charge of incapacity, shown especially in his neglect to bring the enemy to action. His process continued for two years, without any opportunity being allowed to the accused of appearing in his own vindication. It was finally brought to a close by his death,—the consequence, as it is said, of a broken heart. If it were so, it would not be a solitary instance of such a fate in

---

ó bien de intento, terciar llanamente en la conversacion, contra las etiquetas hasta entonces observadas." Rosell, Combate naval de Lepanto, p. 59.

[10] "Y concede dozientos años de perdon a los presentes."--Vanderhammen, Don Juan de Austria, fol. 152.

the annals of the stern republic. Before midsummer the new admiral sailed with his fleet, or as much of it as was then ready, for the port of Messina, appointed as the place of rendezvous for the allies. Here he was soon joined by Colonna, the papal commander, with the little squadron furnished by his holiness; and the two fleets lay at anchor, side by side, in the capacious harbor, waiting the arrival of the rest of the confederates and of John of Austria.

Preparations for the war were now going actively forward in Spain. Preparations on so large a scale had not been seen since the war with Paul the Fourth and Henry the Third, which ushered in Philip's accession. All the great ports in the Peninsula, as well as in the kingdom of Naples, in Sicily, in the Balearic Isles,— in every part of the empire, in short,—swarmed with artisans, busily engaged in fitting out the fleet which was to form Philip's contingent to the armament. By the terms of the treaty he was to bear one-half of the charges of the expedition. In his naval preparations he spared neither cost nor care. Ninety royal galleys, and more than seventy ships of smaller dimensions, were got in readiness in the course of the summer. They were built and equipped in that thorough manner which vindicated the pre-eminence in naval architecture claimed by Spain, and formed a strong contrast to the slovenly execution of the Venetians."

" " *De las mejores que jamas se han visto,*"—" among the best galleys that were ever seen,"—says Don Juan, in a letter from Messina to Don Garcia de Toledo. Documentos inéditos, tom. iii. p. 15.—The earlier part of the third volume of the Documentos inéditos is taken up with the correspondence between John of Austria and Garcia de Toledo, in which the former asks information and advice in respect

Levies of troops were at the same time diligently enforced in all parts of the monarchy. Even a corps of three thousand German mercenaries was subsidized for the campaign. Troops were drawn from the veteran garrisons in Lombardy and the kingdom of Naples. As the Morisco insurrection was fortunately quelled, the forces engaged in it, among whom were the brave Neapolitan battalion and its commander, Padilla, could now be employed in the war against the Turk.

But it can hardly be said to have required extraordinary efforts to fill the ranks on the present occasion; for seldom had a war been so popular with the nation. Indeed, the Spaniards entered into it with an alacrity which might well have suggested the idea that their master had engaged in it on his own account rather than as an ally. It was in truth a war that appealed in a peculiar manner to the sensibilities of the Castilian, familiar from his cradle with the sound of the battle-cry against the infidel. The whole number of infantry raised by the confederates amounted to twenty-nine

to the best mode of conducting the war. Don Garcia de Toledo, fourth marquis of Villafranca, was a man of high family and of great sagacity and experience. He had filled some of the highest posts in the government, and, as the reader may remember, was viceroy of Sicily at the time when Malta was besieged by the Turks. The coldness which on that occasion he appeared to show to the besieged excited general indignation; and I ventured to state, on an authority which I did not profess to esteem the best, that in consequence of this he fell into disgrace, and was suffered to pass the remainder of his years in obscurity. (*Ante,* vol. ii. p. 448.) An investigation of documents which I had not then seen shows this to have been an error. The ample correspondence which both Philip the Second and Don John carried on with him gives undeniable proofs of the confidence he continued to enjoy at court, and the high deference which was paid to his opinion.

thousand. Of this number Spain alone sent over nineteen thousand well-appointed troops, comprehending numerous volunteers, many of whom belonged to the noblest houses of the Peninsula.[12]

On the sixth of June, Don John, after receiving the last instructions of his brother, set out from Madrid on his journey to the south. Besides his own private establishment, making a numerous train, he was escorted by a splendid company of lords and cavaliers, eager to share with him in the triumphs of the Cross. Anxious to reach the goal, he pushed forward at a more rapid rate than was altogether relished by the rest of the cavalcade. Yet, notwithstanding this speed on the road, there were matters that claimed his attention in the towns through which he passed, that occasioned some delay. His journey had the appearance of a royal progress. The castles of the great lords were thrown open with princely hospitality to receive him and his suite. In the chief cities, as Saragossa and Barcelona, he was entertained by the viceroys with all the pomp and ceremony that could have been shown to the king himself. He remained some days in the busy capital of Catalonia, and found there much to engage his attention in the arsenals and dock-yards, now alive with the bustle of preparation. He then made a brief pilgrimage to the neighboring Hermitage of Our Lady of Montserrat, where he paid his devotions, and conversed with the holy fathers, whom he had always deeply reverenced, and had before visited in their romantic solitudes.

[12] Authorities differ, as usual, as to the precise number both of vessels and troops. I have accepted the estimate of Rosell, who discreetly avoids the extremes on either side.

Embarking at Barcelona, he set sail with a squadron of more than thirty galleys,—a force strong enough to guard against the Moslem corsairs in the Mediterranean, and landed, on the twenty-fifth, at Genoa. The doge and the senate came out to welcome him, and he was lodged during his stay in the palace of Andrew Doria. Here he received embassies and congratulatory addresses from the different princes of Italy. He had already been greeted with an autograph letter, couched in the most benignant terms, from the sovereign pontiff. To all these communications Don John was careful to reply. He acquainted his holiness, in particular, with the whole course of his proceedings. While on the way he had received a letter from his brother, giving him a full catalogue of the appropriate titles by which each one of his correspondents should be addressed. Nor was this list confined to crowned heads, but comprehended nobles and cavaliers of every degree.[13] In no country has the perilous code of etiquette been more diligently studied than in Spain; and no Spaniard was better versed in it than Philip.

Pursuing his route by water, Don John, in the month of August, dropped anchor in the beautiful bay of Naples. Arrangements had been made in that city for his reception on a more magnificent scale than any he had witnessed on his journey. Granvelle, who had lately been raised to the post of viceroy, came forth, at the head of a long and brilliant procession, to welcome his royal guest. The houses that lined the streets were hung with richly-tinted tapestries and gayly fes-

---

[13] Vanderhammen has been careful to transcribe this precious catalogue. Don Juan de Austria, fol. 156, et seq.

tooned with flowers. The windows and verandas were graced with the beauty and fashion of that pleasure-loving capital; and many a dark eye sparkled as it gazed on the fine form and features of the youthful hero who at the age of twenty-four had come to Italy to assume the baton of command and lead the crusade against the Moslems. His splendid dress of white velvet and cloth of gold set off his graceful person to advantage. A crimson scarf floated loosely over his breast; and his snow-white plumes, drooping from his cap, mingled with the yellow curls that fell in profusion over his shoulders. It was a picture which the Italian maiden might love to look on. It was certainly not the picture of the warrior sheathed in the iron panoply of war. But the young prince, in his general aspect, might be relieved from the charge of effeminacy by his truly chivalrous bearing and the dauntless spirit which beamed from his clear blue eye. In his own lineaments he seemed to combine all that was most comely in the lineaments of his race. Fortunately, he had escaped the deformity of the heavy Burgundian lip, which he might perhaps have excused, as establishing his claims to a descent from the imperial house of Hapsburg.[14]

Don John had found no place more busy with preparations for the campaign than Naples. A fleet was riding at anchor in her bay, ready to sail under the command of Don Alvaro Bazan, first marquis of Santa Cruz, a nobleman who had distinguished himself by

[14] Vanderhammen, Don Juan de Austria, fol. 159, et seq.—Ferreras, Hist. d'Espagne, tom. x. p. 251.—Herrera, Hist. general, tom. ii. p. 15, et seq.

more than one gallant achievement in the Mediterranean, and who was rapidly laying the foundations of a fame that was one day to eclipse that of every other admiral in Castile.

Ten days Don John remained at Naples, detained by contrary winds. Though impatient to reach Messina, his time passed lightly amidst the *fêtes* and brilliant spectacles which his friendly hosts had provided for his entertainment. He entered gayly into the revels; for he was well skilled in the courtly and chivalrous exercises of the day. Few danced better than he, or rode, or fenced, or played at tennis with more spirit and skill, or carried off more frequently the prizes of the tourney. Indeed, he showed as much ambition to excel in the mimic game of war as on the field of battle. With his accomplishments and personal attractions, we may well believe that Don John had little reason to complain of coldness in the fair dames of Italy. But he seems to have been no less a favorite with the men. The young cavaliers, in particular, regarded him as the very mirror of chivalry, and studiously formed themselves on him as their model. His hair clustered thickly round his temples, and he was in the habit of throwing it back, so as to display his fine forehead to advantage. This suited his physiognomy. It soon became the mode with the gallants of the court; and even those whose physiognomies it did not suit were no less careful to arrange their hair in the same manner.

While at Naples he took part in a ceremony of an interesting and significant character. It was on the occasion of the presentation of a standard sent by Pius the Fifth for the Holy War. The ceremony took place in the church of the Franciscan convent of Santa Chiara. Granvelle officiated on the occasion. Mass was performed by the cardinal-viceroy in his pontificals. *Te Deum* was then chanted, after which Don John, approaching the altar with a slow and dignified step, gracefully knelt before the prelate, who, first delivering to him the baton of generalissimo, in the name of his holiness, next placed in his hands the consecrated standard. It was of azure damask. A crucifix was embroidered on the upper part of the banner, while below were the arms of the Church, with those of Spain on the right and of Venice on the left, united by a chain, from which were suspended the arms of John of Austria. The prelate concluded the ceremony by invoking the blessing of Heaven on its champion and beseeching that he might be permitted to carry the banner of the Cross victorious over its enemies. The choir of the convent then burst forth into a triumphant peal, and the people from every quarter of the vast edifice shouted "Amen!"[15]

It was a striking scene, pregnant with matter for meditation to those who gazed on it. For what could be more striking than the contrast afforded by these two individuals,—the one in the morning of life, his eye kindling with hope and generous ambition, as he looked into the future and prepared to tread the path of glory under auspices as brilliant as ever attended any mortal; the other drawing near to the evening of his day, looking to the past rather than the future, with pale and thoughtful brow, as of one who, after many a

---

[15] "Luego su Alteza, el Coro, y Pueblo dixeron con musica, vozes, y alegria; Amen." Vanderhammen, Juan de Austria, fol. 159.

toilsome day and sleepless night, had achieved the proud eminence for which his companion was panting, —and had found it barren!

The wind having become more favorable, Don John took leave of the gay capital of the South, and embarked for Messina, which he reached on the twenty-fifth of August. If in other places he had seen preparations for war, here he seemed to be brought on the very theatre of war. As he entered the noble port, he was saluted with the thunders of hundreds of pieces of ordnance from the combined fleets of Rome and Venice, which lay side by side awaiting his arrival. He landed beneath a triumphal arch of colossal dimensions, embossed with rich plates of silver and curiously sculptured with emblematical bas-reliefs and with complimentary legends in Latin verse, furnished by the classic poets of Italy.[16] He passed under two other arches of similar rich and elaborate construction, as he rode into the city amidst the ringing of bells, the cheers of the multitude, the waving of scarfs and handkerchiefs from the balconies, and other lively demonstrations of the public joy, such as might have intoxicated the brain of a less ambitious soldier than John of Austria. The festivities were closed in the evening by a general illumination of the city, and by a display of fireworks that threw a light far and wide over the beautiful harbor and the countless ships that floated on its waters.

Nothing could be finer, indeed, whether by day or by night, than the spectacle presented by the port of Messina. Every day a fresh reinforcement of squadrons,

[16] For a minute account of these arches and their manifold inscriptions, see Vanderhammen, Don Juan de Austria, fol. 160-162.

or of single galleys or brigantines, under some brave adventurer, entered the harbor to swell the numbers of the great armada. Many of these vessels, especially the galleys, were richly carved and gilt, after the fashion of the time, and with their many-colored streamers, and their flags displaying the arms of their several states, made a magnificent show as they glanced over the waters. None, in the splendor of their decorations, exceeded the *Real*, as the galley of the commander-in-chief was termed. It was of great size, and had been built in Barcelona, famous for its naval architecture all the world over. The stern of the vessel was profusely decorated with emblems and devices drawn from history. The interior was furnished in a style of luxury that seemed to be designed for pleasure rather than for the rough duties of war. But the galley was remarkable for both strength and speed,—the two most essential qualities in the construction of a ship. Of this she gave ample evidence in her contest with the Turk."[17]

The whole number of vessels in the armada, great and small, amounted to something more than three hundred. Of these full two-thirds were "royal galleys." Venice alone contributed one hundred and six, besides six *galeazzas*. These were ships of enormous bulk, and, as it would seem, of clumsy construction, carrying each more than forty pieces of artillery. The Spaniards counted a score of galleys less than their Venetian confederates. But they far exceeded them in the number of their frigates, brigantines, and vessels of smaller size. They boasted a still greater superiority in the equipment of their navy. Indeed, the Venetian

---

[17] Rosell, Combate naval de Lepanto, p. 84.

squadron was found so indifferently manned that Don John ordered several thousand hands to be drafted from the ships of the other Italian powers, and from the Spanish, to make up the necessary complement. This proceeding conveyed so direct a censure on the remissness of his countrymen as to give great disgust to the admiral, Veniero. But in the present emergency he had neither the power to resist nor to resent it.[18]

The number of persons on board of the fleet, soldiers and seamen, was estimated at eighty thousand. The galleys, impelled by oars more than by sails, required a large number of hands to navigate them. The soldiers, as we have seen, did not exceed twenty-nine thousand; of which number more than nineteen thousand were furnished by Spain. They were well-appointed troops, most of them familiar with war, and officered by men many of whom had already established a high reputation in the service. On surveying the muster-roll of cavaliers who embarked in this expedition, one may well believe that Spain had never before sent forth a fleet in which were to be found the names of so many of her sons illustrious for rank and military achievement. If the same can be said of Venice, we must consider that the present war was one in which the prosperity, perhaps the very existence, of the republic was involved. The Spaniard was animated by the true spirit of the Crusades, when, instead of mercenary motives, the

[18] Don John, in his correspondence with his friend Don Garcia de Toledo, speaks with high disgust of the negligence shown in equipping the Venetian galleys. In a letter dated Messina, August 30th, he says, "Póneme cierta congoja ver que el mundo me obliga á hacer alguna cosa de momento, contando las galeras por número y no por cualidad." Documentos inéditos, tom. iii. p. 18.

guerdon for which men fought was glory in this world and paradise in the next.

Sebastian Veniero, trembling for the possessions of the republic in the Adriatic, would have put to sea without further delay and sought out the enemy. But Don John, with a prudence hardly to have been expected, declined moving until he had been strengthened by all his reinforcements. He knew the resources of the Ottoman empire; he could not doubt that in the present emergency they would be strained to the utmost to equip a formidable armament; and he resolved not to expose himself unnecessarily to the chances of defeat by neglecting any means in his power to prepare for the encounter. It was a discreet determination, which must have met the entire approbation of his brother.

While he was thus detained at Messina, a papal nuncio, Odescalco, bishop of Pena, arrived there. He was the bearer of sundry spiritual favors from the pontiff, whose real object, no doubt, was to quicken the movements of John of Austria. The nuncio proclaimed a jubilee; and every man in the armada, from the captain-general downwards, having fasted three days, confessed and partook of the communion. The prelate, in the name of his holiness, then proclaimed a full remission of their sins; and he conceded to them the same indulgences as had been granted to the deliverers of the Holy Sepulchre. To Don John the pope communicated certain revelations and two cheering prophecies from St. Isidore, which his holiness declared had undoubted reference to the prince. It is further stated that Pius appealed to more worldly feelings, by intimating to the young commander that success could not fail to open the way to the acquisition of some independent sovereignty for himself.[19] Whether this suggestion first awakened so pleasing an idea in Don John's mind, or whether the wary pontiff was aware that it already existed there, it is certain that it became the spectre which from this time forward continued to haunt the imagination of the aspiring chieftain, and to beckon him onward in the path of perilous ambition to its melancholy close.

All being now in readiness, orders were given to weigh anchor; and on the sixteenth of September the magnificent armament—unrivalled by any which had rode upon these waters since the days of imperial Rome—stood out to sea. The papal nuncio, dressed in his pontificals, took a prominent station on the mole; and as each vessel passed successively before him he bestowed on it his apostolic benediction. Then, without postponing a moment longer his return, he left Messina and hastened back to Rome to announce the joyful tidings to his master.[20]

[19] Rosell, Combate naval de Lepanto, p. 82.—The clearest and by far the most elaborate account of the battle of Lepanto is to be found in the memoir of Don Cayetan Rosell, which received the prize of the Royal Academy of History of Madrid, in 1853. It is a narrative which may be read with pride by Spaniards, for the minute details it gives of the prowess shown by their heroic ancestors on that memorable day. The author enters with spirit into the stormy scene he describes. If his language may be thought sometimes to betray the warmth of national partiality, it cannot be denied that he has explored the best sources of information and endeavored to place the result fairly before the reader.

[20] Torres y Aguilera, Chronica de Guerra que ha acontescido en Italia y partes de Levante y Berberia desde 1570 en 1574 (Çaragoça, 1579), fol. 54.—Vanderhammen, Don Juan de Austria, fol. 165, et seq.—Cabrera, Filipe Segundo, lib. ix. cap. 23.

N*

CHAPTER X.

WAR WITH THE TURKS.

Plan of Operations.—Tidings of the Enemy.—Preparations for Combat.—Battle of Lepanto.—Rout of the Turkish Armada.

1571.

As the allied fleet coasted along the Calabrian shore, it was so much baffled by rough seas and contrary winds that its progress was slow. Not long before his departure, Don John had sent a small squadron under a Spanish captain, Gil de Andrada, to collect tidings of the enemy. On his return, that commander met the Christian fleet, and reported that the Turks, with a powerful armament, were still in the Adriatic, where they had committed fearful ravages on the Venetian territories. Don John now steered his course for Corfu, which, however, he did not reach till the twenty-sixth of September. He soon had ample opportunities of seeing for himself the traces of the enemy, in the smoking hamlets and desolated fields along the coast. The allies were welcomed with joy by the islanders, who furnished them with whatever supplies they needed. Here Don John learned that the Ottoman fleet had been seen standing into the gulf of Lepanto, where it lay as if waiting the coming of the Christians.

The young commander-in-chief had now no hesitation as to the course he ought to pursue. But he chose to call a council of his principal captains before deciding. The treaty of alliance, indeed, required him to consult with the other commanders before taking any decisive step in matters of importance; and this had been strenuously urged on him by the king, ever afraid of his brother's impetuosity.

The opinions of the council were divided. Some who had had personal experience of the naval prowess of the Turks appeared to shrink from encountering so formidable an armament, and would have confined the operations of the fleet to the siege of some place belonging to the Moslems. Even Doria, whose life had been spent in fighting with the infidel, thought it was not advisable to attack the enemy in his present position, surrounded by friendly shores, whence he might easily obtain succor. It would be better, he urged, to attack some neighboring place, like Navarino, which might have the effect of drawing him from the gulf, and thus compel him to give battle in some quarter more advantageous to the allies.

But the majority of the council took a very different view of the matter. To them it appeared that the great object of the expedition was to destroy the Ottoman fleet, and that a better opportunity could not be offered than the present one, while the enemy was shut up in the gulf, from which, if defeated, he would find no means of escape. Fortunately, this was the opinion not only of the majority, but of most of those whose opinions were entitled to the greatest deference. Among these were the gallant marquis of Santa Cruz, the Grand Commander Requesens, who still remained near the person of Don John and had command of a galley in his rear, Cardona, general of the Sicilian squadron, Barbarigo, the Venetian *provveditore*, next in authority to the captain-general of his nation, the Roman Colonna, and Alexander Farnese, the young prince of Parma, Don John's nephew, who had come, on this memorable occasion, to take his first lesson in the art of war,—an art in which he was destined to remain without a rival.

The commander-in-chief with no little satisfaction saw himself so well supported in his own judgment; and he resolved, without any unnecessary delay, to give the Turks battle in the position they had chosen. He was desirous, however, to be joined by a part of his fleet, which, baffled by the winds, and without oars, still lagged far behind. For the galley, with its numerous oars in addition to its sails, had somewhat of the properties of a modern steamer, which so gallantly defies both wind and wave. As Don John wished also to review his fleet before coming to action, he determined to cross over to Comenizza, a capacious and well-protected port on the opposite coast of Albania.

This he did on the thirtieth of September. Here the vessels were got in readiness for immediate action. They passed in review before the commander-in-chief, and went through their various evolutions; while the artillerymen and musketeers showed excellent practice. Don John looked with increased confidence to the approaching combat. An event, however, occurred at this time which might have been attended with the worst consequences.

A Roman officer named Tortona, one of those who

had been drafted to make up the complement of the Venetian galleys, engaged in a brawl with some of his crew. This reached the ears of Veniero, the Venetian captain-general. The old man, naturally of a choleric temper, and still smarting from the insult which he fancied he had received by the introduction of the allies on board of his vessels, instantly ordered the arrest of the offender. Tortona for a long while resisted the execution of these orders; and when finally seized, with some of his companions, they were all sentenced by the vindictive Veniero to be hung at the yard-arm. Such a high-handed proceeding caused the deepest indignation in Don John, who regarded it, moreover, as an insult to himself. In the first moments of his wrath he talked of retaliating on the Venetian admiral by a similar punishment. But, happily, the remonstrances of Colonna—who, as the papal commander, had in truth the most reason to complain— and the entreaties of other friends prevailed on the angry chief to abstain from any violent act. He insisted, however, that Veniero should never again take his place at the council-board, but should be there represented by the *provveditore* Barbarigo, next in command,—a man, fortunately, possessed of a better control over his temper than was shown by his superior. Thus the cloud passed away which threatened for a moment to break up the harmony of the allies and to bring ruin on the enterprise.[1]

[1] Torres y Aguilera, Chronica, fol. 64.—Vanderhammen, Don Juan de Austria, fol. 173.—Paruta, Guerra di Cipro, p. 149.—Relacion de la Batalla naval que entre Christianos y Turcos hubo el año 1571, MS.—Otra Relacion, Documentos inéditos, tom. iii. p. 365.

On the third of October, Don John, without waiting longer for the missing vessels, again put to sea, and stood for the gulf of Lepanto. As the fleet swept down the Ionian Sea, it passed many a spot famous in ancient story. None, we may imagine, would be so likely to excite an interest at this time as Actium, on whose waters was fought the greatest naval battle of antiquity. But the mariner, probably, gave little thought to the past, as he dwelt on the conflict that awaited him at Lepanto. On the fifth, a thick fog enveloped the armada and shut out every object from sight. Fortunately, the vessels met with no injury, and, passing by Ithaca, the ancient home of Ulysses, they safely anchored off the eastern coast of Cephalonia. For two days their progress was thwarted by head-winds. But on the seventh, Don John, impatient of delay, again put to sea, though wind and weather were still unfavorable.

While lying off Cephalonia he had received tidings that Famagosta, the second city of Cyprus, had fallen into the hands of the enemy, and this under circumstances of unparalleled perfidy and cruelty. The place, after a defence that had cost hecatombs of lives to the besiegers, was allowed to capitulate on honorable terms. Mustapha, the Moslem commander, the same fierce chief who had conducted the siege of Malta, requested an interview at his quarters with four of the principal Venetian captains. After a short and angry conference, he ordered them all to execution. Three were beheaded. The other, a noble named Bragadino, who had held the supreme command, he caused to be flayed alive in the market-place of the city. The skin of the wretched victim was then stuffed; and with this ghastly trophy dangling from the yard-arm of his galley, the brutal monster sailed back to Constantinople, to receive the reward of his services from Selim.[2] These services were great. The fall of Famagosta secured the fall of Cyprus, which thus became permanently incorporated in the Ottoman empire.[3]

The tidings of these shocking events filled the breast of every Venetian with an inextinguishable thirst for vengeance. The confederates entered heartily into these feelings; and all on board of the armada were impatient for the hour that was to bring them hand to hand with the enemies of the Faith.

It was two hours before dawn, on Sunday, the memorable seventh of October, when the fleet weighed anchor. The wind had become lighter; but it was still contrary, and the galleys were indebted for their progress much more to their oars than their sails. By sunrise they were abreast of the Curzolari, a cluster of huge rocks, or rocky islets, which on the north defends the entrance of the gulf of Lepanto. The fleet moved laboriously along, while every eye was strained to catch the first glimpse of the hostile navy. At length the watch on the foretop of the *Real* called out, "A sail!" and soon after declared that the whole Ottoman fleet was in sight. Several others, climbing up the rigging, confirmed his report; and in a few moments more,

---
[2] Paruta, Guerra di Cipro, pp. 143, 144.—"Despues hizo que lo degollassen vivo, y lleno el pellejo de paja lo hizo colgar de la entena de una galeota, y desta manera lo llevo por toda la ribera de la Suria." Torres y Aguilera, Chronica, fol. 45.

[3] Ibid., fol. 44, 45.—Paruta, Guerra di Cipro, pp. 130-144.—Sagredo, Monarcas Othomanos pp. 283-289.

word was sent to the same effect by Andrew Doria, who commanded on the right. There was no longer any doubt; and Don John, ordering his pennon to be displayed at the mizzen-peak, unfurled the great standard of the League, given by the pope, and directed a gun to be fired, the signal for battle. The report, as it ran along the rocky shores, fell cheerily on the ears of the confederates, who, raising their eyes towards the consecrated banner, filled the air with their shouts.[4]

The principal captains now came on board the *Real*, to receive the last orders of the commander-in-chief. Even at this late hour there were some who ventured to intimate their doubts of the expediency of engaging the enemy in a position where he had a decided advantage. But Don John cut short the discussion. "Gentlemen," he said, "this is the time for combat, not for counsel." He then continued the dispositions he was making for the attack.

He had already given to each commander of a galley written instructions as to the manner in which the line of battle was to be formed in case of meeting the enemy. The armada was now disposed in that order. It extended on a front of three miles. Far on the right, a squadron of sixty-four galleys was commanded by the Genoese admiral, Andrew Doria,—a name of terror to the Moslems. The centre, or *battle*, as it was called, consisting of sixty-three galleys, was led by John of Austria, who was supported on the one side by Colonna, the captain-general of the pope, and on

---

[4] Torres y Aguilera, Chronica, fol. 65.—Documentos inéditos, tom. iii. p. 241.—Rosell, Historia del Combate naval, pp. 93, 94.

the other by the Venetian captain-general, Veniero. Immediately in the rear was the galley of the Grand Commander Requesens, who still remained near the person of his former pupil; though a difference which arose between them on the voyage, fortunately now healed, showed that the young commander-in-chief was wholly independent of his teacher in the art of war.

The left wing was commanded by the noble Venetian, Barbarigo, whose vessels stretched along the Ætolian shore, to which he approached as near as, in his ignorance of the coast, he dared to venture, so as to prevent his being turned by the enemy. Finally, the reserve, consisting of thirty-five galleys, was given to the brave marquis of Santa Cruz, with directions to act in any quarter where he thought his presence most needed. The smaller craft, some of which had now arrived, seem to have taken little part in the action, which was thus left to the galleys.

Each commander was to occupy so much space with his galley as to allow room for manœuvring it to advantage, and yet not enough to allow the enemy to break the line. He was directed to single out his adversary, to close with him at once, and board as soon as possible. The beaks of the galleys were pronounced to be a hinderance rather than a help in action. They were rarely strong enough to resist a shock from an antagonist, and they much interfered with the working and firing of the guns. Don John had the beak of his vessel cut away. The example was followed throughout the fleet, and, as it is said, with eminently good effect. It may seem strange that this discovery should have been reserved for the crisis of a battle.[5]

When the officers had received their last instructions, they returned to their respective vessels; and Don John, going on board of a light frigate, passed rapidly through the part of the armada lying on his right, while he commanded Requesens to do the same with the vessels on his left. His object was to feel the temper of his men, and to rouse their mettle by a few words of encouragement. The Venetians he reminded of their recent injuries. The hour for vengeance, he told them, had arrived. To the Spaniards and other confederates he said, "You have come to fight the battle of the Cross; to conquer or to die. But, whether you are to die or conquer, do your duty this day, and you will secure a glorious immortality." His words were received with a burst of enthusiasm which went to the heart of the commander and assured him that he could rely on his men in the hour of trial. On returning to his vessel, he saw Veniero on his quarter-deck; and they exchanged salutations in as friendly a manner as if no difference had existed between them. At this solemn hour both these brave men were willing to forget all personal animosity in a common feeling of devotion to the great cause in which they were engaged.[6]

The Ottoman fleet came on slowly and with difficulty. For, strange to say, the wind, which had hitherto been

---

[5] Torres y Aguilera, Chronica, fol. 53.—Herrera, Hist. general, tom. ii. p. 30.—Relacion de la Batalla naval, MS.—Rosell, Historia del Combate naval, pp. 95, 99, 100.

[6] Torres y Aguilera, Chronica, fol. 67, et seq.—Relacion de la Batalla naval, MS.—Otras Relaciones, Documentos inéditos, tom. iii. pp. 242, 262.

adverse to the Christians, after lulling for a time, suddenly shifted to the opposite quarter and blew in the face of the enemy.[7] As the day advanced, moreover, the sun, which had shone in the eyes of the confederates, gradually shot its rays into those of the Moslems. Both circumstances were of good omen to the Christians, and the first was regarded as nothing short of a direct interposition of Heaven. Thus ploughing its way along, the Turkish armament, as it came more into view, showed itself in greater strength than had been anticipated by the allies. It consisted of nearly two hundred and fifty royal galleys, most of them of the largest class, besides a number of smaller vessels in the rear, which, like those of the allies, appear scarcely to have come into action. The men on board, of every description, were computed at not less than a hundred and twenty thousand.[8] The galleys spread out, as usual with the Turks, in the form of a regular half-moon, covering a wider extent of surface than the combined fleets, which they somewhat exceeded in number. They presented, indeed, as they drew nearer, a magnificent array, with their gilded and gaudily-painted prows, and their myriads of pennons and streamers fluttering gayly in the breeze; while the rays of the morning sun glanced

[7] Most of the authorities notice this auspicious change of the wind. Among others, see Relacion de la Batalla naval, MS.,—Relacion escrita por Miguel Servia, confesor de Don Juan, Documentos inéditos, tom. xi. p. 368,—Torres y Aguilera, Chronica, fol. 75.—The testimony is that of persons present in the action.

[8] Amidst the contradictory estimates of the number of the vessels and the forces in the Turkish armada to be found in different writers and even in official relations, I have conformed to the statement given in Señor Rosell's *Memoria*, prepared after a careful comparison of the various authorities. Historia del Combate naval, p. 94.

on the polished scimitars of Damascus, and on the superb aigrettes of jewels which sparkled in the turbans of the Ottoman chiefs.

In the centre of the extended line, and directly opposite to the station occupied by the captain-general of the League, was the huge galley of Ali Pasha. The right of the armada was commanded by Mahomet Sirocco, viceroy of Egypt, a circumspect as well as courageous leader; the left, by Uluch Ali, dey of Algiers, the redoubtable corsair of the Mediterranean. Ali Pasha had experienced a difficulty like that of Don John, as several of his officers had strongly urged the inexpediency of engaging so formidable an armament as that of the allies. But Ali, like his rival, was young and ambitious. He had been sent by his master to fight the enemy; and no remonstrances, not even those of Mahomet Sirocco, for whom he had great respect, could turn him from his purpose.

He had, moreover, received intelligence that the allied fleet was much inferior in strength to what it proved. In this error he was fortified by the first appearance of the Christians; for the extremity of their left wing, commanded by Barbarigo, stretching behind the Ætolian shore, was hidden from his view. As he drew nearer and saw the whole extent of the Christian lines, it is said his countenance fell. If so, he still did not abate one jot of his resolution. He spoke to those around him with the same confidence as before, of the result of the battle. He urged his rowers to strain every nerve. Ali was a man of more humanity in his nature than often belonged to his nation. His galley-slaves were all, or nearly all,

Christian captives; and he addressed them in this brief and pithy manner: "If your countrymen are to win this day, Allah give you the benefit of it; yet if I win it, you shall certainly have your freedom. If you feel that I do well by you, do then the like by me."[9]

As the Turkish admiral drew nearer, he made a change in his order of battle, by separating his wings farther from his centre, thus conforming to the dispositions of the allies. Before he had come within cannon-shot, he fired a gun by way of challenge to his enemy. It was answered by another from the galley of John of Austria. A second gun discharged by Ali was as promptly replied to by the Christian commander. The distance between the two fleets was now rapidly diminishing. At this solemn moment a death-like silence reigned throughout the armament of the confederates. Men seemed to hold their breath, as if absorbed in the expectation of some great catastrophe. The day was magnificent. A light breeze, still adverse to the Turks, played on the waters, somewhat fretted by the contrary winds. It was nearly noon; and as the sun, mounting through a cloudless sky, rose to the zenith, he seemed to pause, as if to look down on the beautiful scene, where the multitude of galleys, moving over the water, showed like a holiday spectacle rather than a preparation for mortal combat.

The illusion was soon dispelled by the fierce yells

[9] "Si hoy es vuestro dia, Dios os lo dé; pero estad ciertos que si gano la jornada, os daré libertad: por lo tanto haced lo que debeis á las obras que de mi habeis recebido." Rosell, Historia del Combate naval, p. 101.—For the last pages see Paruta, Guerra di Cipro, pp. 150, 151,—Sagredo, Monarcas Othomanos, p. 292,—Torres y Aguilera, Chronica, fol. 65, 66,—Relacion de la Batalla naval, MS.

which rose on the air from the Turkish armada. It was the customary war-cry with which the Moslems entered into battle. Very different was the scene on board of the Christian galleys. Don John might be there seen, armed *cap-à-pie*, standing on the prow of the *Real*, anxiously awaiting the conflict. In this conspicuous position, kneeling down, he raised his eyes to heaven, and humbly prayed that the Almighty would be with his people on that day. His example was followed by the whole fleet. Officers and men, all prostrating themselves on their knees and turning their eyes to the consecrated banner which floated from the *Real*, put up a petition like that of their commander. They then received absolution from the priests, of whom there were some in every vessel; and each man, as he rose to his feet, gathered new strength, as he felt assured that the Lord of Hosts would fight on his side.[10]

When the foremost vessels of the Turks had come within cannon-shot, they opened their fire on the Christians. The firing soon ran along the whole of the Turkish line, and was kept up without interruption as it advanced. Don John gave orders for trumpet and atabal to sound the signal for action; which was followed by the simultaneous discharge of such of the

[10] This fact is told by most of the historians of the battle. The author of the manuscript so often cited by me further says that it was while the fleet was thus engaged in prayer for aid from the Almighty that the change of wind took place: "Y en este medio, que en la oracion se pedia á Dios la victoria, estaba el mar alterado de que nuestra armada recibia gran daño y antes que se acabase la dicha oracion el mar estuvo tan quieto y sosegado que jamas se a visto, fué fuerça á la armada enemiga amainar y venir al remo."

guns in the combined fleet as could be brought to bear on the enemy. The Spanish commander had caused the *galeazzas*, those mammoth war-ships of which some account has been already given, to be towed half a mile ahead of the fleet, where they might intercept the advance of the Turks. As the latter came abreast of them, the huge galleys delivered their broadsides right and left, and their heavy ordnance produced a startling effect. Ali Pasha gave orders for his galleys to open their line and pass on either side, without engaging these monsters of the deep, of which he had had no experience. Even so their heavy guns did considerable damage to several of the nearest vessels, and created some confusion in the pacha's line of battle. They were, however, but unwieldy craft, and, having accomplished their object, seem to have taken no further part in the combat.

The action began on the left wing of the allies, which Mahomet Sirocco was desirous of turning. This had been anticipated by Barbarigo, the Venetian admiral, who commanded in that quarter. To prevent it, as we have seen, he lay with his vessels as near the coast as he dared. Sirocco, better acquainted with the soundings, saw there was space enough for him to pass, and, darting by with all the speed that oars could give him, he succeeded in doubling on his enemy. Thus placed between two fires, the extreme of the Christian left fought at terrible disadvantage. No less than eight galleys went to the bottom, and several others were captured. The brave Barbarigo, throwing himself into the heat of the fight, without availing himself of his defensive armor, was pierced in the eye by an arrow, and, reluctant to leave the glory of the field to another, was borne to his cabin. The combat still continued with unabated fury on the part of the Venetians. They fought like men who felt that the war was theirs, and who were animated not only by the thirst for glory, but for revenge."

Far on the Christian right a manœuvre similar to that so successfully executed by Sirocco was attempted by Uluch Ali, the dey of Algiers. Profiting by his superiority in numbers, he endeavored to turn the right wing of the confederates. It was in this quarter that Andrew Doria commanded. He had foreseen this movement of his enemy, and he succeeded in foiling it. It was a trial of skill between the two most accomplished seamen in the Mediterranean. Doria extended his line so far to the right, indeed, to prevent being surrounded, that Don John was obliged to remind him that he left the centre too much exposed. His dispositions were so far unfortunate for himself that his own line was thus weakened and afforded some vulnerable points to his assailant. These were soon detected by the eagle eye of Uluch Ali; and, like the king of birds swooping on his prey, he fell on some galleys separated by a considerable interval from their companions, and,

---

[11] Torres y Aguilera, Chronica, fol. 71.—Paruta, Guerra di Cipro. p. 156.—Cabrera, Filipe Segundo, p. 688.—Relacion de la Batalla naval, MS.—Otra Relacion, Documentos inéditos, tom. xi. p. 368.— The inestimable collection of the Documentos inéditos contains several narratives of the battle of Lepanto by contemporary pens. One of these is from the manuscript of Fray Miguel Servia, the confessor of John of Austria, and present with him, in the engagement. The different narratives have much less discrepancy with one another than is usual on such occasions.

sinking more than one, carried off the great *Capitana* of Malta in triumph as his prize."

While the combat opened thus disastrously to the allies both on the right and on the left, in the centre they may be said to have fought with doubtful fortune. Don John had led his division gallantly forward. But the object on which he was intent was an encounter with Ali Pasha, the foe most worthy of his sword. The Turkish commander had the same combat no less at heart. The galleys of both were easily recognized, not only from their position, but from their superior size and richer decoration. The one, moreover, displayed the holy banner of the League; the other, the great Ottoman standard. This, like the ancient standard of the caliphs, was held sacred in its character. It was covered with texts from the Koran, emblazoned in letters of gold, and had the name of Allah inscribed upon it no less than twenty-eight thousand nine hundred times. It was the banner of the sultan, having passed from father to son since the foundation of the imperial dynasty, and was never seen in the field unless the grand seigneur or his lieutenant was there in person."

Both the chiefs urged on their rowers to the top of

[12] Torres y Aguilera, Chronica, fol. 72.—Relacion de la Batalla naval, MS.—The last-mentioned manuscript is one of many left us by parties engaged in the fight. The author of this relation seems to have written it on board one of the galleys, while lying at Petala, during the week after the engagement. The events are told in a plain, unaffected manner, that invites the confidence of the reader. The original manuscript, from which my copy was taken, is to be found in the library of the University of Leyden.

[13] A minute description of the Ottoman standard, taken from a manuscript of Luis del Marmol, is given in the Coleccion de Documentos inéditos, tom. iii. p. 270, et seq.

their speed. Their galleys soon shot ahead of the rest of the line, driven through the boiling surges as by the force of a tornado, and closed with a shock that made every timber crack and the two vessels quiver to their very keels. So powerful, indeed, was the impetus they received that the pacha's galley, which was considerably the larger and loftier of the two, was thrown so far upon its opponent that the prow reached the fourth bench of rowers. As soon as the vessels were disengaged from each other, and those on board had recovered from the shock, the work of death began. Don John's chief strength consisted in some three hundred Spanish arquebusiers, culled from the flower of his infantry. Ali, on the other hand, was provided with an equal number of janizaries. He was followed by a smaller vessel, in which two hundred more were stationed as a *corps de réserve*. He had, moreover, a hundred archers on board. The bow was still as much in use with the Turks as with the other Moslems.

The pacha opened at once on his enemy a terrible fire of cannon and musketry. It was returned with equal spirit and much more effect; for the Turks were observed to shoot over the heads of their adversaries. The Moslem galley was unprovided with the defences which protected the sides of the Spanish vessels; and the troops, crowded together on the lofty prow, presented an easy mark to their enemy's balls. But, though numbers of them fell at every discharge, their places were soon supplied by those in reserve. They were enabled, therefore, to keep up an incessant fire, which wasted the strength of the Spaniards; and, as both Christian and Mussulman fought with indomitable spirit, it seemed doubtful to which side victory would incline.

The affair was made more complicated by the entrance of other parties into the conflict. Both Ali and Don John were supported by some of the most valiant captains in their fleets. Next to the Spanish commander, as we have seen, were Colonna and the veteran Veniero, who, at the age of seventy-six, performed feats of arms worthy of a paladin of romance. In this way a little squadron of combatants gathered round the principal leaders, who sometimes found themselves assailed by several enemies at the same time. Still the chiefs did not lose sight of one another; but, beating off their inferior foes as well as they could, each, refusing to loosen his hold, clung with mortal grasp to his antagonist.[14]

Thus the fight raged along the whole extent of the entrance to the gulf of Lepanto. The volumes of vapor rolling heavily over the waters effectually shut out from sight whatever was passing at any considerable distance, unless when a fresher breeze dispelled the smoke for a moment, or the flashes of the heavy guns threw a transient gleam on the dark canopy of battle. If the eye of the spectator could have penetrated the cloud of smoke that enveloped the combatants, and have embraced the whole scene at a glance, he would have perceived them broken up into small detachments, separately engaged one with another, independently of the rest, and indeed ignorant of all that was doing in other quarters. The contest exhibited few of those

---

[14] Documentos inéditos, tom. iii. p. 265; tom. xi. p. 368.—Torres y Aguilera, Chronica, fol. 70.—Paruta, Guerra di Cipro, pp. 156, 157.—Relacion de la Batalla naval, MS.

large combinations and skilful manœuvres to be expected in a great naval encounter. It was rather an assemblage of petty actions, resembling those on land. The galleys, grappling together, presented a level arena, on which soldier and galley-slave fought hand to hand, and the fate of the engagement was generally decided by boarding. As in most hand-to-hand contests, there was an enormous waste of life. The decks were loaded with corpses, Christian and Moslem lying promiscuously together in the embrace of death. Instances are recorded where every man on board was slain or wounded.[15] It was a ghastly spectacle, where blood flowed in rivulets down the sides of the vessels, staining the waters of the gulf for miles around.

It seemed as if a hurricane had swept over the sea and covered it with the wreck of the noble armaments which a moment before were so proudly riding on its bosom. Little had they now to remind one of their late magnificent array, with their hulls battered, their masts and spars gone or splintered by the shot, their canvas cut into shreds and floating wildly on the breeze, while thousands of wounded and drowning men were clinging to the floating fragments and calling piteously for help. Such was the wild uproar which succeeded the Sabbath-like stillness that two hours before had reigned over these beautiful solitudes.

[15] Herrera notices one galley, "La Piamontesa de Saboya degollada en ella toda la gente de cabo y remo y despedazado con once heridas D. Francisco de Saboya." Another, "La Florencia," says Rosell, "perdió todos los soldados, chusma, galeotes y caballeros de San Esteban que en ella habia, excepto su capitan Tomás de Médicis y diez y seis hombres más, aunque todos heridos y estropeados." Historia del Combate naval, p. 113.

The left wing of the confederates, commanded by Barbarigo, had been sorely pressed by the Turks, as we have seen, at the beginning of the fight. Barbarigo himself had been mortally wounded. His line had been turned. Several of his galleys had been sunk. But the Venetians gathered courage from despair. By incredible efforts, they succeeded in beating off their enemies. They became the assailants in their turn. Sword in hand, they carried one vessel after another. The Capuchin was seen in the thickest of the fight, waving aloft his crucifix and leading the boarders to the assault.[16] The Christian galley-slaves, in some instances, broke their fetters and joined their countrymen against their masters. Fortunately, the vessel of Mahomet Sirocco, the Moslem admiral, was sunk ; and though extricated from the water himself, it was only to perish by the sword of his conqueror, Giovanni Contarini. The Venetian could find in his heart no mercy for the Turk.

The fall of their commander gave the final blow to his followers. Without further attempt to prolong the fight, they fled before the avenging swords of the Venetians. Those nearest the land endeavored to escape by running their vessels ashore, where they abandoned them as prizes to the Christians. Yet many of the fugitives, before gaining the land, perished miserably in the waves. Barbarigo, the Venetian admiral, who

---

[16] "Tomo una Alabarda o Pertesana, y ligando en ella el Sancto Crucifixo, verdadera pendon, se puso delante de todos assi desarmado como estava, y fue el primero que entro en la Galera Turquesca, haziendo con su Alabarda cosas que ponian admiracion." Torres y Aguilera, Chronicas, fol. 75.

was still lingering in agony, heard the tidings of the enemy's defeat, and, uttering a few words expressive of his gratitude to Heaven, which had permitted him to see this hour, he breathed his last.[17]

During this time the combat had been going forward in the centre between the two commanders-in-chief, Don John and Ali Pasha, whose galleys blazed with an incessant fire of artillery and musketry, that enveloped them like "a martyr's robe of flames." The parties fought with equal spirit, though not with equal fortune. Twice the Spaniards had boarded their enemy, and both times they had been repulsed with loss. Still, their superiority in the use of fire-arms would have given them a decided advantage over their opponents if the loss they had inflicted had not been speedily repaired by fresh reinforcements. More than once the contest between the two chieftains was interrupted by the arrival of others to take part in the fray. They soon, however, returned to each other, as if unwilling to waste their strength on a meaner enemy. Through the whole engagement both commanders exposed themselves to danger as freely as any common soldier. In such a contest even Philip must have admitted that it would be difficult for his brother to find, with honor, a place of safety. Don John received a wound in the foot. It was a slight one, however, and he would not allow it to be dressed till the action was over.

---

[17] "Vivió hasta que sabiendo que la vitoria era ganada dijo: que daba gracias á Dios que lo hubiese guardado tanto que viese vencida la batalla y roto aquel comun enemigo que tanto deseó ver destruido." Herrera, Relacion de la Guerra de Cipro, Documentos inéditos, tom. xxi. p. 360.

Again his men were mustered, and a third time the trumpets sounded to the attack. It was more successful than the preceding. The Spaniards threw themselves boldly into the Turkish galley. They were met with the same spirit as before by the janizaries. Ali Pasha led them on. Unfortunately, at this moment he was struck in the head by a musket-ball and stretched senseless in the gangway. His men fought worthily of their ancient renown. But they missed the accustomed voice of their commander. After a short but ineffectual struggle against the fiery impetuosity of the Spaniards, they were overpowered and threw down their arms. The decks were loaded with the bodies of the dead and the dying. Beneath these was discovered the Turkish commander-in-chief, severely wounded, but perhaps not mortally. He was drawn forth by some Castilian soldiers, who, recognizing his person, would at once have despatched him. But the disabled chief, having rallied from the first effects of his wound, had sufficient presence of mind to divert them from their purpose by pointing out the place below where he had deposited his money and jewels; and they hastened to profit by the disclosure before the treasure should fall into the hands of their comrades.

Ali was not so successful with another soldier, who came up soon after, brandishing his sword and preparing to plunge it into the body of the prostrate commander. It was in vain that the latter endeavored to turn the ruffian from his purpose. He was a convict, one of those galley-slaves whom Don John had caused to be unchained from the oar and furnished with arms. He could not believe that any treasure would be worth so much as the head of the pacha. Without further hesitation, he dealt him a blow which severed it from his shoulders. Then, returning to his galley, he laid the bloody trophy before Don John. But he had miscalculated on his recompense. His commander gazed on it with a look of pity mingled with horror. He may have thought of the generous conduct of Ali to his Christian captives, and have felt that he deserved a better fate. He coldly inquired "of what use such a present could be to him," and then ordered it to be thrown into the sea. Far from the order being obeyed, it is said the head was stuck on a pike and raised aloft on board of the captured galley. At the same time the banner of the Crescent was pulled down; while that of the Cross, run up in its place, proclaimed the downfall of the pacha.[18]

The sight of the sacred ensign was welcomed by the Christians with a shout of "Victory!" which rose high above the din of battle.[19] The tidings of the death of

[18] Relacion de la Batalla naval, MS.—Herrera, Hist. general, tom. ii. p. 33.—Paruta, Guerra di Cipro, pp. 157, 158.—Documentos inéditos, tom. iii. p. 244.—Torres y Aguilera tells a rather extraordinary anecdote respecting the great standard of the League in the *Real*. The figure of Christ emblazoned on it was not hit by a ball or arrow during the action, notwithstanding every other banner was pierced in a multitude of places. Two arrows, however, lodged on either side of the crucifix, when a monkey belonging to the galley ran up the mast, and, drawing out the weapons with his teeth, threw them overboard! (Chronica, fol. 75.) Considering the number of ecclesiastics on board the fleet, it is remarkable that no more miracles occurred on this occasion.

[19] Torres y Aguilera, Chronica, fol. 72, et seq.—Relacion de la Batalla naval, MS.—Vanderhammen, Don Juan de Austria, fol. 182.

Ali soon passed from mouth to mouth, giving fresh heart to the confederates, but falling like a knell on the ears of the Moslems. Their confidence was gone. Their fire slackened. Their efforts grew weaker and weaker. They were too far from shore to seek an asylum there, like their comrades on the right. They had no resource but to prolong the combat or to surrender. Most preferred the latter. Many vessels were carried by boarding, others were sunk by the victorious Christians. Ere four hours had elapsed, the centre, like the right wing, of the Moslems might be said to be annihilated.

Still the fight was lingering on the right of the confederates, where, it will be remembered, Uluch Ali, the Algerine chief, had profited by Doria's error in extending his line so far as greatly to weaken it. Uluch Ali, attacking it on its most vulnerable quarter, had succeeded, as we have seen, in capturing and destroying several vessels, and would have inflicted still heavier losses on his enemy had it not been for the seasonable succor received from the marquis of Santa Cruz. This brave officer, who commanded the reserve, had already been of much service to Don John when the *Real* was assailed by several Turkish galleys at once during his combat with Ali Pasha; for at this juncture the marquis of Santa Cruz arriving, and beat-

—Documentos inéditos, tom. iii. p. 247, et seq.—Paruta, Guerra di Cipro, p. 160.—Cabrera, Filipe Segundo, lib. ix. cap. 25, 26.

" Dó el estandarte bárbaro abatido
la Cruz del Redentor fue enarbolada,
con un triunfo solene y grande gloria,
cantando abiertamente la vitoria."
　　　　Ercilla, La Araucana, part ii. canto 24.

O*

ing off the assailants, one of whom he afterwards captured, enabled the commander-in-chief to resume his engagement with the pacha.

No sooner did Santa Cruz learn the critical situation of Doria than, supported by Cardona, "general" of the Sicilian squadron, he pushed forward to his relief. Dashing into the midst of the mêlée, the two commanders fell like a thunderbolt on the Algerine galleys. Few attempted to withstand the shock. But in their haste to avoid it they were encountered by Doria and his Genoese galleys. Thus beset on all sides, Uluch Ali was compelled to abandon his prizes and provide for his own safety by flight. He cut adrift the Maltese *Capitana*, which he had lashed to his stern, and on which three hundred corpses attested the desperate character of her defence. As tidings reached him of the discomfiture of the centre and of the death of Ali Pasha, he felt that nothing remained but to make the best of his way from the fatal scene of action and save as many of his own ships as he could. And there were no ships in the Turkish fleet superior to his, or manned by men under more perfect discipline. For they were the famous corsairs of the Mediterranean, who had been rocked from infancy on its waters.

Throwing out his signals for retreat, the Algerine was soon to be seen, at the head of his squadron, standing towards the north, under as much canvas as remained to him after the battle, and urged forward through the deep by the whole strength of his oarsmen. Doria and Santa Cruz followed quickly in his wake. But he was borne on the wings of the wind, and soon distanced his pursuers. Don John, having disposed of his own assailants, was coming to the support of Doria, and now joined in the pursuit of the viceroy. A rocky headland, stretching far into the sea, lay in the path of the fugitive; and his enemies hoped to intercept him there. Some few of his vessels were stranded on the rocks. But the rest, near forty in number, standing more boldly out to sea, safely doubled the promontory. Then, quickening their flight, they gradually faded from the horizon, their white sails, the last thing visible, showing in the distance like a flock of Arctic sea-fowl on their way to their native homes. The confederates explained the inferior sailing of their own galleys on this occasion by the circumstance of their rowers, who had been allowed to bear arms in the fight, being crippled by their wounds.

The battle had lasted more than four hours. The sky, which had been almost without a cloud through the day, began now to be overcast, and showed signs of a coming storm. Before seeking a place of shelter for himself and his prizes, Don John reconnoitred the scene of action. He met with several vessels too much damaged for further service. These, mostly belonging to the enemy, after saving what was of any value on board, he ordered to be burnt. He selected the neighboring port of Petala, as affording the most secure and accessible harbor for the night. Before he had arrived there, the tempest began to mutter and darkness was on the water. Yet the darkness rendered only more visible the blazing wrecks, which, sending up streams of fire mingled with showers of sparks, looked like volcanoes on the deep.

CHAPTER XI.

WAR WITH THE TURKS.

Losses of the Combatants.—Don John's Generosity.—Triumphant Return.—Enthusiasm throughout Christendom.—Results of the Battle.—Operations in the Levant.—Conquest of Tunis.—Retaken by the Turks.

1571-1574.

LONG and loud were the congratulations now paid to the young commander-in-chief, by his brave companions in arms, on the success of the day. The hours passed blithely with officers and men, while they recounted to one another their manifold achievements. But feelings of gloom mingled with their gayety, as they gathered tidings of the loss of friends who had bought this victory with their blood.

It was indeed a sanguinary battle, surpassing in this particular any sea-fight of modern times. The loss fell much the most heavily on the Turks. There is the usual discrepancy about numbers; but it may be safe to estimate their loss at nearly twenty-five thousand slain and five thousand prisoners. What brought most pleasure to the hearts of the conquerors was the liberation of twelve thousand Christian captives, who had been chained to the oar on board the Moslem galleys, and who now came forth, with tears of joy streaming down their haggard cheeks, to bless their deliverers.[1]

[1] The loss of the Moslems is little better than matter of conjecture,

The loss of the allies was comparatively small,—less than eight thousand.[2] That it was so much less than that of their enemies may be referred in part to their superiority in the use of fire-arms; in part also to their exclusive use of these, instead of employing bows and arrows, weapons on which, though much less effective, the Turks, like the other Moslem nations, seem to have greatly relied. Lastly, the Turks were the vanquished party, and in their heavier loss suffered the almost invariable lot of the vanquished.

As to their armada, it may almost be said to have been annihilated. Not more than forty galleys escaped out of near two hundred and fifty which entered into the action. One hundred and thirty were taken and divided among the conquerors. The remainder, sunk or burned, were swallowed up by the waves. To counterbalance all this, the confederates are said to have lost not more than fifteen galleys, though a much larger number, doubtless, were rendered unfit for service. This disparity affords good evidence of the inferiority of the Turks in the construction of their vessels, as well as in the nautical skill required to manage them. A great amount of booty, in the form of gold, jewels, and brocade, was found on board several of the prizes. The galley of the commander-in-

---

so contradictory are the authorities. The author of the Leyden MS. dismisses the subject with the remark, " La gente muerta de Turcos no se ha podido saber por que la que se hecho en la mar fuera de los degollados fueron infinitos." I have conformed, as in my other estimates, to those of Señor Rosell, Historia del Combate naval, p. 118.

[2] Rosell computes the total loss of the allies at not less than seven thousand six hundred; of whom one thousand were Romans, two thousand Spaniards, and the remainder Venetians. Ibid., p 113.

chief alone is stated to have contained one hundred and seventy thousand gold sequins,—a large sum, but not large enough, it seems, to buy off his life.[3]

The losses of the combatants cannot be fairly presented without taking into the account the quality as well as the number of the slain. The number of persons of consideration, both Christians and Moslems, who embarked in the expedition, was very great. The roll of slaughter showed that in the race of glory they gave little heed to their personal safety. The officer second in command among the Venetians, the commander-in-chief of the Turkish armament, and the commander of its right wing, all fell in the battle. Many a high-born cavalier closed at Lepanto a long career of honorable service. More than one, on the other hand, dated the commencement of their career from this day. Such was Alexander Farnese, prince of Parma. Though he was but a few years younger than his uncle, John of Austria, those few years had placed an immense distance between their conditions, the one filling the post of commander-in-chief, the other being only a private adventurer. Yet even so he succeeded in winning great renown by his achievements. The galley in which he sailed was lying, yard-arm and yard-arm, alongside of a Turkish galley, with which it was hotly engaged. In the midst of the action Farnese sprang on board of the enemy and with his good broadsword hewed down all who opposed him, opening a

---

[3] Rosell, Historia del Combate naval, ubi supra.—Torres y Aguilera, Chronica, fol. 74, et seq.—Documentos inéditos, tom. iii. pp. 246-249; tom. xi. p. 370.—Sagredo, Monarcas Othomanos, pp. 295, 296.—Relacion de la Batalla naval, MS.

path into which his comrades poured one after another, and, after a short but murderous contest, succeeded in carrying the vessel. As Farnese's galley lay just astern of Don John's, the latter could witness the achievement of his nephew, which filled him with an admiration he did not affect to conceal. The intrepidity displayed by the young warrior on this occasion gave augury of his character in later life, when he succeeded his uncle in command and surpassed him in military renown.[4]

Another youth was in that fight, who, then humble and unknown, was destined one day to win laurels of a purer and more enviable kind than those which grow on the battle-field. This was Cervantes, who at the age of twenty-four was serving on board the fleet as a common soldier. He had been confined to his bed by a fever; but, notwithstanding the remonstrances of his captain, he insisted, on the morning of the action, not only on bearing arms, but on being stationed in the post of danger. And well did he perform his duty there, as was shown by two wounds on the breast, and by another in the hand, by which he lost the use of it. Fortunately, it was the left hand. The right yet remained to indite those immortal productions which were to be known as household words, not only in his own land, but in every quarter of the civilized world.[5]

[4] Relacion de la Batalla naval, MS.—Don John notices this achievement of his gallant kinsman in the first letter which he wrote to Philip after the action. The letter, dated at Petala, October 10th, is published by Aparici, Documentos inéditos relativos á la Batalla de Lepanto, p. 26.

[5] Navarete, Vida de Cervantes (Madrid, 1819), p. 19.—Cervantes, in the prologue to the second part of Don Quixote, alluding to Le-

A fierce storm of thunder and lightning raged for four-and-twenty hours after the battle, during which time the fleet rode safely at anchor in the harbor of Petala. It remained there three days longer. Don John profited by the delay to visit the different galleys and ascertain their condition. He informed himself of the conduct of the troops, and was liberal of his praises to those who deserved them. With the sick and the wounded he showed the greatest sympathy, endeavoring to alleviate their sufferings, and furnishing them with whatever his galley contained that could contribute to their comfort. With so generous and sympathetic a nature, it is not wonderful that he should have established himself in the hearts of his soldiers.[6]

But the proofs of this kindly temper were not confined to his own followers. Among the prisoners were two sons of Ali, the Turkish commander-in-chief. One was seventeen, the other only thirteen years of age. Thus early had their father desired to initiate them in a profession which, beyond all others, opened the way to eminence in Turkey. They were not on board of his galley; and when they were informed of his death they were inconsolable. To this affliction was now to be added the doom of slavery.

panto, enthusiastically exclaims that, for all his wounds, he would not have missed the glory of being present on that day: "Quisiera antes haberme hallado en aquella faccion prodigiosa, que sano ahora de mis heridas, sin haberme hallado en ella."

[6] This humane conduct of Don John is mentioned, among other writers, by the author of the Relacion de la Batalla naval, whose language shows that his manuscript was written on the spot: "El queda visitando los heridos y procurando su remedio haziendoles merced y dandoles todo lo que aviase menester." MS.

As they were led into the presence of Don John, the youths prostrated themselves on the deck of his vessel. But, raising them up, he affectionately embraced them, and said all he could to console them under their troubles. He caused them to be treated with the consideration due to their rank. His secretary, Juan de Soto, surrendered his quarters to them. They were provided with the richest apparel that could be found among the spoil. Their table was served with the same delicacies as that of the commander-in-chief; and his chamberlains showed the same deference to them as to himself. His kindness did not stop with these acts of chivalrous courtesy. He received a letter from their sister Fatima containing a touching appeal to Don John's humanity and soliciting the release of her orphan brothers. He had sent a courier to give their friends in Constantinople the assurance of their personal safety; "which," adds the lady, "is held by all this court as an act of great courtesy,—*gran gentileza;* —and there is no one here who does not admire the goodness and magnanimity of your highness." She enforced her petition with a rich present, for which she gracefully apologized, as intended to express her own feelings, though far below his deserts.[7]

In the division of the spoil, the young princes had

---

[7] "Lo qual toda esta corte tuvo á gran gentileza, y no hazen sino alabar la virtud y grandeza de vuestra Alteza."—The letter of Fatima is to be found in Torres y Aguilera, Chronica (fol. 92). The chronicler adds a list of the articles sent by the Turkish princess to Don John, enumerating, among other things, robes of sable, brocade, and various rich stuffs, fine porcelain, carpets and tapestry, weapons curiously inlaid with gold and silver, and Damascus blades ornamented with rubies and turquoises.

been assigned to the pope. But Don John succeeded in obtaining their liberation. Unfortunately, the elder died—of a broken heart, it is said—at Naples. The younger was sent home, with three of his attendants, for whom he had a particular regard. Don John declined keeping Fatima's present, which he gave to her brother. In a letter to the Turkish princess, he remarked that he had done this, not because he undervalued her beautiful gift, but because it had ever been the habit of his royal ancestors freely to grant their favors to those who stood in need of them, but not to receive aught by way of recompense.[8]

The same noble nature he showed in his conduct towards Veniero. We have seen the friendly demonstration he made to the testy Venetian on entering into battle. He now desired his presence on board his galley. As he drew near, Don John came forward frankly to greet him. He spoke of his desire to bury the past in oblivion, and, complimenting the veteran on his prowess in the late engagement, saluted him with the endearing name of "father." The old soldier, not prepared for so kind a welcome, burst into tears; and there was no one, says the chronicler who tells the anecdote, that could witness the scene with a dry eye.[9]

---

[8] "El presente que me embio dexe de rescibir, y le huvo el mismo Mahamet Bey, no por no preciarle como cosa venida de su mano, sino por que la grandeza de mis antecessores no acustumbra rescibir dones de los necessitados de favor, sino darlos y hazerles gracias." Torres y Aguilera, Chronica, fol. 94.

[9] According to some, Don John was induced by the persuasion of his friends to make these advances to the Venetian admiral. (See Torres y Aguilera, Chronica, fol. 75,—Vanderhammen, Don Juan de Austria, fol. 123.) It is certain he could not erase the memory of

While at Petala, a council of war was called to decide on the next operations of the fleet. Some were for following up the blow by an immediate attack on Constantinople. Others considered that, from the want of provisions and the damaged state of the vessels, they were in no condition for such an enterprise. They recommended that the armada should be disbanded, that the several squadrons of which it was composed should return to their respective winter-quarters and meet again in the spring to resume operations. Others, again, among whom was Don John, thought that before disbanding they should undertake some enterprise commensurate with their strength. It was accordingly determined to lay siege to Santa Maura, in the island of Leucadia, — a strongly-fortified place, which commanded the northern entrance into the gulf of Lepanto.

The fleet, weighing anchor on the eleventh of October, arrived off Santa Maura on the following day. On a careful reconnoissance of the ground, it became evident that the siege would be a work of much greater difficulty than had been anticipated. A council of war was again summoned ; and it was resolved, as the season

the past from bis bosom, as appears from more than one of his letters, in which he speaks of the difficulty he should find, in another campaign, in acting in concert with a man of so choleric a temper. In consequence the Venetian government was induced, though very reluctantly, to employ Veniero on another service. In truth, the conduct which had so much disgusted Don John and the allies seems to have found favor with Veniero's countrymen, who regarded it as evidence of his sensitive concern for the honor of his nation. A few years later they made ample amends to the veteran for the slight put on him, by raising him to the highest dignity in the republic. He was the third of his family who held the office of doge, to which he was chosen in 1576, and in which he continued till his death.

was far advanced, to suspend further operations for the present, to return to winter-quarters, and in the ensuing spring to open the campaign under more favorable auspices.

The next step was to make a division of the spoil taken from the enemy, which was done in a manner satisfactory to all parties. One-half of the galleys and inferior vessels, of the artillery and small arms, and also of the captives, was set apart for the Catholic King. The other half was divided between the pope and the republic, in the proportion settled by the treaty of confederation.[10] Next proceeding to Corfu, Don John passed three days at that island, making some necessary repairs of his vessels; then, bidding adieu to the confederates, he directed his course to Messina, which he reached, after a stormy passage, on the thirty-first of the month.

We may imagine the joy with which he was welcomed by the inhabitants of that city, which he had left but little more than six weeks before, and to which he had now returned in triumph, after winning the most memorable naval victory of modern times. The whole population, with the magistrates at their head, hurried down to the shore to witness the magnificent spectacle. As the gallant armament swept into port, it showed the results of the late contest in many a scar. But the consecrated standard was still proudly flying at the

[10] The spoil found on board the Turkish ships was abandoned to the captors. There was enough of it to make many a needy adventurer rich. "Assi por la victoria havida como porque muchos venian tan ricos y prosperados que no havia hombre que se preciasse de gastar moneda de plata sino Zequines ni curasse de regatear en nada que comprasse." To-res y Aguilera, Chronica, fol. 79.

mast-head of the *Real;* and in the rear came the long line of conquered galleys, in much worse plight than their conquerors, trailing their banners ignominiously behind them through the water. On landing at the head of his troops, Don John was greeted with flourishes of music, while salvoes of artillery thundered from the fortresses which commanded the city. He was received under a gorgeous canopy, and escorted by a numerous concourse of citizens and soldiers. The clergy, mingling in the procession, broke forth into the *Te Deum;* and, thus entering the cathedral, they all joined in thanksgivings to the Almighty for granting them so glorious a victory."

Don John was sumptuously lodged in the castle. He was complimented with a superb banquet,—a mode of expressing the public gratitude not confined to our day,—and received a more substantial guerdon in a present from the city of thirty thousand crowns. Finally, a colossal statue in bronze was executed by a skilful artist, as a permanent memorial of the conqueror of Lepanto. Don John accepted the money; but it was only to devote it to the relief of the sick and wounded soldiers. In the same generous spirit, he had ordered that all his own share of the booty taken in the Turkish vessels, including the large amount of gold and rich brocades found in the galley of Ali Pasha, should be distributed among the captors."

[11] For the preceding pages see Vanderhammen, Don Juan de Austria, fol. 186,—Torres y Aguilera, Chronica, fol. 79,—Cabrera, Filipe Segundo, p. 696,—Herrera, Historia general, tom. ii. p. 37,—Ferreras, Hist. d'Espagne, tom. x. p. 261.

[12] An old *romance* thus commemorates this liberal conduct of Don John:

The news of the victory of Lepanto caused a profound sensation throughout Christendom; for it had been a general opinion that the Turks were invincible by sea. The confederates more particularly testified their joy by such extraordinary demonstrations as showed the extent of their previous fears. In Venice, which might be said to have gained a new lease of existence from the result of the battle, the doge, the senators, and the people met in the great square of St. Mark and congratulated one another on the triumph of their arms. By a public decree, the seventh of October was set apart to be observed forever as a national anniversary.

The joy was scarcely less in Naples, where the people had so often seen their coasts desolated by the Ottoman cruisers; and when their admiral, the marquis of Santa Cruz, returned to port with his squadron, he was welcomed with acclamations such as greet the conqueror returning from his campaign.

But even these honors were inferior to those which in Rome were paid to Colonna, the captain-general of the papal fleet. As he was borne in stately procession, with the trophies won from the enemy carried before him, and a throng of mourning captives in the rear, the spectacle recalled the splendors of the ancient Roman

> "Y ansi seda como de oro
> Ninguna cosa ha querido
> Don Juan, como liberal,
> Por mostrar do ha descendido,
> Sino que entre los soldados
> Fuese todo repartido
> En premio de sus trabajos
> Pues lo habian merecido."
>
> Duran, Romancero general (Madrid, 1851), tom. ii. p. 185.

triumph. Pius the Fifth had, before this, announced that the victory of the Christians had been revealed to him from Heaven. But when the tidings reached him of the actual result, it so far transcended his expectations that, overcome by his emotions, the old pontiff burst into a flood of tears, exclaiming, in the words of the Evangelist, "There was a man sent from God; and his name was John."[13]

We may readily believe that the joy with which the glad tidings were welcomed in Spain fell nothing short of that with which they were received in other parts of Christendom. While lying off Petala, Don John sent Lope de Figueroa with despatches for the king, together with the great Ottoman standard, as the most glorious trophy taken in the battle.[14] He soon after sent a courier with further letters. It so happened that neither the one nor the other arrived at the place of their destination till some weeks after the intelligence had reached Philip by another channel. This was the Venetian minister, who on the last of October received despatches from his own government, containing a full account of the fight. Hastening with them to the palace, he found the king in his private chapel, attending vespers on the eve of All-Saints. The news, it cannot be doubted, filled his soul with joy; though *it is said*

[13] Lorea, Vida de Pio Quinto, cap. xxiv. ？ ii.—Torres y Aguilera, Chronica, fol. 80.—Rosell, Historia del Combate naval, pp. 124, 125.

[14] Philip, in a letter to his brother dated from the Escorial in the following November, speaks of his delight at receiving this trophy from the hands of Figueroa. (See the letter, ap. Rosell, Hist. del Combate naval, Apénd. No. 15.) The standard was deposited in the Escorial, where it was destroyed by fire in the year 1671. Documentos inéditos, tom. iii. p. 256.

that, far from exhibiting this in his demeanor, he continued to be occupied with his devotions, without the least change of countenance, till the services were concluded. He then ordered *Te Deum* to be sung.[15] All present joined, with overflowing hearts, in pouring forth their gratitude to the Lord of Hosts for granting such a triumph to the Cross.[16]

That night there was a grand illumination in Madrid. The following day mass was said by the papal legate in presence of the king, who afterwards took part in a solemn procession to the church of St. Mary, where the people united with the court in a general thanksgiving.

[15] "Y S. M. no se alteró, ni demudó, ni hizo sentimiento alguno, y se estuvo con el semblante y serenidad que antes estaba, con el qual semblante estuvo hasta que se acabaron de cantar las vísperas." Memorias de Fray Juan de San Gerónimo, Documentos inéditos, tom. iii. p. 258.

[16] The third volume of the Documentos inéditos contains a copious extract from a manuscript in the Escorial written by a Jeronymite monk. In this the writer states that Philip received intelligence of the victory from a courier despatched by Don John, while engaged at vespers in the palace monastery of the Escorial. This account is the one followed by Cabrera (Filipe Segundo, p. 696) and by the principal Castilian writers. Its inaccuracy, however, is sufficiently attested by two letters written at the time to Don John of Austria, one by the royal secretary Alzamora, the other by Philip himself. According to their account, the person who first conveyed the tidings was the Venetian minister; and the place where they were received by the king was the private chapel of the palace at Madrid, while engaged at vespers on All-Saints' eve. It is worthy of notice that the secretary's letter contains no hint of the nonchalance with which Philip is said to have heard the tidings. The originals of these interesting despatches still exist in the National Library at Madrid. They have been copied by Señor Rosell for his memoir (Apénd. Nos. 13, 15). One makes little progress in history before finding that it is much easier to repeat an error than to correct it.

In a letter from Philip to his brother, dated from the Escorial, the twenty-ninth of November, he writes to him out of the fulness of his heart, in the language of gratitude and brotherly love: "I cannot express to you the joy it has given me to learn the particulars of your conduct in the battle, of the great valor you showed in your own person, and your watchfulness in giving proper directions to others,—all of which has doubtless been a principal cause of the victory. So to you, after God, I am to make my acknowledgments for it, as I now do; and happy am I that it has been reserved for one so near and so dear to me to perform this great work, which has gained such glory for you in the eyes of God and of the whole world."[17]

The feelings of the king were fully shared by his subjects. The enthusiasm roused throughout the country by the great victory was without bounds. "There is no man," writes one of the royal secretaries to Don John, "who does not discern the hand of the Lord in it;—though it seems rather like a dream than a reality, so far does it transcend any naval encounter that the world ever heard of before."[18] The best sculptors and painters were employed to perpetuate the memory of the glorious event. Among the number was Titian, who in the time of Charles the Fifth had passed two

[17] "Y ansi á vos (despues de Dios) se ha de dar el parabien y las gracias della, como yo os las doy, y á mi de que por mano de persona que tanto me toca como la vuestra, y á quien yo tanto quiero, se haya hecho un tan gran negocio, y ganado vos tanta honra y gloria con Dios y con todo el mundo." Rosell, Historia del Combate naval, Apénd. No. 15.

[18] Carta del secretario Alzamora á Don Juan de Austria, Madrid, Nov. 11, 1571, ap. Rosell, Historia del Combate naval, Apénd. No. 13.

years in Spain, and who now, when more than ninety years of age, executed the great picture of "The Victory of the League," still hanging on the walls of the Museo at Madrid."[19] The lofty theme proved a fruitful source of inspiration to the Castilian muse. Among hecatombs of epics and lyrics, the heroic poem of Ercilla [20] and the sublime *cancion* of Fernando de Herrera perpetuate the memory of the victory of Lepanto in forms more durable than canvas or marble,—as imperishable as the language itself.

While all were thus ready to render homage to the talent and bravery which had won the greatest battle of the time, men, as they grew cooler and could criticise events more carefully, were disposed to ask, where were the fruits of this great victory. Had Don John's father, Charles the Fifth, gained such a victory, it was said, he would not thus have quitted the field, but, before the enemy could recover from the blow, would have followed it up by another. Many expressed the conviction that the young generalissimo should at once have led his navy against Constantinople.

There would indeed seem to be plausible ground for criticising his course after the action. But we must remember, in explanation of the conduct of Don John, that his situation was altogether different from that of his imperial father. He possessed no such absolute authority as the latter did over his army. The great

---

[19] See Ford, Handbook for Spain, vol. ii. p. 697.

[20] Ercilla has devoted the twenty-fourth canto of the Araucana to the splendid episode of the battle of Lepanto. If Ercilla was not, like Cervantes, present in the fight, his acquaintance with the principal actors in it makes his epic, in addition to its poetical merits, of considerable value as historical testimony.

leaders of the confederates were so nearly equal in rank that they each claimed a right to be consulted on all measures of importance. The greatest jealousy existed among the three commanders, as there did also among the troops whom they commanded. They were all united, it is true, in their hatred to the Turk. But they were all influenced, more or less, by the interests of their own states, in determining the quarter where he was to be assailed. Every rood of territory wrung from the enemy in the Levant would only serve to enlarge the domain of Venice; while the conquests in the western parts of the Mediterranean would strengthen the empire of Castile. This feeling of jealousy between the Spaniards and the Venetians was, as we have seen, so great in the early part of the expedition as nearly to bring ruin on it.

Those who censured Don John for not directing his arms against Constantinople would seem to have had but a very inadequate notion of the resources of the Porte,—as shown in the course of that very year. There is a remarkable letter from the duke of Alva, written the month after the battle of Lepanto, in which he discusses the best course to be taken in order to reap the full fruits of the victory. In it he expresses the opinion that an attempt against Constantinople, or indeed any part of the Turkish dominions, unless supported by a general coalition of the great powers of Christendom, must end only in disappointment,—so vast were the resources of that great empire.[21] If this

---

[21] The letter, which is dated Brussels, Nov. 17th, 1571, is addressed to Juan de Zuñiga, the Castilian ambassador at the court of Rome. A copy from a manuscript of the sixteenth century, in the library of

were so,—and no better judge than Alva could be found in military affairs,—how incompetent were the means at Don John's disposal for effecting this object, —confederates held together, as the event proved, by a rope of sand, and a fleet so much damaged in the recent combat that many of the vessels were scarcely seaworthy!

In addition to this, it may be stated that Don John knew it was his brother's wish that the Spanish squadron should return to Sicily to pass the winter.[22] If he persisted, therefore, in the campaign, he must do so on his own responsibility. He had now accomplished the great object for which he had put to sea. He had won a victory more complete than the most sanguine of his countrymen had a right to anticipate. To prolong the contest under the present circumstances would be in a manner to provoke his fate, to jeopard the glory he had already gained, and incur the risk of closing the campaign with melancholy cypress, instead of the laurel-wreath of victory. Was it surprising that even an adventurous spirit like his should have shrunk from hazarding so vast a stake with the odds against him?

It is a great error to speak of the victory of Lepanto as a barren victory, which yielded no fruits to those who gained it. True, it did not strip the Turks of an inch of territory. Even the heavy loss of ships and

---

the duke of Ossuna, is inserted in the Documentos inéditos, tom. iii. pp. 292–303.

[22] "Ya havreis entendido la órden que se os ha dado de que inverneis en Meçina, y las causas dello." Carta del Rey á su hermano, ap. Rosell, Historia del Combate naval, Apénd. No. 15.

RESULTS OF THE BATTLE. 341

soldiers which it cost them was repaired in the following year. But the loss of reputation—that tower of strength to the conqueror—was not to be estimated. The long and successful career of the Ottoman princes, especially of the last one, Solyman the Magnificent, had made the Turks to be thought invincible. There was not a nation in Christendom that did not tremble at the idea of a war with Turkey. The spell was now broken. Though her resources were still boundless, she lost confidence in herself. Venice gained confidence in proportion. When the hostile fleets met in the year following the battle of Lepanto, the Turks, though greatly the superior in numbers, declined the combat. For the seventy years which elapsed after the close of the present war, the Turks abandoned their efforts to make themselves masters of any of the rich possessions of the republic, which lay so temptingly around them. When the two nations came next into collision, Venice, instead of leaning on confederates, took the field single-handed, and disputed it with an intrepidity which placed her on a level with the gigantic power that assailed her. That power was already on the wane; and those who have most carefully studied the history of the Ottoman empire date the commencement of her decline from the battle of Lepanto.[73]

[73] See Rosell, Historia del Combate naval, p. 157.—Lafuente, Historia de España (Madrid, 1850), tom. xiii. p. 538.—Ranke, who has made the history of the Ottoman empire his particular study, remarks, "The Turks lost all their old confidence after the battle of Lepanto. They had no equal to oppose to John of Austria. The day of Lepanto broke down the Ottoman supremacy." Ottoman and Spanish Empires (Eng. trans.), p. 23.

The allies should have been ready with their several contingents early in the spring of the following year, 1572. They were not ready till the summer was well advanced. One cause of delay was the difficulty of deciding on what quarter the Turkish empire was to be attacked. The Venetians, from an obvious regard to their own interests, were for continuing the war in the Levant. Philip, on the other hand, from similar motives, would have transferred it to the western part of the Mediterranean and have undertaken an expedition against the Barbary powers. Lastly, Pius the Fifth, urged by that fiery enthusiasm which made him overlook or overleap every obstacle in his path, would have marched on Constantinople and then carried his conquering banners to the Holy Land. These chimerical fancies of a crusader provoked a smile—it may have been a sneer—from men better instructed in military operations than the pontiff.[24]

Pius again labored to infuse his own spirit into the monarchs of Christendom. But it was in vain that he urged them to join the League. All, for some reason or other, declined it. It is possible that they may have had less fear of the Turk than of augmenting the power of the king of Spain. But the great plans of Pius the Fifth were terminated by his death, which occurred on the first of May, 1572. He was the true author of the League. It occupied his thoughts to the

---

[24] "Su Santidad ha de querer que se gane Constantinopla y la Casa Santa, y que tendrá muchos que le querrán adular con facilitárselo, y que no faltarán entre estos algunos que hacen profesion de soldados y que como su Beatitud no pueden entender estas cosas." Carta del Duque de Alba, ap. Documentos inéditos, tom. iii. p. 300.

latest hour of his existence; and his last act was to appropriate to its uses a considerable sum of money lying in his coffers.[75] He may be truly said to have been the only one of the confederates who acted solely for what he conceived to be the interests of the Faith. This soon became apparent.

The affairs of Philip the Second were at this time in a critical situation. He much feared that one of the French faction would be raised to the chair of St. Peter. He had great reason to distrust the policy of France in respect to the Netherlands. Till he was more assured on these points, he was not inclined to furnish the costly armament to which he was pledged as his contingent. It was in vain that the allies called on Don John to aid them with his Spanish fleet. He had orders from his brother not to quit Messina; and it was in vain that he chafed under these orders, which threatened thus prematurely to close the glorious career on which he had entered, and which exposed him to the most mortifying imputations. It was not till the sixth of July that the king allowed him to send a part of his contingent, amounting only to twenty-two galleys and five thousand troops, to the aid of the confederates.

Some historians explain the conduct of Philip not so much by the embarrassments of his situation as by his reluctance to afford his brother the opportunity of adding fresh laurels to his brow, and possibly of achieving for himself some independent sovereignty, like that to which Pius the Fifth had encouraged him to aspire. It may be thought some confirmation of this opinion—at least it infers some jealousy of his

[75] Ranke, History of the Popes (Eng. trans.), vol. i. p. 384.

brother's pretensions—that in his despatches to his ministers in Italy the king instructed them that, while they showed all proper deference to Don John, they should be careful not to address him in speech or in writing by the title of *Highness,* but to use that of *Excellency;* adding that they were not to speak of this suggestion as coming from him.[26] He caused a similar notice to be given to the ambassadors of France, Germany, and England. This was but a feeble thread by which to check the flight of the young eagle as he was soaring to the clouds. It served to show, however, that it was not the will of his master that he should soar too high.

Happily, Philip was relieved from his fears in regard to the new pope by the election of Cardinal Buoncampagno to the vacant throne. This ecclesiastic, who took the name of Gregory the Thirteenth, was personally known to the king, having in earlier life passed several years at the court of Castile. He was well affected to that court, and he possessed in full measure the zeal of his predecessor for carrying on the war against the Moslems. He lost no time in sending his "briefs of fire,"[27] as Don John called them, to rouse him to new exertions in the cause. In France, too, Philip learned with satisfaction that the Guises, the devoted partisans of Spain, had now the direction of public affairs. Thus relieved from apprehensions on these two quarters, Philip consented to his brother's departure with the remainder of his squadron. It amounted to fifty-five galleys and thirty smaller vessels.

[26] Lafuente, Historia de España, tom. xiii. p. 530.
[27] ' Breves de fuego." Ibid., p. 529.

But when the prince reached Corfu, on the ninth of August, he found that the confederates, tired of waiting, had already put to sea, under the command of Colonna, in search of the Ottoman fleet.

The Porte had shown such extraordinary despatch that in six months it had built and equipped a hundred and twenty galleys, making, with those already on hand, a formidable fleet.[28] It was a remarkable proof of its resources, but suggests the idea of the wide difference between a Turkish galley of the sixteenth century and a man-of-war in our day. The command of the armament was given to the Algerine chieftain Uluch Ali, who had so adroitly managed to bring off the few vessels which effected their escape at the battle of Lepanto. He stood deservedly high in the confidence of the sultan, and had the supreme direction in maritime affairs.

The two fleets came face to face with each other off the western coast of the Morea. But, though the Algerine commander was much superior to the Christians in the number and strength of his vessels, he declined an action, showing the same adroitness in eluding a battle that he had before shown in escaping from one.

At the close of August the confederates returned to Corfu, where they were reinforced by the rest of the Spanish squadron. The combined fleet, with this addition, amounted to some two hundred and forty-

---

[28] "E si è veduto, che quando gli fu data la gran rotta, in sei mesi rifabbricò cento venti galere, oltre quelle che si trovavano in essere, cosa che essendo preveduta e scritta da me, fu giudicata piuttosto impossibile che creduta." Relazione di Marcantino Barbaro, 1573. Alberi, Relazioni Venete, tom. iii. p. 306.

seven vessels, of which nearly two-thirds were galleys. It was a force somewhat superior to that of the enemy. Thus strengthened, Don John, unfurling the consecrated banner as generalissimo of the League, weighed anchor, and steered with his whole fleet in a southerly direction. It was not long before he appeared off the harbors of Modon and Navarino, where the two divisions of the Turkish armada were lying at anchor. He would have attacked them separately, but, notwithstanding his efforts, failed to prevent their effecting a junction in the harbor of Modon. On the seventh of October, Uluch Ali ventured out of port and seemed disposed to give battle. It was the anniversary of the fight of Lepanto; and Don John flattered himself that he should again see his arms crowned with victory, as on that memorable day. But if the Turkish commander was unwilling to fight the confederates when he was superior to them in numbers, it was not likely that he would fight them now that he was inferior. After some manœuvres which led to no result, he took refuge under the castle of Modon, and again retreated into port. There Don John would have followed him, with the design of forcing him to a battle. But from this he was dissuaded by the other leaders of the confederates; who considered that the chances of success in a place so strongly defended by no means warranted the risk.

It was in vain that the allies prolonged their stay in the neighborhood, with the hope of enticing the enemy to an engagement. The season wore away with no prospect of a better result. Meantime, provisions were failing, the stormy weather of autumn was drawing nigh, and Don John, disgusted with what he regarded as the timid counsels of his associates, and with the control which they were permitted to exercise over him, decided, as it was now too late for any new enterprise, to break up and postpone further action till the following spring, when he hoped to enter on the campaign at an earlier day than he had done this year. The allies, accordingly, on reaching the island of Paxo, late in October, parted from each other, and withdrew to their respective winter-quarters. Don John, with the Spanish armament, returned to Sicily.[29]

The pope and the king of Spain, nowise discouraged by the results of the campaign, resolved to resume operations early in the spring on a still more formidable scale than before. But their intentions were defeated by the startling intelligence that Venice had entered into a separate treaty with the Porte. The treaty, which was negotiated, it is said, through the intervention of the French ambassador, was executed on the seventh of March, 1573. The terms seemed somewhat extraordinary, considering the relative positions of the parties. By the two principal articles, the republic agreed to pay the annual sum of one hundred thousand ducats for three years to the sultan, and to cede the island of Cyprus, the original cause of the war. One might suppose it was the Turks, and not the Christians, who had won the battle of Lepanto.[30]

Venice was a commercial state, and doubtless had

[29] For the preceding pages see Torres y Aguilera, Chronica, fol. 87-89,—Cabrera, Filipe Segundo, lib. x. cap. 5,—Vanderhammen, Don Juan de Austria, fol. 159, et seq.,—Paruta, Guerra di Cipro, p. 206, et seq.,—Sagredo, Monarcas Othomanos, pp. 301, 302.

[30] It is Voltaire's reflection : " Il semblait que les Turques eussent gagné la bataille de Lépante." Essais sur les Mœurs, chap. 160.

more to gain from peace than from any war, however well conducted. In this point of view, even such a treaty may have been politic with so formidable an enemy. But a nation's interests, in the long run, cannot, any more than those of an individual, be divorced from its honor. And what could be more dishonorable than for a state secretly to make terms for herself with the enemy, and desert the allies who had come into the war at her solicitation and in her defence? Such conduct, indeed, was too much in harmony with the past history of Venice, and justified the reputation for bad faith which had made the European nations so reluctant to enter into the League.[31]

The tidings were received by Philip with his usual composure. "If Venice," he said, "thinks she consults her own interests by such a proceeding, I can truly say that in what I have done I have endeavored to consult both her interests and those of Christendom." He, however, spoke his mind more plainly afterwards to the Venetian ambassador. The pope gave free vent to his feelings in the consistory, where he denounced the conduct of Venice in the most bitter and contemptuous terms. When the republic sent a special envoy to deprecate his anger and to excuse herself by the embarrassments of her situation, the pontiff refused to see him. Don John would not believe in the defection of Venice when the tidings were first announced to him. When he was advised of it by a direct communication from her government, he replied by indignantly commanding the great standard

---

[31] The treaty is to be found in Dumont, Corps diplomatique, tom. v. par. i. pp. 218, 219.

of the League to be torn down from his galley and in its place to be unfurled the banner of Castile.[32]

Such was the end of the Holy League, on which Pius the Fifth had so fully relied for the conquest of Constantinople and the recovery of Palestine. Philip could now transfer the war to the quarter he had preferred. He resolved, accordingly, to send an expedition to the Barbary coast. Tunis was selected as the place of attack,—a thriving city and the home of many a corsair who preyed on the commerce of the Mediterranean. It had been taken by Charles the Fifth in the memorable campaign of 1535, but had since been recovered by the Moslems. The Spaniards, however, still retained possession of the strong fortress of the Goletta, which overlooked the approaches to Tunis.

In the latter part of September, 1574, Don John left the shores of Sicily at the head of a fleet consisting of about a hundred galleys and nearly as many smaller vessels. The number of his troops amounted to not less than twenty thousand.[33] The story of the campaign is a short one. Most of the inhabitants of Tunis fled from the city. The few who remained did not care to bring the war on their heads by offering resistance to the Spaniards. Don John, without so much as firing a shot, marched in at the head of his battalions, through gates flung open to receive him. He found an ample booty awaiting him,—near fifty pieces of artillery, with ammunition and military stores, large quantities of grain, cotton and woollen cloths, rich silks and

---

[32] Rosell, Historia del Combate naval, p. 149.—Cabrera, Filipe Segundo, p. 747.—Torres y Aguilera, Chronica, fol. 95.

[33] Vanderhammen, Don Juan de Austria, fol. 172.

brocades, with various other kinds of costly merchandise. The troops spent more than a week in sacking the place.³⁴ They gained, in short, every thing—but glory; for little glory was to be gained where there were no obstacles to be overcome.

Don John gave orders that no injury should be offered to the persons of the inhabitants. He forbade that any should be made slaves. By a proclamation, he invited all to return to their dwellings, under the assurance of his protection. In one particular his conduct was remarkable. Philip, disgusted with the expenses to which the maintenance of the castle of the Goletta annually subjected him, had recommended, if not positively directed, his brother to dismantle the place and to demolish in like manner the fortifications of Tunis.³⁵ Instead of heeding these instructions, Don

---

³⁴ Cabrera, Filipe Segundo, p. 765.—Vanderhammen, Don Juan de Austria, fol. 174, 175.—Torres y Aguilera, Chronica, fol. 103, et seq. —The author last cited, who was present at the capture of Tunis, gives a fearful picture of the rapacity of the soldiers.

³⁵ The Castilian writers generally speak of it as the *peremptory command* of Philip. Cabrera, one of the best authorities, tells us, " Mandó el Rey Catolico a don Juan de Austria enplear su armada en la conquista de Tunez, i que le desmantelase, i la Goleta." But soon after he remarks, " Olvidando el *buen acuerdo* del Rey, por consejo de lisongeros determinó de conservar la ciudad." (Filipe Segundo, pp. 763, 764.) From this qualified language we may infer that the king meant to give his brother his decided opinion, not amounting, however, to such an absolute command as would leave him no power to exercise his discretion in the matter. This last view is made the more probable by the fact that in the following spring a correspondence took place between the king and his brother, in which the former, after stating the arguments both for preserving and for dismantling the fortress of Tunis, concludes by referring the decision of the question to Don John himself: " Representadas todas estas

John no sooner saw himself in possession of the capital than he commanded the Goletta to be thoroughly repaired, and at the same time provided for the erection of a strong fortress in the city. This work he committed to an Italian engineer, named Cerbelloni, a knight of Malta, with whom he left eight thousand soldiers, to be employed in the construction of the fort, and to furnish him with a garrison to defend it.

Don John, it is said, had been urged to take this course by his secretary, Juan de Soto, a man of ability, but of an intriguing temper, who fostered in his master those ambitious projects which had been encouraged, as we have seen, by Pius the Fifth. No more eligible spot seemed likely to present itself for the seat of his dominion than Tunis,—a flourishing capital surrounded by a well-peopled and fruitful territory. Philip had been warned of the unwholesome influence exerted by De Soto; and he now sought to remove him from the person of his brother by giving him a distinct position in the army, and by sending another to replace him in his post of secretary. The person thus sent was Juan de Escovedo. But it was soon found that the influence which Escovedo acquired over the young prince was both greater and more mischievous than that of his predecessor; and the troubles that grew out of this new intimacy were destined, as we shall see hereafter, to form some of the darkest pages in the history of the times.

Having provided for the security of his new acquisition, and received, moreover, the voluntary submission of the neighboring town of Biserta, the Spanish

dificultades, manda remitir S. M. al Señor Don Juan que él tome la resolucion que mas convenga." Documentos inéditos, tom. iii. p. 139.

commander returned with his fleet to Sicily. He landed at Palermo, amidst the roaring of cannon, the shouts of the populace, and the usual rejoicings that announce the return of the victorious commander. He did not, however, prolong his stay in Sicily. After dismissing his fleet, he proceeded to Naples, where he landed about the middle of November. He proposed to pass the winter in this capital, where the delicious climate and the beauty of the women, says a contemporary chronicler, had the attractions for him that belonged naturally to his age.[36] His partiality for Naples was amply requited by the inhabitants,—especially that lovelier portion of them whose smiles were the well-prized guerdon of the soldier. If his brilliant exterior and the charm of his society had excited their admiration when he first appeared among them as an adventurer in the path of honor, how much was this admiration likely to be increased when he returned with the halo of glory beaming around his brow, as the successful champion of Christendom!

The days of John of Austria glided merrily along in the gay capital of Southern Italy. But we should wrong him did we suppose that all his hours were passed in idle dalliance. A portion of each day, on the contrary, was set apart for study. Another part was given to the despatch of business. When he went abroad, he affected the society of men distinguished for their science, or still more for their knowledge of public affairs. In his intercourse with these persons he showed dignity

[36] "Porque la gentileza de la tierra i de las damas en su conservacion agradaba a su gallarda edad." Cabrera, Filipe Segundo, p. 755. —Also Vanderbammen, Don Juan de Austria, fol. 176.

of demeanor tempered by courtesy, while his conversation revealed those lofty aspirations which proved that his thoughts were fixed on a higher eminence than any he had yet reached. It was clear to every observer that ambition was the moving principle of his actions, —the passion to which every other passion, even the love of pleasure, was wholly subordinate.

In the midst of the gayeties of Naples his thoughts were intent on the best means of securing his African empire. He despatched his secretary, Escovedo, to the pope, to solicit his good offices with Philip. Gregory entertained the same friendly feelings for Don John which his predecessor had shown, and he good-naturedly acquiesced in his petition. He directed his nuncio at the Castilian court to do all in his power to promote the suit of the young chief, and to assure the king that nothing could be more gratifying to the head of the Church than to see so worthy a recompense bestowed on one who had rendered such signal services to Christendom. Philip received the communication in the most gracious manner. He was grateful, he said, for the interest which the pope condescended to take in the fortunes of Don John; and nothing, certainly, would be more agreeable to his own feelings than to have the power to reward his brother according to his deserts. But to take any steps at present in the matter would be premature. He had received information that the sultan was making extensive preparations for the recovery of Tunis. Before giving it away, therefore, it would be well to see to whom it belonged.[37]

[37] Ferreras, Hist. d'Espagne, tom. x. p. 286.—Vanderhammen, Don Jean de Austria, fol. 178.

Philip's information was correct. No sooner had Selim learned the fate of the Barbary capital than he made prodigious efforts for driving the Spaniards from their conquests. He assembled a powerful armament, which he placed under the command of Uluch Ali. As lord of Algiers, that chief had a particular interest in preventing any Christian power from planting its foot in the neighborhood of his own dominions. The command of the land-forces was given to Sinan Pasha, Selim's son-in-law.

Early in July the Ottoman fleet arrived off the Barbary coast. Tunis offered as little resistance to the arms of the Moslems as it had before done to those of the Christians. That city had been so often transferred from one master to another that it seemed almost a matter of indifference to the inhabitants to whom it belonged. But the Turks found it a more difficult matter to reduce the castle of the Goletta and the fort raised by the brave engineer Cerbelloni, now well advanced, though not entirely completed. It was not till the middle of September, after an incredible waste of life on the part of the assailants, and the extermination of nearly the whole of the Spanish garrisons, that both the fortresses surrendered.[38]

No sooner was he in possession of them than the Turkish commander did that which Philip had in vain wished his brother to do. He razed to the ground the

---

[38] Torres y Aguilera, Chronica, fol. 116, et seq.—Relacion particular de Don Juan Sanogera, MS.—Vanderhammen states the loss of the Moslems at thirty-three thousand slain. (Don Juan de Austria, fol. 189.) But the arithmetic of the Castilian is little to be trusted as regards the infidel.

fortress of the Goletta. Thus ended the campaign, in which Spain, besides her recent conquests, saw herself stripped of the strong castle which had defied every assault of the Moslems since the time of Charles the Fifth.

One may naturally ask, Where was John of Austria all this time? He had not been idle, nor had he remained an indifferent spectator of the loss of the place he had so gallantly won for Spain. But when he first received tidings of the presence of a Turkish fleet before Tunis he was absent on a mission to Genoa, or rather to its neighborhood. That republic was at this time torn by factions so fierce that it was on the brink of a civil war. The mischief threatened to extend even more widely, as the neighboring powers, especially France and Savoy, prepared to take part in the quarrel, in hopes of establishing their own authority in the state. At length Philip, who had inherited from his father the somewhat ill-defined title of "Protector of Genoa," was compelled to interpose in the dispute. It was on this mission that Don John was sent, to watch more nearly the rival factions. It was not till after this domestic broil had lasted for several months that the prudent policy of the Spanish monarch succeeded in reconciling the hostile parties and thus securing the republic from the horrors of a civil war. He reaped the good fruits of his temperate conduct in the maintenance of his own authority in the counsels of the republic, thus binding to himself an ally whose navy, in time of war, served greatly to strengthen his maritime resources.[39]

[39] For a brief but very perspicuous view of the troubles of Genoa,

While detained on this delicate mission, Don John did what he could for Tunis, by urging the viceroys of Sicily and Naples to send immediate aid to the beleaguered garrisons.[40] But these functionaries seem to have been more interested in the feuds of Genoa than in the fate of the African colony. Granvelle, who presided over Naples, was even said to be so jealous of the rising fame of John of Austria as not to be unwilling that his lofty pretensions should be somewhat humbled.[41] The supplies sent were wholly unequal to the exigency.

Don John, impatient of the delay, as soon as he could extricate himself from the troubles of Genoa, sailed for Naples, and thence speedily crossed to Sicily. He there made every effort to assemble an armament, of which he prepared, in spite of the remonstrances of his friends, to take the command in person. But nature, no less than man, was against him. A tempest scattered his fleet; and when he had reassembled it, and fairly put to sea, he was baffled by contrary winds, and, taking refuge in the neighboring port of Trapani, was detained

see San Miguel, Hist. de Filipe Segundo (tom. ii. cap. 36). The care of this judicious writer to acquaint the reader with contemporary events in other countries, as they bore more or less directly on Spain, is a characteristic merit of his history.

[40] Torres y Aguilera, Chronica, fol. 113.

[41] The principal cause of Granvelle's coldness to Don John, as we are told by Cabrera (Filipe Segundo, p. 794), echoed, as usual, by Vanderhammen (Don Juan de Austria, fol. 184), was envy of the fame which the hero of Lepanto had gained by his conquests both in love and in war: "La causa principal era el poco gusto que tenia de acudir a don Juan, invidioso de sus favores de Marte i Venus." Considering the cardinal's profession, he would seem to have had no right to envy any one's success in either of these fields.

there until tidings reached him of the fall of Tunis. They fell heavily on his ear. For they announced to him that all his bright visions of an African empire had vanished, like the airy fabric of an Eastern tale. All that remained was the consciousness that he had displeased his brother by his scheme of an independent sovereignty and by his omission to raze the fortress of the Goletta, the unavailing defence of which had cost the lives of so many of his brave countrymen.

But Don John, however chagrined by the tidings, was of too elastic a temper to yield to despondency. He was a knight-errant in the true sense of the term. He still clung as fondly as ever to the hope of one day carving out with his good sword an independent dominion for himself. His first step, he considered, was to make his peace with his brother. Though not summoned thither, he resolved to return at once to the Castilian court,—for in that direction, he felt, lay the true road to preferment.

BOOK VI.

CHAPTER I.

DOMESTIC AFFAIRS OF SPAIN.

Internal Administration of Spain.—Absolute Power of the Crown.—Royal Councils.—Alva and Ruy Gomez.—Espinosa.—Personal Habits of Philip.—Court and Nobles.—The Cortes.—The Guards of Castile.

SEVENTEEN years had now elapsed since Philip the Second ascended the throne of his ancestors,—a period long enough to disclose the policy of his government, longer, indeed, than that of the entire reigns of some of his predecessors. In the previous portions of this work the reader has been chiefly occupied with the foreign relations of Spain, and with military details. It is now time to pause, and, before plunging anew into the stormy scenes of the Netherlands, to consider the internal administration of the country and the character and policy of the monarch who presided over it.

The most important epoch in Castilian history since the great Saracen invasion in the eighth century is the reign of Ferdinand and Isabella, when anarchy was succeeded by law, and from the elements of chaos arose that beautiful fabric of order and constitutional liberty which promised a new era for the nation. In the assertion of her rights, Isabella, to whom this revolution is chiefly to be attributed, was obliged to rely on the support of the people. It was natural that she should requite their services by aiding them in the recovery of their own rights,—especially of those which had been usurped by the rapacious nobles. Indeed, it was the obvious policy of the crown to humble the pride of the aristocracy and abate their arrogant pretensions. In this it was so well supported by the commons that the scheme perfectly succeeded. By the depression of the privileged classes and the elevation of the people, the different orders were brought more strictly within their constitutional limits; and the state made a nearer approach to a well-balanced limited monarchy than at any previous period of its history.

This auspicious revolution was soon, alas! to be followed by another, of a most disastrous kind. Charles the Fifth, who succeeded his grandfather Ferdinand, was born a foreigner,—and a foreigner he remained through his whole life. He was a stranger to the feelings and habits of the Spaniards, had little respect for their institutions, and as little love for the nation. He continued to live mostly abroad; was occupied with foreign enterprises; and the only people whom he really loved were those of the Netherlands, his native land. The Spaniards requited these feelings of indifference in full measure. They felt that the glory of the imperial name shed no lustre upon them. Thus estranged at heart, they were easily provoked to insurrection by his violation of their rights. The insurrection was a failure; and the blow which crushed the insurgents on the plains of Villalar deprived them forever of the few liberties which they had been permitted to retain. They were excluded from all share in the government, and were henceforth summoned to the cortes only to swear allegiance to the heir-apparent or to furnish subsidies for their master. They were indeed allowed to lay their grievances before the throne. But they had no means of enforcing redress; for, with the cunning policy of a despot, Charles would not receive their petitions until they had first voted the supplies.

The nobles, who had stood by their master in the struggle, fared no better. They found too late how short-sighted was the policy which had led them to put their faith in princes. Henceforth they could not be said to form a necessary part of the legislature. For, as they insisted on their right to be excused from bearing any share in the burdens of the state, they could take no part in voting the supplies; and, as this was almost the only purpose for which the cortes was convened, their presence was no longer required in it. Instead of the powers which were left to them untouched by Ferdinand and Isabella, they were now amused with high-sounding and empty titles, or with offices about the person of the monarch. In this way they gradually sank into the unsubstantial though glittering pageant of a court. Meanwhile, the government of Castile, assuming the powers of both making the laws and enforcing their execution, became in its essential attributes nearly as absolute as that of Turkey.

Such was the gigantic despotism which, on the death of Charles, passed into the hands of Philip the Second.

The son had many qualities in common with his father. But among these was not that restless ambition of foreign conquest which was ever goading the emperor. Nor was he, like his father, urged by the love of glory to military achievement. He was of too sluggish a nature to embark readily in great enterprises. He was capable of much labor; but it was of that sedentary kind which belongs to the cabinet rather than the camp. His tendencies were naturally pacific; and up to the period at which we are now arrived he had engaged in no wars but those into which he had been drawn by the revolt of his vassals, as in the Netherlands and Granada, or those forced on him by circumstances beyond his control. Such was the war which he had carried on with the pope and the French monarchy at the beginning of his reign.

But, while less ambitious than Charles of foreign acquisitions, Philip was full as tenacious of the possessions and power which had come to him by inheritance. Nor was it likely that the regal prerogative would suffer any diminution in his reign, or that the nobles or commons would be allowed to retrieve any of the immunities which they had lost under his predecessors.

Philip understood the character of his countrymen better than his father had done. A Spaniard by birth, he was, as I have more than once had occasion to remark, a Spaniard in his whole nature. His tastes, his habits, his prejudices, were all Spanish. His policy was directed solely to the aggrandizement of Spain. The distant races whom he governed were all strangers to him. With a few exceptions, Spaniards were the only persons he placed in offices of trust. His Castilian countrymen saw with pride and satisfaction that they had a native prince on the throne, who identified his own interests with theirs. They contrasted this conduct with that of his father, and requited it with a devotion such as they had shown to few of his predecessors. They not only held him in reverence, says the Venetian minister, Contarini, but respected his laws, as something sacred and inviolable.¹ It was the people of the Netherlands who rose up against him. For similar reasons it fared just the opposite with Charles. His Flemish countrymen remained loyal to the last. It was his Castilian subjects who were driven to rebellion.

Though tenacious of power, Philip had not the secret consciousness of strength which enabled his father, unaided as it were, to bear up so long under the burden of empire. The habitual caution of the son made him averse to taking any step of importance without first ascertaining the opinions of others. Yet he was not willing, like his ancestor the good Queen Isabella, to invoke the co-operation of the cortes, and thus awaken the consciousness of power in an arm of the government which had been so long smitten with paralysis. Such an expedient was fraught with too much danger. He found a substitute in the several councils, the members of which, appointed by the crown and removable at its pleasure, were pledged to the support of the prerogative.

Under Ferdinand and Isabella there had been a

¹ " Questa oppinione, che di lui si hà, rende le sue leggi più sacrosancte et inviolabili." Relazione di Contarini, MS.

complete reorganization of these councils. Their number was increased under Charles the Fifth, to suit the increased extent of the empire. It was still further enlarged by Philip.[2] Under him there were no less than eleven councils, among which may be particularly noticed those of war, of finance, of justice, and of state.[3] Of these various bodies the council of state, charged with the most important concerns of the monarchy, was held in highest consideration. The number of its members varied. At the time of which I am writing, it amounted to sixteen.[4] But the weight of the business devolved on less than half that number. It was composed of both ecclesiastics and laymen. Among the latter were some eminent jurists. A sprinkling of men of the robe, indeed, was to be found in most of the councils. Philip imitated in this the policy of Ferdinand and Isabella, who thus intended to humble the pride of the great lords, and to provide themselves with a loyal militia, whose services would be of no little advantage in maintaining the prerogative.

Among the members of the council of state, two may be particularly noticed for their pre-eminence in that body. These were the duke of Alva and Ruy Gomez de Silva, prince of Eboli. With the former the reader is well acquainted. His great talents, his

[2] A manuscript, entitled "*Origen de los Consejos*," without date or the name of the author, in the library of Sir Thomas Phillips, gives a minute account of the various councils under Philip the Second.

[3] "Sono XI; il consiglio dell' Indie, Castiglia, d' Aragona, d' inquisitione, di camera, dell' ordini, di guerra, di hazzienda, di giustizia, d' Italia, et di stato." Sommario del' ordine che si tiene alla corte di Spagna circa il governo delli stati del Ré Catholico, MS.

[4] Ibid. The date of this manuscript is 1570.

ample experience both in civil and military life, his iron will and the fearlessness with which he asserted it, even his stern and overbearing manner, which seemed to proclaim his own superiority, all marked him out as the leader of a party.

The emperor appears to have feared the ascendency which Alva might one day acquire over Philip. "The duke," wrote Charles to his son in a letter before cited, "is the ablest statesman and the best soldier I have in my dominions. Consult him, above all, in military affairs. But do not depend on him entirely in these or any other matters. Depend on no one but yourself." The advice was good; and Philip did not fail to profit by it. Though always seeking the opinions of others, it was the better to form his own. He was too jealous of power to submit to the control, even to the guidance, of another. With all his deference to Alva, on whose services he set the greatest value, the king seems to have shown him but little of that personal attachment which he evinced for his rival, Ruy Gomez.

This nobleman was descended from an ancient house in Portugal, a branch of which had been transplanted to Castile. He had been early received as a page in the imperial household, where, though he was several years older than Philip, his amiable temper, his engaging manners, and, above all, that tact which made his fortune in later life, soon rendered him the prince's favorite. An anecdote is reported of him at this time, which, however difficult to credit, rests on respectable authority. While engaged in their sports, the page accidentally struck the prince. The emperor, greatly incensed, and conceiving that such an indignity to the heir-apparent was to be effaced only by the blood of the offender, condemned the unhappy youth to lose his life. The tears and entreaties of Philip at length so far softened the heart of his father that he consented to commute the punishment of death for exile. Indeed, it is hard to believe that Charles had ever really intended to carry his cruel sentence into execution. The exile was of no long duration. The society of Gomez had become indispensable to the prince, who, pining under the separation, at length prevailed on his father to recall the young noble and reinstate him in his former situation in the palace.[5]

The regard of Philip, who was not of a fickle disposition, seemed to increase with years. We find Ruy Gomez one of the brilliant suite who accompanied him to London on his visit there to wed the English queen. After the emperor's abdication, Ruy Gomez continued to occupy a distinguished place in Philip's household, as first gentleman of the bedchamber. By virtue of this office he was required to attend his master both at his rising and his going to rest. His situation gave him ready access at all hours to the royal person. It was soon understood that there was no one in the court who exercised a more important influence over the monarch; and he naturally became the channel through which applicants for favors sought to prefer their petitions.[6]

[5] Relazione di Badoer, MS.
[6] Instead of " Ruy Gomez," Badoer tells us they punningly gave him the title of " Rey Gomez," to denote his influence over the king : " Il titolo principal che gli vien dato é di Rey Gomez e non Ruy

Meanwhile, the most substantial honors were liberally bestowed on him. He was created duke of Pastraña, with an income of twenty-five thousand crowns,—a large revenue, considering the value of money in that day. The title of Pastraña was subsequently merged in that of Eboli, by which he has continued to be known. It was derived from his marriage with the princess of Eboli, Anna de Mendoza, a lady much younger than he, and, though blind of one eye, celebrated for her beauty no less than her wit. She was yet more celebrated for her gallantries, and for the tragic results to which they led,—a subject closely connected with the personal history of Philip, to which I shall return hereafter.

Among his other dignities Ruy Gomez was made a member of the council of state, in which body he exercised an influence not inferior, to say the least of it, to that of any of his associates. His head was not turned by his prosperity. He did not, like many a favorite before him, display his full-blown fortunes in the eye of the world ; nor, though he maintained a state suited to his station, did he, like Wolsey, excite the jealousy of his master by a magnificence in his way of living that eclipsed the splendors of royalty. Far from showing arrogance to his inferiors, he was affable to all, did what he could to serve their interests with the king, and magnanimously spoke of his rivals in terms of praise. By this way of proceeding he enjoyed the good fortune, rare for a favorite, of

Gomez, perchè pare che non sia stato mai alcun privato con principe del mondo di tanta autorità e così stimato dal signor suo come egli è da questa Maestà." Relazione, MS.

being both caressed by his sovereign and beloved by the people.[7]

There is no evidence that Ruy Gomez had the moral courage to resist the evil tendency of Philip's policy, still less that he ventured to open the monarch's eyes to his errors. He had too keen a regard to his own interests to attempt this. He may have thought, probably with some reason, that such a course would avail little with the king, and would bring ruin on himself. His life was passed in the atmosphere of a court, and he had imbibed its selfish spirit. He had profoundly studied the character of his master, and he accommodated himself to all his humors with an obsequiousness which does little honor to his memory. The duke of Alva, who hated him with all the hatred of a rival, speaking of him after his death, remarked, "Ruy Gomez, though not the greatest statesman that ever lived, was such a master in the knowledge of the humors and dispositions of kings, that we were all of us fools in comparison."[8]

Yet the influence of the favorite was, on the whole, good. He was humane and liberal in his temper, and inclined to peace,—virtues which were not too common

---

[7] Cabrera, Filipe Segundo, pp. 712, 713.—Cabrera has given us, in the first chapter of the tenth book of his history, a finished portrait of Ruy Gomez, which for the niceness of its discrimination and the felicity of its language may compare with the best compositions of the Castilian chroniclers.

[8] "El señor Ruy Gomez no fué de los mayores consejeros que ha habido, pero del humor y natural de los reyes le reconozco por tan gran maestro, que todos los que por aqui dentro andamos tenemos la cabeza donde pensamos que traemos los pies." Bermudez de Castro, Antonio Perez (Madrid, 1841), p. 28.

in that iron age, and which in the council served much to counteract the stern policy of Alva. Persons of a generous nature ranged themselves under him as their leader. When John of Austria came to court, his liberal spirit prompted him at once to lean on Ruy Gomez as his friend and counsellor. The correspondence which passed between them when the young soldier was on his campaigns, in which he addressed the favorite by the epithet of "father," confessing his errors to him and soliciting his advice, is honorable to both.

The historian Cabrera, who had often seen him, sums up the character of Ruy Gomez by saying, "He was the first pilot who in these stormy seas both lived and died secure, always contriving to gain a safe port." [9] His death took place in July, 1573. "Living," adds the writer, in his peculiar style, "he preserved the favor of his sovereign. Dead, he was mourned by him,—and by the whole nation, which kept him in its recollection as the pattern of loyal vassals and prudent favorites." [10]

Besides the two leaders in the council, there were two others who deserve to be noticed. One of these was Figueroa, count, afterwards created by Philip duke, of Feria, a grandee of Spain. He was one of those who accompanied the king on his first visit to England.

[9] "Fue Rui Gomez el primero piloto que en trabajos tan grandes vivió y murió seguro, tomando sienpre el mejor puerto." Cabrera, Filipe Segundo, p. 713.

[10] "Vivo conservò la gracia de su Rey, muerto le dolió su falta, i la llorò su Reyno, que en su memoria le à conservado para exemplo de fieles vasallos i prudentes privados de los mayores Principes." Ibid., ubi supra.

He there married a lady of rank, and, as the reader may remember, afterwards represented his master at the court of Elizabeth. He was a man of excellent parts, enriched by that kind of practical knowledge which he had gained from foreign travel and a familiarity with courts. He lived magnificently, somewhat encumbering his large estates, indeed, by his profusion. His person was handsome ; and his courteous and polished manners made him one of the most brilliant ornaments of the royal circle. He had a truly chivalrous sense of honor, and was greatly esteemed by the king, who placed him near his person as captain of his Spanish guard. Feria was a warm supporter of Ruy Gomez ; and the long friendship that subsisted between the two nobles seems never to have been clouded by those feelings of envy and jealousy which so often arise between rivals contending for the smiles of their sovereign.

The other member of the council of state was a person of still more importance. This was the Cardinal Espinosa, who, though an ecclesiastic, possessed such an acquaintance with affairs as belonged to few laymen. Philip's eye readily discovered his uncommon qualities, and he heaped upon him offices in rapid succession, any one of which might well have engrossed his time. But Espinosa was as fond of labor as most men are of ease ; and in every situation he not only performed his own share of the work, but very often that of his associates. He was made president of the council of Castile, as well as of that of the Indies, and finally a member of the council of state. He was inquisitor-general, sat in the royal chancery of Seville, and held the bishopric of Siguenza, one of the richest sees in the kingdom. To crown the whole, in 1568, Pius the Fifth, on the application of Philip, gave him a cardinal's hat. The king seems to have taken the greater pleasure in this rapid elevation of Espinosa, that he sprang from a comparatively humble condition, and thus the height to which he raised him served the more keenly to mortify the nobles.

But the cardinal, as is too often the case with those who have suddenly risen to greatness, did not bear his honors meekly. His love of power was insatiable; and when an office became vacant in any of his own departments he was prompt to secure it for one of his dependants. An anecdote is told in relation to a place in the chancery of Granada which had become open by the death of the incumbent. As soon as the news reached Madrid, Hernandez de Córdova, the royal equerry, made application to the king for it. Philip answered that he was too late, that the place had been already given away. "How am I to understand your majesty?" said the petitioner. "The tidings were brought to me by a courier the moment at which the post became vacant; and no one could have brought them sooner unless he had wings." "That may be," said the monarch; "but I have just given the place to another, whom the cardinal recommended to me as I was leaving the council."*

Espinosa, says a contemporary, was a man of noble presence. He had the air of one born to command. His haughty bearing, however, did little for him with

---

* "Puede ser, pero el Cardenal Espinosa me consultó en saliendo del consejo, i proveí la plaça." Cabrera, Filipe Segundo, p. 700.

the more humble suitors, and disgusted the great lords, who looked down with contempt on his lowly origin. They complained to the king of his intolerable arrogance; and the king was not unwilling to receive their charges against him. In fact, he had himself grown to be displeased with his minister's presumption. He was weary of the deference which, now that Espinosa had become a cardinal, he felt obliged to pay him; of coming forward to receive him when he entered the room; of taking off his cap to the churchman, and giving him a seat as high as his own; finally, of allowing him to interfere in all appointments to office. It seemed incredible, says the historian, that a prince so jealous of his prerogatives should have submitted to all this so long."[12] Philip was now determined to submit to it no longer, but to tumble from its pride of place the idol which he had raised with his own hands.

He was slow in betraying his intention, by word or act, to the courtiers, still more to the unfortunate minister, who continued to show the same security and confidence as if he were treading the solid ground, instead of the crust of a volcano.

At length an opportunity offered when Espinosa, in a discussion respecting the affairs of Flanders, made a statement which the king deemed not entirely conformable to truth. Philip at once broke in upon the discourse with an appearance of great indignation, and charged the minister with falsehood. The blow was the more effectual, coming from one who had been scarcely ever known to give way to pas-

---

[12] "Que en principe tan zeloso de su immunidad i oficio pareció increible su tolerancia hasta alli." Cabrera, Filipe Segundo, p. 700.

sion."[13] The cardinal was stunned by it. He at once saw his ruin, and the vision of glory vanished forever. He withdrew, more dead than alive, to his house. There he soon took to his bed; and in a short time, in September, 1572, he breathed his last. His fate was that of more than one minister whose head had been made giddy by the height to which he had climbed.[14]

The council of state, under its two great leaders, Alva and Ruy Gomez, was sure to be divided on every question of importance. This was a fruitful source of embarrassment, and to private suitors, especially, occasioned infinite delay. Such was the hostility of the parties to each other that if an applicant for favor secured the good will of one of the chiefs he was very certain to encounter the ill will of the other.[15] He was a skilful pilot who in such cross seas could keep his course.

Yet the existence of these divisions does not seem to have been discouraged by Philip, who saw in them only the natural consequence of a rivalry for his favor. They gave him, moreover, the advantage of seeing every question of moment well canvassed, and, by furnishing

[13] The anonymous author of a contemporary relation speaks of the king as a person little subject to passions of any kind. The language is striking: " E questo Re poco soggetto alle pasioni, venga ciò, o per inclinazione naturale, o per costume; e quasi non appariscono in lui i primi movimenti nè dell' allegrezza, nè del dolore, nè dell' ira ancora." MS.

[14] " El Rey le habló tan asperamente sobre el afinar una verdad, que le matò brevemente," says Cabrera emphatically. Filipe Segundo, p. 699.

[15] " Perchè chi vuole il favore del duca d'Alva perde quello di Ruy Gomez, e chi cerca il favore di Ruy Gomez, non ha quello del duca d'Alva." Relazione di Soriano, MS.

him with the opposite opinions of his councillors, enabled him the more accurately to form his own. In the mean time, the value which he set on both the great chiefs made him careful not to disgust either by any show of preference for his rival. He held the balance adroitly between them; and if on any occasion he bestowed a mark of his favor on the one, it was usually followed by some equivalent to the other.[16] Thus, for the first twelve years of his reign their influence may be said to have been pretty equally exerted. Then came the memorable discussion respecting the royal visit to the Netherlands. Alva, as the reader may remember, was of the opinion that Philip should send an army to punish the refractory and bring the country to obedience, when the king might visit it with safety to his own person. Ruy Gomez, on the other hand, recommended that Philip should go at once, without an army, and by mild and conciliatory measures win the malecontents back to their allegiance. Each advised the course most congenial to his own temper, and the one, moreover, which would have required the aid of his own services to carry it into execution. Unfortunately, the violent measures of Alva were more congenial to the stern temper of the king, and the duke was sent at the head of his battalions.

But if Alva thus gained the victory, it was Ruy Gomez who reaped the fruits of it. Left without a rival in the council, his influence became predominant over every

---

[16] Ranke has given some pertinent examples of this in an interesting sketch which he has presented of the relative positions of these two statesmen in the cabinet of Philip. Ottoman and Spanish Empires (Eng. trans.), p. 38.

other. It became still more firmly established as the result showed that his rival's mission was a failure. So it continued, after Alva's return, till the favorite's death. Even then his well-organized party was so deeply rooted that for several years longer it maintained an ascendency in the cabinet, while the duke languished in disgrace.

Philip, unlike most of his predecessors, rarely took his seat in the council of state. It was his maxim that his ministers would more freely discuss measures in the absence of their master than when he was there to overawe them. The course he adopted was for a *consulta*, or a committee of two or three members, to wait on him in his cabinet and report to him the proceedings of the council." He more commonly, especially in the later years of his reign, preferred to receive a full report of the discussion, written so as to leave an ample margin for his own commentaries. These were eminently characteristic of the man, and were so minute as usually to cover several sheets of paper. Philip had a reserved and unsocial temper. He preferred to work alone, in the seclusion of his closet, rather than in the presence of others. This may explain the reason, in part, why he seemed so much to prefer writing to talking. Even with his private secretaries, who were always near at hand, he chose to communicate by writing; and they had as large a mass of his autograph notes in their possession as if the correspondence had been

---

17 " Non si trova mai S. M. presente alle deliberationi ne i consigli, ma deliberato chiama una delle tre consulte . . . alla qual sempre si ritrova, onde sono lette le risolutioni del consiglio.' Relazione di Tiepolo, MS.

carried on from different parts of the kingdom.[18] His thoughts too—at any rate his words—came slowly; and by writing he gained time for the utterance of them.

Philip has been accused of indolence. As far as the body was concerned, such an accusation was well founded. Even when young, he had no fondness, as we have seen, for the robust and chivalrous sports of the age. He never, like his father, conducted military expeditions in person. He thought it wiser to follow the example of his great-grandfather, Ferdinand the Catholic, who stayed at home and sent his generals to command his armies. As little did he like to travel, —forming too in this respect a great contrast to the emperor. He had been years on the throne before he made a visit to his great southern capital, Seville. It was a matter of complaint in cortes that he thus withdrew himself from the eyes of his subjects. The only sport he cared for—not by any means to excess—was shooting with his gun or his cross-bow such game as he could find in his own grounds at the Wood of Segovia, or Aranjuez, or some other of his pleasant country-seats, none of them at a great distance from Madrid.

On a visit to such places he would take with him as large a heap of papers as if he were a poor clerk earning his bread; and after the fatigues of the chase he would retire to his cabinet and refresh himself with his despatches.[19] It would indeed be a great mistake to

---

[18] Ranke, Ottoman and Spanish Empires, p. 32.

[19] "El dia que iva à caça bolvia con ansias de bolver al trabajo, como un oficial pobre que huviera de ganar la comida con ello." Los Dichos y Hechos del Rey Phelipe II. (Brusselas, 1666), p. 214.—See also Relazione di Pigafetta, MS.

charge him with sluggishness of mind. He was content to toil for hours, and long into the night, at his solitary labors.[20] No expression of weariness or of impatience was known to escape him. A characteristic anecdote is told of him in regard to this. Having written a despatch, late at night, to be sent on the following morning, he handed it to his secretary to throw some sand over it. This functionary, who happened to be dozing, suddenly roused himself, and, snatching up the inkstand, emptied it on the paper. The king, coolly remarking that "it would have been better to use the sand," set himself down, without any complaint, to rewrite the whole of the letter.[21] A prince so much addicted to the pen, we may well believe, must have left a large amount of autograph materials behind him. Few monarchs, in point of fact, have done so much in this way to illustrate the history of their reigns. Fortunate would it have been for the historian who was to profit by it, if the royal composition had been somewhat less diffuse and the handwriting somewhat more legible.

Philip was an economist of time, and regulated the distribution of it with great precision. In the morning he gave audience to foreign ambassadors. He afterwards heard mass. After mass came dinner, in

---

[20] Relazione di Vandramino, MS.—Relazione di Contarini, MS.— "Distribuia las horas del dia, se puede decir, todas en los negocios, quando yo lo conocí; porque aunque las tenia de oçio ú ocupaciones forçosas de su persona, las gastava con tales criados elegidos tan á proposito que quanto hablava venia à ser informarse mucho, descanso en lo que à otro costara nota y fatiga." MS. Anon. in the Library of the Dukes of Burgundy.

[21] Dichos y Hechos del Rey Phelipe II., pp. 339, 340.

his father's fashion. But dinner was not an affair with Philip of so much moment as it was with Charles. He was exceedingly temperate both in eating and drinking, and not unfrequently had his physician at his side, to warn him against any provocative of the gout,—the hereditary disease which at a very early period had begun to affect his health. After a light repast, he gave audience to such of his subjects as desired to present their memorials. He received the petitioners graciously, and listened to all they had to say with patience,—for that was his virtue. But his countenance was exceedingly grave,—which, in truth, was its natural expression; and there was a reserve in his deportment which made the boldest feel ill at ease in his presence. On such occasions he would say, "Compose yourself,"—a recommendation that had not always the tranquillizing effect intended.[72] Once when a papal nuncio forgot, in his confusion, the address he had prepared, the king coolly remarked, "If you will bring it in writing, I will read it myself, and expedite your business."[73] It was natural that men of even the highest rank should be overawed in the presence of a monarch who held the destinies of so many millions in his hands, and who surrounded himself with a veil of mystery which the most cunning politician could not penetrate.

The reserve so noticeable in his youth increased with age. He became more difficult of access. His public audiences were much less frequent. In the summer he

---

[72] "A estos estando turbados, y desalentados, los animava diziendoles, sossegaos." Dichos y Hechos del Rey Phelipe II., p. 40.

[73] "Diziendole si lo traeis escrito, lo verè, y os harè despachar.' Ibid., p. 41.

would escape from them altogether, by taking refuge in some one of his country places. His favorite retreat was his palace-monastery of the Escorial, then slowly rising under his patronage and affording him an occupation congenial with his taste. He seems, however, to have sought the country not so much from the love of its beauties as for the retreat it afforded him from the town. When in the latter, he rarely showed himself to the public eye, going abroad chiefly in a close carriage, and driving late so as to return to the city after dark.[24]

Thus he lived in solitude even in the heart of his capital, knowing much less of men from his own observation than from the reports that were made to him. In availing himself of these sources of information he was indefatigable. He caused a statistical survey of Spain to be prepared for his own use. It was a work of immense labor, embracing a vast amount of curious details, such as were rarely brought together in those days.[25] He kept his spies at the principal European courts, who furnished him with intelligence; and he was as well acquainted with what was passing in England and in France as if he had resided on the spot. We have seen how well he knew the smallest details of the proceedings in the Netherlands, sometimes even better than Margaret herself. He employed

---

[24] "Quando esce di Palazzo, suole montare in un cocchio coperto di tela incerata, et serrata a modo che non si vede. . . . Suole quando va in villa ritornare la sera per le porte del Parco, senza esser veduto da alcuno." Relazione di Pigafetta, MS.

[25] Ranke, Ottoman and Spanish Empires, p. 32.—Inglis speaks of seeing this work in the library when he visited the Escorial. Spain in 1830, vol. i. p. 348.

similar means to procure information that might be of service in making appointments to ecclesiastical and civil offices.

In his eagerness for information, his ear was ever open to accusations against his ministers, which, as they were sure to be locked up in his own bosom, were not slow in coming to him.[26] This filled his mind with suspicions. He waited till time had proved their truth, treating the object of them with particular favor till the hour of vengeance had arrived. The reader will not have forgotten the terrible saying of Philip's own historian, "His dagger followed close upon his smile."[27]

Even to the ministers in whom Philip appeared most to confide, he often gave but half his confidence. Instead of frankly furnishing them with a full statement of facts, he sometimes made so imperfect a disclosure that, when his measures came to be taken, his counsellors were surprised to find of how much they had been kept in ignorance. When he communicated to them any foreign despatches, he would not scruple to alter the original, striking out some passages and inserting others, so as best to serve his purpose. The copy, in this garbled form, was given to the council. Such was the case with a letter of Don John of Austria, containing an account of the troubles of Genoa, the original of which, with its numerous alterations in the royal handwriting, still exists in the Archives of Simancas.[28]

[26] Ranke, Ottoman and Spanish Empires, p. 33.
[27] See *ante*, vol. ii. p. 493.
[28] Lafuente, Historia de España, tom. xiv. p. 44.—The historian tells us he has seen the original letter, with the changes made in it by Philip.

But, though Philip's suspicious nature prevented him from entirely trusting his ministers, — though with chilling reserve he kept at a distance even those who approached him nearest, — he was kind, even liberal, to his servants, was not capricious in his humors, and seldom, if ever, gave way to those sallies of passion so common in princes clothed with absolute power. He was patient to the last degree, and rarely changed his ministers without good cause. Ruy Gomez was not the only courtier who continued in the royal service to the end of his days.

Philip was of a careful, or, to say truth, of a frugal disposition, which he may well have inherited from his father; though this did not, as with his father in later life, degenerate into parsimony. The beginning of his reign, indeed, was distinguished by some acts of uncommon liberality. One of these occurred at the close of Alva's campaigns in Italy, when the king presented that commander with a hundred and fifty thousand ducats, greatly to the discontent of the emperor. This was contrary to his usual policy. As he grew older, and the expenses of government pressed more heavily on him, he became more economical. Yet those who served him had no reason, like the emperor's servants, to complain of their master's meanness. It was observed, however, that he was slow to recompense those who served him until they had proved themselves worthy of it. Still, it was a man's own fault, says a contemporary, if he was not well paid for his services in the end.[29]

[29] "Chi comincia a servirlo può tener per certa la remunerazione, se il difetto non vien da lui." Relazione Anon., MS.

In one particular he indulged in a most lavish expenditure. This was his household. It was formed on the Burgundian model,—the most stately and magnificent in Europe. Its peculiarity consisted in the number and quality of the members who composed it. The principal officers were nobles of the highest rank, who frequently held posts of great consideration in the state. Thus, the duke of Alva was chief major-domo; the prince of Eboli was first gentleman of the bedchamber; the duke of Feria was captain of the Spanish guard. There was the grand equerry, the grand huntsman, the chief muleteer, and a host of officers, some of whom were designated by menial titles, though nobles and cavaliers of family.[30] There were forty pages, sons of the most illustrious houses in Castile. The whole household amounted to no less than fifteen hundred persons.[31] The king's guard consisted of three hundred men, one-third of whom were Spaniards, one-third Flemings, and the remainder Germans.[32]

The queen had also her establishment on the same scale. She had twenty-six ladies-in-waiting, and, among other functionaries, no less than four physicians to watch over her health.[33]

The annual cost of the royal establishment amounted

[30] Relazione della Corte di Spagna, MS.—Relazione di Badoer, MS.—Etiquetas de Palacio, MS.

[31] Relazione di Badoer, MS.

[32] " Ha tre guardie di 100 persone l' una; la più honorata è di Borgognoni e Fiamminghi, che hanno ad esser ben nati e servono a cavallo, e si dicono Arcieri accompagnando bene il Re per la città a piede non in fila, ma alla rinfusa intorno alla persona reale; l' altri sono d'Albardieri 100 di nazion tedesca, el altri e tanti Spagnuoli." Relazione della Corte di Spagna, MS.

[33] Raumer, Sixteenth and Seventeenth Centuries, vol. i. p. 106.

to full two hundred thousand florins.[34] The cortes earnestly remonstrated against this useless prodigality, beseeching the king to place his household on the modest scale to which the monarchs of Castile had been accustomed.[35] And it seems singular that one usually so averse to extravagance and pomp should have so recklessly indulged in them here. It was one of those inconsistencies which we sometimes meet with in private life, when a man habitually careful of his expenses indulges himself in some which taste, or, as in this case, early habits, have made him regard as indispensable. The emperor had been careful to form the household of his son, when very young, on the Burgundian model; and Philip, thus early trained, probably regarded it as essential to the royal dignity.

The king did not affect an ostentation in his dress corresponding with that of his household. This seemed to be suited to the sober-colored livery of his own feelings, and was almost always of black velvet or satin, with shoes of the former material. He wore a cap, garnished with plumes after the Spanish fashion. He used few ornaments, scarce any but the rich jewel of the Golden Fleece, which hung from his neck. But in his attire he was scrupulously neat, says the Venetian diplomatist who tells these particulars; and he changed his dress for a new one every month, giving away his cast-off suits to his attendants.[36]

---

[34] Raumer, Sixteenth and Seventeenth Centuries, vol. i. p. 105.
[35] Cortes of 1558, peticion 4.
[36] " Questi habiti sempre sono nuovi et puliti, perche ogni mese se gli muta, et poi gli dona quando ad uno, e quando ad un altro." Relazione di Pigafetta, MS.

It was a capital defect in Philip's administration that his love of power and his distrust of others made him desire to do every thing himself,—even those things which could be done much better by his ministers. As he was slow in making up his own opinions, and seldom acted without first ascertaining those of his council, we may well understand the mischievous consequences of such delay. Loud were the complaints of private suitors, who saw month after month pass away without an answer to their petitions. The state suffered no less, as the wheels of government seemed actually to stand still under the accumulated pressure of the public business. Even when a decision did come, it often came too late to be of service; for the circumstances which led to it had wholly changed. Of this the reader has seen more than one example in the Netherlands. The favorite saying of Philip, that "time and he were a match for any other two," was a sad mistake. The time he demanded was his ruin. It was in vain that Granvelle, who, at a later day, came to Castile to assume the direction of affairs, endeavored, in his courtly language, to convince the king of his error, telling him that no man could bear up under such a load of business, which sooner or later must destroy his health, perhaps his life.[37]

[37] Gachard cites a passage from one of Granvelle's unpublished letters, in which he says, "Suplico á V. M., con la humildad que devo, que considerando quanto su vida importa al principe nuestro señor, á todos sus reynos y Estados, y vasallos suyos, y aun á toda la christiandad, mirando en que miserando estado quedaría sin V. M., sea servido mirar adelante más por su salud, descargandose de tan grande y continuo trabajo, que tanto daño le haze." Rapport prefixed to the Correspondance de Philippe II. (tom. i. p. li.), in which

A letter addressed to the king by his grand almoner, Don Luis Manrique, told the truth in plainer terms, such as had not often reached the royal ear. "Your majesty's subjects everywhere complain," he says, "of your manner of doing business,—sitting all day long over your papers, from your desire, as they intimate, to seclude yourself from the world, and from a want of confidence in your ministers.[38] Hence such interminable delays as fill the soul of every suitor with despair. Your subjects are discontented that you refuse to take your seat in the council of state. The Almighty," he adds, "did not send kings into the world to spend their days in reading or writing, or even in meditation and prayer,"—in which Philip was understood to pass much of his time,—"but to serve as public oracles, to which all may resort for answers. If any sovereign have received this grace, it is your majesty; and the greater the sin, therefore, if you do not give free access to all."[39] One may be surprised to find that language

the Belgian scholar, with his usual conscientiousness and care, enters into an examination of the character and personal habits of Philip.

[38] "Habiendo en otra ocasion avisado á vuestra magestad de la publica querella y desconsuelo que habia del estilo que vuestra magestad habia tomado de negociar, estando perpetuamente asido á los papeles, por tener mejor título para huir de la gente, ademas de no quererse fiar de nadie." Carta que escrivio al Señor Rey Felipe Segundo Don Luis Manrique, su limosnero mayor, MS.

[39] "No embio Dios á vuestra magestad y á todos los otros Reyes, que tienen sus veces en la tierra, para que se extravien leyendo ni escribiendo ni aun contemplando ni rezando, si no para que fuesen y sean publicos y patentes oraculos á donde todos sus subditos vengan por sus respuestas. . . . Y si á algun Rey en el mundo dió Dios esta gracia, es á vuestra magestad y por eso es mayor la culpa de no manifestarse á todos." Ibid.—A copy of this letter is preserved among the Egerton MSS. in the British Museum.

such as this was addressed to a prince like Philip the Second, and that he should have borne it so patiently. But in this the king resembled his father. Churchmen and jesters—of which latter he had usually one or two in attendance—were privileged persons at his court. In point of fact, the homilies of the one had as little effect as the jests of the other.

The pomp of the royal establishment was imitated on a smaller scale by the great nobles living on their vast estates scattered over the country. Their revenues were very large, though often heavily burdened. Out of twenty-three dukes, in 1581, only three had an income so low as forty thousand ducats a year.[40] That of most of the others ranged from fifty to a hundred thousand, and that of one, the duke of Medina Sidonia, was computed at a hundred and thirty-five thousand. Revenues like these would not easily have been matched in that day by the aristocracy of any other nation in Christendom.[41]

The Spanish grandees preferred to live on their estates in the country. But in the winter they repaired to Madrid, and displayed their magnificence at the court of their sovereign. Here they dazzled the eye by the splendor of their equipages, the beauty of their horses, their rich liveries, and the throng of their retainers. But with all this the Castilian court was far from appearing in the eyes of foreigners a gay one,—

---

[40] Nota di tutti li Titolati di Spagna con li loro casate el rendite, etc., fatta nel 1581, MS.

[41] Ibid.—The Spanish aristocracy, in 1581, reckoned twenty-three dukes, forty-two marquises, and fifty-six counts. All the dukes and thirteen of the inferior nobles were grandees.

forming in this respect a contrast to the Flemish court of Margaret of Parma. It seemed to have imbibed much of the serious and indeed sombre character of the monarch who presided over it. All was stately and ceremonious, with old-fashioned manners and usages. "There is nothing new to be seen there," write the Venetian envoys. "There is no pleasant gossip about the events of the day. If a man is acquainted with any news, he is too prudent to repeat it."[42] The courtiers talk little, and for the most part are ignorant,—in fact, without the least tincture of learning. The arrogance of the great lords is beyond belief; and when they meet a foreign ambassador, or even the nuncio of his holiness, they rarely condescend to salute him by raising their caps.[43] They all affect that imperturbable composure, or apathy, which they term *sosiego*."[44]

They gave no splendid banquets, like the Flemish nobles. Their chief amusement was gaming,—the hereditary vice of the Spaniard. They played deep, often to the great detriment of their fortunes. This did not displease the king. It may seem strange that a society so cold and formal should be much addicted

[42] "La corte è muta; in publico non si ragiona di nuove, et chi pure le sa, se le tace." Relazione di Pigafetta, MS.

[43] "Sono d' animo tanto elevato . . . che è cosa molto difficile da credere . . . e quando avviene che incontrino o nunzi del pontefice o ambasciadori di qualche testa coronata o d' altro stato, pochissimi son quelli che si levin la berreta." Relazione di Badoero, MS.

[44] "Non si attende à lettere, ma la Nobilità è a maraviglia ignorante e ritirata, mantenendo una certa sua alterigia, che loro chiamano *sussiego*, che vuol dire tranquillità et sicurezza, et quasi serenità." Relazione di Pigafetta, MS.

to intrigue.⁴⁵ In this they followed the example of their master.

Thus passing their days in frivolous amusements and idle dalliance, the Spanish nobles, with the lofty titles and pretensions of their ancestors, were a degenerate race. With a few brilliant exceptions, they filled no important posts in the state or in the army. The places of most consideration to which they aspired were those connected with the royal household; and their greatest honor was to possess the empty privileges of the grandee, and to sit with their heads covered in the presence of the king.⁴⁶

From this life of splendid humiliation they were nothing loath to escape into the country, where they passed their days in their ancestral castles, surrounded by princely domains, which embraced towns and villages within their circuit, and a population sometimes reaching to thirty thousand families. Here the proud lords lived in truly regal pomp. Their households were formed on that of the sovereign. They had their major-domos, their gentlemen of the bedchamber, their grand equerries, and other officers of rank. Their halls were filled with hidalgos and cavaliers, and a throng of inferior retainers. They were attended by body-guards of one or two hundred soldiers. Their dwell-

---

⁴⁵ "Non si convita, non si cavalea, si giuoca, et si fa all' amore." Relatione di Pigafetta, M.S.—See also the Relazioni of Badoero and Contarini.

⁴⁶ Dr. Salazar y Mendoza takes a very exalted view of the importance of this right to wear the hat in the presence of the king.—"a prerogative," he remarks, "so illustrious in itself, and so admirable in its effects, that it alone suffices to stamp its peculiar character on the dignity of the grandee." Dignidades de Castilla, p. 34.

ings were sumptuously furnished, and their sideboards loaded with plate from the silver quarries of the New World. Their chapels were magnificent. Their wives affected a royal state. They had their ladies of honor; and the page who served as cup-bearer knelt while his mistress drank. Even knights of ancient blood, whom she addressed from her seat, did not refuse to bend the knee to her.[47]

Amidst all this splendor, the Spanish grandees had no real power to correspond with it. They could no longer, as in the days of their fathers, engage in feuds with one another; nor could they enjoy the privilege, so highly prized, of renouncing their allegiance and declaring war upon their sovereign. Their numerous vassals, instead of being gathered as of yore into a formidable military array, had sunk into the more humble rank of retainers, who served only to swell the idle pomp of their lord's establishment. They were no longer allowed to bear arms, except in the service of the crown; and after the Moriscoes had been reduced, the crown had no occasion for their services,—unless in foreign war.[48]

The measures by which Ferdinand and Isabella had broken the power of the aristocracy had been enforced with still greater rigor by Charles the Fifth, and were now carried out even more effectually by Philip the Second. For Philip had the advantage of being always in Spain, while Charles passed most of his time in other parts of his dominions. Thus ever present, Philip was as prompt to enforce the law

[47] Ranke, Ottoman and Spanish Empires, p. 57.
[48] Relazione di Tiepolo, MS.—Relazione Anon., MS.—Relazione di Contarini, MS.

against the highest noble as against the humblest of his subjects.

Men of rank commanded the armies abroad, and were sent as viceroys to Naples, Sicily, Milan, and the provinces of the New World. But at home they were rarely raised to civil or military office. They no longer formed a necessary part of the national legislature, and were seldom summoned to the meetings of the cortes; for the Castilian noble claimed exemption from the public burdens, and it was rarely that the cortes were assembled for any other purpose than to impose those burdens. Thus without political power of any kind, they resided like so many private gentlemen on their estates in the country. Their princely style of living gave no umbrage to the king, who was rather pleased to see them dissipate their vast revenues in a way that was attended with no worse evil than that of driving the proprietors to exactions which made them odious to their vassals.[49] Such, we are assured by a Venetian envoy,—who, with great powers of observation, was placed in the best situation for exerting them,—was the policy of Philip. "Thus," he concludes, "did the king make himself feared by those who, if they had managed discreetly, might have made themselves feared by him."[50]

While the aristocracy was thus depressed, the strong arm of Charles the Fifth had stripped the Castilian commons of their most precious rights. Philip, happily for himself, was spared the odium of having reduced

---

[49] "Che per contrario affligiono i loro proprii sudditi onde incorrono nel loro odio." Relazione di Contarini, MS.

[50] "Temono Sua Maesta, dove, quando si governassero prudentemente, sarieno da essa per le loro forze temuti." Ibid.

them to this abject condition. But he was as careful as his father could have been that they should not rise from it. The legislative power of the commons, that most important of all their privileges, was nearly annihilated. The Castilian cortes were, it is true, frequently convoked under Philip,—more frequently, on the whole, than in any preceding reign. For in them still resided the power of voting supplies for the crown. To have summoned them so often, therefore, was rather a proof of the necessities of the government than of respect for the rights of the commons.

The cortes, it is true, still enjoyed the privilege of laying their grievances before the king; but, as they were compelled to vote the supplies before they presented their grievances, they had lost the only lever by which they could effectually operate on the royal will. Yet when we review their petitions, and see the care with which they watched over the interests of the nation and the courage with which they maintained them, we cannot refuse our admiration. We must acknowledge that under every circumstance of discouragement and oppression the old Castilian spirit still lingered in the hearts of the people. In proof of this, it will not be amiss to cite a few of these petitions, which, whether successful or not, may serve at least to show the state of public opinion on the topics to which they relate.

One, of repeated recurrence, is a remonstrance to the king on the enormous expense of his household,— "as great," say the cortes, "as would be required for the conquest of a kingdom."[51] The Burgundian estab-

---

[51] "Que bastarán para conquistar y ganar un reyno." Cortes of Valladolid of 1558, pet. 4.

lishment, independently of its costliness, found little favor with the honest Castilian; and the cortes prayed his majesty to abandon it, and to return to the more simple and natural usage of his ancestors. They represented "the pernicious effects which this manner of living necessarily had on the great nobles and others of his subjects, prone to follow the example of their master."[52] To one of these petitions Philip replied that "he would cause the matter to be inquired into, and such measures to be taken as were most for his service." No alteration took place during his reign; and the Burgundian establishment, which in 1562 involved an annual charge of a hundred and fifty-six millions of maravedis, was continued by his successor.[53]

Another remonstrance of constant recurrence—a proof of its inefficacy—was that against the alienation of the crown lands and the sale of offices and the lesser titles of nobility. To this the king made answer in much the same equivocal language as before. Another petition besought him no longer to seek an increase of his revenue by imposing taxes without the sanction of the cortes required by the ancient law and usage of the realm. Philip's reply on this occasion was plain enough. It was, in truth, one worthy of an Eastern despot. "The necessities," he said, "which have compelled me to resort to these measures, far from having ceased, have increased, and are still increasing, allowing me no alternative but to pursue the course I have adopted."[54] Philip's embarrassments

[52] Cortes of Toledo of 1559, pet. 3.
[53] Lafuente, Historia de España, tom. xiii. p. 118.
[54] Ibid., tom. xiv. p. 397.

were indeed great,—far beyond the reach of any financial skill of his ministers to remove. His various expedients for relieving himself from the burden, which, as he truly said, was becoming heavier every day, form a curious chapter in the history of finance. But we have not yet reached the period at which they can be most effectively presented to the reader.

The commons strongly urged the king to complete the great work he had early undertaken, of embodying in one code the municipal law of Castile.[55] They gave careful attention to the administration of justice, showed their desire for the reform of various abuses, especially for quickening the despatch of business, proverbially slow in Spain, and, in short, for relieving suitors as far as possible from the manifold vexations to which they were daily exposed in the tribunals. With a wise liberality, they recommended that, in order to secure the services of competent persons in judicial offices, their salaries — in many cases wholly inadequate — should be greatly increased.[56]

The cortes watched with a truly parental care over the great interests of the state,—its commerce, its husbandry, and its manufactures. They raised a loud, and, as it would seem, not an ineffectual, note of remonstrance against the tyrannical practice of the crown in seizing for its own use the bullion which, as elsewhere stated, had been imported from the New World on their own account by the merchants of Seville.

Some of the petitions of the cortes show what would be thought at the present day a strange ignorance of the

---

[55] Cortes of Valladolid of 1558, pet. 12.
[56] Lafuente, Historia de España, tom. xiii. p. 125.

true principles of legislation in respect to commerce. Thus, regarding gold and silver, independently of their value as a medium of exchange, as constituting in a peculiar manner the wealth of a country, they considered that the true policy was to keep the precious metals at home, and prayed that their exportation might be forbidden. Yet this was a common error in the sixteenth century with other nations besides the Spaniards. It may seem singular, however, that the experience of three-fourths of a century had not satisfied the Castilian of the futility of such attempts to obstruct the natural current of commercial circulation.

In the same spirit, they besought the king to prohibit the use of gold and silver in plating copper and other substances, as well as for wearing-apparel and articles of household luxury. It was a waste of the precious metals, which were needed for other purposes. This petition of the commons may be referred in part, no doubt, to their fondness for sumptuary laws, which in Castile formed a more ample code than could be easily found in any other country.[57] The love of costly and ostentatious dress was a passion which they may have caught from their neighbors the Spanish Arabs, who delighted in this way of displaying their opulence. It furnished, accordingly, from an early period, a fruitful theme of declamation to the clergy, in their invectives against the pomp and vanities of the world.

Unfortunately, Philip, who was so frequently deaf to

[57] The history of luxury in Castile, and of the various enactments for the restraint of it, forms the subject of a work by Sempere y Guarinos, containing many curious particulars, especially in regard to the life of the Castilians at an earlier period of their history Historia del Luxo (Madrid, 1788, 2 tom. 1.mo).

the wiser suggestions of the cortes, gave his sanction to this petition; and in a *pragmatic* devoted to the object he carried out the ideas of the legislature as heartily as the most austere reformer could have desired. As a state paper it has certainly a novel aspect, going at great length into such minute specifications of wearing-apparel, both male and female, that it would seem to have been devised by a committee of tailors and milliners rather than of grave legislators.[58] The tailors, indeed, the authors of these seductive abominations, did not escape the direct animadversion of the cortes. In another petition they were denounced as unprofitable persons, occupied with needle-work, like women, instead of tilling the ground or serving his majesty in the wars, like men.[59]

In the same spirit of impertinent legislation, the cortes would have regulated the expenses of the table, which, they said, of late years had been excessive. They recommended that no one should be allowed to have more than four dishes of meat and four of fruit

[58] " Anssi mismo mandamos que ninguna persona de ninguna condicion ni calidad que sea, no pueda traer ni traya en ropa ni en vestido, ni en calzas, ni jubon, ni en gualdrapa, ni guarnicion de mula ni de cavallo, ningun genero de bordado ni recamado, ni gandujado, ni entorchado, ni chaperia de oro ni de plata, ni de oro de cañutillo, ni de martillo, ni ningun genero de trenza ni cordon ni cordoncillo, ni franja, ni pasamano, ni pespunte, ni perfil de oro ni plata ni seda, ni otra cosa, aunque el dicho oro y plata sean falsos," etc. Pracmatica expedida á peticion de la Cortes de Madrid de 1563.

[59] " Ocupados en este oficio y género de vivienda de coser, que habia de ser para las mugeres, muchos hombres que podrian servir á S. M. en la guerra dejaban de ir á ella, y dejaban tambien de labrar los campos." Cortes of 1573, pet. 75, ap. Lafuente, Hist. de España, tom. xiv. p. 407.

served at the same meal. They were further scandalized by the increasing use of coaches, a mode of conveyance which had been introduced into Spain only a few years before. They regarded them as tempting men to an effeminate indulgence which most of them could ill afford. They considered the practice, moreover, as detrimental to the good horsemanship for which their ancestors had been so renowned. They prayed, therefore, that, considering "the nation had done well for so many years without the use of coaches, it might henceforth be prohibited."[60] Philip so far complied with their petition as to forbid any one but the owner of four horses to keep a coach. Thus he imagined that, while encouraging the raising of horses, he should effectually discourage any but the more wealthy from affecting this costly luxury.

There was another petition, somewhat remarkable, and worth citing as it shows the attachment of the Castilians to a national institution which has often incurred the censure of foreigners. A petition of the cortes of 1573 prayed that some direct encouragement might be given to bull-fights, which of late had shown symptoms of decline. They advised that the principal towns should be required to erect additional circuses, and to provide lances for the combatants and music for the entertainments at the charge of the municipalities. They insisted on this as important for mending the breed of horses, as well as for furnishing a chivalrous exercise for the nobles and cavaliers. This may excite some surprise in a spectator of our day, accustomed to

[60] Cortes of 1573, pet. 75, ap. Lafuente, Hist. de España, tom. xiv. p. 408.

see only the most wretched hacks led to the slaughter and men of humble condition skirmishing in the arena. It was otherwise in those palmy days of chivalry, when the horses employed were of a generous breed, and the combatants were nobles, who entered the lists with as proud a feeling as that with which they would have gone to a tourney. Even so late as the sixteenth century it was the boast of Charles the Fifth that, when a young man, he had fought like a *matador* and killed his bull. Philip gave his assent to this petition with a promptness which showed that he understood the character of his countrymen.

It would be an error to regard the more exceptionable and frivolous petitions of the cortes, some of which have been above enumerated, as affording a true type of the predominant character of Castilian legislation. The laws, or, to speak correctly, the petitions, of that body, are strongly impressed with a wise and patriotic sentiment, showing a keen perception of the wants of the community and a tender anxiety to relieve them. Thus, we find the cortes recommending that guardians should be appointed to find employment for such young and destitute persons as, without friends to aid them, had no means of getting a livelihood for themselves.[61] They propose to have visitors chosen, whose duty it should be to inspect the prisons every week and see that fitting arrangements were made for securing the health and cleanliness of the inmates.[62] They desire

[61] Ranke, Ottoman and Spanish Empires, p. 59.
[62] "Que cada semana ó cada mes se nombren en los ayuntamientos de cada ciudad ó villa destos Reynos, dos Regidores, los quales se hallen á la vision y visitas de la carcel." Cortes of Toledo of 1559, 1560, pet. 102.

that care should be taken to have suitable accommodations provided at the inns for travellers.[63] With their usual fondness for domestic inquisition, they take notice of the behavior of servants to their masters, and, with a simplicity that may well excite a smile, they animadvert on the conduct of maidens who, "in the absence of their mothers, spend their idle hours in reading romances full of lies and vanities, which they receive as truths for the government of their own conduct in their intercourse with the world."[64] The books thus stigmatized were doubtless the romances of chivalry, which at this period were at the height of their popularity in Castile. Cervantes had not yet aimed at this pestilent literature those shafts of ridicule which did more than any legislation could have done towards driving it from the land.

The commons watched over the business of education as zealously as over any of the material interests of the state. They inspected the condition of the higher seminaries, and would have provision made for the foundation of new chairs in the universities. In accordance with their views, though not in conformity to any positive suggestion, Philip published a pragmatic

[63] Provision real para que los mesones del reyno esten bien proveidos de los mantenimientos necesarios para los caminantes, Toledo, 20 de Octubre de 1560.

[64] "Como los mancebos y las donzellas por su ociosidad se principalmente ocupan en aquello [leer libros de mentiras y vanidades], desvanecense y aficionanse en cierta manera á los casos que leen en aquellos libros haver acontescido, ansi de amores como de armas y otras vanidades: y afficionados, quando se offrece algun caso semejante, danse á el mas á rienda suelta que si no lo huviessen leydo.' Cortes of 1558, pet. 107, cited by Ranke, Ottoman and Spanish Empires, p. 60.

in respect to these institutions. He complained of the practice, rapidly increasing among his subjects, of going abroad to get their education, when the most ample provision was made for it at home. The effect was eminently disastrous; for, while the Castilian universities languished for want of patronage, the student who went abroad was pretty sure to return with ideas not the best suited to his own country. The king, therefore, prohibited Spaniards from going to any university out of his dominions, and required all now abroad to return. This edict he accompanied with the severe penalty of forfeiture of their secular possessions for ecclesiastics, and of banishment and confiscation of property for laymen.[65]

This kind of pragmatic, though made doubtless in accordance with the popular feeling, inferred a stretch of arbitrary power that cannot be charged on those which emanated directly from the suggestion of the legislature. In this respect, however, it fell far short of those ordinances which proceeded exclusively from the royal will, without reference to the wishes of the commons. Such ordinances—and they were probably more numerous than any other class of laws during this reign—are doubtless among the most arbitrary acts of which a monarch can be guilty; for they imply nothing less than an assumption of the law-making power into his own hands. Indeed, they met with a strong remonstrance in the year 1579, when Philip was besought by the commons not to make any laws but such as had first received the sanction of the cortes.[66] Yet Philip might

[65] Pracmatica para que ningun natural de estos reynos vaya á estudiar fuera de ellos, Aranjuez, 22 de Noviembre de 1559.
[66] Marina, Teoria de las Cortes, tom. ii. p. 219.

vindicate himself by the example of his predecessors,— even of those who, like Ferdinand and Isabella, had most at heart the interests of the nation.[67]

It must be further admitted that the more regular mode of proceeding, with the co-operation of the cortes, had in it much to warrant the idea that the real right of legislation was vested in the king. A petition, usually couched in the most humble terms, prayed his majesty to give his assent to the law proposed. This he did in a few words; or, what was much more common, he refused to give it, declaring that in the existing case "it was not expedient that any change should be made." It was observed that the number of cases in which Philip rejected the petitions of the commons was much greater than had been usual with former sovereigns.

A more frequent practice with Philip was one that better suited his hesitating nature and habit of procrastination. He replied, in ambiguous terms, that "he would take the matter into consideration," or "that he would lay it before his council and take such measures as would be best for his service." Thus the cortes adjourned in ignorance of the fate of their petitions. Even when he announced his assent, as it was left to him to prescribe the terms of the law, it might be more or less conformable to those of the petition. The cortes having been dismissed, there was

---

[67] See the "Pragmaticas del Reyno," first printed at Alcalá de Henares, at the close of Isabella's reign, in 1503. This famous collection was almost wholly made up of the ordinances of Ferdinand and Isabella. After passing through several editions, it was finally absorbed in the "Nueva Recopilacion" of Philip the Second.

no redress to be obtained if the law did not express their views, nor could any remonstrance be presented by that body until their next session, usually three years later. The practice established by Charles the Fifth, of postponing the presenting of petitions till the supplies had been voted, and the immediate adjournment of the legislature afterwards, secured an absolute authority to the princes of the house of Austria, that made a fearful change in the ancient constitution of Castile.

Yet the meetings of the cortes, shorn as that body was of its ancient privileges, were not without important benefits to the nation. None could be better acquainted than the deputies with the actual wants and wishes of their constituents. It was a manifest advantage for the king to receive this information. It enabled him to take the course best suited to the interests of the people, to which he would naturally be inclined when he did not regard them as conflicting with his own. Even when he did, the strenuous support of their own views by the commons might compel him to modify his measures. However absolute the monarch, he would naturally shrink from pursuing a policy so odious to the people that, if persevered in, it might convert remonstrance into downright resistance.

The freedom of discussion among the deputies is attested by the independent tone with which in their petitions they denounce the manifold abuses in the state. It is honorable to Philip that he should not have attempted to stifle this freedom of debate; though perhaps this may be more correctly referred to his policy, which made him willing to leave this safety-valve open for the passions of the people. He may have been content to flatter them with the image of power, conscious that he alone retained the substance of it. However this may have been, the good effect of the exercise of these rights, imperfect as they were, by the third estate, must be highly estimated. The fact of being called together to consult on public affairs gave the people a consideration in their own eyes which raised them far above the abject condition of the subjects of an Eastern despotism. It cherished in them that love of independence which was their birthright, inherited from their ancestors, and thus maintained in their bosoms those lofty sentiments which were the characteristics of the humbler classes of the Spaniards beyond those of any other nation in Christendom.

One feature was wanting to complete the picture of absolute monarchy. This was a standing army,—a thing hitherto unknown in Spain. There was, indeed, an immense force kept on foot in the time of Charles the Fifth, and many of the troops were Spaniards. But they were stationed abroad, and were intended solely for foreign enterprises. It is to Philip's time that we are to refer the first germs of a permanent military establishment, designed to maintain order and obedience at home.

The levies raised for this purpose amounted to twenty companies of men-at-arms, which, with the complement of four or five followers to each lance, made a force of some strength. It was further swelled by five thousand *ginetes*, or light cavalry.[68] These corps were a heavy charge on the crown. They were called "the Guards

[68] Relazione di Contarini, MS.

of Castile." The men-at-arms, in particular, were an object of great care, and were under admirable discipline. Even Philip, who had little relish for military affairs, was in the habit of occasionally reviewing them in person. In addition to these troops there was a body of thirty thousand militia, whom the king could call into the field when necessary. A corps of some sixteen hundred horsemen patrolled the southern coasts of Andalusia, to guard the country from invasion by the African Moslems; and garrisons established in fortresses along the frontiers of Spain, both north and south, completed a permanent force for the defence of the kingdom against domestic insurrection, as well as foreign invasion.

CHAPTER II.

DOMESTIC AFFAIRS OF SPAIN.

The Clergy.—Their Subordination to the Crown.—The Escorial.—
Queen Anne.

A REVIEW of the polity of Castile would be incomplete without a notice of the ecclesiastical order, which may well be supposed to have stood pre-eminent in such a country and under such a monarch as Philip the Second. Indeed, not only did that prince present himself before the world as the great champion of the Faith, but he seemed ever solicitous in private life to display his zeal for religion and its ministers. Many anecdotes are told of him in connection with this. On one occasion, seeing a young girl going within the railing of the altar, he rebuked her, saying, "Where the priest enters is no place either for me or you."[1] A cavalier who had given a blow to a canon of Toledo he sentenced to death.[2]

Under his protection and princely patronage, the Church reached its most palmy state. Colleges and convents—in short, religious institutions of every kind —were scattered broadcast over the land. The good fathers loved pleasant and picturesque sites for their

[1] "Vos ni yo no avemos de subir donde los Sacerdotes." Dichos y Hechos de Phelipe II., p. 96.
[2] Cabrera, Filipe Segundo, p. 894.

dwellings; and the traveller, as he journeyed through the country, was surprised by the number of stately edifices which crowned the hill-tops or rested on their slopes, surrounded by territories that spread out for many a league over meadows and cultivated fields and pasture-land.

The secular clergy, at least the higher dignitaries, were so well endowed as sometimes to eclipse the grandees in the pomp of their establishments. In the time of Ferdinand and Isabella, the archbishop of Toledo held jurisdiction over fifteen principal towns and a great number of villages. His income amounted to full eighty thousand ducats a year.[3] In Philip's time the income of the archbishop of Seville amounted to the same sum, while that of the see of Toledo had risen to two hundred thousand ducats, nearly twice as much as that of the richest grandee in the kingdom.[4] In power and opulence the primate of Spain ranked next in Christendom to the pope.

The great source of all this wealth of the ecclesiastical order in Castile, as in most other countries, was the benefactions and bequests of the pious,—of those, more especially, whose piety had been deferred till the close of life, when, anxious to make amends for past delinquencies, they bestowed the more freely that it was at the expense of their heirs. As what was thus bequeathed was locked up by entail, the constantly accumulating property of the Church had amounted in Philip's time, if we may take the assertion of the cortes, to more than one-half of the landed property

---

[3] L. Marineo Siculo, Cosas memorables, fol. 23.
[4] Nota di tutti li Titolati di Spagna, MS.

in the kingdom.⁵ Thus the burden of providing for the expenses of the state fell with increased heaviness on the commons. Alienations in mortmain formed the subject of one of their earliest remonstrances after Philip's accession, but without effect; and, though the same petition was urged in very plain language at almost every succeeding session, the king still answered that it was not expedient to make any change in the existing laws. Besides his good will to the ecclesiastical order, Philip was occupied with the costly construction of the Escorial; and he had probably no mind to see the streams of public bounty, which had hitherto flowed so freely into the reservoirs of the Church, thus suddenly obstructed, when they were so much needed for his own infant institution.

While Philip was thus willing to exalt the religious order, already far too powerful, he was careful that it should never gain such a height as would enable it to overtop the royal authority. Both in the Church and in the council,—for they were freely introduced into the councils,—theologians were ever found the most devoted servants of the crown. Indeed, it was on the crown that they were obliged to rest all their hopes of preferment.

Philip perfectly understood that the control of the clergy must be lodged with that power which had the right of nomination to benefices. The Roman see, in its usual spirit of encroachment, had long claimed the exercise of this right in Castile, as it had done in other European states. The great battle with the Church was fought in the time of Isabella the Catholic. For

⁵ Lafuente, Historia de España, tom. xiv. p. 416.

tunately, the sceptre was held by a sovereign whose loyalty to the Faith was beyond suspicion. From this hard struggle she came off victorious; and the government of Castile henceforth retained possession of the important prerogative of appointing to vacant benefices.

Philip, with all his deference to Rome, was not a man to relinquish any of the prerogatives of the crown. A difficulty arose under Pius the Fifth, who contended that he still had the right, possessed by former popes, of nominating to ecclesiastical offices in Milan, Naples, and Sicily, the Italian possessions held by Spain. He complained bitterly of the conduct of the councils in those states, which refused to allow the publication of his bulls without the royal *exequatur*. Philip, in mild terms, expressed his desire to maintain the most amicable relations with the see of Rome, provided he was not required to compromise the interests of his crown. At the same time he intimated his surprise that his holiness should take exceptions at his exercise of the rights of his predecessors, to many of whom the Church was indebted for the most signal services. The pope was well aware of the importance of maintaining a good understanding with so devoted a son of the Church; and Philip was allowed to remain henceforth in undisturbed possession of this inestimable prerogative.[6]

The powers thus vested in the king he exercised with great discretion. With his usual facilities for information, he made himself acquainted with the characters of the clergy in the different parts of his dominions.

[6] Lafuente, Historia de España, tom. xiii. p. 261.—Cabrera, Filipe Segundo, pp. 432, 433.

He was so accurate in his knowledge that he was frequently able to detect an error or omission in the information he received. To one who had been giving him an account of a certain ecclesiastic, he remarked, "You have told me nothing of his amours." Thus perfectly apprised of the characters of the candidates, he was prepared, whenever a vacancy occurred, to fill the place with a suitable incumbent.[7]

It was his habit, before preferring an individual to a high office, to have proof of his powers by trying them first in some subordinate station. In his selection he laid much stress on rank, for the influence it carried with it. Yet frequently, when well satisfied of the merits of the parties, he promoted those whose humble condition had made them little prepared for such an elevation.[8] There was no more effectual way to secure his favor than to show a steady resistance to the usurpations of Rome. It was owing, in part at least, to the refusal of Quiroga, the bishop of Cuença, to publish a papal bull without the royal assent, that he was raised to the highest dignity in the kingdom, as archbishop of Toledo. Philip chose to have a suitable acknowledgment from the person on whom he conferred a favor; and once when an ecclesiastic, whom he had made a bishop, went to take possession of his see without first expressing his gratitude, the king sent for him back, to

[7] Cabrera, Filipe Segundo, lib. xi. cap. 11 ; lib. xii. cap. 21.—Relazione Anon., 1588, MS.

[8] " Otras vezes presentaba para Obispos Canonigos tan particulares i presbiteros tan apartados no solo de tal esperança, mas pensamiento en si mismos, i en la comun opinion, que la cedula de su presentacion no admitia su rezelo de ser engañados ó burlados. Eligia á quien no pedia, i merecia." Cabrera, Filipe Segundo, p. 891.

remind him of his duty.[9] Such an acknowledgment was in the nature of a homage rendered to his master on his preferment.

Thus, gratitude for the past and hopes for the future were the strong ties which bound every prelate to his sovereign. In a difference with the Roman see, the Castilian churchman was sure to be found on the side of the sovereign rather than on that of the pontiff. In his own troubles, in like manner, it was to the king, and not to the pope, that he was to turn for relief. The king, on the other hand, when pressed by those embarrassments with which he was too often surrounded, looked for aid to the clergy, who for the most part rendered it cheerfully and in liberal measure. Nowhere were the clergy so heavily burdened as in Spain.[10] It was computed that at least one-third of their revenues was given to the king. Thus completely were the different orders, both spiritual and temporal, throughout the monarchy, under the control of the sovereign.

A few pages back, while touching on alienations in mortmain, I had occasion to allude to the Escorial, that "eighth wonder of the world," as it is proudly styled by the Spaniards. There can be no place more proper to give an account of this extraordinary edifice than the part of the narrative in which I have been desirous to throw as much light as possible on the character and occupations of Philip. The Escorial engrossed the leisure of more than thirty years of his

---

[9] Cabrera, Filipe Segundo, lib. xi. cap. 11.
[10] Relazione di Contarini, MS.—Ranke, Ottoman and Spanish Empires, p. 61.

life; it reflects in a peculiar manner his tastes and the austere character of his mind; and, whatever criticism may be passed on it as a work of art, it cannot be denied that, if every other vestige of his reign were to be swept away, that wonderful structure would of itself suffice to show the grandeur of his plans and the extent of his resources.

The common tradition that Philip built the Escorial in pursuance of a vow which he made at the time of the great battle of St. Quentin, the tenth of August, 1557, has been rejected by modern critics, on the ground that contemporary writers, and among them the historians of the convent, make no mention of the fact. But a recently discovered document leaves little doubt that such a vow was actually made.[11] However this may have been, it is certain that the king designed to commemorate the event by this structure, as is intimated by its dedication to St. Lawrence, the martyr on whose day the victory was gained. The name given to the place was *El Sitio de San Lorenzo el Real*. But the monastery was better known from the hamlet near which it stood,—*El Escurial*, or *El Escorial*,—which latter soon became the orthography generally adopted by the Castilians.[12]

[11] The document alluded to is a letter, without date or signature, but in the handwriting of the sixteenth century, and purporting to be written by a person intrusted with the task of drafting the necessary legal instruments for the foundation of the convent. He inquires whether in the preamble he shall make mention of his majesty's vow. " *El voto que S. M. hijo,* si S. M. no lo quiere poner ni declarar, bien puede, porque no hay para que; pero si S. M. quisiere que se declare en las escrituras, avísemelo v. m." Documentos inéditos, tom. xxviii. p. 567.

[12] Examples equally ancient of both forms of spelling the name may

The motives which, after all, operated probably most powerfully on Philip, had no connection with the battle of St. Quentin. His father the emperor had directed by his will that his bones should remain at Yuste until a more suitable place should be provided for them by his son. The building now to be erected was designed expressly as a mausoleum for Philip's parents, as well as for their descendants of the royal line of Austria. But the erection of a religious house on a magnificent scale, that would proclaim to the world his devotion to the Faith, was the predominant idea in the mind of Philip. It was, moreover, a part of his scheme to combine in the plan a palace for himself; for, with a taste which he may be said to have inherited from his father, he loved to live in the sacred shadows of the cloister. These ideas, somewhat incongruous as they may seem, were fully carried out by the erection of an edifice dedicated at once to the threefold purpose of a palace, a monastery, and a tomb.[13]

Soon after the king's return to Spain, he set about carrying his plan into execution. The site which, after careful examination, he selected for the building, was among the mountains of the Guadarrama, on the borders of New Castile,[14] about eight leagues northwest of

be found; though *Escorial*, now universal in the Castilian, seems to have been also the more common from the first. The word is derived from *scoriæ*, the dross of iron-mines, found near the spot. See Ford, Handbook for Spain (3d edition), p. 751.

[13] A letter of the royal founder, published by Siguença, enumerates the objects to which the new building was to be specially devoted. Historia de la Orden de San Geronimo, tom. iii. p. 534.

[14] "The Escorial is placed by some geographers in Old Castile; but the division of the provinces is carried on the crest of the *Sierra* which rises behind it." Ford, Handbook for Spain, p. 750.

Madrid. The healthiness of the place and its convenient distance from the capital combined with the stern and solitary character of the region, so congenial to his taste, to give it the preference over other spots which might have found more favor with persons of a different nature. Encompassed by rude and rocky hills, which sometimes soar to the gigantic elevation of mountains, it seemed to be shut out completely from the world. The vegetation was of a thin and stunted growth, seldom spreading out into the luxuriant foliage of the lower regions; and the winds swept down from the neighboring sierra with the violence of a hurricane. Yet the air was salubrious, and the soil was nourished by springs of the purest water. To add to its recommendations, a quarry, close at hand, of excellent stone somewhat resembling granite in appearance, readily supplied the materials for building,—a circumstance, considering the vastness of the work, of no little importance.

The architect who furnished the plans, and on whom the king relied for superintending their execution, was Juan Bautista de Toledo. He was born in Spain, and, early discovering uncommon talents for his profession, was sent to Italy. Here he studied the principles of his art, under the great masters who were then filling their native land with those monuments of genius that furnished the best study to the artist. Toledo imbibed their spirit, and under their tuition acquired that simple, indeed severe, taste which formed a contrast to the prevalent tone of Spanish architecture, but which, happily, found favor with his royal patron.

Before a stone of the new edifice was laid, Philip had taken care to provide himself with the tenants who were to occupy it. At a general chapter of the Jeronymite fraternity, a prior was chosen for the convent of the Escorial, which was to consist of fifty members, soon increased to double that number. Philip had been induced to give the preference to the Jeronymite order, partly from their general reputation for ascetic piety, and in part from the regard shown for them by his father, who had chosen a convent of that order as the place of his last retreat. The monks were speedily transferred to the village of the Escorial, where they continued to dwell until accommodations were prepared for them in the magnificent pile which they were thenceforth to occupy.

Their temporary habitation was of the meanest kind, like most of the buildings in the hamlet. It was without window or chimney, and the rain found its way through the dilapidated roof of the apartment which they used as a chapel, so that they were obliged to protect themselves by a coverlet stretched above their heads. A rude altar was raised at one end of the chapel, over which was scrawled on the wall with charcoal the figure of a crucifix.[15]

The king, on his visits to the place, was lodged in the house of the curate, in not much better repair than the other dwellings in the hamlet. While there he was punctual in his attendance at mass, when a rude seat was prepared for him near the choir, consisting of a

---

[15] Sigüença, Hist. de la Orden de San Geronimo, tom. iii. p. 549.
—Memorias de Fray Juan de San Geronimo, Documentos inéditos, tom. vii. p. 22.

three-legged stool, defended from vulgar eyes by a screen
of such old and tattered cloth that the inquisitive spectator might without difficulty see him through the holes
in it.[16] He was so near the choir that the monk who
stood next to him could hardly avoid being brought
into contact with the royal person. The Jeronymite
who tells the story assures us that Brother Antonio
used to weep as he declared that more than once, when
he cast a furtive glance at the monarch, he saw his eyes
filled with tears. "Such," says the good father, "were
the devout and joyful feelings with which the king, as
he gazed on the poverty around him, meditated his
lofty plans for converting this poverty into a scene of
grandeur more worthy of the worship to be performed
there."[17]

The brethren were much edified by the humility
shown by Philip when attending the services in this
wretched cabin. They often told the story of his one
day coming late to matins, when, unwilling to inter-
rupt the services, he quietly took his seat by the entrance, on a rude bench, at the upper end of which a
peasant was sitting. He remained some time before

[16] "Tenia de ordinario una banquetilla de tres pies, bastísima y
grosera, por silla, y cuando iba á misa porque estuviese con algun
decencia se le ponia un paño viejo francés de Almaguer el contador,
que ya de gastado y deshilado hacia harto lugar por sus agujeros á
los que querian ver á la Persona Real." Memorias de Fray Juan de
San Geronimo, Documentos inéditos, tom. vii. p. 22.

[17] "Jurábame muchas veces llorando el dicho fray Antonio que
muchas veces alzando cautamente los ojos vió correr por los de S. M.
lágrimas: tanta era su devocion mezclada con el alegria de verse en
aquella pobreza y ver trás esto aquella alta idea que en su mente tenia
de la grandeza á que pensaba levantar aquella pequeñez del divino
culto." Ibid., ubi supra.

his presence was observed, when the monks conducted him to his tribune.[18]

On the twenty-third of April, 1563, the first stone of the monastery was laid. On the twentieth of August following, the corner-stone of the church was also laid, with still greater pomp and solemnity. The royal confessor, the bishop of Cuença, arrayed in his pontificals, presided over the ceremonies. The king was present, and laid the stone with his own hands. The principal nobles of the court were in attendance, and there was a great concourse of spectators, both ecclesiastics and laymen; the solemn services were concluded by the brotherhood, who joined in an anthem of thanksgiving and praise to the Almighty, to whom so glorious a monument was to be reared in this mountain-wilderness.[19]

The rude sierra now swarmed with life. The ground was covered with tents and huts. The busy hum of labor mingled with the songs of the laborers, which, from their various dialects, betrayed the different, and oftentimes distant, provinces from which they had come. In this motley host the greatest order and decorum prevailed; nor were the peaceful occupations of the day interrupted by any indecent brawls.

As the work advanced, Philip's visits to the Escorial were longer and more frequent. He had always shown his love for the retirement of the cloister, by passing some days of every year in it. Indeed, he was in the

[18] "¡Para levantar tanta fábrica menester eran actos de humildad tan profunda!" Memorias de Fray Juan de San Geronimo, Documentos inéditos, tom. vii. p. 23.

[19] Ibid., p. 25, et seq.—Siguença, Hist. de la Orden de San Geronimo, tom. ii. p. 546.

habit of keeping Holy Week not far from the scene of his present labors, at the convent of Guisando. In his present monastic retreat he had the additional interest afforded by the contemplation of the great work, which seemed to engage as much of his thoughts as any of the concerns of government.

"Philip had given a degree of attention to the study of the fine arts seldom found in persons of his condition. He was a connoisseur in painting, and, above all, in architecture, making a careful study of its principles, and occasionally furnishing designs with his own hand.[20] No prince of his time left behind him so many proofs of his taste and magnificence in building. The royal mint at Segovia, the hunting-seat of the Pardo, the pleasant residence of Aranjuez, the alcazar of Madrid, the "Armeria Real," and other noble works which adorned his infant capital, were either built or greatly embellished by him. The land was covered with structures, both civil and religious, which rose under the royal patronage. Churches and convents—the latter in lamentable profusion—constantly met the eye of the traveller. The general style of their execution was simple in the extreme. Some, like the great cathedral of Valladolid, of more pretension, but still showing the same austere character in their designs, furnished excellent models of architecture to counteract the meretricious tendencies of the age. Structures of a different

---

[20] " Tenia tanta destreça en disponer las traças de Palacios, Castillos, Jardines, y otras cosas, que quando Francisco de Mora mi Tio Traçador mayor suyo, y Juan de Herrera su Antecessor le traian la primera planta, assi mandava quitar, ò poner, ò mudar, como si fuera un Vitrubio." Dichos y Hechos de Phelipe II., p. 181.

kind from these were planted by Philip along the frontiers in the north and on the southern coasts of the kingdom; and the voyager in the Mediterranean beheld fortress after fortress crowning the heights above the shore, for its defence against the Barbary corsair. Nor was the king's passion for building confined to Spain. Wherever his armies penetrated in the semi-civilized regions of the New World, the march of the conqueror was sure to be traced by the ecclesiastical and military structures which rose in his rear.

Fortunately, similarity of taste led to the most perfect harmony between the monarch and his architect in their conferences on the great work which was to crown the architectural glories of Philip's reign. The king inspected the details, and watched over every step in the progress of the building, with as much care as Toledo himself. In order to judge of the effect from a distance, he was in the habit of climbing the mountains at a spot about half a league from the monastery, where a kind of natural chair was formed by the crags. Here, with his spy-glass in his hand, he would sit for hours and gaze on the complicated structure growing up below. The place is still known as the "king's seat."[31]

It was certainly no slight proof of the deep interest which Philip took in the work that he was content to exchange his palace at Madrid for a place that afforded him no better accommodations than the poverty-stricken village of the Escorial. In 1571 he made an important change in these accommodations, by erecting a chapel which might afford the monks a more decent house of

[31] Lafuente, Historia de España, tom. xiii. p. 253.

worship than their old weather-beaten hovel; and with this he combined a comfortable apartment for himself. In these new quarters he passed still more of his time in cloistered seclusion than he had done before. Far from confining his attention to a supervision of the Escorial, he brought his secretaries and his papers along with him, read here his despatches from abroad, and kept up a busy correspondence with all parts of his dominions. He did four times the amount of work here, says a Jeronymite, that he did in the same number of days in the capital.[22] He used to boast that, thus hidden from the world, with a little bit of paper, he ruled over both hemispheres. That he did not always wisely rule is proved by more than one of his despatches relating to the affairs of Flanders, which issued from this consecrated place. Here he received accounts of the proceedings of his heretic subjects in the Netherlands, and of the Morisco insurgents in Granada. And as he pondered on their demolition of church and convent, and their desecration of the most holy symbols of the Catholic faith, he doubtless felt a proud satisfaction in proving his own piety to the world by the erection of the most sumptuous edifice ever dedicated to the Cross.

In 1577 the Escorial was so far advanced towards completion as to afford accommodations not merely for Philip and his personal attendants, but for many of the court, who were in the habit of spending some time there with the king during the summer. On one of

---

[22] "Sabese de cierto que se negociava aqui mas en un dia que en Madrid en quatro." Siguença, Hist. de la Orden de San Geronimo, tom. iii. p. 575.

these occasions an accident occurred which had nearly been attended with most disastrous consequences to the building.

A violent thunder-storm was raging in the mountains, and the lightning struck one of the great towers of the monastery. In a short time the upper portion of the building was in a blaze. So much of it, fortunately, was of solid materials that the fire made slow progress. But the difficulty of bringing water to bear on it was extreme. It was eleven o'clock at night when the fire broke out, and in the orderly household of Philip all had retired to rest. They were soon roused by the noise. The king took his station on the opposite tower, and watched with deep anxiety the progress of the flames. The duke of Alva was one among the guests. Though sorely afflicted with the gout at the time, he wrapped his dressing-gown about him and climbed to a spot which afforded a still nearer view of the conflagration. Here the "good duke" at once assumed the command, and gave his orders with as much promptness and decision as on the field of battle.[73]

All the workmen, as well as the neighboring peasantry, were assembled there. The men showed the same spirit of subordination which they had shown throughout the erection of the building. The duke's orders were implicitly obeyed; and more than one instance is recorded of daring self-devotion among the

[73] "El buen Duque de Alba, aunque su vejez y gota no le daban lugar, se subió á lo alto de la torre á dar ánimo y esfuerzo á los oficiales y gente; . . . y esto lo hacia S. E. como diestro capitan y como quien se habia visto en otros mayores peligros en la guerra." Memorias de Fray Juan de San Geronimo, Documentos inéditos, tom. vii. p. 197.

workmen, who toiled as if conscious they were under the eye of their sovereign. The tower trembled under the fury of the flames; and the upper portion of it threatened every moment to fall in ruins. Great fears were entertained that it would crush the hospital, situated in that part of the monastery. Fortunately, it fell in an opposite direction, carrying with it a splendid chime of bells that was lodged in it, but doing no injury to the spectators. The loss which bore most heavily on the royal heart was that of sundry inestimable relics which perished in the flames. But Philip's sorrow was mitigated when he learned that a bit of the true cross, and the right arm of St. Lawrence, the martyred patron of the Escorial, were rescued from the flames. At length, by incredible efforts, the fire, which had lasted till six in the morning, was happily extinguished, and Philip withdrew to his chamber, where his first act, we are told, was to return thanks to the Almighty for the preservation of the building consecrated to his service.[24]

The king was desirous that as many of the materials as possible for the structure should be collected from his own dominions. These were so vast, and so various in their productions, that they furnished nearly every article required for the construction of the edifice, as well as for its interior decoration. The gray stone of which its walls were formed was drawn from a neighboring quarry. It was called *berroqueña*,—a stone bearing a resemblance to granite, though not so hard. The blocks hewn from the quarries, and dressed there,

---

[24] Memorias de Fray Juan de San Geronimo, Documentos inéditos, tom. vii. p. 201.

were of such magnitude as sometimes to require forty or fifty yoke of oxen to drag them. The jasper came from the neighborhood of Burgo de Osma. The more delicate marbles, of a great variety of colors, were furnished by the mountain-ranges in the south of the Peninsula. The costly and elegant fabrics were many of them supplied by native artisans. Such were the damasks and velvets of Granada. Other cities, as Madrid, Toledo, and Saragossa, showed the proficiency of native art in curious manufactures of bronze and iron, and occasionally of the more precious metals.

Yet Philip was largely indebted to his foreign possessions, especially those in Italy and the Low Countries, for the embellishment of the interior of the edifice, which, in its sumptuous style of decoration, presented a contrast to the stern simplicity of its exterior. Milan, so renowned at that period for its fine workmanship in steel, gold, and precious stones, contributed many exquisite specimens of art. The walls were clothed with gorgeous tapestries from the Flemish looms. Spanish convents vied with each other in furnishing embroideries for the altars. Even the rude colonies in the New World had their part in the great work, and the American forests supplied their cedar and ebony and richly-tinted woods, which displayed all their magical brilliancy of color under the hands of the Castilian workman.[75]

Though desirous as far as possible to employ the products of his own dominions and to encourage native

---

[75] Siguença, Hist. de la Orden de San Geronimo, tom. iii. p. 596.—Dichos y Hechos de Phelipe II., p. 289.—Lafuente, Hist. de España, tom. xiv. p. 427.

art, in one particular he resorted almost exclusively to foreigners. The oil-paintings and frescos which profusely decorated the walls and ceilings of the Escorial were executed by artists drawn chiefly from Italy, whose schools of design were still in their glory. But, of all living painters, Titian was the one whom Philip, like his father, most delighted to honor. To the king's generous patronage the world is indebted for some of that great master's noblest productions, which found a fitting place on the walls of the Escorial.

The prices which Philip paid enabled him to command the services of the most eminent artists. Many anecdotes are told of his munificence. He was, however, a severe critic. He did not prematurely disclose his opinion. But when the hour came, the painter had sometimes the mortification to find the work he had executed, it may be with greater confidence than skill, peremptorily rejected, or at best condemned to some obscure corner of the building. This was the fate of an Italian artist, of much more pretension than power, who, after repeated failures according to the judgment of the king,—which later critics have not reversed,—was dismissed to his own country. But even here Philip dealt in a magnanimous way with the unlucky painter. "It is not Zuccaro's fault," he said, "but that of the persons who brought him here;" and when he sent him back to Italy he gave him a considerable sum of money in addition to his large salary.[26]

Before this magnificent pile, in a manner the creation of his own taste, Philip's nature appeared to expand, and to discover some approach to those generous

---

[26] Stirling, Annals of the Artists of Spain, tom. i. p. 211.

sympathies for humanity which elsewhere seem to have been denied him. He would linger for hours while he watched the labors of the artist, making occasional criticisms, and laying his hand familiarly on his shoulder.[27] He seemed to put off the coldness and reserve which formed so essential a part of his character. On one occasion, it is said, a stranger, having come into the Escorial when the king was there, mistook him for one of the officials, and asked him some questions about the pictures. Philip, without undeceiving the man, humored his mistake, and good-naturedly undertook the part of *cicerone*, by answering his inquiries and showing him some of the objects most worth seeing.[28] Similar anecdotes have been told of others. What is strange is that Philip should have acted the part of the good-natured man.

In 1584 the masonry of the Escorial was completed. Twenty-one years had elapsed since the first stone of the monastery was laid. This certainly must be regarded as a short period for the erection of so stupendous a pile. St. Peter's church, with which one naturally compares it as the building nearest in size and magnificence, occupied more than a century in its erection, which spread over the reigns of at least eighteen popes. But the Escorial, with the exception of the subterraneous chapel constructed by Philip the Fourth for the burial-place of the Spanish princes, was executed in the reign of one monarch. That monarch held in his hands the revenues of both the Old World and the New; and, as he gave in some sort a personal

---

[27] Stirling, Annals of the Artists of Spain, tom. i. p. 203.
[28] Dichos y Hechos de Phelipe II., p. 81.

supervision to the work, we may be sure that no one was allowed to sleep on his post.

Yet the architect who designed the building was not permitted to complete it. Long before it was finished, the hand of Toledo had mouldered in the dust. By his death it seemed that Philip had met with an irreparable loss. He felt it to be so himself, and with great distrust consigned the important task to Juan de Herrera, a young Asturian. But, though young, Herrera had been formed on the best models; for he was the favorite pupil of Toledo, and it soon appeared that he had not only imbibed the severe and elevated tastes of his master, but that his own genius fully enabled him to comprehend all Toledo's great conceptions, and to carry them out as perfectly as that artist could have done himself. Philip saw with satisfaction that he had made no mistake in his selection. He soon conferred as freely with the new architect as he had done with his predecessor. He even showed him greater favor, settling on him a salary of a thousand ducats a year, and giving him an office in the royal household, and the cross of St. Iago. Herrera had the happiness to complete the Escorial. Indeed, he lived some six years after its completion. He left several works, both civil and ecclesiastical, which perpetuate his fame. But the Escorial is the monument by which his name, and that of his master, Toledo, have come down to posterity as those of the two greatest architects of whom Spain can boast.

This is not the place for criticism on the architectural merits of the Escorial. Such criticism more properly belongs to a treatise on art. It has been my object simply to lay before the reader such an account of the execution of this great work as would enable him to form some idea of the object to which Philip devoted so large a portion of his time, and which so eminently reflected his peculiar cast of mind.

Critics have greatly differed from each other in their judgments of the Escorial. Few foreigners have been found to acquiesce in the undiluted panegyric of those Castilians who pronounce it the eighth wonder of the world.[29] Yet it cannot be denied that few foreigners are qualified to decide on the merits of a work, to judge of which correctly requires a perfect understanding of the character of the country in which it was built, and of the monarch who built it. The traveller who gazes on its long lines of cold gray stone, scarcely broken by an ornament, feels a dreary sensation creeping over him, while he contrasts it with the lighter and more graceful edifices to which his eye has been accustomed. But he may read in this the true expression of the founder's character. Philip did not aim at the beautiful, much less at the festive and cheerful. The feelings which he desired to raise in the spectator were of that solemn, indeed sombre complexion which corresponded best with his own religious faith.

Whatever defects may be charged on the Escorial, it is impossible to view it from a distance, and see the mighty pile as it emerges from the gloomy depths of the mountains, without feeling how perfectly it conforms in its aspect to the wild and melancholy scenery

---

[29] One of its historians, Father Francisco de los Santos, styles it, on his title-page, " *Unica Maravilla del Mundo.*" Descripcion del Real Monasterio de San Lorenzo de el Escorial (Madrid, 1698).

of the sierra. Nor can one enter the consecrated precincts without confessing the genius of the place, and experiencing sensations of a mysterious awe as he wanders through the desolate halls, which fancy peoples with the solemn images of the past.

The architect of the building was embarrassed by more than one difficulty of a very peculiar kind. It was not simply a monastery that he was to build. The same edifice, as we have seen, was to comprehend at once a convent, a palace, and a tomb. It was no easy problem to reconcile objects so discordant and infuse into them a common principle of unity. It is no reproach to the builder that he did not perfectly succeed in this, and that the palace should impair the predominant tone of feeling raised by the other parts of the structure, looking in fact like an excrescence, rather than an integral portion of the edifice.

Another difficulty, of a more whimsical nature, imposed on the architect, was the necessity of accommodating the plan of the building to the form of a gridiron, —as typical of the kind of martyrdom suffered by the patron saint of the Escorial. Thus, the long lines of cloisters, with their intervening courts, served for the bars of the instrument; the four lofty spires at the corners of the monastery represented its legs inverted; and the palace, extending its slender length on the east, furnished the awkward handle.

It is impossible for language to convey any adequate idea of a work of art. Yet architecture has this advantage over the sister arts of design, that the mere statement of the dimensions helps us much in forming a conception of the work. A few of these dimensions will serve to give an idea of the magnitude of the edifice. They are reported to us by Los Santos, a Jeronymite monk, who has left one of the best accounts of the Escorial.

The main building, or monastery, he estimates at seven hundred and forty Castilian feet in length by five hundred and eighty in breadth. Its greatest height, measured to the central cross above the dome of the great church, is three hundred and fifteen feet. The whole circumference of the Escorial, including the palace, he reckons at two thousand nine hundred and eighty feet, or near three-fifths of a mile. The patient inquirer tells us there were no less than twelve thousand doors and windows in the building; that the weight of the keys alone amounted to fifty *arrobas*, or twelve hundred and fifty pounds; and, finally, that there were sixty-eight fountains playing in the halls and courts of this enormous pile.[30]

The cost of its construction and interior decoration, we are informed by Father Siguença, amounted to very near six millions of ducats.[31] Siguença was prior of the monastery, and had access, of course, to the best sources of information. That he did not exaggerate, may be inferred from the fact that he was desirous to relieve the building from the imputation of any excessive expenditure incurred in its erection,—a common theme of complaint, it seems, and one that was urged with strong marks of discontent by contemporary writers. Probably no single edifice ever contained such an amount and variety of inestimable treasures as

---

[30] Los Santos, Descripcion del Escorial, fol. 116.
[31] Siguença, Hist. de la Orden de San Geronimo, tom. iii. p. 862.

the Escorial,—so many paintings and sculptures by the greatest masters,—so many articles of exquisite workmanship, composed of the most precious materials. It would be a mistake to suppose that when the building was finished the labors of Philip were at an end. One might almost say they were but begun. The casket was completed; but the remainder of his days was to be passed in filling it with the rarest and richest gems. This was a labor never to be completed. It was to be bequeathed to his successors, who, with more or less taste, but with the revenues of the Indies at their disposal, continued to lavish them on the embellishment of the Escorial.[32]

Philip the Second set the example. He omitted nothing which could give a value, real or imaginary, to his museum. He gathered at an immense cost several hundred cases of the bones of saints and martyrs, depositing them in rich silver shrines of elaborate workmanship. He collected four thousand volumes, in various languages, especially the Oriental, as the basis of the fine library of the Escorial.

The care of successive princes, who continued to

[32] The enthusiasm of Fray Alonso de San Geronimo carries him so far that he does not hesitate to declare that the Almighty owes a debt of gratitude to Philip the Second for the dedication of so glorious a structure to the Christian worship! " Este Templo, Señor, deve á Filipo Segundo vuestra Grandeza; con que gratitud le estará mirando, en el Impireo, vuestra Divinidad!"—This language, so near akin to blasphemy as it would be thought in our day, occurs in a panegyric delivered at the Escorial on the occasion of a solemn festival in honor of the hundredth anniversary of its foundation. A volume compiled by Fray Luis de Santa Maria is filled with a particular account of the ceremonies, under the title of " Octava sagradamente culta, celebrada en la Octava Maravilla," etc. (Madrid, 1664, folio).

spend there a part of every year, preserved the palace-monastery and its contents from the rude touch of Time. But what the hand of Time had spared the hand of violence destroyed. The French, who in the early part of the present century swept like a horde of Vandals over the Peninsula, did not overlook the Escorial. For in it they saw the monument designed to commemorate their own humiliating defeat. A body of dragoons under La Houssaye burst into the monastery in the winter of 1808; and the ravages of a few days demolished what it had cost years and the highest efforts of art to construct. The apprehension of similar violence from the Carlists, in 1837, led to the removal of the finest paintings to Madrid. The Escorial ceased to be a royal residence. Tenantless and unprotected, it was left to the fury of the blasts which swept down the hills of the Guadarrama.

The traveller who now visits the place will find its condition very different from what it was in the beginning of the century. The bare and mildewed walls no longer glow with the magical tints of Raphael and Titian and the sober pomp of the Castilian school. The exquisite specimens of art with which the halls were filled have been wantonly demolished, or more frequently pilfered for the sake of the rich materials. The monks, so long the guardians of the place, have shared the fate of their brethren elsewhere since the suppression of religious houses, and their venerable forms have disappeared. Silence and solitude reign throughout the courts, undisturbed by any sound save that of the ceaseless winds, which seem to be ever chanting their melancholy dirge over the faded glories of the Escorial. There is little now to remind one of the palace or of the monastery. Of the three great objects to which the edifice was devoted, one alone survives,—that of a mausoleum for the royal line of Castile. The spirit of the dead broods over the place, —of the sceptred dead, who lie in the same dark chamber where they have lain for centuries, unconscious of the changes that have been going on all around them.

During the latter half of Philip's reign he was in the habit of repairing with his court to the Escorial and passing here a part of the summer. Hither he brought his young queen, Anne of Austria,—when the gloomy pile assumed an unwonted appearance of animation. In a previous chapter the reader has seen some notice of his preparations for his marriage with that princess, in less than two years after he had consigned the lovely Isabella to the tomb. Anne had been already plighted to the unfortunate Don Carlos. Philip's marriage with her afforded him the melancholy triumph of a second time supplanting his son. She was his niece; for the Empress Mary, her mother, was the daughter of Charles the Fifth. There was, moreover, a great disparity in their years; for the Austrian princess, having been born in Castile during the regency of her parents, in 1549, was at this time but twenty-one years of age,— less than half the age of Philip. It does not appear that her father, the Emperor Maximilian, made any objection to the match. If he felt any, he was too politic to prevent a marriage which would place his daughter on the throne of the most potent monarchy in Europe.

It was arranged that the princess should proceed to Spain by the way of the Netherlands. In September, 1570, Anne bade a last adieu to her father's court, and with a stately retinue set out on her long journey. On entering Flanders she was received with great pomp by the duke of Alva, at the head of the Flemish nobles. Soon after her arrival, Queen Elizabeth despatched a squadron of eight vessels, with offers to transport her to Spain, and an invitation for her to visit England on her way. These offers were courteously declined; and the German princess, escorted by Count Bossu, captain-general of the Flemish navy, with a gallant squadron, was fortunate in reaching the place of her destination, after a voyage of less than a week. On the third of October she landed at Santander, on the northern coast of Spain, where she found the archbishop of Seville and the duke of Bejar, with a brilliant train of followers, waiting to receive her.

Under this escort, Anne was conducted by the way of Burgos and Valladolid to the ancient city of Segovia. In the great towns through which she passed, she was entertained in a style suited to her rank; and everywhere along her route she was greeted with the hearty acclamations of the people. For the match was popular with the nation; and the cortes had urged the king to expedite it as much as possible.[33] The Spaniards longed for a male heir to the crown; and since the death of Carlos, Philip had only daughters remaining to him.

In Segovia, where the marriage-ceremony was to be performed, magnificent preparations had been made for

---

[33] Florez, Reynas Catholicas, tom. ii. p. 905.

the reception of the princess. As she approached that city, she was met by a large body of the local militia, dressed in gay uniforms, and by the municipality of the place, arrayed in their robes of office and mounted on horseback. With this brave escort she entered the gates. The streets were ornamented with beautiful fountains, and spanned by triumphal arches, under which the princess proceeded, amidst the shouts of the populace, to the great cathedral.[34]

Anne, then in the bloom of youth, is described as having a rich and delicate complexion. Her figure was good, her deportment gracious, and she rode her richly-caparisoned palfrey with natural ease and dignity. Her not very impartial chronicler tells us that the spectators particularly admired the novelty of her Bohemian costume, her riding-hat gayly ornamented with feathers, and her short mantle of crimson velvet richly fringed with gold.[35]

After *Te Deum* had been chanted, the splendid procession took its way to the far-famed *alcazar*, that palace-fortress, originally built by the Moors, which now served both as a royal residence and as a place of confinement for prisoners of state. Here it was that the unfortunate Montigny passed many a weary month of captivity; and less than three months had elapsed since he had been removed from the place which was so soon to become the scene of royal festivity, and consigned to the fatal fortress of Simancas, to perish by the hand of the midnight executioner. Anne, it

[34] Florez, Reynas Catholicas, tom. ii. p. 908.

[35] " Realzada con gracia por el mismo trage del camino, sombrero alto matizado con plumas, capotillo de terciopelo carmesí, bordado de oro á la moda Bohema." Ibid., p. 907.

may be remembered, was said, on her journey through the Low Countries, to have promised Montigny's family to intercede with her lord in his behalf. But the king, perhaps willing to be spared the awkwardness of refusing the first boon asked by his young bride, disposed of his victim soon after her landing, while she was yet in the north.

Anne entered the *alcazar* amidst salvoes of artillery. She found there the good Princess Joanna, Philip's sister, who received her with the same womanly kindness which she had shown twelve years before to Elizabeth of France, when, on a similar occasion, she made her first entrance into Castile. The marriage was appointed to take place on the following day, the fourteenth of November. Philip, it is said, obtained his first view of his betrothed when, mingling in disguise among the cavalcade of courtiers, he accompanied her entrance into the capital.[36] When he had led his late queen, Isabella, to the altar, some white hairs on his temples attracted her attention.[37] During the ten years which had since elapsed, the cares of office had wrought the same effect on him as on his father, and turned his head prematurely gray. The marriage was solemnized with great pomp in the cathedral of Segovia. The service was performed by the archbishop of Seville. The spacious building was crowded to overflowing with spectators, among whom were the highest dignitaries of the Church and the most illustrious of the nobility of Spain.[38]

[36] Florez, Reynas Catholicas, ubi supra.
[37] *Ante*, vol. i. p. 415.
[38] Florez, Reynas Catholicas, tom. ii. p. 908.—Cabrera, Filipe Segundo, p. 661.

During the few days which followed, while the royal pair remained in Segovia, the city was abandoned to jubilee. The auspicious event was celebrated by public illuminations and by magnificent *fêtes*, at which the king and queen danced in the presence of the whole court, who stood around in respectful silence.[39] On the eighteenth, the new-married couple proceeded to Madrid, where such splendid preparations had been made for their reception as evinced the loyalty of the capital.

As soon as the building of the Escorial was sufficiently advanced to furnish suitable accommodations for his young queen, Philip passed a part of every summer in its cloistered solitudes, which had more attraction for him than any other of his residences. The presence of Anne and her courtly train diffused something like an air of gayety over the grand but gloomy pile, to which it had been little accustomed. Among other diversions for her entertainment we find mention made of *autos sacramentales*, those religious dramas that remind one of the ancient Mysteries and Moralities which entertained our English ancestors. These *autos* were so much in favor with the Spaniards as to keep possession of the stage longer than in most other countries; nor did they receive their full development until they had awakened the genius of Calderon.

It was a pen, however, bearing little resemblance to that of Calderon which furnished these edifying dramas. They proceeded, probably, from some Jeronymite gifted with a more poetic vein than his brethren. The actors

[39] "En el sarao bailaron Rey y Reyna, estando de pie toda la Corte." Florez, Reynas Catholicas, tom. ii. p. 908.

were taken from among the pupils in the seminary established in the Escorial. Anne, who appears to have been simple in her tastes, is said to have found much pleasure in these exhibitions, and in such recreation as could be afforded her by excursions into the wild, romantic country that surrounded the monastery. Historians have left us but few particulars of her life and character,—much fewer than of her lovely predecessor. Such accounts as we have represent her as of an amiable disposition and addicted to pious works. She was rarely idle, and employed much of her time in needle-work, leaving many specimens of her skill in this way in the decorations of the convents and churches. A rich piece of embroidery, wrought by her hands and those of her maidens, was long preserved in the royal chapel, under the name of "Queen Anne's tapestry."

Her wedded life was destined not to be a long one, —only two years longer than that of Isabella. She was blessed, however, with a more numerous progeny than either of her predecessors. She had four sons and a daughter. But all died in infancy or early childhood except the third son, who as Philip the Third lived to take his place in the royal dynasty of Castile.

The queen died on the twenty-sixth of October, 1580, in the thirty-first year of her age and the eleventh of her reign. A singular anecdote is told in connection with her death. This occurred at Badajoz, where the court was then established, as a convenient place for overlooking the war in which the country was at that time engaged with Portugal. While there the king fell ill. The symptoms were of the most alarming character. The queen, in her distress, implored the Almighty to spare a life so important to the welfare of the kingdom and of the Church, and instead of it to accept the sacrifice of her own. Heaven, says the chronicler, as the result showed, listened to her prayer.[40] The king recovered; and the queen fell ill of a disorder which in a few days terminated fatally. Her remains, after lying in state for some time, were transported with solemn pomp to the Escorial, where they enjoyed the melancholy pre-eminence of being laid in the quarter of the mausoleum reserved exclusively for kings and the mothers of kings. Such was the end of Anne of Austria, the fourth and last wife of Philip the Second.

[40] " El efecto dijo, que oyó Dios su oracion: pues mejorando el Rey, cayó mala la Reyna." Florez, Reynas Catholicas, tom. ii. p. 913.

END OF THE THIRD VOLUME.

www.ingramcontent.com/pod-product-compliance
Lightning Source LLC
Chambersburg PA
CBHW022137300426
44115CB00006B/230